General Editor's Introduction

This volume is published in collaboration with the Center for the Study of World Christian Revitalization Movements at Asbury Seminary. Building on the work of the previous Wesleyan/Holiness Studies Center at the Seminary, the Center provides a focus for research in the Wesleyan Holiness and other related Christian renewal movements, including Pietism and Pentecostal movements, which have had a world impact. The research seeks to develop analytical models of these movements, including their biblical and theological assessment. Using an interdisciplinary approach, the Center bridges relevant discourses in several areas in order to gain insights for effective Christian mission globally. It recognizes the need for conducting research that combines insights from the history of evangelical renewal and revival movements with anthropological and religious studies literature on revitalization movements. It also networks with similar or related research and study centers around the world, in addition to sponsoring a three-year research project (through 2011) under the funding of the Henry Luce Foundation.

This study focuses on the United Brethren in Christ, an important church tradition which began as a pioneering movement of interdenominational revitalization in the decades immediately following the first Great Awakening in eighteenth century America. Its ministry in Sierra Leone West Africa is generally recognized as establishing the most influential and vital Christian presence in that former British colony that had been a key cog in the eighteenth century British slave trade.

Jeremy Smith's treatment of his subject comes from a quite different angle of interest from previous scholarship on the subject. Drawing from the philosophical pragmatism of William James and the phenomenology of Husserl, among others, he probes the dynamics of what it means to inculcate a "sense of the life of living beings around us from within", as seen in the context of the missionary work of Lloyd Mignerey, an early twentieth century American UB missionary to Sierra Leone. Here is the first treatment of this key mission in the development of indigenous Christianity among West African tribal society that approaches its subject from an epistemological perspective. In doing so, it honors the faithful missional efforts of Mignerey and the hundreds of others who served in that important UB mission field for almost 160 years. Yet, in addition to that, it also contributes to a larger discussion of what religious dynamics are involved in the deeper quest for God that transcends the limitations of religious language and social ethos. Viewed in the ethos of the United Brethren in Christ, this was also a quest for the new humanity that is formed out of the Christian experience of Pentecost—a theme to which the United Brethren explicitly appealed in their missional self-understanding. Viewed from that perspective, this sensitive study also contributes to the deeper meaning of Christian revitalization.

> —J. Steven O'Malley, General Editor and Director
> Center for the Study of World Christian Revitalization Movements
> Asbury Theological Seminary

"The only impression made upon the nobler spirits by this display of material superiority and the condescending patronage it suggests is that stated by Dante, that no food is so bitter as the bread of dependence and no ascent so painful as the staircase of a patron, and they shrink from the proffered coddling."
–E.W. Blyden

The Staircase of a Patron

Sierra Leone and The United Brethren in Christ

Jeremy H. Smith

Asbury Theological Seminary Series:
The Study of World Christian Revitalization Movements in
Pietist/Wesleyan Studies (No. 4)

EMETH PRESS
www.emethpress.com

The Staricase of a Patron: Sierra Leone and The United Brethren in Christ

Library of Congress Cataloging-in-Publication Data

Smith, Jeremy H.
 The staircase of a patron : Sierra Leone and the United Brethren in Christ / Jeremy H. Smith.
    p. cm. -- (Asbury Theological Seminary series. The study of world Christian revitalization movements in pietist/wesleyan studies ; No. 4)
 Includes bibliographical references and index.
 ISBN 978-1-60947-016-6 (alk. paper)
 1. United Brethren Church--Missions--Sierra Leone--History--20th century. 2. Missions--Sierra Leone. 3. Mignerey, Lloyd. 4. Sierra Leone--Church history--20th century. 5. Sierra Leone--Religion. I. Title.
 BV3625.S4S65 2011
 266'.99664--dc22   2011008288

The cover photograph comes from the collection of J.R. King, a United Brethren missionary to Sierra Leone from 1894 to 1912. Two Western women—probably missionaries—stand on either side of a masked African figure. The purpose of the photograph does not seem to be disrespectful—yet the juxtaposition is startling and strange. The mask is immediately recognizable as that of the spirit of either the Bondo or the Sande society. The Bondo (for the Temne) and the Sande (for the Mende) societies included all adult women, and along with the Poro society for males, represent the heart and soul of traditional African society and religion in Sierra Leone. The Bondo or Sande mask is only worn by women. The cultures of Sierra Leone are, for Africa, relatively unusual in assigning women such an important role—or indeed any role—as masked, dancing, representatives of the spirit world. (It is unusual for the masquerader to be wearing a dress, in this case a typical African "wrapper" beneath the raffia, but the black stockings she is wearing, as well as the whip she is carrying, identify her as a genuine masquerader). It has not proved possible to positively identify the two missionaries. (The figure on the left is probably J.R. King's wife, Zella King). But the photograph suggests in a striking way the theme of this book: a confrontation of radically different cultural worlds which resulted in a kind of peaceful coexistence imbued with underlying tension.

Contents

Foreword

In the "Introduction" to this book, *The Staircase of a Patron: Sierra Leone and the United Brethren In Christ*, Jeremy Smith has explained how and why he wrote the book. He and I have been colleagues in the English Department of Otterbein College (now Otterbein University) since 1988. I am an appreciative witness to the intensive research and gifts of thought Jeremy has invested in this book over a period of at least fifteen years.

I was baptized in the United Brethren Church in Christ before it merged to form the Evangelical United Brethren Church (1946), and then again merged to form the United Methodist Church (1968). As a child, I recall the excitement with which the congregation welcomed a visit from Charles Leader and his wife, who were on sabbatical from their missionary duties in Sierra Leone. I do not recall anything the Leaders said in their talk to the congregation, but I do recall the veneration with which the congregation listened. Here was a couple who was truly doing the Lord's work in the world.

What was it like to be a United Brethren missionary in Sierra Leone under British colonialism? At the core of *The Staircase of a Patron* is Jeremy's commentary on the diaries of Lloyd Mignerey, (pronounced min'-uh-ree), who was a diligent recorder of his experiences as a United Brethren missionary in Sierra Leone from 1922 to 1924. Mignerey went to Sierra Leone as a missionary inspired by "social Gospel" ideals associated with the liberal theology of Walter Rauschenbusch. The story that Jeremy weaves out of Mignerey's diaries reveals a man who was caught between those ideals and the realities of a culture to which those ideals did not easily relate. Mignerey was a man, says Jeremy, "who thought about things, and took very seriously his responsibility to follow his thoughts wherever they might lead, regardless of the consequences." One of those consequences was Mignerey's realization that he personally was not free of cultural and racial prejudice, in spite of his commitment to the liberal Christian principle that all humans of all races are equal in the eyes of God. He struggled within himself to understand, without outright condemnation, certain African religious and social practices that his own structure of moral values did not accommodate. Jeremy speaks of Mignerey's life as a spiritual journey "out of racism," and in the "Epilogue" details how Mignerey, after having ascended and descended the "staircase," ascended it again through the remaining years of his long life as an outspoken advocate for racial social justice that was embodied in the work of Martin Luther King, Jr. and the Civil Rights Movement. It is a fascinating story that Jeremy tells with keen intelligence and passion.

When Jeremy discovered Mignerey's diaries in the archives of the Otterbein College library, he was teaching a course in African literature and culture that featured among other texts Chinua Achebe's great novels *Things Fall Apart* and *Arrow of God*. "I knew," he writes, "I had gotten hold of a gripping personal account, from one man's perspective, of a social and historical situation I found fascinating, and that I felt impelled to explore further." When I read books by scholars, I often find myself asking a biographical question about what personal experiences might have shaped a scholar's interest in the subject he or she is pursuing. Jeremy sheds light on that biographical question in relation to his book by telling of a personal experience that reaches back to his school days.

> I grew up in the 1960s, in Indianapolis, Indiana. The "other culture" we heard about most was also a name given to a war. Colonialism per se is not something I recall hearing much about. But racism was a reality of everyday life. The most vicious racist in my memory is my sixth grade teacher, who mercilessly persecuted the Black students in our class, and got away with it. I also could hardly miss the presence of Christians sure of who was going to hell. Like many, I was deeply disturbed by the arrogance of power, the cruelty of racism, the pride of religious exclusivism. Yet those who identified these evils with the essence of our civilization seemed to me themselves to be succumbing to their own kind of prejudice and pride. As I now look back I realize that it was finally these experiences of youth that impelled me to complete this project.

On a personal level, *The Staircase of a Patron* represents Jeremy's *agon*, or conflict, with racism as a fact of life in human culture. On a scholarly level, it is a study of how missionaries like Mignerey, though well intentioned, were ill adjusted to grasp the "African point of view" of religious experience.

Before I turn to discuss Chapter Four, the book's most theoretical and challenging chapter, let me offer an overview of the book's structure. It is not until we reach the third of the book's five chapters that we get a detailed discussion of Mignerey's diaries. Jeremy carefully prepares for this chapter in Chapter One by describing the contrast between liberal and conservative theological parties in the United Brethren Church, and by situating Mignerey as a member of the liberal party. In Chapter Two, he presents a picture of Sierra Leone under the rule of British colonialism up to the time of Mignerey's arrival there in 1922. In Chapter Four, he offers an understanding of religious experience in general, and of traditional African religious experience in particular. This chapter lays the groundwork for Chapter Five, in which Jeremy discusses the way African religious experience interacted with the religious experience of Mignerey and other missionaries.

Chapter Four, titled "Traditional African Religion and Society in Sierra Leone," is an ethnographical study, which focuses on the religious beliefs and practices of the two largest ethnic groups in Sierra Leone, the Mende and the Temne. "My aim," Jeremy writes, "is to understand those beliefs and practices . . . empathetically as well as intellectually, to make sense of them personally as well as to explain them objectively. To do this, I need to work out a basic understanding of the nature of religious experience as such." In working out this basic understanding of religious experience, Jeremy's insights assume the shape of a philosophy of religion. I will do no more here than highlight four propositions on which that philosophy of religion rests.

1. He rejects the post-modernist assumption that there is "no set of terms that can define an essence of religion or human nature that all cultures and humans share." In his opposition to post-modernism, Jeremy aligns himself with such thinkers as William James, Michel Henry, Edmund Husserl, Alfred North Whitehead, Maurice Merleau-Ponty, Louis Lavelle, Michael Polanyi, and H. Richard Niebuhr. This is quite a rich cast of thinkers, each of whom contributes in a distinctive way to a large conversation that affirms the principle of essence and the capacity of humans at the deepest levels of personal experience to participate in it.

2. "Participation" is a key word here. How do we participate in essence? First, we participate by being the kind of creatures that we are. Human nature does not stand apart from physical nature, but is part of the realm of essences that constitutes reality. Second, we participate in essence by experiencing it, which above all—put simply—involves paying devoted, conscious attention to essence as it is manifested in things of this world. Jeremy's brief characterization of Husserl's phenomenology (which he has written on extensively in other venues) features the idea that "the essence of human nature is the experience of being an 'I,' from the perspective of 'I.'" Below, I cite independently of Jeremy's text a quote from Husserl's *Ideas*, translated by W. R. Boyce Gibson (London: George Allen & Unwin, 1967).

> What things are . . . *they are as things of experience*. Experience alone prescribes their meaning, and indeed when we are dealing with things , . . it is actual experience in its definitely ordered . . . connexions which does the prescribing. (147-48)

From a Husserlian point of view, to which Jeremy is partial, everything, whether it is a physical entity or a thought, is potentially a thing of human experience. This does not mean that the world has no objectivity in its own right, but that it is human experience that prescribes the essence of things in the world. One might say that things in the world realize the status of essence when they are joined, or participated in, by the consciousness of an "I," which in itself belongs to the realm of essences.

3. Emphasis on the consciousness of the "I" as the means to participation in essence leads to a difficult question, "How can I know other "I"'s"—other human beings' experience of life? This is a question philosophers wrestle with under the rubric of "other minds." To what extent is it possible for me to know or identify with the experience of another "I"? One might try to answer this

question by saying that every individual is locked into a private consciousness that has no way of transcending itself. Or, one might try to answer the question by saying that all humans share and participate in a common experience of life. This latter attempt to answer the question is the one that Jeremy advances. Drawing upon the thought of William James, he presses the Jamesian insight that at the primordial level of our "I" experience is a feeling, or intuition, of "more." This "more" is something that defies scientific verification, but nonetheless suggests itself in the human capacity to reach beyond the immediacies of personal consciousness and to participate in, or to enter empathetically into, the joys and sorrows of others. The Jamesian intuition of "more," Jeremy insists, is one that "inspires and requires a deliberate, active response . . . not only a relatively passive sense of a powerful 'more,' but also an active 'getting on board of' [James' phrase] that more." Jeremy relates this idea of "getting on board of" the "more" to the religious thought of H. Richard Niebuhr, for whom as a confessional Christian thinker getting on board means loyalty, trust and faith in God as "the ultimate and absolute value and power which gives meaning to life in spite of its inexplicable tragedy."

4. In the remainder of Chapter Four, Jeremy observes how principles of *more, loyalty, trust,* and *faith* are expressed in the African Mende and Temne religions. These principles are expressed in reliance on ancestors, magic, and spirits, in bonds of social loyalty and trust, in medical practices, in secret societies, and in funeral practices. For all the dense particulars of Jeremy's observations in this chapter, of which I have only scratched the surface, the thought that rules is that principles of *more, loyalty, trust* and *faith* are inherent to religious experience generally. All expressions of religious experience are not the same, but all expressions of religious experience have their origin in the human consciousness of a great mystery of the essence of life that surrounds us. That seems to me to be a central message of Chapter Four of Jeremy's book, and a therapeutic message, I might add, in a world that elevates religious particularity and conflict over religious universality and peace.

The concluding chapter of the book draws together Jeremy's sociological-historical conclusions of how the Christianity of the missionaries in Sierra Leone interacted with traditional African religion, "each of which had its own notions of God and morality, its own sets of rituals, and its own ways of defining and valuing social groups." A generously documented piece of scholarship, this chapter contains roughly one third of the of the book's banquet of footnotes, which by my casual count total around 750. Jeremy seems to have left no stone unturned in trying to understand and appreciate, through reading, interviews, and a personal study trip to Sierra Leone, how African Christians assimilated the Christianity of the missionaries to their own religious traditions, and how Christianity remains alive in those traditions as a branch grafted onto an ancient trunk.

The Staircase of a Patron is a book that will repay reading specifically by persons who are interested in the history of the missionary enterprise of the United Brethren church in Sierra Leone. But it reaches well beyond that specific audience to speak to persons who are in the real life situation of cultural contact with religious and social principles different from their own. Jeremy writes, "There is always available to us the sense of the life of the living beings around us *from within*. If we let ourselves, we can feel what they feel from their perspective." Letting ourselves feel what others feel from their perspective is fundamental to the religious ethos that pervades this book.

—Norman Chaney

Acknowledgements

John Conteh-Morgan, who passed away in 2008, was an invaluable source of advice, encouragement, and inspiration throughout this project. I still remember the day in 1993 we together first opened Mignerey's diary in the Otterbein archive. The excitement we found in that moment—which included discovering the role of his grandfather, Ross Lohr—has seen me through from beginning to end.

I would also like to thank John, as well as Arthur Abraham, for making my visit to Freetown in 1996 possible. My many discussions with John and Arthur were indispensable to my effort to understand the history and culture of Sierra Leone. My thanks go to them, as well as Rosalind Hackett, Howard Mueller, Abhijat Joshi, Norman Chaney, Sylvia Vance, Allan Cooper, Gene Lawlis, and Betsy MacLean, for reading the manuscript at various stages. I would especially like to thank Howard Mueller for making available to me 450 pages of interview transcripts of United Brethren pastors and teachers in Sierra Leone. Elinor Mignerey Brown graciously made available to me additional relevant material, including her mother's diary.

The Otterbein University Archive and the Center for Evangelical United Brethren Heritage at United Theological Seminary have played a central role in this project. I would also like to thank the student assistants at Otterbein who patiently worked on tasks such as transcription and proofreading at various stages: Brian Worra, Beth Honeycutt, Caitlin Ward, and Sarah Tucker.

I am grateful to Frederick Lamp for his help with the explanation of the cover photograph.

INTRODUCTION

"The Staircase of a Patron"

The theme of this book is how Christianity was introduced and adopted in Sierra Leone. I approach this theme through the study of the United Brethren in Christ (who were probably the single most influential missionary presence there), and of the ethnic groups they mostly interacted with, the Mende and the Temne.[1] I base the story of the interaction of these radically different traditions upon a thorough exploration of each religious culture on its own terms, and I place this interaction in the context of the political reality of colonization.

E.W. Blyden was in the late nineteenth and early twentieth centuries one of the most prominent worldwide spokesmen for Africa and Africans. Though himself a Christian, Blyden proclaimed unequivocally that the Western missionary enterprise had one, perhaps fatal, flaw: its attitude of cultural and racial superiority. This attitude of superiority is a central factor in the story of cultural interaction I wish to tell. As Blyden summed up the situation between Africans and missionaries: "If they would come to Christ they must go upstairs."

The United Brethren missionary Lloyd Mignerey served in Sierra Leone from 1922–24, and left a remarkably detailed record of his thoughts, experiences, and personal struggles. His writings provide a unique perspective on this story of cultural interaction, not least because Mignerey discovered Blyden's works while in Sierra Leone, and through a painful process of self-examination, came to accept many of Blyden's positions. Even the most well-intentioned and progressive missionaries were still upstairs, and their attitude could be very patronizing. As Mignerey put it: "Our attitudes of helpfulness, nevertheless, have been marked too often by a spirit of thinly-disguised condescension. Beneath the surface we have assumed that the cream of the earth is undoubtedly white."

Origins of the Project

I would like to start with a few words about how this book came to be written. Otterbein College (or, as of 2010, University) is a small, midwestern liberal arts school founded by the United Brethren Church in 1847 that has always included in its student body a large proportion of first generation college students. Lloyd Mignerey, a United Brethren minister and missionary, had left his papers to Otterbein, his alma mater, shortly before his death in 1988. I began teaching English there in the same year. (My doctoral degree in Comparative Literature was in the area of religion and literature.) In the summer of 1993 I attended a six week NEH sponsored seminar in African literature at Ohio State University, and the Otterbein archivist, hearing of this, told me I might be interested in Mignerey's papers. Despite the fact that I had other research interests, I found myself drawn more and more deeply into the world they opened up.

Mignerey had graduated from Otterbein in 1917, and had served as a missionary in Sierra Leone from 1922–24. His voice, his thoughts, his mind emerge out of his writings with startling clarity. And he represents a standpoint almost totally forgotten in our contemporary culture: an evangelical Christian who was theologically and politically liberal, committed to the social gospel, prohibition, and converting Africa to Christianity. The world and historical situation he entered in Sierra Leone was much like the situation portrayed in Chinua Achebe's great novels *Things Fall Apart* and *Arrow of God*. I knew I had gotten hold of a gripping personal account, from one man's perspective, of a social and historical situation I found fascinating, and that I felt impelled to explore further. So many of the genuinely serious and disturbing questions raised by our own historical situation were at stake. That situation is one in which the diversity of cultural perspectives that make up our world is readily available to those who will pay attention. And those who pay attention can see that the original historical reason for this intercultural fluidity is colonialism.

I grew up in the 1960s, in Indianapolis, Indiana. The "other culture" we heard about most was also the name given to a war. Colonialism per se is not something I recall hearing much about. But racism was a reality of everyday life. The most vicious racist in my memory is my sixth grade teacher, who mercilessly persecuted the Black students in our class, and got away with it. I also could hardly miss the presence of Christians sure of who was going to hell. Like many, I was deeply disturbed by the arrogance of power, the cruelty of racism, the pride of religious exclusivism. Yet those who identified these evils with the essence of our civilization seemed to me themselves to be succumbing to their own kind of prejudice and pride. As I now look back I realize that it was finally these experiences of youth that impelled me to complete this project.

I am convinced that reality is inescapably personal. Empathy with actual individuals through narrative and dialogue is comprehension of history at the deepest level. Mignerey's writings open a path to comprehension of this sort. As the self-conscious effort of a highly intelligent and reflective individual to make sense of his religious beliefs and of his experience in a world alien to him, Mignerey's writings have an intrinsic historical interest that far outstrips that of the typical missionary diary. My original plan was simply to publish an edition of Mignerey's papers. But I wanted to understand the impact of the United Brethren mission on Sierra Leone. What were the belief systems of the people the United Brethren tried to convert? How did the socio-political situation of colonization relate to the work of the church? How did Africans react to the Western missionaries and to the Christianity they preached? Thanks to a large body of existing research on Sierra Leone, I was able to answer these questions. Especially important are Harris and Sawyerr on Mende belief, Abraham on the precolonial and colonial political situation of the Mende, and the work of Reeck and of Mueller specifically on the United Brethren Church in Sierra Leone. Without Mueller's research in particular I would have had less than half a worthwhile project. In 1971–72 Mueller interviewed 52 African pastors and teachers who had worked with the United Brethren Missions from the 1920s on. His work, including his dissertation and the interviews upon which it is based (filling 450 single spaced pages), uniquely open up access to the African perspective on the United Brethren missions.

Mignerey's experience in 1922–24 is the focal point of my treatment of the theme of cultural interaction. The particular time and place of Mignerey's missionary experience does provide an instructive and useful perspective for a study of the reception of Christianity in Sierra Leone and Africa generally. By the early 1920s both British colonial power and Christian missions had become firmly established. And yet the memory of colonial conquest (1898) was still fairly fresh and decolonization was a long way off. The specific locations of Mignerey's work are well suited for an accurate overview of missionary endeavors in Africa: during the first year he served as missionary in charge of a station at an important "upcountry" town, Rotifunk. The station included a school, a church, and a dispensary. And Rotifunk was very much a crossroads in Sierra Leone, where several major ethnic groups regularly mingled. During his second year he served in the capital, Freetown, as principal of Albert Academy, one of the most important secondary schools in Sierra Leone. A large proportion of the country's future leaders were to graduate from this institution, including Milton Margai and Siaka Stevens, the first and third presidents of independent Sierra Leone.

Chapter Outlines

The core of this book is the third chapter, which focuses on Mignerey's experience in Sierra Leone from 1922–24. The first and second chapters set the stage by presenting the historical background of the United Brethren Church and of the colonization of Sierra Leone, through 1922. The fourth chapter is a detailed study of the traditional religion and society of the Mende and the Temne. The fifth chapter draws all of these strands together, exploring both the religious and the social impact of both missions and political colonization.

In Chapter One, I define the religious and ideological outlook of the United Brethren Church as it existed through the 1920s. I identify two distinct theological traditions within the church, which I label "liberal" and "conservative." The tension between these two traditions more or less defines the history of Protestantism in America in the late nineteenth and the early twentieth century. What is remarkable about these two traditions is what they had in common until about 1920, and to lesser degree afterwards: a commitment to Prohibition, to missions, and to an extent to the social gospel; and along with that, a healthy dose of racism and ethnocentrism.

In Chapter Two, I provide a historical introduction beginning with the founding of the original Colony of Sierra Leone in 1787, following the interaction between British power and Mende and Temne states through the nineteenth century, and culminating with the decisive imposition of colonial rule through the Hut Tax War of 1898. In addition, I trace the beginnings of the United Brethren missions in the context of British expansion and of missionary activity as a whole.

In Chapter Three, I tell Mignerey's story and begin to place it in context, making extensive use of his writing as well as of other material, especially Mueller's research. Mignerey describes his interactions with a wide variety of individuals representing all the major social groups involved in the colonial situation: John F. Musselman, the American head of the United Brethren missions in Sierra Leone; other missionaries such as Nurse Nora Vesper at Rotifunk and his friend Glen Rosselot (stationed at Shenge); the African pastor at Rotifunk John Karefa-Smart; African teachers such as Ross Lohr and mission "boys" at Rotifunk; Paramount Chief A.G. Caulker and section chief Santigi Bundu; residents of villages where he travels to preach; the students and African teachers at Albert Academy; and even Alexander Remeford Slater, the Governor of Sierra Leone.

Mignerey had thought carefully about his motivations for becoming a missionary, and ended up embracing a very specific interpretation of Christianity as the foundation of his work. His outlook is one of consistent theological and political liberalism. His theological loyalties were with the doctrine of "the fatherhood of God and the brotherhood of man," and his political loyalties were with socialism. All the same, he speaks with evangelical fervor of converting Africa to Jesus, and his sincerest desire was for the passage of the eighteenth amendment inaugurating Prohibition. Research into his own cultural context reveals two things: there was nothing unusual about a liberalism that combined those particular commitments; and there was nothing unusual about the presence of a strident liberal, or in fact of a strong liberal minority, in a predominantly conservative religious group.

As Mignerey began his work in Sierra Leone, he made an effort to understand the cultures he encountered there. In the diary, he describes in some detail incidents of conflict in which he was involved. He views his situation in Sierra Leone as a whole, attempting to grasp it from a religious, cultural, political, and economic perspective. Mignerey had begun his diary several months before actually leaving for Africa. He planned a coherent narrative. As it turned out, his story does finally have a clear beginning, middle, and end. But it was not one he could have at first anticipated. The theme of this unexpected narrative is another, to us striking, characteristic of Mignerey's original mindset: unacknowledged racial prejudice. And again, research into his American social context reveals that there was nothing at all unusual in this. Across the board, American society from 1880–1920 simply took for granted a set of explicit attitudes toward African Americans which after the 1960s would be almost universally recognized as racist. Liberals and Progressives such as Mignerey were for the most part by no means an exception to this. The story of Mignerey that emerges from his diary and later writings taken as a whole is the story of how he came to recognize this racism. The story's conclusion can be found in an article he wrote for his denomination's magazine in 1933 very explicitly attacking racism in American society, in the Christian church, and among missionaries (himself included). He showed exceptional courage in making a very public and brutally honest attack on racism in a day long before the civil rights movement transformed discourse about race in his country.

In the same chapter, I also begin to place Mignerey's story in its African context. Making use of Mueller's interviews, I demonstrate that the African pastors and teachers, despite the high regard in which they held the missionaries, were anything but blind to the racist and ethnocentric attitudes the missionaries brought with them from America. At one point in the 1930s, the African pastors even took action against another missionary for his ruthless persecution of polygamous teachers employed by the mission. The missionaries were in general stymied in their efforts to abolish both polygamy and slavery. However, they were clearly successful in a number of ways: in introducing a new religion into Sierra Leone which then took root there; in establishing a system of Western education; and in contributing to the development of a small Western-educated elite.

In Chapter Four, I leave Lloyd Mignerey's story behind, and turn to the African world with which he and the United Brethren came into contact. In attempting to portray the African cultural environment upon which the United Brethren impinged, I have focused on the two largest ethnic groups of Sierra Leone: the Mende and the Temne. I present a survey of their beliefs about God, creation, ancestors, and spirits, and present an account of the religious bases of their social systems. This survey I hope will deepen one's appreciation of the overall situation described in Chapter Three. Also, the material I present sets the stage for the story of cultural interaction I tell in Chapter Five.

In the course of this discussion I engage Robin Horton's contention that the primary basis of traditional African religion is the prediction and control of events rather than communion. The available evidence for the Mende and the Temne supports Horton's contention about the central role of prediction and control in the case of magic, and also about the relative absence of communion in the case of the traditional creator god. But I also claim, contra Horton, that communion with the immediate human community is in fact the central focus of religious experience and practice in Mende and Temne culture, and that the human community includes the living dead. I interpret communion with the immediate human community both in terms of Niebuhr's notion of loyalty and trust, and in terms of James's notion of the "more" which I relate to Durkheim's notion of "effervescence."

I conclude with a discussion of the religious basis of the Poro and Sande/Bondo societies and their central role in the cohesion of traditional society among the Mende and the Temne. I also show how the Poro society functions as a fundamentally democratic political institution. This survey lays the basis for my concluding exploration of the interaction of missionary activity with traditional culture, and of the interaction of colonial power with the political structures of traditional society.

The fifth and final chapter is the synthesis and conclusion of everything that has gone before. The core of Chapter Five is the section titled "The African Encounter with Missionary Christianity." In that section I explore in detail the reaction of pastors and teachers to the missionaries with whom they worked, and the nature of their participation in the missionary endeavor. Lamin Sanneh has said that the task of scholarship in the study of traditional African religions in the colonial context should not simply be to defend them, but to study in detail how they interacted with Christianity.[2] Howard Mueller's interviews provide detailed evidence about the nature of this interaction in Sierra Leone. Sanneh also claims that the stereotype is mistaken according to which Africans were the passive recipients of a religion imposed upon them by missionaries. He wants to encourage a movement of scholarship that will "demonstrate the role of Africans as pioneers in the adaptation and assimilation of Christianity in their societies, with a corresponding scaling down of the role of Western missionaries in that process."[3] Mueller's interviews make it clear that in the case of the United Brethren and Sierra Leone, Sanneh's assertion is fully justified. The African United Brethren pastors he interviewed provide a remarkable glimpse of the way that Africans used their own traditions to interpret Christianity, and also often wove those traditions together into their own Christian religious life. I demonstrate that the pastors played a more important role than missionaries in the propagation of Christianity; that conversions were voluntary and not coerced; that even pastors retained, in varying degrees, traditional African beliefs, often without the missionaries' knowledge or understanding; that even conservative pastors did not demonize traditional African belief; and that pastors regularly used analogies from traditional African religion to help explain Christianity to potential converts. Also, the interviews show that there were a number of serious and clearly defined conflicts between the pastors and the missionaries, especially as in the case of polygamy.

While the main focus of this work is on religion, I have endeavored throughout to place religious interaction in its social and political context. In Chapter Five I include a study of the political and social effects of colonization from the 1920s to the time of independence in 1961. The overall conclusion one reaches with the benefit of hindsight is that the effect of colonization on the political and social integrity of African society was mainly destructive. The involvement of Christian missions in colonization was not the most significant factor in the disruption of the religious basis of traditional African society. The key factor in this disruption was the marginalization of the Poro society through the policy of indirect rule. And this must count as religious disruption, since the Poro is a religious institution. The religious function of Poro is communion with one's immediate human community, which is the central focus, as I argue, of traditional African religion among the Mende and the Temne. From the available evidence, it appears that the relationship between traditional African religion and United Brethren Christianity in Sierra Leone was on the whole one of accommodation and synthesis rather than conflict and disruption. For example, even United Brethren pastors were Poro members, and the missionaries' campaign against polygamy had virtually no effect beyond that on mission workers.

Though in so many ways things have turned out differently in post-colonial Sierra Leone than a great many well-intentioned people desired, missionaries and Africans together did succeed in establishing Christianity and modern Western education in Sierra Leone. The United Brethren mission also made a marked contribution to the formation of a new nation through the education of its future leaders. In the final section of the fifth chapter, I complete the story of the pastors' struggle to win autonomy for their church—a struggle carried out against the resistance of many missionaries, who, though committed in theory to eventual autonomy, were after all quite reluctant to let go. Autonomy for the African church lagged behind the political independence of Sierra Leone by more than ten years, despite the fact that many of the Africans who led the way to independence emerged out of the United Brethren mission schools.

I hope that the overall effect of this book will be to provide a comprehensive picture of a certain time and place in history in which enormous social forces came into dynamic interaction. The same forces, of course, were coming together all over Africa at that same time in more or less similar ways. My interest is in the particular way this interaction played out in one corner of Africa, from the different perspectives of a number of individuals the record whose experiences is fortunately extant.

Philosophy of Religion, Social Science, and History: A Note on Method

The approach I have taken to the study of history and of the history of ideas affirms that empathy with personal voices and personal stories plays an irreplaceable role in the understanding of the past. The basis of this work is the voices of particular human individuals—most prominently Mignerey and the African pastors Mueller interviewed. But of course it is imperative see any individual's experience within the context of the overall experience of the groups he or she may belong to. I have worked to relate these voices to the context of the religious belief and social ideology of the United Brethren church in the United States and Africa, as well as of the traditional society and religion of the Mende and the Temne.

The sources I have drawn upon to illuminate the cultural interaction I study fall into the categories of history, sociology, anthropology, political science, and philosophy. These sources have provided not only information or "data" but also explanatory ideas. To attempt to understand religious and cultural interaction is to attempt to understand human beliefs and human actions, including beliefs and actions attributable to groups. The approach I am taking to this understanding is phenomenological. But the phenomenological tradition upon which I am relying calls into question the meaning of social science as such. For example, Husserl claims that in fact psychology does not exist—there is only transcendental phenomenology.[4] Husserl does not mean that psychological research as it is usually carried out has no meaning or value—but rather that when a "science of the mind" is seen as but one science among others, something absolutely essential has been overlooked.

Social science takes as its object individual and collective human action and belief. For Husserl, consciousness is itself that which knows and understands; its knowing and understanding is an ability to act; and action intends conscious goals. This means that social science intends to understand understanding itself. What does it mean to understand understanding as such, and what does it mean to understand anyone's particular understanding of anything? Phenomenology focuses on the issues that arise when we ask just these questions.

The phenomenological approach I am taking holds that the fundamental human situation is that of the pre-objectively self-aware individual human being to whom the world appears as composed of objects which are values, and to whom other pre-objectively self-aware conscious beings appear as values in a more fundamental sense. There will always be dispute about what really exists, and in what way, and about what is really valuable, and in what way. But value as such, world as such, and consciousness as such cannot be in dispute and cannot be explained in any more fundamental terms. Understanding another person's values and beliefs, or the beliefs and values of a group, can begin in no other way than the attempt to empathize with the other's understanding. The idea that knowing can be explained as the mere result of blind physical forces is nonsense. And the idea that social "forces" explain individual action needs strict qualification: A society only exists insofar as its constituent individuals believe it does and are willing to act as if it does. "Society" as that which limits and supports any individual arises only in and through the beliefs and loyalties of its members. Action is inescapably individual. It is only the existence of shared interpretations of the meaning of an individual's actions that gives meaning to society as an agent.

Human beings are motivated by the values that mean something to them. The primary source of my understanding of what a value means to another is my empathy with that person's experience of that value. Through such empathy, the value which means something must appear as a possibly a genuine value—a value I might possibly also embrace and affirm. The essence of human consciousness is that truthfulness is at issue for it. The activity of valuing, which means the experience of human motivation as such, is essentially an effort to embrace that which truly matters. To say that empathy is the necessary starting point for the understanding of human motivation is to say that I can only understand another by trying to participate in his or her very activity of valuing. This is why human experience can never be a mere object of study. To regard human experience, including human culture, merely as one object acted upon by another—as an effect to be explained by a cause—is simply to ignore human experience as human experience. In my study of the interaction of culture and religion, I am assuming that culture and religion are primarily the human activity of valuing. Understanding radically contrasting cultural and religious values involves first attempting to empathize with individuals who embrace those values. Such empathy is the source of insight into how it is that the values in question could mean something to someone.

The task of tracing the interaction of religious traditions raises the fundamental question of how it may even be possible to compare disparate traditions as well as the question of the nature of social groups and of the nature of religious experience itself. My aim accordingly has also been to work out a philosophical approach to the question of a definition of religion within which religious diversity may be understood. (I explain this outlook in detail in Chapter Four.) I locate religious experience in the personal experience of value and in a lived questioning of origins that arises out of that experience. The experience of value involves both a passive dimension of feeling, and an active dimension of commitment. The roots of my notion of religious feeling lie in William James's notion of the "more." I draw my notion of commitment from H. Richard Niebuhr's appropriation of the outlook of Kierkegaard. This definition of religion in terms of feeling and commitment encompasses both religions for whom a transcendent God is the center of faith and religious feeling, and those whose center is the immediate human community, inclusive of ancestors.

In my study, I have endeavored to pay detailed attention to the social and historical dimensions of religion, and have drawn upon sociological theory to some extent. However, my final perspective is neither sociological nor theological. I say that my *final* perspective in this work is not sociological because I view religious experience not as a mere object of study, but as that through which a certain kind of truth can be disclosed. However, my final perspective in this work is not theological either, since, while I take religious truth seriously, I am not here endeavoring to evaluate the material at hand in terms of some particular religious commitment, perhaps that of a particular denomination or creed. The perspective into which I attempt to integrate a great deal of sociological, anthropological, historical, and religious material is best named "philosophy of religion."

Notes

1. I should note that "The United Brethren in Christ" here signifies the church of that name which merged with the Evangelical Church in 1946 to form the Evangelical United Brethren Church, which itself merged with the Methodist church in 1968 to form the United Methodist Church. I follow the story of this church in Sierra Leone through 1973, when it gained autonomy. In 1889, a small group split off from the United Brethren in Christ and remains a distinct denomination to this day, maintaining some missionary presence in Sierra Leone. In this volume, I do not follow the history of that denomination, which has always retained the name "The United Brethren in Christ."

2. Lamin Sanneh, *West African Christianity* (Maryknoll, NY: Orbis Books, 1983), 242.

3. Ibid., 244.

4. Edmund Husserl, *The Crisis of European Sciences and Transcendental Phenomenology,* trans. David Carr (Evanston, Il.: Northwestern Univ. Press, 1972), sec. 72.

CHAPTER ONE

Theological Diversity and Missionary Ideology in the United Brethren Church (1800–1922)

A widespread stereotype closely associates missionaries with a conservative or fundamentalist religious outlook that would reject all that is not Christian as the work of the devil. Certainly such a stereotype can be expected to come to mind on the basis of the bare facts of Lloyd Mignerey's early career: born in 1898, he grew up in a small southern Ohio town in a conservative, pietistic religious environment, and felt called to preach as early as his teenage years. The two dreams of his youth were to work in the service of the great causes of Prohibition and of foreign missions. When opportunities opened up in each of these fields, he embraced them with fervor. "Africa for Jesus!" he exclaimed in his diary as he was about to set off on his voyage to Sierra Leone. But this same Mignerey who embraced missions also embraced the most liberal version of nineteenth century liberal theology. This same Mignerey who embraced Prohibition also embraced socialism. His liberal Christian outlook was not at all unusual for the liberal Christianity of his time. And though liberal Christianity was a minority outlook in his own as well as in many other Protestant denominations, it was not a persecuted or even a marginalized one.

As an example of how Mignerey helps shatter stereotypes I can point to what was in some ways the climax of Mignerey's experience in Sierra Leone. During his second year in that country, he had served as principal of Albert Academy, a highly regarded secondary school located in the capital city, Freetown. As the time of commencement approached, he became inspired with an idea to revolutionize the commencement ceremony. He would write an allegorical pageant in which the Spirit of Christian Education would rescue the Spirit of Africa whom the Spirit of Ignorance had enslaved. The Spirit of Africa would appear in chains. Mignerey quickly wrote up a draft and shared it with the African teachers in the Academy. They did not like it, letting him know that the people would not take kindly to seeing the Spirit of Africa on stage in the chains of ignorance. But they insisted they liked the idea of having a pageant. After much discussion he revised the play, which became a great success. The draft had been an almost perfect reflection of the prejudices about Africa he had been taught by his church, his schools, and his whole social environment. But the draft, rather than being forced down the Africans' throats, had become an occasion of dialogue. And for Mignerey the dialogue continued. He obtained in Freetown the works of Edward W. Blyden, one of the most prominent Black anti-imperialists of his time. Mignerey ended up becoming a great admirer of Blyden, and even tried to spread Blyden's views in the United Brethren Church when he returned to Ohio. There is evidence his attempts at enlightening Americans met with some frustration.

In this chapter I attempt to describe the religious environment in which Mignerey grew up and was educated. I explore the currents of theological and social thought and opinion in the United Brethren Church in the late nineteenth and early twentieth centuries, especially as they were evident at Otterbein College in Westerville, Ohio, which was the church's flagship institution of higher education at the time. There was a wide range of thought and opinion even within this one small denomination, a range that confounds in one way or another the way we in the present generally understand terms such as 'liberal,' 'conservative,' and even 'fundamentalist.'

In the following sections, I attempt to define two contrasting movements in nineteenth and early twentieth century American Protestantism, which I designate "liberalism" and "conservatism." Mignerey's diaries and papers offer a unique perspective on education at Otterbein College from 1913–1917, and specifically on the place of liberalism and conservatism in the world of thought into which faculty would have introduced the college's students. The liberalism and conservatism of the time had some perhaps surprising commonalities: Many conservatives and even fundamentalists embraced the social gospel along with liberals; and the dominant racism and ethnocentrism of the time went largely unchallenged by liberals and conservatives alike.

United Brethren Christianity:
Conservatism and Liberalism

Mignerey's interpretation of Christianity and his motivation for missionary work grew out of the influence of the United Brethren Church and his education at Otterbein College, the oldest and most respected of the denomination's six institutions of higher learning. While the theological outlook of the United Brethren Church was certainly predominantly conservative, it was by no means monolithic, especially by the late nineteenth century. The church had arisen in the United States in the eighteenth century through the coalescence of groups of German immigrants, many of whom lived isolated from established congregations, and who came out of the pietistic tradition in the Lutheran and Reformed churches. Phillip William Otterbein, a graduate of Herborn University, "the citadel of pietism in the German Reformed Church,"[1] was brought to the colonies in 1752, and became the leader who united the immigrant groups into a single organization, which was formally founded in 1800.[2] William Henry Naumann, in his careful study of the role of theology in the United Brethren (and Evangelical) churches defines the "central core of their convictions" as "their commitment to the supreme importance of Christian experience, usually interpreted to accent the emotions....To confront Christ squarely was to be convulsively converted, and this meant transformation of the whole man, not least of which were his feelings."[3] Naumann also notes that "the religious feelings of a Christian could be used to prove the truth of certain Christian doctrines," or to refute others, such as the Calvinistic doctrine of predestination.[4] This kind of high valuation of feeling in religion is certainly typical of pietism (as well as of British and American Methodism). But neither pietists nor Methodists based their religious life and religious convictions on feeling alone. As Naumann points out, for pietists Christian experience had to be evaluated against the authority of scripture and of common sense, as well as in terms of the fruits of experience in good works.[5]

Naumann shows how the United Brethren and Evangelical churches, as they increased in numbers and as their members became increasingly educated over the course of the nineteenth century, moved from a position of anti-intellectualism and even fear of education, to a position that valued education highly, and promoted serious engagement with theological issues.[6] The United Brethren Church, for example, founded six colleges and one theological seminary between 1847 and 1905.[7] (Indeed, United Brethren could look back to the example of the close association between the highly educated Phillip William Otterbein, and Martin Boehm, the untutored preacher, who together were the most important leaders of the movement that led to the founding of their church[8]). Early in the nineteenth century, the emphasis on Christian experience and on biblicism led to a downplaying of the importance of creeds, while in the sixties and seventies, increasing contact with the wider world of competing viewpoints led to a greater sense of the importance of creeds, and of the importance of theological reflection, as a defense against heterodox views. After 1885, there was increasing acceptance within the church of the idea that creeds are not absolute statements of truth and that it may at times be appropriate to revise them.[9] Naumann also points out that, at least during the period 1841–1890 "purity of doctrine remained a prime concern for most Evangelicals and United Brethren."[10] The climate of religious thought and belief in the United Brethren Church from its beginnings at least through 1930 (the period covered by Naumann's study) was certainly predominantly conservative. But by the 1880s, the denominational literature had come to include a number of distinctly liberal voices. Naumann points out that "although never in the majority, liberal voices did make themselves heard....Bishops Hott [1889–1902], Mills [1893–1909], and Bell [1905–1929] of the United Brethren frequently expressed liberal sentiments. Mills was widely known as being on the liberal side of almost every question."[11]

What is involved in gaining a sense of the predominant or prevailing view-point of a religious group? In stating that the predominant viewpoint of the United Brethren at least until 1930 was "conservative" or "orthodox" it is important to keep certain, perhaps obvious, things in mind. The conservatism or orthodoxy of one group or one era may well be the heresy of another group or era. (For example, the United Brethren, a church with a Calvinistic heritage, on the whole rejected the orthodox Calvinistic doctrine of predestination, although unanimity was lacking here[12]). Also, the fact that members of a group accept a set of belief statements (such as the Apostles' Creed or the Nicene Creed) as true does not imply that what those statements mean to their adherents is identical in each case, that each adherent understands the statement in the same way, that each adherent has an clear understanding of the statement, or has reflected sufficiently for the meaning of the statement to even be an issue.

The pages of *The Religious Telescope* (which form the primary basis for Naumann's generalizations about the predominant viewpoints of the United Brethren church, from 1834–1930) are filled with a remarkable range of articles written by laymen, ministers, bishops, and professors, that reveal fairly wide differences in viewpoint, sensibility, knowledge, and intellectual sophistication. Prior to 1841, Naumann does find in these views the common assumption that "all parts of scripture [are]... of equal value and authority," that "the Bible [is] a collection of eternal truths, the language of which [is] equally comprehensible and relevant to peoples of all time."[13] This assumption, along with the emphasis on emotional, life-changing conversion, discouraged theological discussion altogether in the church in the early nineteenth century.

But even as more explicit viewpoints emerge in the mid-to-late nineteenth century, it is impossible to precisely define an "orthodox" view—simply because any statement of belief will be interpreted, experienced, and applied in a variety of different ways by those who affirm it, and some of those who affirm it will reflect upon it seriously, while others will not. But it is possible to define certain general emphases as a basis for a rough classification of "liberal" and "conservative" viewpoints. In general, liberals and conservatives in the United Brethren Church shared a very strong emphasis on the inner experience of conversion as central to their religion. Liberals tended to view creeds as human productions, changeable and relative, while among conservatives there was a range of opinion regarding the mutability or immutability of creeds. Among both groups of United Brethren, correct beliefs are viewed as meaningless without a changed heart and a changed life. Both groups affirmed the importance, not only of experience, but also of the revelation of God through Jesus Christ, and both groups understood that revelation in specific ways, and expressed their understanding in specific language. The difference between liberalism and conservatism among United Brethren in the late nineteenth and early twentieth centuries can best be defined, I think, in relationship to nineteenth century German liberal theology. What makes this liberal theological movement, as a whole, distinctive is the new emphasis it introduced. In the simplest terms, this liberalism places primary emphasis on the life and teachings of Jesus. In doing so it contrasts with a conservatism that places primary emphasis on Jesus' death and atonement.

One possible measure of conservatism or orthodoxy might be closeness of adherence to the Apostles' and/or Nicene Creeds. But interestingly, the Apostles' Creed has nothing to say about "atonement," and the doctrine of atonement explicit in the Nicene creed goes no further than the assertion that Christ was crucified "for our sake." The conservative view is perhaps better defined in terms of what it most emphasizes in its understanding of the creeds. The topics covered in the Nicene creed, for example, are: the nature and relationship between God and Christ; the birth, death, resurrection, and second coming of Jesus Christ (the creeds mention nothing about his life or teaching); the church; baptism; afterlife. The conservatism of the United Brethren church is evident in a statement by one its early leaders, to the effect that "This church shall be free and open to all denominations of Christendom, who live, teach, and believe in the doctrine of the Trinity and preach the doctrine of Atonement."[14] United Brethren Bishop Jonathan Weaver's *Christian Theology: A Concise and Practical View of the Cardinal Doctrines and Institutions of Christianity* (1900), which is basically a collection of Weaver's essays on various theological topics, may be taken as an example of a typically conservative view.[15] According the Weaver, "the doctrine of atonement, deep, mysterious and wonderful as it is...should ever be considered as the leading doctrine of Christianity."[16] And Weaver understands atonement as "vicarious." Man has sinned against God's law, and man cannot be pardoned unless "satisfaction" has been rendered to God, which is to say, unless someone is punished, for man's disobedience. Jesus Christ

> the eternal Son of God, volunteered to come into the world and take upon himself human nature, and become obedient unto death. His relation to God, in his divine nature, and his relation to man, in his human nature, made it possible for him to render satisfaction to the law, and provide a way whereby man could escape from the guilt and punishment of sin.[17]

In *Outlines of Doctrinal Theology* (1914), the only other theological manual published by the United Brethren, A.W. Drury teaches a slightly more flexible conservatism. The typical emphasis of conservatism is explicit: "The life of purity, obedience, and service might be regarded a part of this work [the work of the Redeemer], but it was rather a condition or preparation for it. It is the passive righteousness of Christ, his sufferings and death in man's behalf, that claims our attention. It is here that we come to the very heart of the gospel."[18] But Drury's exposition includes implicit as well as explicit acknowledgement of conflicting positions. For example, a statement such as the following could be seen as an attempt to find common ground with liberalism: "Those who seek to find the basis of redemption in the sufferings and death, or passive righteousness of Christ, and those who seek it in the acts of Christ might harmonize on the statement that the merit is in his obedience unto death."[19] In his exposition of the atonement, Drury briefly (and indeed, somewhat vaguely) sketches four different theories of the atonement. Drury supports what he calls "the Anselmic view" of vicarious atonement, while also finding some truth in other views. He contrasts his "moderate Anselmic view" with what he calls the "ultra-evangelical view." According to the "moderate Anselmic view," the atonement is not a matter of

Christ being "punished in our stead," but rather represents "the cost to God of man's salvation."[20] Although conservative, Drury wants to avoid what he considers to be extremism, and he makes some effort to find common ground with those who hold views different from his own. Drury also includes in his manual pietism's clear rejection of the Calvinistic doctrine that the benefits of the atonement are limited to a predetermined band of the elect.[21]

Like the Nicene and Apostles' Creeds upon which it relies, the conservative view places primary emphasis on the death of Christ, and in its understanding of that death, the conservative view emphasizes the idea of "vicarious" or "substitutionary" atonement (an idea not explicitly present in the creeds). But even Weaver emphasizes that "creeds and confessions are not to be considered sources of theology."[22] The authority behind the creeds is the Bible. But he is also critical of "those who oppose creeds....They insist that the Bible alone is the one only standard of faith and practice. This sounds well, but it is not the Bible alone, but the Bible *as they interpreted it.*"[23] Creeds are not only necessary but inevitable, because anyone who is teaching the truths of the Bible is thereby stating an interpretation of the Bible. Creeds are important also because they promote the unity of church organizations. Conservative though he is, Weaver implicitly acknowledges the necessity and relativity of interpretation.

The liberalism that gained prominence in American Protestantism in the late nineteenth century represents a specific movement and tradition within Protestant Christianity. The movement began with the German theologian Friedrich Schleiermacher, whose most well known successors were the German theologians Albrecht Ritschl, his student Adolf Harnack, and the American theologian Walter Rauschenbusch. This movement came to dominate most mainline protestant seminaries in the United States after 1880.[24] While the United Brethren remained, of course, predominantly conservative, a minority within the church did embrace liberalism. The most noteworthy United Brethren liberal of this time was also one of the denomination's most revered bishops, J.S. (Job Smith) Mills, who served as bishop from 1893 till his death in 1909.

Liberalism is often defined in terms of acceptance of or openness to various intellectual movements of the nineteenth century. For example, nineteenth century liberals were responsible for developing the biblical scholarship which made tremendous advances in understanding the process through which the Bible was written, and which rejected the idea that each book had the authorship traditionally assumed for it, and that every statement was factual and infallible. But conservatives at times accepted that scholarship in some ways and to some extent. Liberals emphasized the importance of feeling in religion as a reality deeper than mere belief statements, but, especially in the pietistic tradition, conservatives did as well. Liberals could be counted on to reject a literalistic understanding of scripture, but not all conservatives were literalists. Liberals were certainly open to the idea of evolution, interpreting it in a theistic context, but many conservatives shared that interpretation. What perhaps most reliably distinguishes the liberal from the conservative viewpoint is a difference in what each emphasizes as of primary (though not necessarily exclusive) importance. The central emphasis of the conservative view is on Christ's death and atonement, while the central emphasis of the liberal view is on Christ's life and teachings. The Apostles' and the Nicene creeds are silent about the life and teachings of Jesus. The liberal view does not necessarily involve the rejection of those creeds, but the central focus of the liberal view is precisely upon what the creeds ignore. Liberal theology is based on a close study of the biblical texts themselves, and makes constant reference to them. It finds the essence of Christianity in what Jesus actually said and did, drawing its greatest inspiration from the sermon on the mount and the parables.[25]

Harnack, in his tremendously influential *What is Christianity* (1901) [*Das Wesen des Christentums*, 1900] identified the three main subjects of the teachings of Jesus as "1) the kingdom of God and its coming, 2) God the Father and the Infinite Value of the Human Soul; 3) the higher righteousness and the commandment of love."[26] According to Ritschl, "the kingdom of God is the divinely vouched for highest good of the community founded through his revelation in Christ" and "the righteous conduct in which the members of the Christian community share in the bringing in the kingdom of God has its universal law and its personal motive in love to God and to one's neighbor."[27] But for Ritschl, "the highest good of the community" and the "personal motive [of] love to God and to one's neighbor" are not merely 'man's highest ethical ideals' (as theologians critical of liberalism, such as H.R. Niebuhr, claim) but bear a unique relationship to Jesus Christ. Ritschl does not reject the doctrine of the trinity, but interprets the relationship between God and Jesus as unique in this way: "Now Jesus, being the first to realize in His own personal life the final purpose of the kingdom of God, is therefore alone of his kind, for should any other fulfill the same task as perfectly as He, yet he would be unlike Him because dependent on Him."[28] Jesus is the son of God in the sense that he uniquely *initiates* the human relationship to God as Father, which itself is the essence of the Kingdom of God. Ritschl also explicitly rejects the doctrine of vicarious atonement.[29] Ritschl interprets the significance of Christ's death not in terms of judicial satisfaction but in terms of the uniqueness of Jesus' relationship toward God the Father. Jesus freely obeyed his calling, to the point of death, "for the purpose of bringing mankind into the same relation toward God as their Father which He occupied. For this very purpose He accepted with patience and resignation to God's will increased suffering and even death as a proof of His fellowship with God."[30] Ritschl believes Christ's death can be understood only in the context of his life. Noting the virtual absence of Christ's life from the epistles, Ritschl notes that "it appears as if the emphasizing of His death as the act of redemption counted upon an interpretation of this act which is in complete contrast to the thought of His life. Yet is it plain that the apostles understood the divinely purposed death of Christ to be a sacrifice only as it was connected with His obedience to His life-calling."[31]

Bishop J.S. Mills (1848–1909) was the most prominent liberal in the United Brethren Church of his time. Mills was born on a farm in rural Washington County in southeast Ohio and was sickly as a child. Due to his ill health, and the fact that common schools were open only three or four months a year, he did not learn to read until age 11. But he applied himself assiduously to study, and became a United Brethren minister at age 20. At age 26, his assignment as pastor to Otterbein College gave him the opportunity to further his self-education. Thomas J. Sanders, who later became Otterbein's philosophy professor, re-members: "The dominant impression I have of him is as a thinker, a student, a scholar—the typical scholar, pale as the proverbial potato sprout in the cellar. He lived much and intensely with his books, in his study. It was my first conspi-cuous example of a student preacher. Once he took me into his study 'den'—a square room and in its center a kind of hollow square desk where he sat with books all around him."[32] Mills received the A.M. from Otterbein, the D.D. from Lebanon Valley and Westfield, and the Ph.D. from Illinois Wesleyan Univ. (probably through correspondence study). In pursuit of his studies he gained a reading knowledge of German, French, Italian, and Spanish.[33] He served as Pro-fessor of English literature and rhetoric, Professor of Philosophy, and President at Western College (a UBC college in Toledo, Iowa, later called Leander Clark College, which eventually merged with Coe College). For the last 16 years of his life he served as bishop. Mills' wide and intense study made him familiar with all the major philosophical views of the day. The limited writing he has left behind is startling not only for its liberalism, but for its subtlety, sophistication, and eloquence.

BISHOP JOB SMITH MILLS, A.M., Ph.D., D.D.

J.S. Mills

In 1913, the church produced a 270 page biographical volume in his honor. The volume's introduction is not stinting in its praise of Mills:

> The life of a Christian is a revelation from God; it is the gospel in action. The bi-
> ography of a great man is...an exhibition of the power of the gospel....Bishop J.S.
> Mills, D.D...had large revelations from God for the work of His church. The re-
> cord of his struggle, rise, service, and achievements as here set forth is most in-
> spiring. But few men have overcome such giant difficulties, and risen to such su-
> preme heights in scholarship and service.[34]

The volume does not attempt to conceal or downplay Mills' liberal views.
Indeed, the last chapter includes the full text of an address Mills gave before
students at the Union Biblical Seminary, titled "The Kingdom of God, the True
Socialism" which is a clear and unambiguous presentation of the essentials of
liberal theology. In the chapter on Mills' role as churchman and bishop, we find
a clear discussion of Mills' viewpoint:

> Bishop Mills was a liberal. His spirit and life were in sympathy with the pro-
> gressive movements for the betterment of society and the enlargement of the use-
> fulness of the church to which he belonged.[35]
>
> Bishop Mills was never a conservative or middle-of-the-road man; he was
> always on the constructive, progressive side of every question that touched his
> life. Hence, he was considered by some as being so progressive that he was un-
> safe. Indeed, some called him visionary and others were inclined to say of him
> that he was seeking these things for his own advancement and preferment. How-
> ever, those who were near him—those who understood him—quickly refuted this
> charge as unfair to him as a Church leader.[36]

The volume includes a series of eulogies and reminiscences, even including
one from W.M. Weekley, who later became the leader of United Brethren fundamentalists. Weekley says: "We did not always agree on everything. No two
men will who think independently, but I found him gentlemanly and brotherly in
his bearing, willing to listen, and when convinced, ready to yield."[37] It is noteworthy that an individual whose theological viewpoint differed drastically from
those of the majority of his denomination rose to a position of leadership and
honor, and that differences could be the topic of open dialogue carried out in an
atmosphere of civility and respect.

Mills' outlook is unmistakably that of liberalism in theology. He had direct acquaintance with German Biblical and theological scholarship[38] and he
expressed his commitment to liberal theology forthrightly and persuasively. The
address he gave to students at Union Biblical seminary in 1891, titled "The
Kingdom of God, or True Socialism" is an eloquent summing up of all the major
tenets of that movement. Regarding "the fundamental idea" of the kingdom of
God, he says:

> This is not the fact of human sinfulness, though it shows why sin is so great a
> matter. This is not the possibility of an eternal loss through sin, though it shows
> why that possibility is such a fearful one. This is not the offer of salvation to all
> men, though it shows why God was pleased to make the offer. This is not the joy
> of the redeemed in heaven, though it reveals the source and ground of that joy.
> This fundamental idea upon which the kingdom of God rests is the fatherhood of
> God, and the childhood of all men to him, and the brotherhood of all men to each
> other. Phillips Brooks says, "Upon the race and upon the individual, Jesus is al-
> ways bringing into more and more perfect revelation the certain truth that man,

and every man, is the child of God." This is the sum of the word, of the incarnation. A hundred other statements concerning him are true; but all statements concerning him hold their truth within this truth—that Jesus came to restore the fact of God's fatherhood to man's knowledge, and to its central place of power over man's life.

Jesus is mysteriously the word of God made flesh. He is the worker of amazing miracles upon the bodies and souls of men. He is the Savior by suffering; but behind all these, as the purpose for which he is all these, he is the redeemer of man into the fatherhood of God...The power of Jesus, in founding a kingdom, is the idea of Jesus multiplied by, and projected through his personality. That idea is, the relation of childhood and fatherhood between man and God, and the relation of brotherhood between all men. Man is the child of God even though he is sinful and rebellious. He is the prodigal child of God, ignorant of his father. But his rebellion breaks not that first relationship. To reassert this fatherhood, childhood, and brotherhood as an everlasting truth, and to re-establish its power as the central, formative idea of society was the mission of Jesus to earth.[39]

Mills' view is evidently very close indeed to Ritschl's.[40] The meaning of Jesus' sonship cannot be separated from his mission to bring all human beings into the relationship of sonship. The understanding of Jesus' mission so defined does not mean rejecting, say, the creeds, or the "hundred other statements" that are true of Jesus, but it does mean that everything in the creeds has its root and meaning only in that mission. And in particular, the kingdom of God is not limited to the afterlife or an apocalyptic millennium, but is "the spirit of Christ in human society, remedying its ills and uniting it into social unity, ultimately redeemed and perfected."[41]

In the *Manual of Family Worship* Mills compiled and wrote, the scripture selections he presents also illustrate his liberal theology. Mills notes that the Bible "has no equal and can have no substitute" but also that since it "is a large book of unequal parts, a selection has been made of the most valuable portions." Just before the scripture selections begin Mills places the Apostles' Creed, which he describes as "a brief expression of what the early church believed the Bible teaches." The scripture selections begin with eleven "summaries of religion and ethics." And these passages are exactly those upon which liberal theology places the greatest emphasis. Three represent versions of the love commandment. He chose the first three from the Old Testament, including Micah 6:8: "He hath shewed thee, O man, what is good; and what doth the lord require of thee, but to do justly, and to love mercy, and walk humbly with your God?"[42] He includes this New Testament version of the love commandment: "Master, which is the great commandment in the law? And he said unto him, thou shalt love the Lord thy God with all thy heart, and with all thy soul, and with all thy mind. This is the great and first commandment. And a second like unto it is this, Thou shalt love thy neighbor as thy self. On these two commandments hangeth the whole law, and the prophets" (Matt. 22:36–40). The following passage illustrates the idea that all human beings are children of God: "For in him we live, and move, and have our being....For we are also his offspring. Being then the offspring of God, we ought not to think that the Godhead is like unto gold, or silver, or stone, graven by art and device of man" (Acts 17: 28, 29). None of the eleven selections refers to the crucifixion or atonement.

Liberalism and Conservatism at Otterbein College (1913–1917)

Lloyd Mignerey was born, raised, and educated in a predominantly conservative denomination in which a minority of liberal voices were accorded a hearing and even a significant degree of respect and influence. Liberals like Mills, far from being ostracized, could even become bishops. Among the faculty of Otterbein College as well, liberal and conservative viewpoints were accorded respect and flourished side by side. As a major in Philosophy and Education[43] Mignerey must have become well acquainted with the intellectual roots of the contradictions in his church. Otterbein's faculty was fairly distinguished. Of 15 faculty in 1914 (not counting eight music and art faculty), six held Ph.D.'s and one (the president) held the D.D. In his diary, Mignerey makes frequent positive mention of two professors whose classes he attended—the English Professor Sarah M. Sherrick (Ph.D. Yale, 1896; Ph.B. Otterbein, 1889), and the professor of Sociology and Economics Charles Snavely (Ph.D. Johns Hopkins, 1902; A.B. Otterbein, 1894; LL.D. Otterbein, 1934). (In all there were three faculty with degrees [A.M. or Ph.D.] from Yale. A tradition of attendance of United Brethren at Yale divinity school, which lasted into the twentieth century, began in the 1870s.[44]) As a philosophy and education major, Mignerey took many courses with Thomas J. Sanders (Ph.D. Wooster, 1888; M.A. Otterbein, 1881; B.A. Otterbein, 1878), and like all students at Otterbein, he took the required two years of "Bible" with Edmund Jones, Professor of Bible and Education (A.M. Amherst, 1871; Ph.D. Ohio Univ., 1903). He makes no mention of the latter three professors in his diary. From course descriptions, diary entries, and college compositions Mignerey preserved, a clear picture emerges of Thomas Sanders (who had been president of Otterbein from 1891–1901) as a representative of an intellectually sophisticated, and relatively moderate, conservatism, and of Charles Snavely as a critically minded advocate of the social gospel. Upon Mignerey, Snavely evidently made much the deeper impression of the two.

George Marsden, in *The Soul of the American University*, demonstrates the intimate involvement of Protestantism in the development of American higher education. The domination of American colleges by a conservative, often Calvinist Protestantism was challenged by the liberalism of the Jeffersonian enlightenment in the late eighteenth century. Marsden shows how the major colonial institutions and the new universities founded in the nineteenth century reasserted the dominance of Protestantism by embracing the assumption that biblical truth and the truths uncovered through scientific and scholarly inquiry will in the long run necessarily harmonize even if in the short run they do not. An essential thrust of Protestantism itself, they agreed, is free inquiry. This intellectual compromise enabled them, as leaders of an evangelical Protestantism that still dominated national culture, to maintain allegiance to that Protestantism while modernizing their institutions in ways that the economy, if nothing else, required. The leaders of American higher education in the nineteenth century, whether they were relatively conservative (like James McCosh and Francis Patton of Princeton, Noah Porter of Yale, or Henry Tappan of the University of Michigan) or relatively liberal (like Andrew White of Cornell, Daniel Coit Gilman of Johns Hopkins, or Charles Eliot of Harvard), shared this basic assumption. Marsden shows how these major universities found it increasingly difficult to maintain their distinctively Christian character as they moved toward, and into, the twentieth century. Men like McCosh, Patton, and Porter attempted to foster free inquiry while still ensuring that Christian, or at least theistic, perspectives would remain dominant. The delicate balance they achieved could not be maintained once they had left the scene. A small denominational college like Otterbein in the first two decades of the twentieth century, while it had an up-to-date curriculum, was still able to present that curriculum as a whole within the context of Christian belief. The differences of opinion about the meaning and interpretation of that belief could be significant, but those differences represented just that—an internal struggle about the meaning of a shared heritage.

The intellectual outlook that Thomas Sanders conveyed in the philosophy courses Mignerey attended in 1915 and 1916 in many ways represented the compromise embraced by academic leaders like McCosh and Porter in the 1870s and 1880s. Mignerey had eleven semesters of courses in philosophy, education, and psychology, most of which would have been taught by Sanders. The descriptions of these courses in Otterbein's catalogue, evidently written by Sanders, summarize, in devout tones, the main text for each class. Especially notable among the philosophy courses taken by Mignerey are the courses in *Logic* and *Grounds of Theistic and Christian Belief.* The text for *Logic* is by James McCosh, the renowned Scottish philosopher who came to the United States in 1868 and served as president of Princeton University from 1868–1888. Princeton was closely associated with the Presbyterian Church, and McCosh attempted to preserve the conservative Calvinist character of the institution.[45] McCosh was also "America's greatest (indeed its last great) exponent" of Scottish Common Sense philosophy.[46]

This tradition begins with Thomas Reid's (1710–1796) "common sense" response to the radical skepticism of David Hume about the existence of the world and of the human soul.[47] Against Hume, Reid maintained that there is a whole range of basic beliefs—such as the existence of the world, the existence of the soul, and the reality of moral obligations—that are imposed upon us by the constitution of our minds, and of whose truth we can therefore be certain. We know the reality of the world and the truth of our basic beliefs directly—ideas and sensations do not play the role of intermediary between the mind and reality. (Reid did not grapple with the wide range of considerations introduced by, for example, Kant, which call into question any neat distinction between experience and the world, and suggest that experience itself fashions, or has a role in fashioning, the reality of the world). Everything we know, according to Reid, is objective and factual.

The tradition of Scottish Common Sense realism was warmly and widely embraced by Americans in the nineteenth century.[48] Before the 1880s German idealism had a much smaller following.[49] The Protestant establishment relied upon Common Sense philosophy as the intellectual underpinning of its conviction that biblical truth and the truths of scholarship and scientific inquiry must necessarily be in harmony. Protestant conservatives like McCosh viewed biblical truth and scientific truth as two sets of objective facts, each possessing firm, inherent authority, and each confirming the other.[50] But for all his conservatism, McCosh nevertheless supported the theory of evolution, interpreted in a theistic context.[51]

The text for Sanders' course *Grounds of Theistic and Christian Belief* is the volume by George Park Fisher of the same title. In Sanders' words, "this is a work in Theistic and Christian Evidences, masterly and profound. There is constant endeavor to justify in the student the conviction that the argument for Christianity is one of impregnable strength." Fisher was a professor at Yale University under President Noah Porter. Porter, though more open to German idealism that McCosh, was nevertheless a conservative. He believed both that biblical and scientific truth are in harmony, and also that anti-Christian viewpoints ought not to be espoused by Yale faculty.[52] Fisher's volume was one of the most widely known expositions of the doctrine of harmony. Published in 1883, it had gone through at least twelve editions by 1913, including a 1902 revision. But Fisher's view departs significantly both from straight Common Sense realism and from conservative biblicism. Philosophically, Fisher favors the viewpoint of William Hamilton (1788–1856), who attempted to combine the insights of Kant with Common Sense realism.[53] (Sanders' writings show that he shared with Fisher this basic philosophical orientation.[54]) Theologically, it is difficult to classify Fisher (and Sanders) either as conservative or as liberal, even according to 'liberal' or 'conservative' standards of his day. Fisher believed that nature and the human conscience involve a natural revelation of God, that the supernatural revelation reported in the Bible exceeds the natural one, while fulfilling a longing inherent in it, and that the two revelations are in harmony. The basis of the doctrine of the trinity, for Fisher, is Jesus' consciousness "of a unity with God altogether exceptional" which grew and developed over the course of his life. Fisher deals with the atonement, but advocates no particular theory of the atonement.[55] The Bible is the record of a progressive revelation. Over the course of both the Old Testament and the New, we find the record of God revealing himself ever more profoundly to humans as their capacity to receive the revelation also grew. For Fisher, this means the clear rejection of biblical inerrancy. The authority of the Bible lies in the Bible as a whole, and not in each statement in the Bible taken individually. The revelation recorded in the bible regards moral and religious matters. The geology and cosmology the Hebrews absorbed from their Mesopotamian environment, reflected in Genesis, is not part of revelation. Fisher supports the doctrine of theistic evolution. Christian faith need have nothing to fear from biblical criticism carried out according to strict standards of historical research. However, those standards err if they assume that miracles are impossible. Fisher develops a philosophically sophisticated defense of the possibility of miracles. But he argues that the authority of miracles, rather than being the basis for the authority of the bible (as Paley had), is rather itself based upon the trustworthiness of the witnesses to the miracles (Christ and his apostles).[56] On the basis of these assumptions, Fisher attempts to develop a rational argument to support many of the traditional beliefs about biblical authorship and reliability that biblical criticism had challenged. Finally, Fisher, sounding very much like a proponent of the social gospel, asserts that: "the fundamental reality is not the Bible, it is the Kingdom of God,"[57] and that "no view of the divine kingdom is adequate which fails to see that the end of its establishment is the transformation of human society."[58] But while disparities in wealth cannot be reconciled with the kingdom of God, the remedy cannot involve any "infraction of the right of property" such as, Fisher implied, socialism recommends.[59]

Mignerey took Sanders' course in *Theism* in Fall semester of his junior year. At the end of that year, he records the following reflections on his spiritual and intellectual struggle:

> In these months of serious, sober thot,[60] my experience is growing richer and richer in the Christian life. It is richer because simpler. I must confess that I have come to the place of disgust and rejection of many of the petty traditional beliefs concerning religion which heretofore have made it a heavy, speculative subject. I am impressed that much good time and energy has been lost in quibbling over subjects which are not yet settled or yet to be. One of the sincerest struggles of my soul in these past months has been for a more satisfying faith—one that could conform more closely to the inward revelation to my own consciousness. To my supreme happiness that is coming to pass with the passing days. It makes no difference to me whether Christ was virgin born or whether his body rose from the grave. I do rest assured that his life and teachings reveal a lofty standard of living that approximates our best ideas of God himself; and that that these simple, profound teachings are suited to the needs of all life, my life, as nothing else; and that the very nature of my soul testifies to its immortality whether the body is raised or not. To see the way clear and simple means discarding the infallibility of the Bible; it also implies questioning the verbal inspiration of the collection. As best I see it now the most reliable of the books of the bible upon which to build a true system of Christianity are the gospels, and especially those that record the direct words of Jesus. Other of the New Testament books are comments upon the teachings of Christ being put into practice by the zealous leaders of the early church. Only as these harmonize with the gospel words of Jesus should they be given as universal gospel. As to the Old Testament, it is merely interesting from a historical standpoint as leading up to the coming of the Perfect Man. Many ideas of the Old Testament are much less satisfying than those of the new. For example the anthropomorphic idea of God as being a god of anger, hate, jealousy, God of Battles, is quite different from the N.T. "God is love."[61]

Mignerey never mentions Sanders in his diary but in his "disgust and rejection of many of the petty traditional beliefs concerning religion which heretofore have made it a heavy, speculative subject," Mignerey may well be throwing up his hands in frustration at the intricate, even contorted argumentation pursued by men like Fisher and in their attempt to reconcile liberal and conservative viewpoints.

Mignerey's familiarity with, and decision in favor of, theological liberalism, could not be more clear. The sources of that familiarity would have included the classes he took with Professor Charles Snavely, where he certainly encountered and intensively studied the ideas of the major proponents of the social gospel. Charles Snavely had graduated from Otterbein in 1894. On the recommendation of Professor George Scott (whose Ph.D. from Yale was in Latin, and was still at Otterbein during Mignerey's time), Snavely attended Johns Hopkins University, received a Ph.D. there in 1902, and then returned to Otterbein to fill its newly created chair in history. Johns Hopkins University had been founded in 1878 as "the first school to make graduate and professional education the center of its enterprise."[62] As Marsden points out, Daniel Coit Gilman, the University's first president, did want religion to be part of the University's identity, especially for its undergraduate college.[63] But the graduate school of the University was the first to be consciously organized on the basis of complete freedom of inquiry, which meant in practice, to be completely secular in orientation. The model for the Johns Hopkins graduate school was the rigorous scholarly professionalism of the German university. Indeed, Snavely's dissertation on "A History of the City Government of Cleveland Ohio" is a work of careful historical scholarship.[64] In his dissertation, Snavely focused in particular on the history of city government reform. Committed to putting ideals of local government reform into practice, Snavely ran for mayor of Westerville, Ohio (where Otterbein is located), and in 1905 became the first Democratic mayor of that conservative town since the Civil War.

Clear statements of Snavely's religious and political views are not extant, but the kinds of issues he raised are obvious from his course descriptions. Mignerey had four semesters of work with Snavely, in Sociology, American History, and Economics. For first semester economics, Snavely states that "special emphasis will be given to the social character of economic activity" and in second semester economics, "special attention will be given to some of the more important present day problems, such as the factory system, corporations, monopoly, and socialism." In his diary, Mignerey repeatedly refers to this latter course simply as "Socialism." Mignerey preserved the final paper he wrote for that class, titled "A Son of Democracy." The son of democracy, Mignerey maintains, is socialism, and in his paper he argues, both fervently and carefully, and from a Christian perspective, in favor of that economic system. The paper is based partly on lecture notes, and quotes Snavely's classroom definition of socialism: "Socialism is a proposed economic system to supplant the present economic system; under this system all material instruments of production are to be owned and operated by society." The paper's bibliography lists the following books, at least some of which must have been texts for the class: Richard Theodore Ely, *Socialism and Social Reform*; Morris Hillquit, *Socialism in Theory and Practice*; John Spargo, *Socialism*; F.M. Sprague, *Socialism from Genesis to Revelation*; *Communist Manifesto*; *Encyclopaedia of Social Reform*; Shailer Matthews, *The Social Teachings of Jesus*; John Graham Brooks, *The Social Unrest: Studies in Labor and Socialist Movements*; Walter Rauschenbusch, *The Social Principles of Jesus*. Snavely himself was probably not a thoroughgoing socialist; it is likely that his views were close to those of Richard Ely (most of the references in Mignerey's paper are to Ely). Ely taught at Johns Hopkins from 1881–1892 (just before Snavely's time) and "was particularly influential in shaping the views of a number of the founders of the American social sciences."[65] Ely's text, (evidently *Socialism: An Examination Of Its Nature, Its Strength And Its Weakness, With Suggestions For Social Reform*) is a careful examination of the main theories of, and objections to, socialism, and Ely presents socialism in a very positive light. When it comes to specific suggestions for "practicable social reform," though, Ely believes that only "natural monopolies" such as railway transportation and telegraph communication, should be socialized. For other areas of industry, Ely advocates reform and regulation rather than government ownership. Writing in 1894, the reforms he proposes include a six day work week, abolition of sweatshops, and restriction of the workday for persons under eighteen.[66] (By contrast, Spargo's text *Socialism*, which Mignerey also studied in Snavely's class, presents a clear endorsement of the entire socialist program.[67]) Ely also makes it clear that his view of society grows out of his Christian belief. An article by Ely appeared even in the United Brethren's *Quarterly Review*. Ely there states that "Christianity is a social force above everything else," and that "the Church is the universal anti-poverty society, or she is false to her founder."[68]

Thomas J. Sanders   **Charles Snavely**

Ely was a prominent social scientist who embraced the social gospel, but its foremost exponent was Walter Rauschenbusch. On the basis of the liberal theology of Ritschl and Harnack, Rauschenbusch developed a Christian approach to the social problems of contemporary industrial America. Mignerey was inspired by Rauschenbusch's *The Social Principles of Jesus,* a volume "written under the direction of sub-Committee of college courses Sunday school council of evangelical denominations and committee on voluntary study council of north American student movements."[69] Rauschenbusch and the social gospel were very widely known and highly influential in the United Brethren church of the time. Study courses for ministers between 1905 and 1917 included Rauschenbusch's *Christianity and the Social Crisis* and *Christianizing the Social Order,* and Ely's

Social Aspects of Christianity.[70] Mignerey received his copy of *The Social Principles of Jesus* as a present from the young lady who was his seat-mate in chapel. It is also noteworthy that Mignerey took advantage of the opportunity he had to hear the preaching of Washington Gladden, one of the most important and well-known exponents of the social gospel in the United States. Gladden was active until 1917 in his First Congregational church in downtown Columbus (about 15 miles from Westerville, and accessible at that time by trolley). Mignerey writes in his college diary of Gladden as "a man I have come to admire as a man of peace and love." In addition to hearing him preach, Mignerey could read summaries of his sermons each week in the *Ohio State Journal.*[71]

Ritschl emphasized that the kingdom of God is supernatural, but that it "forms at the same time the ethical ideal, for whose attainment the members of the community bind themselves together through their definite reciprocal action."[72] This implies that the message of Jesus about the Kingdom of God pertains not merely to individual, otherworldly salvation, but also to the actions of individuals, *and* to the organization of societies, here and now. As Harnack put it "the Gospel aims at founding a community among men as wide as life itself and as deep as human need. As has been truly said, its object is to transform the socialism which rests on the basis of conflicting interests into the socialism which rests on the consciousness of a spiritual unity. In this sense its social message can never be outbid."[73] Rauschenbusch's debt to German theology is clear. In *The Social Principles of Jesus*, he states that

> "Jesus Christ was the first to bring the value of every human soul to light, and what he did no one can any more undo" (Harnack)....We shall be at one with the spirit of Christianity and of modern civilization if we approach all men with the expectation of finding beneath commonplace, sordid, or even repulsive externals some qualities of love, loyalty, heroism, aspiration, or repentance, which prove the divine in man. Kant expressed that reverence for personality in his doctrine that we must never treat a man as a means only, but always as an end in himself. So far as our civilization treats men merely as labor force, fit to produce wealth for few, it is not yet Christian.[74]

Even more than for Ritschl and Harnack, Rauschenbusch's focus is on Jesus' teaching about the kingdom of God. Chapter four of *The Social Principles of Jesus* is titled, "The Kingdom of God: Its Values: The Right Social Order is the Highest Good for All." Rauschenbusch there makes it clear that Jesus' teaching applies to the social order as a whole, and not just to individual private life: "Since he [Jesus] loved men and believed in their solidarity, the conception of a God-filled humanity living in a righteous social order, which would give free play to love and would bind all in close ties, would be the only satisfying outlook for him....If a man is of flawless private life, but is indifferent to any social ideal, or even hostile to all attempts at better justice and greater fraternity, is he really good?"[75] Rauschenbusch would probably not directly call Jesus a "socialist" since "the idea of the Kingdom of God is not identified with any special social theory."[76] But the particular social issues Rauschenbusch draws attention to are very much the kind raised by socialists. Rauschenbusch expresses his interpretation of Jesus' message to us today by applying Jesus' sayings of the form "you have heard it said...but I say to you," to modern industrial conditions: "It was said of old 'thou shalt not commit murder.' It is said to us, 'Ye shall not wear down life in the young by premature hard labor; nor let the fear of poverty freeze the fountain of life; and ye shall put a stop to war.' It was said of old, 'Thou shalt not steal.' It is said to us, 'Ye shall make no unearned gain from your fellows, but pay to society in productive labor what ye take from it in goods.'"[77] Rauschenbusch attempts to awaken American society from the complacent belief that it is a "Christian" society (as Ely also does, for example, in his article in the United Brethren's *Quarterly Review*[78]): "The separation of humanity into classes on the line of wealth is so universal and so orthodox that few of us ever realize that it flouts all the principles of Christianity and humanity."[79]

Common Ground: The Social Gospel and Missions

Writing in his diary several years after graduation, when he was deeply involved in the cause of Prohibition, Mignerey expresses his commitment to the social gospel, which he had first formed during his senior year at college, in no uncertain terms:

> These hirelings of the liquor business are certainly dying hard! The "principle" for which they are struggling is the *right to make money*. Every other consideration is lost sight of. And this fight is a history of morals against money. It illustrates the extreme to which money-maddened men will go when their interests collide with the public welfare. Viewing the struggle from this angle I see a grim forecast of the future. The liquor traffic is only one of many in which the love of gain is the motive power. And if their interests ever collide with public interests they will be just as heartless as the liquor interests have been.
>
> There are those of our students of social science who see that such monstrous private monopolies as the Steel Trust, the Standard Oil Company, and the Railroads are fundamentally opposed to public welfare—as private enterprises. And this raises a number of moral question concerning the stewardship of property and the collective care of our neighbors, in which big industries, like the big liquor industry, will prove lacking—as they have already proved lacking when put to the test—in moral vision. And since these big monopolies also control the sources of publicity the truth of the proper relations of these big interests to the public welfare will filter thru[80] slowly. In this fight against the liquor interests little gain was made until there was established a means of publicity thru school text-books and "dry" newspapers which counteracted the poisoned press of the big business.
>
> Viewing this struggle from the angle of right and wrong involved, I am convinced that *right is bound to win*. When our good friend Dr. Russell[81] trudged down the streets of Columbus twenty-five years ago he carried all there was of the Anti-Saloon League in a black hand-bag and a big white soul. And because he was Right his divinely inspired organization of the Church in Action has become the most-feared, most effective instrument of righteousness in the world.
>
> No amount of persecution could drown the spread of the great Truth of Prohibition. And there were many men who gave their lives in cold blood for the righteousness of this cause. For the Big Business did not hesitate to stoop to slanders and persecutions and cold blooded murder when its interests clashed with the public welfare.

Kindred Big Businessmen are just now doing the same thing to those brave few who have dared to raise their strength of mind and soul in protest against these titanic public outrages. In the case of these, as with the liquor business, the Truth is seeping thru. And I have not the least doubt in the world that the Right will triumph against these other soul-less money interests as it has in the past, from the coming of the Master Meddler with Unrighteousness to the triumph of the Prohibition cause.

I am as certain of this as that God lives! I am profoundly more certain than I otherwise might be of the coming triumph of the public over selfish financial demigogs [demagogues] because the first glimpses of that future "Kingdom come on earth as in heaven" have been caught by our leading *religious* thinkers. Once the prohibition cause was moving with the power of religious conviction there was nothing to stop it. The "social gospel" will be as equally omnipotent now that such brave thinkers as Coe, Rauschenbusch, and Mathews have dared to interpret present industrial conditions in the light of Christian teaching. It is to me the only gospel worth while. It is a gospel the preaching of which will doom me, like the Master Meddler, to abuse and poverty. It is a gospel which offers the finest fight for the Kingdom. It is a gospel that does not shrink from the use of the latest and the best of the discoveries of modern science for the welfare and happiness not of a few but of the people.

These are in reality some of the issues that have been involved in this desperate struggle of the organized church of God armed with all the scientific discoveries of the past hundred years had to offer against organized iniquity. It has been and is the social gospel in action. (From *Crumbs*).

It is worth noting that Mignerey adopts a liberal argument for prohibition—drawing upon Ely as well as Rauschenbusch and others. The consumption of alcohol is not wrong because it violates one of the rules ordained by a monarchical God. It is wrong because alcohol destroys lives, and each human life is of infinite value. One of the ways capitalism destroys lives is through the aggressive production, marketing, and sale of alcoholic beverages for the sake of the profit of the few, without regard to the devastating effects of this business upon human beings, each and every one a child of God.

Between 1880 and 1920, the Church of the United Brethren (like American Protestantism generally) contained within its membership and leadership persons with a wide range of conflicting views, especially in terms of the liberalism and conservatism I have outlined. (In 1889 a very small group on the conservative side did split off, but the division that led to this split was by no means simply between liberal and conservative.[82]) On the whole the denomination remained united. Those who differed from the predominant conservatism were apparently generally accorded acceptance, respect, and at times even a high degree of influence. The leadership of Otterbein College, for example, was not really conservative at all, but rather moderate to liberal.

During the early 1920s this situation changed, both for the United Brethren and in American Protestantism generally. The fundamentalist movement, which had taken shape after World War One, brought the tension between conservative and liberal viewpoints to the forefront, but by 1924 had failed in its ambition to take control the United Brethren, or of any mainline Protestant denomination, and thereafter subsided. But the fundamentalist campaign did have the effect of driving liberals and conservatives farther apart than they previously had been. Marsden notes that "by the 1920s the one really unifying factor in fundamentalist political and social thought was the overwhelming predominance of political conservatism."[83] But, as Marsden points out, prior to the 1920s conservative theology had not been nearly so rigidly aligned with conservative politics as it later came to be. In the realm of social issues, theological liberals and conservatives had often found much more to agree on. Liberals like Mignerey supported causes such as prohibition. A large number of Progressives, including advocates of the social gospel such as Rauschenbusch, supported Prohibition as a natural part of their overall program. Even the Unitarians joined the cause.[84] And conservatives often supported many of the other kinds of social reforms called for by the social gospel.[85] William Jennings Bryan, whose religious conservatism brought him ridicule during the Scopes trial in 1924, was one of Mignerey's heroes, precisely for his radical stand on social issues. Marsden provides numerous examples of prominent conservative evangelical leaders who were committed to liberal social reform prior to the 1920s. For example,

> Charles Blanchard, although a convert to premillennial and holiness views, had not yet abandoned—as he eventually would—progressive reform ideals, or even the idea of 'Christian civilization,' inherited from his father. 'Christian men should lead,' he urged in 1897, in fighting such injustices as unequal taxation, benefits to favored railroads and other corporations, delays in justice in the courts, justice denied to the poor because of excessive legal expenses, and pardons for corrupt officials while poor immigrants served out jail terms.[86]

Ferenc Szasz, in *The Divided Mind of American Protestantism,* addresses this issue much more comprehensively than Marsden. According to Szasz, "historians' traditional separation of the clergy between those concerned with the Social Gospel and those concerned only with individual salvation is not accurate for this period. From 1901 to about 1917, both liberal and conservative Protestant groups worked to alleviate social ills, each in its own way."[87] Szasz shows that, for the years 1901–1917, "from North to South, from liberals and conservatives, lectures and books poured forth the new message of social salvation and the Kingdom of God. The journals of the period also devoted numerous articles to such concerns. Although the various denominations arrived at the Social Gospel at different times, from different paths, and with different degrees of conviction, by 1910 every major denominational publication was addressing social concerns."[88]

Christian missions represented another cause that united religious conservatives and religious liberals. William R. Hutchinson, in *Errand to the World,* traces the history of American Protestant missionary ideology from its beginnings through the 1930s. The first three decades of the twentieth century represented a period of tremendous popular enthusiasm for, coupled with tremendous growth in, missionary activity, and especially by American Protestants. Hutchinson notes that "by 1900 the sixteen American missionary societies of the 1860s had swelled to about ninety."[89] In 1900, the number of American and Canadian Protestant missionaries overseas was 4891, 27% of all Protestant missionaries. By 1925, that number had grown to 13,608, which by then constituted

49% of all Protestant missionaries.[90] Surveying missionary ideology in the first two decades of the twentieth century Hutchinson concludes that "the leaders spoke with remarkable unanimity across the theological spectrum."[91] And despite "contrasts in theory and general tendency, conservative Protestants often found themselves undertaking the same chaplaincy as that to which their liberal colleagues felt called."[92] The two most prominent leaders of interdenominational missionary groups in the early twentieth century, Robert Speer and John Mott, both avoided defining missionary ideology in exclusively liberal or conservative terms. The Student Volunteer Movement for Foreign Missions, the most influential organization of its kind, was founded at Dwight Moody's Mount Hermon School in 1886. Mott was one of the founding members, and became chairman within two years. Speer was the organization's traveling secretary. Mott, a Methodist, continued as chair until 1920, and Speer became the head of the Presbyterian Board of Foreign Missions.[93]

The most conservative missionaries took as the basis of their calling Jesus' "great commission" to "teach all nations" (Mt. 28:18–20). The commission was to be obeyed because Jesus commanded it, and because non-Christians are destined for hell if they do not have the opportunity to hear the gospel. But both Mott and Speer, themselves relatively conservative, publicly emphasized that their movement should not be based on any single, narrow ideology. The movement embraced as its slogan or "watchword" "the evangelization of the world in this generation." Mott had published a book with that same title in 1900. But 'the watchword' Mott wrote, "does not necessitate a belief in the premillenial view" or "stand in the service of any other particular theory or eschatology."[94] For Speer, "the supreme argument for foreign missions is not any word of Christ's [such as the great commission]—it is Christ Himself."[95] Hutchinson notes that "in the opening paragraphs of a major defense of missions he [Robert E. Speer] insisted that Christian obligation would be the same even if Christ had never pronounced a great commission."[96]

A liberal like Mignerey is not motivated to be a missionary by any belief that conversion to Christianity is the necessary qualification for entrance into heaven and escape from hell. Nor were liberals motivated merely by social concerns. While the liberalism of Ritschl, Harnack, and the social gospel is free from the exclusivism that takes "the great commission" literally, it does assign a position to Jesus that is unique. In Ritschl's words, "now Jesus, being the first to realize in His own personal life the final purpose of the kingdom of God, is therefore alone of his kind, for should any other fulfill the same task as perfectly as He, yet he would be unlike Him because dependent on Him."[97] Jesus has a unique and unprecedented role in bringing the kingdom of God to earth. This assumption, while not implying the condemnation of non-Christian religions, does provide a justification for efforts of conversion.[98] And the basic idea of the social gospel is that conversion cannot be a merely spiritual matter, but is inseparable from improvements in social well-being. The social gospel implied for liberals the imperative to reform social conditions not only at home, but also in foreign lands through missions. The missions themselves typically did in fact have a significant educational and medical, in addition to evangelizing, component.

And in general, both conservatives and liberals found it appropriate that bringing the gospel to non-Christians should go hand in hand with bringing what were considered the benefits of Western civilization.[99]

Both conservatives and liberals felt they were part of Western civilization, either identifying Western civilization with civilization as such, or believing that Western civilization was the best form of civilization to have yet arisen. Neither liberals or conservatives necessarily believed that Western civilization was free from evils, but both were confident that Western civilization had something essential to offer the rest of the world that the world desperately needed. The shared view would be that Western civilization offers a plan for transforming non-Christian societies the like of which those societies themselves have never produced (if it is even acknowledged that non-Western societies and traditions contain anything of value at all in the realm of social ethics), and that Christianity offers a revelation which is superior to any revelation that may already be known within non-Christian societies (if it is even acknowledged that non-Christian religions include any truth at all).

The consensus of the missionary movement of the first two decades of the twentieth century, embraced by both conservatives and liberals, is expressed by John R. Mott in his 1910 volume *The Decisive Hour of Christian Missions* (published by the Student Volunteer Movement for Foreign Missions).[100] In the first chapter of this work, titled "The Non-Christian Nations Plastic and Changing," Mott surveys the condition of the entire world of his time. Mott identifies as the most significant factor in the contemporary situation the growing and inescapable influence of Western countries on non-Western countries. But one could come away from his book with little awareness that the force behind that influence had been the force of military conquest and intimidation. One is left instead with the impression that the most important thing about the accelerating contact with Western civilization throughout the world is that an opportunity has opened for positive social change. Mott gives the impression that prior to contact with the West, non-Western societies were static, and only contact with Western ideas and institutions has opened those societies up to change. But this book does include the beginnings of an attitude critical of colonialism. Mott includes among positive changes a growing sense of nationalism in the non-Western world. Without endorsing anything like decolonization (or even mentioning the word "colony") he nevertheless sees this growing nationalism as something positive, and indeed as emerging from "the discovery of the worth and rights of the individual man", an idea introduced, he asserts, by Christian missionaries.[101]

For Mott and the Student Volunteer Movement he lead, the new openness of non-Christian societies to outside influences represented a unique opportunity in history for the spread of Christianity. This situation was the background of the movement's "watchword": "the evangelization of the world in this generation."[102] Writing in 1914, four years later, Mott becomes much more directly critical of colonialism. He openly condemns the Western world for its program of colonial military conquest and commercial exploitation. His views are made clear in a chapter titled "The Unchristian Aspects of our Western Civilization" in *The Present World Situation: With Special Reference Made Upon the Chris-*

tian Church in Relation to Non-Christian Lands. Mott continues to believe that the growing interconnectedness of the world created by colonialism offers a unique opportunity for the spread of Christianity. But the policies of the colonial powers are "closing the peoples' hearts to the teachings of Christianity." The "unchristian aspects of the present day impact of Western civilization on the non-Christian world" include the "seizure or stealing of territory" including "ninety six percent of the African continent," and "considerable areas of China."[103] "Is it strange" Mott asks "that many of the better informed of the peoples of the weaker countries say, 'Christianity is the religion of the lands which have thus insulted, injured and robbed us. We want none of it.'"[104] Among the "wrong practices in commercial and industrial relations" practiced by Western nations, he includes discrimination against native Africans in South Africa, "the cruel [commercial] exploitation" in the Congo, the "complicity" of Western governments and commercial firms "in helping to fasten the opium curse upon China," as well as in the introduction of alcohol to Africa.[105]

But despite the moral outrage he expresses over colonialism, Mott never suggests that the Western powers simply pack up and leave. His response is somewhat different: "Enough has already been stated to make it evident that by far the greatest obstacle to the world-wide spread of the Christian religion is the unchristian impact of our Western civilization. That impact must be Christianized." Under these conditions missions need to be *expanded* to counteract the "bad influences of Western civilization."[106] And this includes working to transform the unchristian aspects of our civilization at home as well, especially in the areas of race prejudice and "social injustice."[107] Mott seems to have been unaware of just how tangled his position was. Colonialism has given Christianity the greatest opportunity to expand that has ever been offered it, but the greatest obstacle to that expansion is the unchristian aspect of Western civilization, including the military conquest and political subversion that in fact define colonialism. The greatest opportunity was apparently identical to the greatest obstacle. And the tone of his exhortations remained eager and triumphalist: "the evangelization of the world in our generation!" He somehow held onto a faith that colonialism could be redeemed from within.

Common Ground: Ethnocentrism and Racism

As high school students, Lloyd Mignerey and Glen Rosselot learned about Africa from *Our Foreign Missionary Enterprise*, published in 1908 by the United Brethren Publishing House as part of the United Brethren Mission Study Course. The chapter on Sierra Leone was written by W.R. Funk, who had made one brief visit to Africa, and includes extensive quotations from J.R. King, who had served as a missionary for many years. This volume instructs that Africans in Sierra Leone are "very decidedly the children of nature, and live in squalid habitations....Since the houses are entirely lacking in conveniences, of course the women are poor housekeepers." The African "is not naturally an energetic person. Nature has been so kind to him in the abundant supply of food...he has not felt the need of being industrious in order to obtain a livelihood."[108] The African is religious but "nearly all the pagan's gods are demons....The cruel barbarities of the pagan do not necessarily spring from an inborn brutality of nature, but from his ideas of gods and religion." However, Funk soon insinuates that the inferiority of Africans just might be biological as well as cultural: "There can be little doubt that there has been a development of parts of the human race and a retrogression of another part. The former is seen at its best in the Anglo-Saxon, while the latter is seen in its awfulness in the degraded lives of the raw Africans."[109] Funk quotes J.R. King's description of the Mende rebellion of 1898. King sees the war simply as a matter of Africans showing their true nature, "giving complete license to their old habit of loot and plunder." The African converts "have seen in this cruel insurrection the awfulness of heathen life when unrestrained."[110] Missing of course is any sense that the war might have been a rebellion against foreign invasion and military domination. The implicit idea is that cruelty and violence represent the true nature of Africans, and that the intervention of white Christians is required if there is to be any hope of restraining Africans, with their inherently savage nature.

The ethnocentrism and racism taught in this book represents a standard, almost unquestioned view in the United States between 1880 and 1920. It was by no means limited to any one group with a particular viewpoint, but was the common assumption of conservatives and liberals alike. Most Progressive advocates of the social gospel did not challenge the prevailing racism. Even the most radical proponents of the social gospel during the progressive era had little or nothing to say about racism and racial injustice. Some were even racists, although that cannot be said about Rauschenbusch or Gladden. (Gladden, contrary to the norm, became relatively outspoken about racial problems, especially after the turn of the century.[111]) According to Thomas F. Gossett's definitive study, *Race: The History of an Idea in America*: "Whereas the Social Gospel ministers spoke out openly and fearlessly against other injustices of society, they said nothing with real meaning about racial injustice."[112] It is hardly surprising that Mignerey should have absorbed perceptions of race that were standard across the board in the society of his day.

How did the United Brethren's most prominent liberal, J.S. Mills, view race and culture? His outlook is by no means as crude as that of Funk and King, but it too can only be classified as racist and ethnocentric. Mills originally had wanted to be a missionary but was turned down by the mission board because of his frail constitution. As bishop he devoted significant effort to missions, including two journeys to Sierra Leone, one from October 1896 to March 1897 and a second from November 1903 to January 1904; visits to Puerto Rico in 1902 and 1906; and a journey to China, Japan, and the Philippines lasting from October 1907 to May 1908.[113] These journeys were the basis both for his contributions to *Our Foreign Missionary Enterprise* and an earlier volume he wrote and edited titled *Mission Work in Sierra Leone, West Africa* (1898).[114] (The chapter on Sierra Leone in *Our Foreign Missionary Enterprise*, however, was not written by Mills, but by Funk.) Mills bases his conclusions both on extensive study and on first hand observations. His discussion of Africa is probably about as objective and fair minded a report as could be expected from anyone of the era. His writing is free of the ethnocentrism of the absurdly careless kind (evident in Funk's chapter on Sierra Leone) that concludes, for example, that African women are poor housekeepers because they lack modern conveniences. And his understanding of African religion is much more accurate that Funk's. For example, he is aware that traditional African religion includes belief in "a supreme god" to whom "the creation of the world is ascribed," and he is aware in general terms of the role of ancestor veneration (or "worship"), and of the role of 'medicine' (or "fetishes"). Mills asserts that the creator god "is rarely worshiped or even referred to."[115]

Another volume available to Mignerey in the Otterbein library, published eight years after Mills', was Robert Nassau's *Fetichism in West Africa: Forty Years' Observation of Native Customs and Superstitions,* published by the Young Peoples' Missionary Movement, 1904 (acquired by the Otterbein library in 1906). Nassau had been for forty years a missionary in "the Gabun district of Congo-Francaise." Nassau makes it clear that all of the Africans he has ever encountered believe in a supreme creator God, and he points out several factors that have lead Westerners to overlook this fact or to underestimate the importance of the creator God in African religions. The idea of God in Africa is related to Christianity, for Nassau, in this way: "But while it is therefore undeniable that a knowledge of this Great Being exists among the natives, and that the belief is held that he is a superior and even a supreme being, that supremacy is not so great as what we ascribe to Jehovah. Nevertheless, I believe that the knowledge of their Anzam or Anyambe has come down—clouded though it be and fearfully obscured and marred, but still a revelation—from Jehovah Himself."[116] Even United Brethren missionary D.K. Flickinger, in *Ethiopia, or Twenty Six Years of Missionary Life in Western Africa* conceded that "they all believe in the existence of a supreme Jehovah, who is the creator of the world, and of all things therein; that he is almighty, and just in all his ways."[117] But Flickinger inaccurately observes that "they hold that a being whom they call the devil is the author of all providence, and that he is able to bring good and bad luck upon them—especially ill luck." And Flickinger concludes that "they are emphatically devil worshipers; they are most profoundly selfish in their worship, as in most other things. We must not forget, however, that in their present condition they are not capable of exercising other than selfish motives."[118]

Mills is free from the sneering tone discernible in Flickinger and Funk, but his attitude toward "paganism" is no less condescending. Paganism "is the cry for light of a soul groping in the dark; it is the tendrils of the heart, designed to cling to that which would lift man up into the sunlight, now binding him face downward to the earth; it is the perversion and abuse of man's religious nature, thereby bringing his whole nature into bondage to evil."[119] Indeed, paganism is for Mills one of Africa's "six great curses." The other five are "Mohammedanism," polygamy, war, rum, and slavery.

At this point it is worth noting that Mills' criticisms of Africans and African religion come from an individual whose liberal theological views included an openness to religious truth outside of the bounds of the explicitly Christian. In his address to Union Seminarians in 1891, he asks "what is the kingdom of heaven?" Part of his answer is that "there is no difference between natural virtue and Christian virtue....all goodness is a beam of that light, and is therefore essentially Christian....In the old world and the modern heathen world, in their systems of morality, religion, and philosophy are found many gleams of this true light, a sort of unconscious Christian faith in the better things to come."[120] In his essay on China, Mills calls Lao-tze "a great and good man, one of the prophets outside of Israel," and Confucius "is one of the greatest of the sons of men."[121] Mills seems to have had less understanding of Buddhism—but he at least refrains from wholesale condemnation. Mills' learning and open-mindedness is in general remarkable for a member of his denomination or indeed for any American of his time. It is instructive that even an individual as intellectually responsible as he, was caught up in the tide of prejudice against African culture.

Funk's and Mills' accounts of Africa teach prejudice not merely about culture, but also about race. The unquestioned racism their descriptions convey was of a kind that pervaded the American society of their time. In many ways, the period 1880–1920 marks the low point for race relations in the U.S. This was the era during which African-Americans, now no longer literally enslaved, were decisively forced back into a subordinate and marginal place in American society. And the imposition of the system of segregation encountered no major opposition anywhere in white society. In general, as Gossett points out, "the decision of the South to segregate and disenfranchise the Negro encountered no really strong opposition in the North."[122] The period 1880–1920 was one in which racism and racist attitudes were not only taken for granted at all levels of society, but also went almost unchallenged. In Gossett's words: "what is noticeable is that American thought of the period 1880–1920 generally lacks any perception of the Negro as a human being with potentialities for improvement. Most of the people who wrote about Negroes were firmly in the grip of the idea that intelligence and temperament are racially determined and unalterable."[123] Neither the conventional, conservative Funk, nor the unconventional, liberal Mills constituted exceptions to Gosset's generalization. Funk concludes his discussion of "general conditions" in Sierra Leone with a paragraph titled "effects of sin":

> That sin has wrought great havoc in the life and character of the people no one will doubt who has been brought in touch with them, although it must be remembered that their vices, in the main, are not very different from those found among civilized people. The only question is that of degree. There can be little doubt that there has been a development of parts of the human race and a retrogression of another part. The former is best seen in the Anglo-Saxon, while the latter is seen in its awfulness in the degraded lives of the raw Africans. This is especially true of the Hottentot, where the lowest strata of human life may be found.[124]

One particularly chilling aspect of this quotation is that it points directly to a specific source, Nott and Gliddon's *Types of Mankind* (1854). This book was extremely popular during the nineteenth century, having gone through nine editions before 1900.[125] It is perhaps the most blatant example we have of racist pseudoscience. That approach in fact dominated anthropology until its shoddy methods, faulty logic, and specious, self-serving assumptions were decisively exposed by researchers such as Franz Boas in the 1920s. The scientific consensus since Boas is that it is impossible to establish any kind of ranking of races.[126] Nott himself actually claimed that Blacks are a separate *species* with inferior capabilities. He also claimed that there is a gradation among the inhabitants of Africa, with those occupying the southernmost part (the Hottentots) being the most inferior, and those furthest north (the Berbers), the least. It is very likely that Funk was familiar with the kinds of ideas Nott and Gliddon advocated, and was drawing, either directly or indirectly, on the following passages from *Types of Mankind*:

> We shall show, that not only is that vast continent [Africa] inhabited by types quite as varied as those of Europe or Asia, but that there exists a regular *gradation* from the Cape of Good Hope to the Isthmus of Suez, of which the Hottentot and Bushman form the lowest, and the Egyptian and Berber types the highest links.[127]
>
> It is here [Cape Colony] that we find the lowest and most beastly specimens of mankind: viz. the *Hottentot* and the *Bushman*. The latter, in particular, are but little removed, both in moral and physical characters, from the orang-outan.[128]

Mills also surveys the African "races" from north to south. Mills says nothing about a gradation, but he does say that south of the equator, "all the earliest stages of progress are met," and that "the Bushmen in the extreme south are savages of the rawest type."[129] Neither Mills nor Funk compares Africans to animals, as Nott and Gliddon do. For Funk, "Negroes" represent a part of the human race that has retrogressed, while "Anglo-Saxons" represent a part of the human race that has developed. Mills is characteristically reluctant to sneer or to condemn, but his racism is no less blatant for its smiling paternalism:

> They [the African races] are a vast quantity of raw material, elemental germs, embryonic possibilities, now being brought into contact with the higher races, that the work of redemption and evolution may be accomplished.[130]
>
> The one word that most fully expresses his [the Negro's] nature in heathenism is, with few exceptions, childhood. He is as affectionate, trustful, hopeful, excitable, impulsive, vivacious, and thoughtless—lives in his senses and emotions—as a child.[131]

Lloyd Mignerey, by the time he arrived in Africa, had fully absorbed the racist assumptions of his society. That Mignerey himself was certainly aware of, and had been influenced by either Nott and Gliddon's (738 page) work, or at least others like it, becomes apparent in one entry in his diary made at Rotifunk. But notable in his observations is a hint of questioning:

> This has awakened me to the problem of the subnormal pupil in our school. I believe that were the subject investigated fully, it would be found that a large number of the older pupils in our day school come easily into this classification. It is a matter of common knowledge that the children of the first, second, and third standard, show a mental brilliance that begins to diminish rapidly with the fourth standard, and in many cases, is entirely extinguished before the sixth standard is reached or completed. It is said by learned men who write the big, red-backed books that this early retarded development is especially characteristic of the black race. I do not wish to take their word for it so much as to make actual,

scientific observation of it for myself, with a view of adapting the school curriculum to the needs of the abnormal child.

Nott and Gliddon do not discuss the concept of "retarded development" in *Types of Mankind*, but they were certainly among the "learned men" who produced the many tomes of racist pseudoscience. At another point, Mignerey seems to more unambiguously adopt the viewpoint he learned from sources such as *Our Foreign Missionary Enterprise*, and perhaps from Mills' book on Africa:

> Much of the intellectual and spiritual stupidity of the black race in Africa can be traced to the diseases and the excesses and the senility of its diabolical system of polygamy and immorality. The race here is above the animal mostly in theory, and in the possibilities for improvement. This is the justification of Christian missions. It is not to gain more adherents for the sake of numbers. Their lives and their collective standards of life must be reborn.

From these two quotations, a number of points emerge concerning the state of Mignerey's thinking about Africa and Africans. He is certainly not firmly committed to any specific set of racist ideas. At times he seems to feel that Blacks are inherently inferior, and at other times that they simply happen to be inferior now, but are capable of advancing through contact with Western knowledge and religion. The racism anyone would absorb from American society was confirmed by the religious and educational leaders of his denomination and of the country at large.

Notes

1. James O. Bemesderfer, *Pietism and its influence upon the Evangelical United Brethren Church* (Annville, Pa.: Bemesderfer, 1966), 118.

2. J. Bruce Behney and Paul H. Eller, *The History of the Evangelical United Brethren Church* (Nashville: Abington, 1979), 25, 97.

3. William Henry Naumann, *Theology and German-American Evangelicalism: The Role of Theology in the Church of the United Brethren in Christ and the Evangelical Association* (Diss. Yale Univ., 1966), 9.

4. Ibid., 10.

5. Ibid., 19–30.

6. See Naumann, *Theology*, 105, 134. Naumann bases his study on a careful and exhaustive examination of the denominational literature—most notably, its periodical *The Religious Telescope* (for the years 1834–1930). That periodical is remarkable for the depth and breadth of discussion it includes of ecclesiastical, theological, and political issues. Naumann points out that "after 1850, however, this anti-intellectualism rapidly became only a minor theme. The warfare against reason all but ceased. So much is said in favor of reason and philosophy that one is tempted to talk about a growing alliance between religion and reason among evangelicals and United Brethren" (134). While early in the century, the pietistic emphasis on the conversion experience and the commitment to a devotional biblicism led the denomination to be suspicious of any theological inquiry (62–68), "the period of 1841 to 1890 was one of broadening theological awareness for Evangelicals and United Brethren. They gradually came to agree on the importance of theological study" (105).

7. The extent of both its educational and missionary endeavor is remarkable for what was a relatively small church. Membership was: 25,000 in 1841; 94,453 in 1861; 204, 492 in 1889; 370,000 in 1921. Behney, *History*, 155, 230, 243, 255.

8. Behney, *History*, 39–40.

9. Naumann, *Theology*, 189–95.

10. Ibid., 125.

11. Ibid., 214.

12. Ibid., 57.

13. Ibid., 50.

14. Naumann, *Theology*, 52.

15. See ibid., 348.

16. Jonathon Weaver, *Christian Theology: A Concise and Practical View of the Cardinal Doctrines and Institutions of Christianity* (Dayton, Ohio: United Brethren Publishing House, 1900), 133.

17. Ibid., 135.

18. A.W. Drury, *Outlines of Doctrinal Theology* (Dayton, Oh.: Otterbein Press, 1914), 108.

19. Ibid.,110.

20. Ibid., 117.

21. Ibid., 121.

22. Weaver, *Christian Theology*, 354.

23. Ibid., 355.

24. Kenneth Cauthen, *The Impact of American Religious Liberalism* (Washington, DC: University Press of America, 1983), 4–5.

25. Liberal biblical scholarship was committed to a careful reading of these texts on their own terms, and in making careful distinctions between what Jesus himself most likely said and did, and later interpretations of, and beliefs about, Jesus. In defining these movements in this way, I am deliberately avoiding the kind of classification that sees liberalism as something like an 'accommodation to secular culture' and conservatism as something like 'being true to Christian distinctiveness.' For example, liberalism certainly owes something to Kant, but the Nicene creed just as certainly owes something to Greek philosophy, and the doctrine of vicarious atonement owes just as much to the emphasis on developing of secular law in the 12th century. The sheer fact that an idea or way of thinking is widespread in a particular time and culture does not disqualify it as an interpretation of an ancient text. H. Richard Niebuhr, in *Christ and Culture* (New York: Harper, 1951), criticizes Ritschl for "selecting among the attributes of the God of Jesus Christ the one quality of love at the expense of his attributes of power and of justice," with the result that that his theology is "a caricature" of Christian theology, though it is still "recognizably Christian" (99). Niebuhr does not explain why this emphasis on love should be assigned to the category of 'accommodation to culture.' Niebuhr also apparently thinks that the subordination of power and justice to love is somehow well characterized as a nineteenth century cultural ideal—albeit the best the nineteenth century had to offer. Niebuhr does have one valid criticism of Ritschl—he is claiming that Ritschl does not confront the question of how it is possible for God as the creator and ruler of the world as it is to also be the God that leads the world and human society towards what it ought to be. Niebuhr does wrestle with this question in his own theology. But Niebuhr's final statements are really not very far from Ritschl. While Niebuhr does confront the dimensions of power and judgment in a way liberalism in general did not, he himself nevertheless still subordinates power and judgment to love. Radical monotheism, "as faith, is reliance on the source of all being for the significance of the self and of all that

exists. It is the assurance that because I am, I am valued, and because you are, you are beloved, and because whatever is has being, therefore it is worthy of love," *Radical Monotheism and Western Culture* (New York: Harper, 1970), 32. This seems to me a very clear and accurate definition of the very doctrine Niebuhr criticizes in *Christ and Culture*: the Fatherhood of God and the Brotherhood of Man. H.R. Niebuhr's view clearly is that the ultimate nature of God is love, and that love is deeper in God than judgment or wrath. Reinhold Niebuhr has a similar view, stated explicitly in *The Nature and Destiny of Man, I* (New York: Scribner's 1964): "Christian faith sees in the cross of Christ the assurance that judgment is not the final word of God to man" (142). George Rupp, in *Culture-Protestantism: German Liberal Theology at the Turn of the Twentieth Century* (Missoula, Montana: Scholar's Press, 1977), is critical of Niebuhr's classification of nineteenth century liberal theology as the "Christ of Culture" type, and its exclusion from the "Christ the Transformer of Culture" type. "In assigning all 'conversionist' tendencies to this fifth type, Niebuhr in effect programmatically confines the Christ of Culture motif to a legitimation of the cultural status quo" (10–11). One might well add that it is extremely odd to classify Walter Rauschenbusch as a defender of the status quo!

26. Adolf Harnack, *What is Christianity?*, trans. Thomas Bailey Saunders (New York, Putnam, 1901), vii.

27. Albrecht Ritschl, *Instruction in the Christian Religion*, trans. Alice Mead Swing, in Albert Temple Swing, *The Theology of Albrecht Ritschl* (New York: Longmans, 1901), 174, 175.

28. Ibid., 197.

29. Ibid., 220–21 n.

30. Ibid., 220.

31. Ibid., 219n.

32. William R. Funk, *Life of Bishop J.S. Mills, D.D.* (Dayton, Ohio: Otterbein Press, 1913), 59.

33. Naumann, *Theology*, 216–17; see Funk, *Life*, 114, 117.

34. Funk, *Life*, 4.

35. Ibid., 133.

36. Ibid.,130.

37. Ibid., 191–92.

38. Mills' specific reference to German liberal theology is in the [United Brethren] *Quarterly Review* 6 (Jan. 1895) "The Essence of Christianity," 33–47. He there quotes Otto Pfleiderer: "The characteristic feature of the religious personality of Jesus was his consciousness of sonship of God" (41).

39. Funk, *Life*, 214–15.

40. In his article in the [United Brethren] *Quarterly Review* on "The Essence of Christianity" Mills asserts that "The essence of Christianity is the sprit of God in man's soul, attesting to his divine sonship" (40). Mills quotes approvingly Otto Pfleiderer's version of the liberal doctrine of sonship as "a universal human religious relation—which first in [Jesus] became completely real, but can and should be realized in all of us, by him and through him.....It is evident that we must consider the divine sonship which formed the fundamental character of the religious self-consciousness of Jesus, not as a unique metaphysical relation between him and God, but as the first actual and typical realization of that religious relation in general in which all men should stand to God because of their divine origin and destination, and which becomes a real experience in all who believe in Christ—that is, make their own his filial spirit" (41–42). Mills takes this quote from an article by Pfleiderer entitled "The Essence of Christianity" in *The New World: A Quarterly Review of Religion, Ethics, and Theology* 1 no. 3 (Sept. 1892): 403–404.

41. Funk, *Life,* 208.

42. J.S. Mills, *A Manual of Family Worship With an Essay on the Christian Family* (Dayton, Ohio: United Brethren Publishing House, 1900), 71, 72, 73.

43. The two fields together constituted one of the seven "groups"—what we now call a major—that students could choose from.

44. Naumann, *Theology*, 92–97.

45. George M. Marsden, *The Soul Of The American University: From Protestant Establishment To Established Nonbelief* (New York: Oxford University Press, 1994), 196 ff.

46. George M. Marsden, *Fundamentalism and American Culture: The Shaping of Twentieth Century Evangelicalism, 1870–1925* (New York: Oxford University Press, 1980), 18.

47. Marsden, *Soul,* 91.

48. Ibid., 196–97.

49. Ibid.

50. Ibid., 92.

51. Ibid., 202–204.

52. Ibid., 126–28.

53. George Park Fisher, *Grounds of Theistic and Christian Belief* (New York: Scribner, 1909), 83–86.

54. See Thomas Jefferson Sanders, *The Philosophy of the Christian Religion: A Thesis,* Ph.D. Thesis, Univ. of Wooster (Dayton, Ohio: United Brethren Publishing House, 1890).

55. Fisher, *Grounds,* 1883 ed., 358–61.

56. Fisher, *Grounds,* 1909 ed. 116ff.; 1883 ed.; 174ff.

57. Ibid., 328, 1909 ed.

58. Ibid., 331, 1909 ed.

59. Ibid., 111, 1909 ed.

60. In his diary, Mignerey consistently adheres to certain simplified spelling reforms, especially "o" or "u" for "ough." I have not altered these spellings in the extracts I include. The movement for simplified spelling had some currency in his time. For example, in 1906, the Simplified Spelling Board was founded. The board had 30 members, including prominent leaders from publishing, academia, and philanthropy, politics, business, and the law. Members included Andrew Carnegie, Mark Twain, and William James, as well as the presidents of Columbia University, the University of Michigan, and Stanford University. "Carnegie Assaults the Spelling Book," *New York Times* (March 12, 1906); "Latest Effort to Simplify the Spelling of our Language," *New York Daily Tribune* (March 18, 1906). Even Mignerey's spelling is a sign of his adherence to Progressivism.

61. *Crumbs* [Otterbein], May 18, 1916, pp. 65–66.

62. George Marsden, *Soul,* 153.

63. Ibid., 150–56, 153.

64. See Charles Snavely, "A History of the City Government of Cleveland Ohio" (Ph.D. Thesis, Johns Hopkins Univ., 1902).

65. Marsden, *Soul,* 253.

66. Richard T. Ely, *Socialism: An Examination Of Its Nature, Its Strength And Its Weakness, With Suggestions For Social Reform* (New York: Crowell, 1894), 314 ff.

67. John Spargo, *Socialism: A Summary and Interpretation of Socialist Principles* (New York: MacMillan, 1912).

68. Richard T. Ely, "Christianity as a Social Force," [United Brethren] *Quarterly Review* 5 (Jan. 1894), 66–69.

69. Walter Rauschenbusch, *The Social Principles of Jesus* (New York: National Board of the Young Women's Christian Associations, 1916; New York: Association Press, 1916).

70. Naumann, *Theology,* 204.

71. "From the first, Gladden announced his evening sermon topics in the local press. Many of the sermons appeared in the Monday papers, which from the 1890s on gave considerable space to extensive reports. In 1912 one paper [Ohio State Journal] began to print them under the boxed heading 'Dr. Gladden's sermon.'" Jacob H. Dorn, *Washington Gladden: Prophet of the Social Gospel* (Columbus: Ohio State University Press, 1967), 84. In [Otterbein] *Crumbs* 87) Mignerey includes a clipping from "State Journal" 6–26–16 about a speech by Washington Gladden.

72. Ritschl, *Instruction,* 174–75.

73. Harnack, *What is Christianity?,* 108.

74. Walter Rauschenbusch, *The Social Principles of Jesus* (New York: National Board of the Young Women's Christian Associations, 1916, New York: Association press, 1916), 13–14.

75. Rauschenbusch, *Social Principles,* 59–60.

76. Ibid., 75.

77. Ibid., 91.

78. Ely, "Christianity," 70.

79. Rauschenbusch, *Social Principles,* 125. George M. Marsden in *Fundamentalism and American Culture: The Shaping of Twentieth Century Evangelicalism, 1870–1925* (New York: Oxford University Press, 1980), sheds a great deal of light upon this era of American Protestant church history. However, I do not think Marsden's understanding of the relation of the social gospel and religious liberalism is entirely accurate. According to Marsden, "The implication was that theological doctrine and affirmation of faith in Christ and his deeds were irrelevant, except as an inspiration to moral action, more specifically social action" (92). Then, "to my mind, the test of a genuine example of the Social Gospel is whether other aspects of Christianity are subordinated to, and in effect incidental to, its social aspects" (255–56, note to p. 92). Marsden's understanding of the social gospel is flawed. The whole issue hinges precisely on how one defines those "other aspects." "The Fatherhood of God and the Brotherhood of Man" is the liberal protestant slogan for those "other aspects." The conservative slogan for the other aspects is "Christ died for your sins." Even Luther says that "love flows from faith as heat and light from a fire." What liberal Protestant Christianity specifically denies is a particular theory of atonement—that the punishment due the human race is taken upon himself by Christ and hence taken away from humans. For liberal Protestantism, moral action does have its origin in God, and the ultimate dimension of reality is love—the same love that is at the heart of moral action.

80. In his diary, Mignerey consistently adheres to certain simplified spelling reforms, especially "o" or "u" for "ough." I have not altered these spellings in the extracts I include. The movement for simplified spelling had some currency in his time. For example, in 1906, the Simplified Spelling Board was founded. The board had 30 members, including prominent leaders from publishing, academia, and philanthropy, politics, business, and the law. Members included Andrew Carnegie, Mark Twain, and William James, as well as the presidents of Columbia University, the University of Michigan, and Stanford University. "Carnegie Assaults the Spelling Book," *New York Times* (March 12, 1906); "Latest Effort to Simplify the Spelling of our Language," *New York Daily Tribune* (March 18, 1906). Even Mignerey's spelling is a sign of his adherence to Progressivism.

81. Dr. Howard H. Russell founded the Ohio Anti-Saloon League in 1893, and was one of the co-founders of the Anti-Saloon League of America in 1895. Russell pursued temperance work in Columbus for three years from 1893. See Louis Albert Banks, *The Lincoln Legion: The Story of its Founder and Forerunners* (New York: Mershon, 1903), 185, 214.

82. This group continues as a distinct denomination to this day, retaining the name "United Brethren in Christ," with headquarters in Huntington, Indiana, and a membership of about 47,000. See www.ub.org/ (as of 1–11–10). The cause of the split was a disagreement over the procedure by which a new constitution was adopted (in 1888–89), and especially over a provision in the new constitution which withdrew the prohibition against membership in secret societies such as the Freemasons. A ballot was sent out to the entire church membership of about 200,000. The vote on the proposal to allow secret society membership was 46,994 for/7,298 against. The membership of the churches which rejected the new constitution, and which adopted the name The United Brethren Church (Old Constitution) was about 20,000. The majority in favor of the changes was called the "liberal" faction in this controversy, but clearly the issue here was not the conflict between theological liberalism and conservatism. J. Bruce Behney and Paul H. Eller, *The History of the Evangelical United Brethren Church* (Nashville: Abington, 1979), 181–87, 227.

83. Marsden, *Fundamentalism,* 92.

84. See James H. Timberlake, *Prohibition and the Progressive Movement: 1900–1920* (Cambridge, Mass.: Harvard Univ. Press, 1963), e.g. 2, 18–29.

85. Marsden, *Fundamentalism,* 93.

86. Ibid., 88–89.

87. Ferenc Szasz, *The Divided Mind of Protestant America 1880–1930* (University, Al.: Univ. of Alabama Press, 1982), 56.

88. Ibid., 65.

89. William R.Hutchinson, *Errand to the World: American Protestant Thought and Foreign Missions* (Chicago: Univ. of Chicago Press, 1987), 91.

90. See W. Richie Hogg, "The Role of American Protestantism in World Mission," in *American Missions in Bicentennial Perspective,* edited by R. Pierce Beaver (South Pasadena, California: William Carey Library, 1977), 369.

91. Hutchinson, *Errand,* 95.

92. Ibid., 112.

93. See Hogg, "The Role," 383–384; see also Charles W. Forman, "A History of Foreign Mission Theory in America," in *American Missions in Bicentennial Perspective,* edited by R. Pierce Beaver (South Pasadena, California: William Carey Library, 1977), 89–93.

94. John R. Mott, *The Evangelization of the World in this Generation* (N.Y.: Student Volunteer Movement, 1905), 9; Hutchinson notes that "'Pre-millennialism' was a view embraced by many, but not all, conservatives" (*Errand,* 120).

95. Robert E. Speer, *Christianity and the Nations* (New York: Laymen's Missionary Movement, 1910), 17.

96. Hutchinson, *Errand,* 113.

97. Ritschl, *Instruction,* 197.

98. See Hutchinson, *Errand*: "Most liberals, even if they got out of the business of personal evangelization, continued to express ultimate aims in the terminology not only of world evangelization but of Christian finality and right of conquest" (111).

99. See also Hutchinson, "A Moral Equivalent for Imperialism," in *Missionary Ideologies in the Imperialist Era, 1880–1920: Papers from the Durham Consultation, 1981,*

edited by Torben Christensen and William R. Hutchinson (Århus, Denmark: Aros,1983), 169, 174; and *Errand*, 111.

100. This volume probably served as a text for Otterbein's course *History of Christian Missions*, which, according to the catalogue, "emphasizes the present as the 'Decisive Hour of Christian Missions.'" Mignerey took neither this course, nor the other two in the category of "Missions": *Modern Missions*, and *Non-Christian Religions*.

101. Mott, John R., *The Decisive Hour of Christian Missions* (New York: Student Volunteer Movement for Foreign Missions, 1910), 33; See Clifton J. Phillips's discussion in "Changing Attitudes in the Student Volunteer Movement of Great Britain and North America, 1886–1928," 131–45, in *Missionary Ideologies in the Imperialist Era, 1880–1920*, edited by Torben Christensen and Willliam R. Hutchinson (Århus, Denmark: Aros, 1983), 137.

102. Hutchinson, *Errand,* 91 ff.

103. John R. Mott, *The Present World Situation: With Special Reference to the Demands Made upon the Christian Church in Relation to Non-Christian Lands* (New York: Student Volunteer Movement, 1915), 102.

104. Ibid., 101–103.

105. Ibid., 110, 112.

106. Ibid., 120, 127.

107. Ibid., 135, 148.

108. J.S. Mills, W. R. Funk, and S. S. Hough, *Our Foreign Missionary Enterprise* (Dayton, Ohio: United Brethren Publishing House, 1908), 4, 5 (Hereafter OFME).

109. OFME, 7–8.

110. OFME, 43–44.

111. See Dorn, *Washington Gladden*, 291–302.

112. Thomas F.Gosset, *Race: The History of an Idea in America* (New York: Oxford Univ. Press, 1997) 197. According to Szasz, "Progressive reformers generally ignored the issue of race" (43).

113. Funk, *Life*, 90 ff.

114. Job Smith Mills, *Mission Work in Sierra Leone, West Africa* (Dayton, Ohio, United Brethren Publishing House, 1898).

115. Ibid., 61, 29.

116. Robert Nassau, *Fetichism [sic] in West Africa: Forty Years' Observation of Native Customs and Superstitions* (New York: Young Peoples' Missionary Movement, 1904), 37–38.

117. D.K. Flickinger, *Ethiopia: Or Twenty Six Years of Missionary Life in Western Africa* (Dayton, Ohio: United Brethren Publishing House, 1882), 76.

118. Ibid., 78, 79.

119. Mills, *Mission Work,* 30.

120. in Funk, *Life*, 211.

121. OFME, 88.

122. Gossett, *Race*, 285.

123. Ibid., 286.

124. OFME, 7–8.

125. Gossett, *Race*, 65.

126. See Gossett, *Race*, 409–430.

127. Josiah Clark Nott and George R. Gliddon, *Types of Mankind* (Philadelphia: Lippincott, 1854), 180.

128. Ibid., 182.

129. Mills, *Mission work*, 24.

130. Ibid., 25.
131. Ibid., 53.

CHAPTER TWO

History of Sierra Leone 1787 – 1922: African States, Colonial Rule, and Missions

In the late nineteenth and early twentieth centuries, the political reality upon which Christian missionary expansion in Africa depended was colonial conquest through the use of military force. This was especially true in Sierra Leone, since the British were able to annex the Protectorate in 1898 only through a military response to a violent rebellion which was waged throughout the extent of the Protectorate. This war was still within living memory at the time of Mignerey's service in 1922-24. In this chapter, I will trace the history of Sierra Leone from 1787-1922. Through this historical survey, I will attempt to portray the political, economic, and military situation that emerged in the nineteenth century in order to set the stage for the more detailed treatment of the situation in the 1920s which is the focus of the present study. My overall aim is in fact to understand the religious experience of those involved in this situation and I do not see that experience as being simply determined by political, social, or economic factors. However, I am also endeavoring to understand the exact role that those factors really played. Three distinct political realities are at the heart of the story of the colonization of Sierra Leone: the original Colony of Sierra Leone, founded in 1787; the Mende, Temne, and Sherbro states of the nineteenth century which grew up in various regions of what was to become the Protectorate; and the gradual expansion of British power into those states, culminating in the formal imposition of the Protectorate in 1896, and war in 1898. I will also trace the development of missions, and especially of the United Brethren mission, in relationship to these three factors.

The original colony of 1789 was established on a completely different basis than the later Protectorate. Its geographical extent was limited to Freetown and its surrounding peninsula, and it was founded not as a bridgehead for imperial expansion but as a haven for freed slaves. The Protectorate was established in the heat of the late nineteenth century imperial "scramble for Africa." The "hinterland" that was eventually to become the Protectorate, and later, joined with the former colony, the independent nation of Sierra Leone, was and is home to approximately fifteen different ethnic groups, concentrated in fairly distinct areas. The two largest ethnic groups are the Mende and the Temne. The Temne, who were, by the way, the original inhabitants of the peninsula, occupy roughly the north-central and north-eastern area of the modern country (including the coast north of Freetown), the Mende most of the southern area, and the Sherbro or Bullom occupy the coast south of Freetown. The Kono, Kuranko, Lokko, Limba, Yalunka and Susu occupy the area to the north of the Mende and to the East of the Temne.

Mignerey served for about 16 months (January 1922-April 1923) in Rotifunk, at one of the United Brethren's earliest, largest, and most successful mission stations. Rotifunk is in an area that had been part of the precolonial Sherbro state. Mignerey observed that it was a town of "many languages," which is not surprising considering it was an important trading center and is close to the edge of both the Temne and Mende areas of Sierra Leone. The Paramount Chief of the region was Sherbro, but the town chief of Rotifunk was Lokko, and the chief and inhabitants of nearby Yenkissa were Kuranko. It would be instructive to focus on Rotifunk even had Mignerey not chanced to be sent there, since Rotifunk brings together in one place the predominant ethnic groups of the area: Mende, Temne, Sherbro, and Krio. United Brethren missionary activity was concentrated in the area of the Mende, with significant work in Sherbro country as well.

The nineteenth century saw the development of a number of states in the area of what is now Sierra Leone. Some had Mende rulers and were predominantly Mende, others had Temne rulers and were predominantly Temne, but there was never a state that simply encompassed the entirety of either ethnic group. Nor does there seem to have been any sort of special ethnic consciousness which militated for the unification of a people under a state. And the states were often multiethnic. Certain traditions and institutions, most notably the Poro society, crossed ethnic divisions. But while the Poro society could form the basis of very widespread collective action, it had nothing like a unified organization, and was itself nothing like a state. The history of Sierra Leone in the nineteenth century is the story of the gradual consolidation of states in a small region that was and is characterized by a great deal of cultural continuity—even across languages and ethnic groups—but also by a great deal of cultural diversity. This story is interwoven with the story of the gradual expansion of British power over these states, followed by the abrupt imposition of colonial rule during 1896-1898. The port city of Freetown was the center from which British power emanated. The original Colony of Sierra Leone was in fact limited to this city and the peninsula on which it is located. The area formally annexed to the British Empire in 1896-1898, corresponding to the present day boundaries of the nation, became known as the Protectorate. But the British founders of the original Colony of Sierra Leone did not envision their project as a staging ground for the further expansion of the Empire.

The Original Colony of Sierra Leone and the Emergence of the Krio

The original Colony of Sierra Leone owed its founding to the efforts of the British anti-slavery activist Granville Sharp, who persuaded the British government to undertake a settlement in Africa of ex-slaves who had been living in London, many of whom had earlier been freed by the British during the United States Revolutionary War.[1] The initial settlement, undertaken in 1787, of 411 people, at the site which would later become Freetown, ended in failure within a year. Granville Sharp then joined with other anti-slavery activists in 1791 to form the Sierra Leone Company, which this time successfully established a settlement at the site now named Freetown. Slavery and the slave trade were forbidden in the settlement. The new settlement included three groups: some of the original settlers from London; North American slaves who had been freed by the British during the Revolutionary War and had been settled in Nova Scotia afterwards[2] and, in 1795, a group of Jamaican slaves who had successfully rebelled and fled to the mountains, where they had established their own state and remained until moving to Sierra Leone as a result of negotiations.[3]

In 1806 Britain legally abolished the slave trade, and in 1808 Britain formally took over the Colony of Sierra Leone from the Sierra Leone Company.[4] At this time the population of the colony was under 2000. The Anti-Slave-Trade Act had empowered the British navy to seize slave ships. Freetown became the base for this activity, and also the place of residence for those who were freed.[5] Between 1808 and 1864, 84,000 Africans were liberated from slave ships and settled in Freetown.[6] While this constituted only about 8% of the slaves shipped from Africa during that period, the effects of the naval activity may have been more far-reaching. According to the calculations of one researcher, the overall deterrent effect of the activity of the naval squadron may have been that as many as 825,000 fewer slaves were exported than would have been otherwise (i.e. a difference of 43%).[7]

The unique form that settlement took in the Sierra Leone Colony resulted in the eventual fusion of peoples from over 100 different ethnic groups, among whom the Yoruba and Igbo were predominant.[8] The many differences that existed—between settlers and "recaptives," as well as among the many "recaptive" groups of liberated Africans—did lead to some conflicts. However, the result was that over the century, a new and cohesive group identity did emerge, with its own unique synthesis of various African cultural traditions with European traditions. The Krio language which emerged can be classified as a dialect of English, but approximately twenty percent of its vocabulary is African, and both pronunciation and syntax are strongly influenced by African patterns. Krio is in fact a fully developed language and not a 'pidgin' dialect.[9]

The British, mostly through the Church Missionary Society (C.M.S.), introduced Western education and Christianity to the Liberated Africans, who, for
the most part, did become Christians. A fifth of the Krio population of children
were in school by 1840. (Fyfe points out that at this time only three fifths of the
population of England was literate.[10]) In 1827 the C.M.S. founded Fourah Bay
College, the first European style institution of higher learning in Sub-Saharan
Africa. (Islamic universities, such as the one at Timbuktu, were of course much
older.) Over the course of the century, Fourah Bay produced not only many
teachers and priests, but at least 25 medical doctors and at least 15 lawyers.[11]
The British did not rule their colony democratically: selected citizens served in
at most an advisory role in the government. However, until the 1890s educated
Krios served in the British colonial administration.[12]

At the same time as the Krios were energetically absorbing European culture, they were also creating a shared African tradition. For example, the Krio
ceremonies marking birth (*komojade*), engagement (*put stop*), and death (*awujoh*) are clearly African in origin. The *awujoh* ceremony, for example, clearly
maintains traditional African beliefs about ancestors, especially the notion that
there is communication between the living and ancestors, and that ancestors can
influence the fortunes of the living.[13]

The real prosperity of the Krio, including the Liberated Africans, began in
1835. The British at that point decided that ships needed only to be fitted out for
slaving to be liable for capture, and that any goods they had been carrying for
trade were open to auction in Freetown. Krio traders were able to outbid and
undersell competing European merchants.[14] From this beginning Krio prosperity
continually grew, expanding first into the groundnut and palm oil trade with the
hinterland.[15] Between 1850 and 1880, Krio traders established at least seven
outposts on the plain south of the peninsula, none more than forty to fifty miles
from the coast.[16] Fyfe cites a tax list from 1853 which gives a clear picture of
the prosperity and relative status in Freetown of the Krio merchant elite at that
time: "Of the nineteen biggest owners of houses and land only five were Europeans," and among the fifteen non-Europeans there were 7 recaptives, one (or
more) came from an original settler family, four were half-African, one was Caribbean, and one was African-American. In addition "of the 175 next largest
owners, over 100 were recaptives, disbanded soldiers, or their children."[17]

Mende, Temne, and Sherbro States

One of the justifications for colonial conquest often put forward was that only
the colonial state could unify and pacify an area essentially in chaos, with no
level of political organization above that of the war-town. Decisively refuting
this view, Arthur Abraham demonstrates that prior to colonization there were
approximately eight states in the Mende area, and that the imposition of colonial
rule dismantled these states. According to Abraham, "the war-town was the
smallest unit of local administration, and was under the jurisdiction of a chief
who had had some military experience."[18] The head of the town or village was
usually male, but it was not uncommon for women to fill that role.[19] At the next

level, a chief might exercise jurisdiction over a group of walled towns and villages. This level is the one that most closely resembles the colonial chiefdom. Among them, the population of such a polity might be as high as 7000 (Jama) to 10,000 (Taiama). The third level of political organization is that of states—which were intentionally or inadvertently dismantled by the British. Abraham identifies two basic kinds of states in Mendeland: personal-amorphous states, and territorial states. Personal amorphous states were basically the creations of the military activity of effective leaders, and territorial states were based on traditions of kingship, and had more stable boundaries. In both kinds of state, "the office of king was not hereditary. Election determined the incumbent to the office." [20] While "it was not uncommon...to have women as town or village heads," [21] only men over 40 were considered candidates for leadership at the higher levels. The leaders of the personal-amorphous states wielded greater personal power than the leaders of territorial states. However, the position of each was basically that of first among equals. Abraham notes that for both, "the king was responsible for the external relations of the state and also for war, and he heard appeals from his chiefs or against his chiefs." However, "In terms of the actual exercise of day-to-day administrative authority, the kings wielded power almost equal to that of their chiefs...The kings did not interfere with the administration of their chiefs over their direct and immediate subjects." [22] The largest Mende state was that of the Kpa-Mende, centered at Taiama. [23] In addition to Kpa-Mende, Abraham also identifies Sherbro, Bumpe, Lugbu, and Gallinas as territorial states with traditional systems of kingship. These states existed in the western half of the Sierra Leone area, while the four personal-amorphous states existed in the eastern half. [24]

The Temne as well had achieved political organization at a level higher than the town, even prior to the nineteenth century. In 1822, one observer noted that there were "four districts in Temne country, each under one supreme chief." [25] From Kenneth Wylie's and Adeleye Ijagbemi's discussions it is clear that such chiefdom organization persisted into the nineteenth century, but that the chiefdoms perhaps then became somewhat fragmented. There were clearly at least six, and perhaps as many as ten or twelve, [26] chiefdoms that were still each relatively unified and had traditional systems of kingship. In the traditional Temne governmental organization the *Obai* (or *Alikali*) is paramount in power. The *Kapr* (or *Alimami* and *Santigi*) whom he appoints consist of two groups—his immediate advisers, and section chiefs, who are responsible for regions of the state. Along with the section chiefs, appointed by the *Obai* (*Bai*) or *Alikali*, there are also headmen, who are elected and had authority over villages or sections of villages or towns. [27] Among the Temne, kingship traditions and titles that were especially influential in the nineteenth century were that of the Alikali of Maforki; Bai Simera of Masimera; Bai Koblo of Marampa; and Bai Komp of Kolifa. [28] The Koya chiefdom lay to the immediate West of the Sierra Leone peninsula, and indeed originally included that peninsula. The original colony was carved out of that chiefdom, and the entire chiefdom was militarily conquered by the British in 1862, more than three decades before the establishment of the Protectorate. [29]

The Sherbro (also, and originally, known as the Bullom) are an ethnic group occupying the coastal areas to the north and to the south of the Sierra Leone penninsula. The Sherbro to the south had a much longer history of contact and involvement with European powers than any other group, and their political history was shaped from very early by that contact, primarily in the form of the slave trade. From a very early date ruling houses emerged as a result of inter-marriage with Europeans. In 1684, an individual named Thomas Corker came from England to Sherbro country in the service of The Company of Merchants Trading in Africa. The main form of trade at that time was the slave trade. Slave traders lived safely under the protection of local chiefs.[30] Corker married Seni-ora Doll, the daughter of a politically powerful family in the area that controlled the bay just to the south of the Sierra Leone penninsula. This family came to dominate the area well into the twentieth century.

The history of the Caulker family (as the Corkers soon came to be called) is riven with internal conflict, which Fyfe traces in detail. For example, in the mid-eighteenth century, another branch emerged through the marriage of a Corker daughter to another man from England, William Cleveland. His son James, who controlled the Banana Islands, attacked and beheaded a chief Charles Corker.[31] At the time, William and Stephen Caulker controlled the rest of the Sherbro area. Upon William's death, Stephen attacked the Banana Islands and drove out William Cleveland, the son of James Cleveland, who had since died.[32] William Cleveland continued to fight Stephen Caulker, and many Sherbro chiefs were drawn into the conflict on either side. And as Fyfe puts it, "European slave traders supplied arms, and reaped a rich harvest of slaves captured from devas-tated villages all over the country."[33] In 1805 the British interceded and nego-tiated a truce in which "the Sherbro people agreed that the ancient British right to York Island...gave the Governor the right to interfere, even to crown their king."[34]

Stephen Caulker's son George Stephen I had been educated in England. When Stephen Caulker died in 1810, his brother Thomas Stephen (Kon Tham) was to succeed him. But with the pressure of the British Governor, Thomas Ste-phen (Kon Tham) was persuaded to divide the chiefdom with his nephew George Stephen (I), the Banana islands and the mainland going to Thomas Ste-phen (Kon Tham), and the Plantain islands to George Stephen (I).[35] Both the Banana and the Plantain Islands were important slave-trading centers. What was at stake in the intense and violent competition for power in the area had much to do with competition for the lucrative control of the slave trade, and by the 1840s, of the timber trade as well, which by that time had become equally lucra-tive.[36] In 1820 the Caulkers agreed to lease the Banana Islands to the British, and "Thomas [Stephen] Caulker [Kon Tham] moved to Bumpe on the main-land."[37] George Stephen Caulker (I) had to face continued harrassment from the Clevelands, who brought in Mende on their side. He appealed to the British for help, and "in ... 1825 ...[Governor] Turner bought two condemned slave ships, filled them with troops, ..and..sailed to the Plantains where [George Stephen] Caulker [I] had gathered some Sherbro chiefs. He explained that he could do nothing unless they agreed to give up the slave trade and cede their country to the Crown. So ... they made a treaty by which the Caulkers...gave up sovereignty between the Kamaranka and Kamalay ... and became British subjects."[38]

George Stephen Caulker (I) of the Plantains died in 1831, and was succeeded by his uncle Thomas Stephen (Ba Tham), who in 1854 moved from the Plantains to Shenge on the mainland and ruled from there until his death in 1871. Thomas Stephen (Ba Tham) was the chief who granted permission for the first United Brethren mission in 1857, but converted to Christianity only shortly before his death. At Bumpe on the mainland, Charles Caulker succeeded his father Thomas Stephen Caulker (Kon Tham) in 1832, and Charles was succeeded at his death by Canreba Caulker in 1842.[39] Canreba's reign initiated another bitter, protracted, and violent conflict between the two branches of the Caulker family, ruling from Bumpe (Canreba) and Shenge (Thomas Stephen— Ba Tham) respectively. The conflict continued into the next generation as well: Canreba's son Richard Canreba Caulker of Bumpe came to rule in 1864.[40] But when Thomas Stephen Caulker (Ba Tham) of Shenge was succeeded in 1871 by his son George Stephen Caulker II (at the behest of the British), Richard Canreba Caulker contested the succession on behalf of William Caulker (grandson of George Stephen I), even though the whereabouts of William were at the time unknown.[41] When William returned four years later he began to fight for power.[42] The United Brethren missionary Joseph Gomer attempted to mediate to no avail.[43] George Stephen Caulker II captured William and the British held him as a political prisoner from 1878-1882. George Stephen Caulker II died in 1881, and was succeeded, again at the behest of the British, by his half-brother Thomas Neale Caulker, who then publicly reconciled with William and had him released.[44] As Fyfe makes clear, this was an action Thomas Neale came to regret:

> William and Thomas Neale Caulker... remained bitter enemies. Thomas accused William of abetting robbery in 1883 and sent him to Freetown for trial; through Macfoy, he retained Lewis and was acquitted..... On his returned he determined on revenge. Thomas Neale, oppressive and harsh, as a servant is traditionally when he is king, was hated by many of his chiefs: William eagerly incited them against him.... With the connivance, it was believed, of Richard Caulker of Bumpe, William hired Mende mercenaries....Then while the Creoles were celebrating their centenary, William's followers swept through the country, slaughtering and devastating with the ferocity of the earlier Caulker wars.[45]

William also planned to capture and kill Joseph Gomer at Shenge, but the attack was beaten off and William was apprehended by the British. William was brought to Freetown where he was tried for murder, convicted, and hanged. Richard Canreba Caulker of Bumpe town was sent into exile in Gambia, but was reinstated as Paramount Chief of Bumpe chiefdom in 1895. He was removed by the British after the Hut Tax war, and replaced by his cousin James Canraybah Caulker (whose son A.G. Caulker was Bumpe Paramount Chief when Mignerey arrived in Rotifunk).[46] Richard died in a Freetown jail in 1901.[47]

The hanging of William Caulker had been against the wishes of the jury, which had recommended mercy. The verdict and execution were unpopular in Freetown. As Fyfe puts it, "they saw William as the victim of a greedy, irresponsible power which denied its subjects the protection of law, but punished them for taking it into their own hands."[48] And in Sherbro country, Thomas Neale was unpopular. Many supported William's claim to rule, regarding Thomas Neale as a "usurper," and William as a "martyr."[49] During the Hut Tax War of 1898, when the mission at Shenge was attacked, Thomas Neale refused the missionaries' pleas to escape with them. He instead waited grimly for his relatives to arrive and avenge themselves on him.[50]

Caulker Succession, Nineteenth to Early Twentieth Century[51]	
Stephen and Thomas Stephen (Kon Tham)	
1796-1810	Stephen Caulker
1810-1832	Thomas Stephen Caulker (Kon Tham), brother of Stephen Caulker
Plantain-Shenge Caulkers	
1810-1831	George Stephen I, son of Stephen. Shared rule with Thomas Stephen (Kon Tham)
1831-1871	Thomas Stephen (Ba Tham), son of Stephen, brother of George Stephen I.
1871-1881	George Stephen II, son of Thomas Stephen (Ba Tham)
1881-1898	Thomas Neale, half brother of George Stephen II.
Bumpe Caulkers	
1832-42	Charles, brother of Thomas Stephen (Kon Tham)
1842-57	Canreba, son of Thomas Stephen (Kon Tham)
1857-1864	Thomas Theophilus, brother of Canreba
1864-1898	Richard Canreba, son of Canreba
1899-1903	James Canreba, son of Richard Canreba
1904-1907	John Canreba, brother of James Canreba
1907-1921	Thomas Canreba, brother of John Canreba
1921-1954	Albert George, son of James Canreba

Warfare and Trade in the Nineteenth Century

The hinterland of Sierra Leone during the nineteenth century was plagued by warfare. One of the main justifications advanced by the factions in the colonial government proposing the Protectorate was in fact the pacification of the interior. And the warfare was often ascribed in this context to the "savage" nature of the "tribes" that were fighting what were indeed often called "tribal" wars. But this stereotyped account, propagated on down into the twentieth century, misunderstands both the nature and the cause of these wars. The wars involved one chiefdom or kingdom against another, or disputes about chiefdom leadership, and also alliances among chiefdoms, in a way that was as likely to pit various chiefdoms of like ethnicity against one another, as it was to involve conflicts between chiefdoms belonging to different linguistic and cultural groups. Indeed, it is unlikely that prior to colonization, either the Temne or the Mende ethnic groups even "existed" in the sense of being named or being loci of group allegiance. There were indeed cultural traditions within each group, but there was also cultural diversity within each group, and there were traditions shared by segments of both of the two groups as well as by the Sherbro and others. The primary reason for the proliferation of these wars was competition for control of the burgeoning "legitimate trade" between the hinterland and the coast that followed upon the successful prohibition of external trade in slaves. Indeed, the whole history of Sierra Leone in the nineteenth century can be understood in this context, once it is recognized that the British too were players in this struggle, and in fact were the ones who finally prevailed with the military imposition of the Protectorate in 1898.[52]

Ijagbemi points out that "from about 1828, by which time legitimate trading was firmly established, to 1887, when the trade wars came to an end in Temne country, the territories adjoining the Colony of Freetown knew very little peace."[53] The disruption of trade by recurrent warfare was a pressing issue for both the Freetown traders and hinterland rulers. But at the same time, the nineteenth century saw a marked and continuous expansion of that trade. The initial crisis for the hinterland economy was the cutting off of external slave trade in 1807, which made necessary a transition to "legitimate" commerce.[54] This transition began with the production and export of timber, which flourished from the 1840s to the 1860s.[55] The cash crop production for trade with Freetown by small scale farmers of palm products, peanuts, kola, benniseed and rubber began roughly in the 1840s. Peanut cultivation for trade rose until the 1870s, benniseed until the 1870s, and kola into the 1890s.[56] The international depression of the 1880s had a much more significant effect on trade than the interior wars—but calls for the Protectorate by trading interests focused on the wars rather than the depression.[57]

While warfare had at times and in places a depressing effect on trade, most of the warfare was rooted in competition for participation in trade and for control of trade routes and crucial trading towns and regions. Howard points out that "the political fortunes of big men-traders located along the main corridors improved during the 1870s and 1880s, in good measure through their own astute use of war, diplomacy, and alliance to safeguard roads and mobilize trade."[58] Also, the growing opportunities for trade throughout the nineteenth century prompted those in the hinterland already in positions of power and authority to take advantage of that power to extract labor more intensively, especially through the increased acquisition of slaves through warfare. The prohibition of external slave trade may have had the paradoxical effect of promoting slavery internally, as opportunity increased for cash-crop trade, and big-men realized that capturing and retaining slaves could be even more profitable than the selling of slaves.[59]   The numerous local wars of the nineteenth century could be very destructive in that they often involved the burning and plunder of towns and the taking of many captives. But from the sources available to Abraham, Ijagbemi, and Wylie, it is difficult to come to a definite conclusion about just how destructive the wars were in terms of loss of life. It appears that the wars did not in fact involve a great deal of loss of life. In general, the fact that the wars typically aimed not at vengeance or complete subjugation, but at the control of trade and the gaining of wealth, supports the claim that loss of life was not extensive. According to Abraham,

> the nature of these wars did not take on the character of bloody casualties, except when Europeans were involved, deploying their superior fire-power against the Africans, as will be shown in chapter II. Otherwise, the general picture has been

well described thus: "The wars of these people are, however, not attended with any sanguinary results, they consist mainly in surprising a few individuals where they can be suddenly come upon. Sometimes, the roads are waylaid wherever their respective traders are supposed to pass. These, together with other petty annoyances, constitute their principal mode of warfare. The large walled towns are seldom taken. Pitched battles are seldom fought; and even when these people may be said to take the open field, most is done by some war Chief by way of displaying his individual prowess."[60]

While the description Abraham quotes (Anderson's) may be accurate as far as it goes, the reports cited by Abraham, Wylie, and Ijagbemi consistently report the extensive burning of towns and taking of captives. Abraham elsewhere reports that when villages were conquered "women and children were always taken as dependents, while the male defenders were usually killed or sold."[61]

The situation in the Sierra Leone hinterland in the nineteenth century appears to have been one of great political instability, but far from total chaos—various chiefdoms and regions retained enough integrity to act to promote their individual interests and gain wealth. (Ijagbemi consistently uses the word "chaos" to describe the situation in the Temne area, but the evidence he cites for actual conditions—while it does indicate a situation of frequent upheaval and military conflict—does not suggest a situation in which order and commerce had by any means completely broken down.) And the origin of this instability appears to have been the significant economic change introduced by the transition in international trade from a basis in slave trade to a basis in "legitimate" trade, and in the continuous increase in that trade. The conflict was one between local regions that flared up at various places and times for various specific reasons. So while a particular area might appear to be devastated at a particular point, it could quickly recover. Ijagbemi cites one case in particular which well illustrates how it could be that on the one hand, colonial officials could get the impression that the hinterland was in chaos, and yet at the same time, trade overall kept flourishing and growing. Referring to the situation in the Rokel river area in 1882, one official stated that "the country is actually desolate and ruined, all the flourishing towns ruined, broken and depopulated, and are now the habitation of elephants and wild beasts."[62] But by 1884, another official visiting the same region wrote that "almost the whole of the towns that had been destroyed by the late war are rebuilt—the country is full of trade, produce of all descriptions is coming down in abundance."[63] Another British officer discovered that, in the midst of the renewed wars on the Rokel River in 1886, "trade was still brisk, and life normal" which, as Ijagbemi notes, was "a sharp and disappointing contrast to what [the officer] expected, and a pointer to the degree of exaggeration that usually accompanied reports of warring activities of the 'savage hordes' of the interior."[64] Anderson, whose journey to Musadu in 1868 traversed the hinterland region just to the south of Mende country, between the Mano and St. Paul rivers, writes that:

Many stories were rife of the unsettled state of the country: that the roads between us and the interior tribes were infested with banditti; that war was raging between interior tribes themselves; that between all these jarring forces, it was impossible for the expedition to survive forty miles.... But as the expedition was pushed on in the very localities where these difficulties were said to exist, it was found that there were disturbances, but not of a character to entirely prohibit our progress.[65]

Expansion of British Power to 1890

Throughout the nineteenth century, trade was continually expanding between the Colony and the hinterland, and was for most of the century largely in the hands of Krio merchants. The desire to protect and to foster this trade motivated calls by both Krios and Europeans involved in Freetown government and commerce for increased British political and military influence in the hinterland. However, until as late as 1890, the British metropolitan government and colonial office consistently resisted calls for the expansion of British territorial holdings. The established policy was that the responsibilities and expense of an expanded empire would bring no net gain for Britain either economically or politically.

Despite the official policy against annexation, British military and political involvement in the hinterland gradually expanded hand in hand with economic involvement through most of the nineteenth century. Many of the 28 British governors who served during the nineteenth century actively promoted this involvement. Once the Colony had been established, the first treaties with rulers outside of the peninsula were with the Alikali of Port Loko in 1825[66] and with the Sherbro chiefs in 1826.[67] The latter, which claimed annexation, was overturned by the colonial office.

The governors began, in 1831, to make series of treaties with rulers near the Colony that promised the protection of traders in return for stipends from the government.[68] Without being formally annexed, Koya chiefdom (to the immediate east of the Colony) was already in the British sphere of influence by 1830.[69] The first formal annexation, with the consent of the colonial office, took place in 1861, when a 200 square mile area around the coastal town of Bendu in the Sherbro area was acquired. In 1862, at the end of a military campaign, the British imposed a peace treaty that annexed the Koya area in all but name.[70] By 1883 the British had effectively annexed the entire coastline south of the peninsula.[71]

The arguments made for expanding influence and annexation were economic. A European depression starting in 1873 that continued into the 1880s reduced demand and lowered prices for palm produce, the primary export from Sierra Leone.[72] But the trading interests affected attributed their declining fortunes to the internecine warfare in the interior rather than to the international depression. This lead to repeated involvement by the British military in that warfare. Also, the revenue of the Colony government itself was primarily derived from export duties. The annexation of the coastline was carried out in order to collect export duties all along the coast instead of only in Freetown.[73]

The Expansion of Missionary Influence and
The Role of United Brethren Missions

The Church Missionary Society (C.M.S.) was founded in 1799 by the antislavery activist William Wilberforce. It was in fact in Sierra Leone that the C.M.S. first began its work, sending three German missionaries to Rio Pongas in the Susu area. In 1811 the Wesleyan Missionary Society (W.M.S.) sent its first missionaries directly to Freetown.[74] In 1816 Governor MacCarthy persuaded the C.M.S. to move its mission to Freetown in order to convert the Liberated Africans. The C.M.S. missionaries came to function as government superintendents for the numerous villages established for the Liberated Africans on the peninsula.[75] The missionary efforts at conversion in the Colony were in fact very successful, so that "by 1840 there was scarcely a village in the colony that did not have at least one church"[76] and most of the Liberated Africans had become Christians.[77] By 1839 the W.M.S. had churches in fourteen peninsula villages.[78]

Missionary efforts outside of the Colony were less successful. The C.M.S. mission established in 1840 at Port Loko (in an area of Temne country where the influence of Islam was strong) produced no converts, and was moved to the less Muslim town of Magbele in 1851.[79] The C.M.S. sent individual missionary representatives to regions as they were annexed in 1869 and 1870: Koya in the Temne area in Bendu, Bonthe and Victoria in the Sherbro area.[80] By 1894 the C.M.S. had established three more missions in the north.[81] But by the 1890s "in the north, long under Muslim influence, Christian missions had made little progress," and there was only one even nominally Christian chief.[82] By late in the century, the only hinterland Roman Catholic missions were in the area to the north under the French sphere of influence, and there was only one small Roman Catholic Church in Freetown.[83] By the 1890s the W.M.S. had missions in the Mabanta, Rokel and Limba regions in the north, and an additional mission in the Sherbro area. By 1890, the African Methodist Episcopal Church had established missions at Mange and Magbele in the north.[84] The United Free Methodists had two missions in the Mende area, at Senehun and Tikonko.[85] The United Brethren, whose missions were concentrated in the Mende area, were the most successful of all the churches who made missionary efforts in the hinterland. By 1892, as Fyfe observes "the most flourishing, best equipped missions were still those affiliated to the U.B.C."[86] The U.B.C. was also apparently the only organization, besides the United Free Methodists, to develop missions in the south—which is surprising given the much greater prevalence of Islam in the north.

The first missionary society of the United Brethren Church was organized at Otterbein University in 1852, and the "Home, Frontier, and Foreign Missionary Society of the United Brethren in Christ" was established at the General Conference in 1853.[87] Three United Brethren missionaries, lead by D.K. Flickinger, arrived in Sierra Leone in 1855, and their attempts to start a mission in the Sherbro region were not successful until 1857, when Flickinger persuaded Chief Thomas Stephen Caulker (Ba Tham) to allow a mission to be opened at Shenge. The Caulker family had long been prominent in the Sherbro region. The Caulkers were involved, at various times throughout the nineteenth century and before, in disputes, alliances, intrigues, and violent conflict on every level: within the family, with other powerful families and chiefdoms, with both the British and the French. Thomas Stephen Caulker (Ba Tham) had at the time thrown his lot in with the British. As Fyfe summarizes the story, when the missionaries first made their request, "Caulker was unfriendly, but realized that with missionaries under his protection at Shenge, his own claim to live there, which was being contested, would be strengthened....During the first decade there were only two converts. One was Caulker's daughter Lucy. Furious at her conversion, he packed her off to York Island as mistress to a European trader who had no more Christian principles than he."[88] Lucy Caulker was 14 at the time of her conversion, and, according to one United Brethren source "because of her stand for Christ, suffered great persecution."[89] She left her "husband" after her father became a Christian (about 1871), remarried, and worked for the church at Shenge until her death in 1910.[90]

The mission floundered for the next fifteen years. During that time, the church sent nine missionaries, including Flickinger, none of whom was able to remain for more than about two years.[91] Flickinger, who journeyed to Sierra Leone twice and was a passionate advocate at home, was one of the individuals crucial to the initial survival of the mission. The other was J.A. Williams, a Krio minister from Freetown originally affiliated with the Huntingtonians.[92] Williams served for about ten years, starting in 1858 or 1859. He was the only individual able to remain consistently at the helm throughout this period, and Flickinger credits him with saving the mission. He ran the mission on his own for as much as two years at a time.[93] But the mission was barely holding on, counting only two converts between 1857 and about 1870.[94] The mission board seemed to be on the verge of abandoning its efforts in Sierra Leone, even resolving, in 1870, to transfer control of the mission, ostensibly temporarily, to the American Missionary Association. Williams had run the mission on his own from 1869, but upon his death in 1870, the board had a change of heart, and appointed Joseph Gomer, an African American, to carry on the work.[95] Gomer and his wife arrived in Shenge in 1871. Gomer was able to befriend and in fact convert Thomas Stephen Caulker (Ba Tham) and "now politically entrenched, he was able to build up the mission in succeeding years."[96] J.A. Evans, another African American, worked with Gomer at Shenge from 1871 to 1873.[97] (D.F. Wilberforce was brought from Bonthe in 1871 at age 19, given a high school education in Dayton, and sent back to serve in Sierra Leone, eventually becoming principal of Rufus Clark and Wife Training School at Shenge.[98]) Gomer succeed where his nine predecessors had failed. By 1875, the United Brethren had two churches with 24 members, and his impact extended far beyond sheer numbers of converts.[99] He clearly deserves credit as the individual most responsible for the original establishment of the United Brethren mission in Sierra Leone—in fact the one individual without whom the mission would have failed. Gomer served until his death in 1892.[100] The early United Brethren chroniclers (Flickinger, McKee, and Mills) give him full and unstinting credit for this achievement, and regard him as a model missionary. And yet the Gomers and Evans were not only the first African-American missionaries sent by the United Brethren. They were also the last.

Gomer's story is significant both because he more than any other was the founder of United Brethren missions in Sierra Leone, and because of the light it sheds on the recrudescence of racism in American society during the period 1880-1920, a recrudescence to which the United Brethren were not immune. But a little earlier the story was quite different. At the end of the 1860s, the United Brethren had a deliberate policy of recruiting African-American missionaries.[101] The United Brethren had taken a strongly abolitionist stand from early in the pre-civil war period. For example, in 1837, copies of *The Religious Telescope* were confiscated in Virginia due to the editors' willingness to openly advocate abolitionist views, and in 1850 the *Telescope* openly condemned the Fugitive Slave Bill.[102] The United Brethren leadership regarded the antislavery cause, and the cause of missions, as closely related.[103] As Americans they felt complicit in the sin of slavery. They also felt that complicity gave them a special obligation toward Africa, an obligation not only to obey the Great Commission, but also to offer redress for the collective sin of slavery. There is a refreshing moral clarity in Flickinger's proclamation of this position, made in full acknowledgement not only of the horror of slavery, but of its disastrous effect on Africa itself:

> Now if those from enlightened countries and of our own color, have done so much to debase that people, ought we not to do something to elevate them? .... For my part I cannot explain how we can be guiltless, in the sight of High Heaven, unless we put forth our hands to raise them from the dreadful dilemma in which we have helped place them? Is it not to be feared that the Savior will say to us 'inasmuch as ye did it not unto one of the least of these, ye did it not to me?'[104]

It is true that Flickinger, in his writings, exhibits an extremely ethnocentric attitude towards African culture: he finds no value in traditional African religion, even identifying it with devil worship, and he regards the Poro society as something to be abolished. (Gomer, by the way, shared exactly the same cultural attitudes.) However, Flickinger seems quite free of specifically *racial* prejudice—a prejudice much more in evidence in the subsequent generation, including Funk and even Mills. (Indeed, in the subsequent two or three generations of missionaries, there seems on the whole some decrease in ethnocentrism, coupled with an increase in race prejudice.) Flickinger, in his *Ethiopa*, quotes extensively from Gomer's letters—and his expressed admiration for Gomer has no hint of condescension. (The same can be said of the extensive treatment of Gomer in the volume by McKee, *The History of the Sherbro Mission*, and the volume on which Flickinger collaborated with McKee, *History of the Origin, Development, and Condition of Missions Among the Sherbro and Mendi Tribes*.) And Flickinger backed up his words with actions—he was probably the single person most responsible for the promotion of the mission from the very outset, and for the recruitment of African-Americans as missionaries.

Gomer was born in Ann Arbor, Michigan, where his educational opportunities were limited because of his race. He served as a cook in the Union army during the Civil War, and after the war moved to Dayton, Ohio, where he worked as a foreman in a carpet factory, and was very active in a leadership role at the Third United Brethren Church of Dayton, an African-American congregation.[105] He was not an ordained minister at the time he was sent to Sierra Leone. Once he had arrived there, in response to his repeated requests, an ordained minister had been sent, in the person of J.A. Evans. Of course when he arrived he found the mission in a shambles. He immediately set to work by reestablishing the school, and engaging in a project of preaching and itineration. His quick and continuing success had much to do with his ardent faith, his determination, and his self-confidence. But beyond these characteristics, which most if not all missionaries shared, Gomer had an exceptional ability to work with Africans at all levels of society. He was able to gain their confidence and cooperation, and to resolve conflicts of all kinds, even the most seemingly intractable.[106] And clearly his race had something to do with his success. Africans were receptive to a Black missionary in a way they might not have been to a white one—openly expressing their gratitude to the mission for employing someone of their own race.[107] And Gomer made a point of reaching out to Africans not only in meetings or at church—and his meetings were very well attended—but of frequently visiting their farms and homes, and involving himself in their everyday concerns—to an extent that few if any white missionaries were willing to do.[108]

Gomer's ability to work with people included his ability to work with leaders. His first significant accomplishment was the conversion of the Shenge chief Thomas Stephen Caulker (Ba Tham). When Caulker died within a year, he was succeeded by his son George Stephen Caulker II. Even while working closely with the Caulkers, Gomer maintained a critical eye toward how they conducted themselves as leaders. For example, he is not too eager to take Thomas Stephen Caulker's word for it about his conversion:

> I had a long talk with old Mr. Caulker last night. He makes fair promises, if only he will keep them. He says Lucy Caulker, his daughter, was converted in this mission and is a Christian. [Gomer must be aware of how Caulker had treated her at the time!] He seems proud of her. God only knows the old man's heart. I leave all with God.[109]

Gomer was evidently not entirely convinced of the sincerity of the father's conversion. And while his son George Caulker had not converted, Gomer did gain his support for the mission.[110] Gomer was committed to the ending of polygamy and slavery. But, as he put it "I have to go slow." Gomer had the patience and pragmatism to accept that he had to work diplomatically with imperfect individuals if there was to be hope for any real accomplishment. And he was aware of just how imperfect George Caulker was. Only a few weeks after the younger Caulker became chief, Gomer writes:

> I attended the meeting in town yesterday morning and evening. At night there was a large attendance, many having come in from their farms. George interpreted for me all day. At the close of the evening meeting he wished to read a text to the people. He read, with a few remarks, Proverbs 16:15 and 19:12. The slaves all seem to have a sort of dread of him. He may be trying to deceive me.[111]

Gomer's suspicion of Caulker gains added credibility when one considers the texts from *Proverbs* Caulker wished to proclaim. *Proverbs* 16:15 and 19:12, in the King James version, read: "In the light of the king's countenance is life; and his favor is as a cloud of the latter rain"; "The king's wrath is as the roaring of a lion; but his favor is as dew upon the grass." It is probably dawning on Gomer that Caulker's support of the mission may have more to do with the political advantage of alliance with Western power than with any kind of sincere change of heart. In December of 1871, three new missionaries arrived: J.A. Evans, Mrs. M. B. Hadley, and Miss P. Williams. Mrs. Hadley's naive, almost gushing, response to Caulker contrasts distinctly with Gomer's astute assessment:

> Even the young ruler is very favorably impressed [by Gomer], and renders most valuable service in our mission work. He wields great influence and power over the people to bring them under religious teaching. And we have bright hopes that he will soon be led into this great work, like Paul. He is a man of fine talent and education and can turn Scriptures into the Sherbro language in a ready and fluent manner.[112]

Gomer did not let his realistic assessment of Caulker interfere with his work. This fact gains its most striking confirmation when one considers the very significant political role Gomer came to play in the affairs of Shenge especially in its relations with neighboring chiefdoms. Gomer developed an intimate knowledge of the intricate political tangle of the region in which he lived, especially of the complicated and vexed relationships among various members of the Caulker family who were politically powerful in that region. Most notably, he attempted to bring peace between the rival Caulkers. In 1872, the accession of George Stephen Caulker (II) of Shenge was contested by Richard Canreba Caulker, who had ruled in Bumpe (town) since 1864. Richard claimed he should rule the whole chiefdom until William Caulker, whom he claimed to regard as the rightful heir, could be found. George and Richard had not spoken since 1866.[113] Gomer attempted to bring them together to resolve their differences. As Gomer describes the situation:

> On the 1st of December Richard, with between two and three hundred war men, and a great train of Murrymen and Mohammedan priests as his counsellors, arrived at Molacket, a small town on the opposite side of the river from Genda Mah. Molacket is in Richard's territory. Richard refused to cross the river to George at Genda Mah, and George refused to go over to Richard. Richard was afraid that George was playing some trick on him, and George stood on his dignity. So I think. The situation soon became known throughout the country, and all the chief men soon assembled at Genda Mah to try to effect a reconciliation between the parties, for all feared the consequences.[114]

Gomer shuttled back and forth repeatedly, and finally persuaded the feuding relatives to meet. Gomer does not point to the specifics of any sort of agreement reached between the two. But he did manage to bring them to display a public show of reconciliation. The enthusiastic way it was received suggests there was indeed popular support for that reconciliation:

Bannah Bandah first shook hands with Richard; next George went to him and embraced him ; and now the scene that followed, I can not describe. Several hundred persons were present, to witness the proceedings. Guns were fired, drums were beaten, and the air was filled with the shouts of the people. The women formed in companies, danced, clapped their hands, and sung songs. After the first outburst of joy was over, the two chiefs drank each other's health, in water, each making a short speech, promising that the past should all be forgotton and buried forever, and thanking us for what we had done.[115]

Unfortunately, this mood of harmony did not last, especially after the return of William Caulker.

Earlier in 1872, Gomer resolved a dangerous situation that arose between George Stephen Caulker II and another chief, Bannah Banda. It appears that someone from Caulker's territory had been accused of a crime in Banda's territory, had fled to Caulker, and then left Caulker. Bannah Banda had sent a sword and a lock of hair in order to ask Caulker to judge the situation, but his delegates had used this as an excuse to plunder. At any rate, this is the story Gomer got out of Banda after traveling for more than thirty miles to meet him. He found him very sick with leprosy. Once Gomer explained what was happening, Banda immediately sent a messenger to his people in Caulker's territory, and was able to make them desist.[116] Gomer obviously had both a high level of diplomatic skill, and an ability to communicate and create trust in the cultural environment in which he was placed. Gomer seems to know how to exploit his unique position. He has more credibility than other missionaries because he is black, but on the other hand, he is at times taken "as a white man" by Africans because he is a missionary, in a way that gives him an edge. As Gomer remarks upon his successful resolution of the situation with Bannah Banda:

The next day the people in Shengay thanked me very much for "that walker that I do walk." The people had changed their conduct toward Mr. Caulker. He was again at liberty to go where he pleased. One man that came from Mr. Caulker said that when the people heard that the "white man" had gone to Bannah Bandah, "they all got coward."[117]

The remarkable success acheived by Joseph Gomer, one might think, would if anything have inclined the United Brethren leadership in the United States to continue to seek out African Americans for service in Africa. But quite the opposite occurred. Gomer, his wife, Evans, and Wilberforce were the only African Americans ever sent. Deliberately *not* to send African Americans in fact became mission policy. In a private letter of 1923, S.R. Ziegler, the General Secretary of the Mission Board, disclosed what was probably the core motivation for this policy:

We find it more or less of a problem to send colored workers from America and place them on an equality with our white workers on the field, because the native church does not exactly understand why these colored men should be in full relation to the Mission Council and all its work while they are not.[118]

In other words, Ziegler believes that the presence of African American missionaries would provide an occasion for African pastors to question the missionaries' superior position in the church hierarchy in Africa. In the course of the twentieth century, the pastors did come to chafe against this hierarchy, and slowly struggle for a position of equality. So Ziegler's perception is probably correct. But it bears closer examination. Ziegler is in fact attempting to justify racial discrimination by claiming it is needed in order to maintain the missionaries' position of privilege in a colonial situation. One wonders what has become in his mind of the ideal of racial equality he should have learned from Flickinger, and the ideal of African leadership that was supposedly the mission's goal. That the presence of African American missionaries in Africa might create "difficulties" might well be true. But why could he not have said: we will *embrace* and *deal with* those difficulties when they come, in the interest of something of much greater importance? Ziegler's statement more likely has the nature of a mere excuse. Because of the cultural recrudescence of racism which had taken place over the previous forty years, it is much more likely that the sending of African American missionaries to Africa was something that was *just not done*. Ziegler probably had the instinct for the status quo and the ability to make plausible excuses for betraying one's ideals which is part of the mental equipment of any conventional administrator.

Once Gomer had gotten the mission on its feet again, it continued to expand. In 1876, the United Brethren Women's Missionary Association was founded. Its first accomplishment was the establishment of the station at Rotifunk in 1878, with the cooperation of Chief Sorie Kessebeh (Suri Kesebe).[119] The United Brethren were active at eight locations by 1883 when the American Missionary Association transferred control to them of its three stations, together known as the "Mendi Mission."[120] The American Missionary Association had grown out of the efforts of Lewis Tappan, an American businessman and anti-slavery activist who had formed a committee to defend the Africans who had been aboard the *Amistad*. (The story of the Africans, mostly Mende, who, in 1839, mutinied and took control of the slave ship *Amistad*, only to be then tricked by the ship's owners, taken to New York, put on trial, and finally freed, gained some popular currency through Stephen Spielberg's 1997 movie *Amistad*.[121]) Tappan's committee arranged to send the Mende from the *Amistad* back to their homeland, accompanied by missionaries. A station was founded near Komende. However, "once returned to African soil the *Amistad* people began drifting away, so that the mission started with the disappointment of losing what had seemed a valuable nucleus of converts."[122] Tappan's committee then joined with other organizations to form the American Missionary Association.[123] During the 1850s, the A.M.A. managed to establish three stations, even though the original one was abandoned,[124] and these three were the ones transferred to the United Brethren.

The United Brethren missions continued to develop and expand. "In 1892 they opened a school at Rotifunk in the latest American style, surpassing anything yet seen in Sierra Leone, equipped to teach anatomy, astronomy, and brick-making."[125] In 1886, The Rufus Clark and Wife Training School was founded at Shenge, and a school for girls was opened at Rotifunk.[126] By 1908 the two United Brethren mission boards were active at 24 locations between them (ten operated by the women's board), with 22 churches claiming 2400 adherents.[127] It is significant that both before and after the imposition of the Protectorate, the missionaries had, in each case, to negotiate with local chiefs in order to obtain permission, and land, to operate their stations.

British Policy after 1890, The Imposition of the Protectorate, and War

1890 marked a shift in British policy toward the interior. The making of treaties accelerated. Two Traveling Commissioners were appointed to make treaties in the north, and T.J. Alldridge, who had been the commissioner of the Sherbro, worked in the south.[128] Their assigned task was to gain signatures for a standard treaty throughout the hinterland area. These treaties bound the chiefs: to be at peace with Britain; to give British subjects free access; to submit to the Governor for final decision any dispute with a British subject; to cease warfare that interferes with trade; and to not cede territory to any foreign power.[129] The British provided troops and also stipends to chiefs who signed treaties. These treaties created the appearance of alliance formation, while in fact laying the basis for colonial conquest. Abraham points out that the commissioners often did not really understand with whom they were making treaties. "The distinction between king and chief, the latter being the subordinate of the king, was lost....By signing treaties with their subordinates, the British detached the allegiance of the chiefs from their kings."[130]

The establishment in 1890 of the Frontier Police was the clearest sign of the British government's new assertion of power over the interior. The first 32 stations were spread along the road created by Governor Rowe in 1889 along the entire edge of the Colony's sphere of influence. That sphere of influence included the region up to roughly 80 miles from the coast. The force was recruited from districts bordering the Colony.[131] On assuming office in 1894, Governor Cardew proposed expanding the number of privates in the force from 300 to 500.[132] The chiefs at first welcomed the force believing it would bolster the guarantees they expected from the treaties. But complaints from the chiefs began to pour in as soon as the force was put in place. The "incessant abuse of their powers" included kidnapping, rape, extortion, indiscriminate flogging, and unauthorized deputization.[133] The colonial government was aware of the woeful lack of discipline of the force, and tried in vain, through the issuing of increasingly detailed regulations, to keep it under control. Cardew himself reported that, because of inadequate supervision "the men get out of hand, they deteriorate as a military body...often behave extorionably [sic] and are always open to the temptations of bribes."[134] Nevertheless, even in his first two years in office, Cardew made it clear to the hinterland chiefs that they would not be allowed to expel the Frontiers, and that the Frontiers were there to enforce the Governor's orders, as in the case of the suppression of the slave trade.[135] Though the Protectorate had not yet been declared, the chiefs within the British sphere of influence had already been robbed of their sovereignty.

The last decade of the nineteenth century also marked a radical change in British, and indeed European, colonial policy toward Africa as a whole. The idea of colonialism is rooted in the racist idea that it is the right and the destiny of a putative European Anglo-Saxon race to dominate other races, especially Africans, either because the Anglo-Saxons are the fittest to survive, or because it is their duty to civilize those who are inferior. This idea did not prevail among those responsible for the British Empire during most of the nineteenth century, and when Britain finally did accede to the pressure of the colonialist ideologues, the action was as much motivated by the political judgment that French expansion needed to be counterbalanced as it was by enthusiastic adherence to colonialist ideology. The French military expansion in West Africa was made possible by the relative independence within the French government of the Marine, which was dominated by fervent colonialists to an extent that other institutions were not. And of course, the interest groups favoring colonial expansion were not limited to the racist ideologues, but included those whose motives and rationale were purely economic. Crowder believes that the best explanation for why the scramble for Africa occurred when it did is not that it was an inevitable result of the popularity of colonialist ideology but rather that "the mutual suspicions of the interested European powers of each other's intentions had reached such a pitch that none of them was willing to hold off the undesirable for fear their own interests might be pre-empted by another."[136] At the Berlin Conference of 1884-85, the colonial powers reached a comprehensive agreement regarding their respective claims to almost the entire continent of Africa. Crowder asserts that the Conference, "rather than initiating the Scramble for Africa, ...tried to bring some form of discipline to a situation that looked as though it might rapidly get out of hand."[137] But, on the whole, the last two decades of the nineteenth century were a time in which the ideology of racism and colonialism was clearly winning the day.[138] With the ascension of Joseph Chamberlain as Colonial Secretary in 1895 the British change in policy was complete, and a Governor like Cardew finally had a colonial administration in tune with his ambitions.

One manifestation of the now dominant racist ideology was the official marginalization of the Krios. Throughout the century, Krios had played an important part in the colonial administration. But, as Fyfe reports, "Cardew's policy of appointing Europeans to senior posts, continued by his successors, slowly squeezed out Creole officials"[139]; "In 1892 Creoles held eighteen of some forty senior posts; in 1912 the service had so expanded that there were ninety-two such posts...but Creoles only held fifteen, five of which were abolished within the next five years as their holders retired."[140] Along with this official marginalization there developed an attitude toward the Krios among colonial officials and in Britain generally of sneering mockery. Racism was becoming an unquestioned assumption held especially by educated Western elites. A racist in fact had no option but to have a special contempt for the Krios—for the achievements of the Krios constituted such an obvious refutation of the ideology of racism that their reality and significance had somehow to be denied. The slippery turn of consciousness that allowed racists to close their eyes to Krio achievements expressed itself in the idea that Africans were somehow making fools of themselves by adopting English culture. Neither the vicious social-Darwinian racists, nor the humanitarian condescending racists, could stand to look in the face the reality that Africans were in every respect the equal of Englishmen, and in the case of the educated Krio, the equal even on the Englishmen's own terms.

Cardew was an individual whose time had come. While the colonial office felt he was going too fast, and exercised some restraining influence, the abrupt, decisive, and violent action he took to impose the Protectorate in 1896 was fully in accord with that office's changed assumptions. The criticisms to which he was subjected both during the imposition and after the war it provoked only concerned the haste with which he acted, and not at all the fact of the imposition of the Protectorate itself. Cardew's forcefulness was combined with a contempt for Africans in line with the racism of the day. Abraham quotes Cardew's words to the effect that he felt he was dealing "with a people that are practically savages—some are cannibals—quite illiterate and very degraded by ignorance and gross superstition...accustomed to the most despotic sway on the part of their chiefs."[141]

The idea behind the Protectorate Ordinance of 1896 was to rule the Protectorate not directly, but indirectly through the traditional chiefs. The government would divide the Protectorate into chiefdoms, and appoint a "Paramount Chief," who would serve at the pleasure of the government, for each. Chiefdoms were grouped into five districts, each presided over by a British District Commissioner.[142] The powers of the chiefs were also substantially reduced—Abraham estimates at least by half.[143] Specifically, a new court system was instituted, in which the chiefs would now play a distinctly subordinate role. There would be three levels of jurisdiction: The Court of Native Chiefs could now hear only civil cases between "natives." The Court of the District Commissioner and Native Chiefs would now try criminal offenses. The District Commissioner did sit on this court together with two native chiefs. However, those chiefs were selected by the District Commissioner, and the power of decision rested with him alone. The Court of the District Commissioner would hear all civil and criminal cases involving non-natives, all land title cases, as well as all cases involving Poro laws. In addition, the Protectorate Ordinance of 1896 outlawed the slave trade, but not domestic slavery, and instituted a tax levied on houses to pay for the new government.

The effect was both to strip chiefs of much of their traditional authority, and to strip communities of their power to check the chiefs' authority, since the chiefs were now to serve at the pleasure of the British government.[144] The ordinance in no way acknowledges or incorporates the traditional democratic role of the chiefs' council and the Poro society. In fact, the ordinance actively undermined the authority of the Poro by placing cases involving the Poro directly under the jurisdiction of the District Commissioner alone. The British Attorney General justified this subordination of the Poro by asserting that "the 'poroh' custom, which while beneficial in many ways, is open to great abuses, besides being...decidedly dangerous to constituted authority."[145] It was, of course, dangerous because it represented the branch of indigenous government that could not readily be brought under control by the colonial usurper.

The announcement of the ordinance created a storm of protest throughout the Protectorate. The protest began with petitions from chiefs against the tax. It had become clear to the chiefs that the attitude of friendship and alliance between equals the British had tried to project had been a sham. The Protectorate Ordinance explicitly and unmistakably placed the government of the declared Protectorate under British control—and required the newly subjugated society to pay for its own subjugation. The chiefs were now obligated to collect the tax for the British government. Only one chief, Madam Yoko of Kpa-Mende, who already owed her position to the British, accepted the ordinance with its provision of tax collection.[146] There is documented evidence that at least two United Brethren pastors preached sermons supporting the tax in at least four locations.[147] In particular, "at Bumpe and Palli a Creole UBC agent, Joseph B.W. Johnson, advised that God said that people must pay the tax."[148]

Cardew responded to the widespread resistance to tax collection by the chiefs with violent force, carried out by the Frontier Police. According to Abraham, "the precise extent of the barbarities committed against the chiefs and their people may never be known, but it may be assumed that it was of such dimensions as to convert apathy to active resistance."[149] Fyfe characterizes the situation in these terms:

> All over the Protectorate Frontiers assumed despotic powers, terrorized chiefs and people, seized their goods, brutalized those who protested. In some places the sight of a uniform was enough to drive people into the bush. A District Surgeon who investigated charges against them in Bandajuma found most admitted their guilt freely, apparently imagining they had a right to oppress.[150]

The war of resistance to the imposition of foreign rule began in the north in February of 1898, under the leadership of Bai Bureh, a prominent war chief of unusual ability. Bai Bureh's well-disciplined forces waged a guerrilla war against the British army. The entire uprising in the North was under the control of Bureh and his forces, and their discipline prevented the occurrence of atrocities against civilians. (Only four civilians were killed by forces loyal to Bureh.) But the British response was brutal. When the Frontier Police proved no match for Bureh's forces, the British brought in the West Indian Regiment. The British campaign attempted to gain control of roads linking major towns, and its methods turned more and more to the destruction of any village offering resistance. Bureh's forces waged an effective guerrilla war, inflicting heavy casualties upon British columns from the cover of the dense bush. The British campaign in April to gain control of the area around Port Loko and Karene was particularly intense. All 97 villages in the Kasse area were destroyed.[151] The British finally prevailed by November, forcing the surrender of Bai Bureh himself. Bureh, who has become a national hero in post-colonial Sierra Leone, was exiled to the Gold Coast but allowed to return to Freetown in 1905 three years before his death.

The war took a very different course in the south. While the war in the north was a guerrilla war waged against the colonial army alone, the war in the south was essentially a campaign of mass terrorism. The sudden, simultaneous outbreak of the terror on the 27th or 28th of April all over the south points to the existence of a central organized plan, and in all likelihood this coordinated effort was accomplished through the Poro society.[152] The intended victims included anyone at all associated with the British colonial presence. The targets were "officials, missionaries, traders, and their families (Creole, European, and American alike)." Two of the three chiefs who cooperated—Madam Yoko of Kpa-Mende and Nancy Tucker of Bagru escaped death. However, Thomas Neale Caulker of Shenge waited for his relatives to come and kill him even though he could have escaped safely with the fleeing U.B.C. missionaries.[153] The U.B.C. missions at Shenge, Rotifunk, Taiama, and Mano Bagru were destroyed. The murdered included the five missionaries who were at Rotifunk, and the two at Taiama at the time of the uprising.[154] At least 1000 people in all were killed in the terror campaign.[155] The planned resistance took the form of terror alone—no preparation at all had been made to make a sustained military effort of the kind waged in the north. As a result, within two months, the British, through the Frontier Police and the West India Regiment, and finally with some participation from the West African Regiment (recruited locally) were able to regain control.[156] The British campaign in the south included the complete destruction of Taiama, the center of Kpa-Mende, which once had a population of 10,000. Taiama was destroyed in May "with great loss of life,"[157] in a campaign that involved the destruction of many other towns as well.[158] The British succeeded in completely putting down the Mende rebellion in two months, in contrast to the north where Bai Bureh did not surrender until November.[159]

The British government eventually hanged eighty three people for the crime of murder. But the show of force at the conclusion of the war was peaceful.[160] In February 1899, three columns of 995 troops, mostly from the newly recruited West African Force, covered 2629 miles, in order to make itself known in every region. "When the people realized the troops were advancing peaceably they lost their fears and welcomed them: there was none of the opposition Chalmers prophesied, nor any mass flight into French Guinea or Liberia....So, with a speed and ease that in mid-1898 could scarcely have been imagined, the Hut Tax War ended."[161]

The actual imposition of the Protectorate was finally accomplished, in Sierra Leone as elsewhere, only through the assertion of military force. That military force was indeed the force of the British army, but the soldiers in that army were almost all either African or Caribbean—the forces of the Frontier Police, the West Indian Regiment, and the West African Regiment. By the 1840s, the British had tried to recruit troops in the Colony from among the original settlers and from recaptives, but had great difficulty in raising the numbers of men needed. The original members of the West Indian Regiment were recruited from the Caribbean, but from 1810 to 1870 the recruits were Freetown recaptives who were then sent to the West Indies for training. From 1870, the forces were recruited and trained locally. "Police" forces were raised in Sierra Leone, the Gold Coast, and Nigeria throughout the century. In all of the British West African colonies, the primary pool of recruits consisted of men fleeing slavery. As a result, and especially since these men were often sent back to the districts from which they had fled, abuses of power by the recruits were rampant. The colonial government and military commanders recognized this, but found they had no alternative but to continue to recruit ex-slaves even though there was no way to enforce enough discipline to curb the continuing abuses.[162] The British were victorious in their scramble for Africa not simply because of superior firepower and organization, but also to an extent because they were able to pursue a policy of divide and rule: The British made alliances that exploited indigenous conflicts and were able to recruit Africans to serve in the forces that backed up those alliances and that also later defeated resistance to the imposition of outright colonial rule.

Joseph Chamberlain, the Colonial Secretary from 1895, believed that, in the imposition of colonial rule, force should be used with caution. But he at the same time believed that some force would in fact be necessary. Punitive expeditions "were the only system of civilizing and practically of developing the trade of Africa."[163] The expeditions ranged in scale from "a patrol of about 100 men to operate in a clearly defined locality," to a full scale war "against a king or territory (technically or legally) not owing allegiance to the Crown."[164] Some wars, which were really wars of overt conquest, were waged ostensibly to enforce treaties (as in the Sierra Leone Protectorate), others to maintain free trade, others in pursuit of ostensibly humanitarian aims (such as ending the slave trade), others in order to "avenge the death of a colonial official."[165] Some punitive expeditions were carried out in the Sierra Leone hinterland even before the 1898 war, and much of the British military action during the war consisted in the destruction of villages. S.C. Ukpabi deals in some detail with the question of the degree of inhumanity that ought to be ascribed to the British wars and punitive expeditions in West Africa. He concludes that

> the overriding factor determining the amount of destruction done to life and property was the nature of the resistance met. Where the inhabitants showed any friendly disposition …the officers did all they could to keep themselves and the men under control… But whenever the authority of the government was challenged, or where any European had lost his life, the troops were generally ruthless.[166]

How were those countless villages destroyed during the hut tax war? Were families warned to leave before their dwellings were burnt down? Were the villages fired upon in addition to being burnt? It seems very likely that this war was a case where the officers and troops quite often and willingly let themselves get out of control. Ukpabi refers, for example to "the actions of Captains Moore and Fairtlough [during the Sierra Leone war] in carrying out indiscriminate destruction and in using every opportunity to initiate combat with people who did not offer any resistance."[167]

J.R. King and J.S. Mills

The Rebuilding of the United Brethren Missions

During the Hut Tax War, seven United Brethren missionaries were murdered and the rest escaped and returned to the United States. In addition, "the insurgents had destroyed the buildings at the stations, stolen all of the movable property and burned the entire set of documents and records." Most of the African converts associated with the stations had abandoned the church.[168] The Government had originally intended to destroy every town in which missionaries had been killed: Rotifunk, Ronietta, Taiama, Bumpe, and Shenge. But the United Brethren prevailed upon Governor Cardew to spare Rotifunk and Shenge.[169] The United Brethren were determined not to be discouraged and immediately got to work on the task of reconstruction. The Home, Frontier and Foreign Missionary Association and the Women's Missionary Association together charged Mr. and Mrs. J.R. King with the responsibility of heading up the reconstruction effort. They arrived in Freetown in October, 1898—a time just a few months after the defeat of the Mende uprising, and in fact before Bai Bureh had finally surrendered in the north. J.R. King set to work with single-minded determination and a great deal of energy. He embarked on an ambitious building campaign. The church aimed not just at reconstruction but expansion. King's work culminated in the founding of Albert Academy in 1904. The church also sent an unprecedented number of new missionaries to Sierra Leone in the post-war period (1898-1912). "Forty-one additional missionaries arrived on the field, only ten less than the total number in the previous forty three years!"[170] But King's energy and single-minded determination was autocratic, and many of the missionaries eventually came to feel that his style was no longer conducive to the progress of the mission. The conflict came to a head in 1911—one of King's opponents even threatening to resign over the matter. King's opponents strongly criticized not only his autocratic methods, but specifically his failure to give any attention to the development of African leadership, and his overemphasis upon material development at the expense of spiritual growth in the church. King went home on furlough in 1912, and during that year the missionaries in the field finally convinced the mission board to relieve King of his responsibilities in Sierra Leone. (He was appointed head of a retirement home instead.)[171] By 1912, as a result of King's building program, the mission "had more chapels, schools, and houses than there had been at the start of the uprising in 1898."[172] Communicant membership had grown from 327 in 1901 to 988 in 1912. By 1922, membership had grown to 1525.

In 1912 Lloyd Mignerey was a junior in High School in Mowrystown, Ohio. In Sunday school he and his classmates had learned of their church's missionary efforts through the volume *Our Foreign Missionary Enterprise*, published in 1908 by the United Brethren Publishing House. This was the book that inspired him to become a missionary, especially in Africa, for "that is where there is the greatest need." The section on Sierra Leone of course includes a description of the Hut Tax War and the mission's heroic reconstruction efforts under the leadership of J.R. King. The chapter quotes King's account directly:

> In 1898 the interior tribes arose in rebellion against the British government and swept down over the country, slaughtering the civilized inhabitants, destroying property, and giving complete license to their old habit of loot and plunder....Would the remnant of native Christians fall away?....It was a crisis. The native Christians stood steadfast....We now have a more consecrated band of native teachers and evangelists. They have seen in this cruel insurrection the awfulness of the heathen life when unrestrained, and are putting forth greater efforts to deliver their fellow countrymen from the power of the evil one.[173]

It does not begin to cross his mind that the war originated in the attempt to resist the imposition of colonial rule, and he seems completely unaware of the difference between the cruel terrorism of the rebellion in the south and the disciplined guerilla warfare in the north. The explanation for the rebellion lies instead in what he sees as the essential nature of African people. They have simply reverted to their "old habit of loot and plunder." The rebellion was an expression of the essential "awfulness" of "heathen life" which will simply come out unless restrained. And of course the mission of the missionaries is to introduce that very restraint. *Our Foreign Missionary Enterprise* includes helpful study questions at the end of each chapter. Question number three for the chapter on "Missions in Sierra Leone" leaves no doubt as to the church's understanding of the war and its outcome: "How did God overrule the uprising of 1898 for good?"[174]

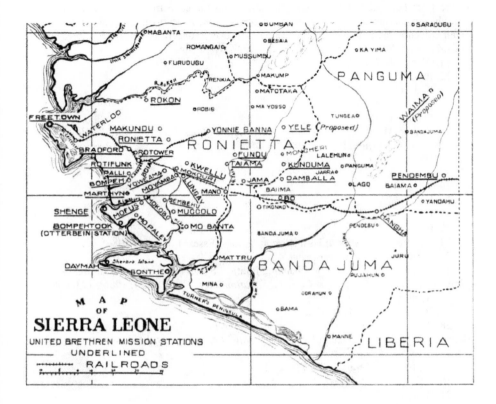

MAP
OF
SIERRA LEONE
UNITED BRETHREN MISSION STATIONS
UNDERLINED
.... RAILROADS

Notes

1. Christopher Fyfe, *A Short History of Sierra Leone* (London: Longmans, 1962), 26–27 (hereafter SHSL).

2. SHSL, 32, 3.

3. SHSL, 38.

4. SHSL, 43.

5. SHSL, 50.

6. Akintola Wyse, *The Krio of Sierra Leone: An Interpretive History* (London: Hurst, 1987), 2.

7. A.G. Hopkins, *An Economic History of West Africa* (New York: Columbia University Press, 1973), 113 note, in reference to E. Phillip LeVeen, *British Slave Trade Suppression Policies, 1821–1865: Impact and Implications* (Univ. of California, Berkeley Ph.D. Thesis, 1971).

8. Wyse, *The Krio*, 2.

9. Ibid.,12; see also Clifford Fyle, *A Krio-English Dictionary* (Suffolk: Oxford Univ. Press, 1980).

10. Christopher Fyfe, *A History of Sierra Leone* (Oxford: Oxford Univ. Press, 1962), 213 (hereafter HSL). The historical overview of the history of the Colony of Sierra

Leone I am here presenting, focused selectively on the concerns of the present study, relies heavily, as any study of the history of Sierra Leone must, upon the wealth of factual detail woven together to clearly delineate almost every conceivable historical dimension in Christopher Fyfe's monumental *A History of Sierra Leone.*

11. Wyse, *The Krio,* 34–35.

12. Ibid., 41.

13. Ibid., 11.

14. HSL, 202–204.

15. SHSL, 70–72.

16. Arthur Abraham, *Mende Government and Politics Under Colonial Rule* (Freetown: Sierra Leone Univ. Press, 1978), 43–44.

17. HSL, 257.

18. Abraham, *Mende Government,* 30.

19. Ibid., 36.

20. Ibid., 35.

21. Ibid., 36.

22. Ibid., 37.

23. Adu Boahen, *Topics in West African History* (Essex: Longman, 1986), 98.

24. Abraham, *Mende Government,* 40.

25. Vernon R. Dorjahn, "The Changing Political System of the Temne," in Immanuel Wallerstein, *Social Change: The Colonial Situation* (New York: Wiley, 1966), 173, note.

26. Boahen, *Topics,* 98.

27. Dorjahn, "Changing," 176.

28. Adeleye Ijagbemi, *A History of the Temne in the Nineteenth Century* (Univ. of Edinburgh, 1968), and KennethWylie, *The Political Kingdoms of the Temne* (New York: Africana, 1977).

29. Ijagbemi, *A History of the Temne,* 176.

30. HSL, 8.

31. HSL, 10.

32. HSL, 81.

33. HSL, 96.

34. HSL, 96.

35. HSL, 113.

36. HSL, 248.

37. HSL, 133.

38. HSL, 156.

39. HSL, 248, 284.

40. George Maxmillan Domingo, "The Caulker Manuscript," Pt. 2. *Sierra Leone Studies* (old series) 6 (1922): 6.

41. Ibid., 7–8.

42. Ibid., 22.

43. Ibid., 24–25.

44. Ibid., 27–29.

45. HSL, 472.

46. HSL, 604.

47. HSL, 472–73.

48. HSL, 474.

49. HSL, 569.

50. HSL, 575.

51. Based on "Summary of the Caulker Rulers, 1789-1999," Appendix 1 in Imodale Caulker-Burnett, *The Caulkers of Sierra Leone: The Story of a Ruling Family and Their Times* (Xlibris, 2010).

52. See Hopkins, *Economic History*, chap. 4.

53. Adeleye Ijagbemi, "The Freetown Colony and the Development of Legitimate Commerce in the Adjoining Territories," *Journal of the Historical Society of Nigeria* 5, no.2 (1970), 253.

54. See Hopkins, *Economic History,* 124–25.

55. Allen M. Howard, "Production, Exchange, and Society in Northern Coastal Sierra Leone," in Vernon R. Dorjahn and Barry L. Isaac, eds., *Essays on the Economic Anthropology of Sierra Leone* (Philadelphia: Institute for Liberian Studies, 1979), 56.

56. Howard, "Production," 56–57.

57. Abraham, *Mende Government*, 81.

58. Howard, "Production," 58.

59. Ijagbemi, "Freetown," 253; see also Abraham, *Mende Government*, 11.

60. Abraham, *Mende Government,* 14–15, quoting Benjamin Anderson, *Narrative of a Journey to Musadu, the Capital of the Western Mandingoes* (New York: n.p., 1870), 116.

61. Arthur Abraham, "Pattern of Warfare and Settlement Among the Mende in the Second Half of the Nineteenth Century," *Africa* 2 (1975), 134.

62. Ijagbemi, *History*, 242.

63. Ibid., 243.

64. Ibid., 264–65.

65. Anderson, *Narrative*, 11.

66. Wylie, *Political Kingdoms*, 95.

67. Abraham, *Mende Government,* 48.

68. Ibid., 48.

69. Ibid., 48.

70. Ijagbemi, *History*, 76.

71. Abraham, *Mende Government,* 68.

72. Ibid., 50–51.

73. Ibid., 50–53.

74. SHSL, 51.

75. SHSL, 52.

76. SHSL, 62, see also HSL, 200–202.

77. HSL, 70.

78. HSL, 214

79. HSL, 214, 254

80. HSL, 372, 419.

81. HSL, 531.

82. HSL, 554.

83. HSL, 419.

84. HSL, 532.

85. HSL, 419, 532.

86. HSL, 532.

87. J.S. Mills, W. R. Funk, and S. S. Hough, *Our Foreign Missionary Enterprise* (Dayton, Oh.: United Brethren Publishing House, 1908), 37–38 (hereafter OFME).

88. HSL, 285; See Fyfe's source D.K. Flickinger, *Ethiopia: Or Twenty Six Years of Missionary Life in Western Africa* (Dayton, Ohio: United Brethren Publishing House, 1882), 134, 143.

89. Samuel S. Hough, *Our Church Abroad* (Dayton: United Brethren Publishing House, 1918), 33.

90. Hough, *Our Church,* 33; OFME, 41; Flickinger, *Ethiopia,* 143.

91. Samuel R. Ziegler, *History of the United Brethren Board of Missions,* chap. III, 14 [Ms. at Center for EUB Heritage].

92. Ibid., chap. III, 16.

93. Flickinger, *Ethiopia,* 141.

94. Ibid., 144.

95. D.K. Flickinger, *Our Missionary Work from 1853 to 1889* (Dayton, Ohio: United Brethren Publishing House, 1889), 88–89; Ziegler, chap. IV, 1.

96. HSL, 373.

97. Flickinger, *Ethiopia,* 154–55, 166; HSL, 373.

98. HSL, 420–21; Flickinger, *Ethiopia,* 166; William McKee, *History of the Sherbro Mission, West Africa, Under the Direction of the Missionary Society of the United Brethren in Christ* (Dayton, Ohio: United Brethren Publishing House, 1874), 180–82.

99. Hough, *Our Church,* 36.

100. J.S. Mills, *Mission work in Sierra Leone, West Africa* (Dayton, Ohio: United Brethren Publishing House, 1898), 228.

101. Ziegler, chap. IV, 2.

102. Ziegler, chap. III, 6–7.

103. See J. Steven O'Malley, "The Role of African Americans in the Millenial Vision of the United Brethren in Christ: The Case of Joseph and Mary Gomer," *The A.M.E. Church Review* 119, no. 389 (Jan.–Mar. 2003): 62–63.

104. D.K. Flickinger, *Off Hand Sketches of Men and Things in Western Africa* (Dayton, Oh.: United Brethren Printing Establishment, 1857), 122.

105. Mills, *Mission Work,* 221–22.

106. O'Malley identifies three essential reasons for Gomer's success: 1) "In contrast with the experience of other denominations, the Gomers maintained close relations with the Caucasian UB leaders and also with the Africans." 2) "Gomer was convinced of his calling, and moved decisively, even when his support base lagged behind." 3) "Gomer's skills as a craftsman helped him forge a hands-on approach to missions. He linked community development with preaching and biblical training." "The Role of African Americans," 61–62.

107. Cf. McKee, 148.

108. Ibid., 115–17, 167–68.

109. Ibid., 130.

110. Ibid., 158.

111. Ibid., 163.

112. Ibid., 168.

113. Ibid., 205.

114. Ibid., 206.

115. Ibid., 211.

116. Ibid., 187–193.

117. Ibid., 192.

118. Quoted in Howard Mueller, *Formation of a Mission Church in an African Culture: The United Brethren in Sierra Leone* (Diss. Northwestern University, 1973), 94.

119. HSL, 420; OFME, 60–64.

120. OFME, 43; HSL, 420.

121. See HSL, 222.

122. HSL, 223.

123. HSL, 246.

124. HSL, 285.

125. HSL, 532.

126. Hough, *Our Church,* 38.

127. OFME, 45–70.

128. T. J. Alldridge, *The Sherbro and its Hinterland* (London: Macmillan, 1901), 165.

129. Abraham, *Mende Government,* 96.

130. Ibid., 103.

131. Ibid., 105.

132. Ibid., 108.

133. Ibid., 106.

134. Quoted in Abraham, *Mende Government,* 109.

135. Abraham, *Mende Government,* 107–108.

136. Michael Crowder, *West Africa Under Colonial Rule* (London: Hutchinson, 1968), 60.

137. Ibid., 62.

138. See Hopkins, *Economic History,* 161–62; Crowder, *West Africa,* 51–55.

139. HSL, 615.

140. Ibid.

141. Abraham, *Mende Government,* 132.

142. Ibid., 129.

143. Ibid.

144. Ibid.

145. Ibid., 127.

146. Ibid., 137.

147. Darrell Reeck, *Deep Mende: Religious Interaction in a Changing African Rural Society* (Leiden: Brill, 1976), 56; HSL, 555.

148. Reeck, *Deep Mende,* 56.

149. Abraham, *Mende Government,* 145.

150. HSL, 553.

151. HSL, 586; see also LaRay Denzer and Michael Crowder, "Bai Bureh and the Hut Tax War of 1898," in *Protest and Power in Black Africa,* edited by Robert I. Rotberg and Ali A. Mazrui (New York: Oxford Univ. Press, 1970), 169–212.

152. Abraham, *Mende,* 147, 158–59.

153. HSL, 575.

154. Abraham, *Mende* 147; HSL, 572–73.

155. HSL, 589.

156. Abraham, *Mende* 151–56.

157. Ibid. 182.

158. HSL, 583.

159. Abraham, *Introduction,* 193.

160. HSL, 589.

161. HSL, 591.

162. See S.C. Ukpabi, "Recruiting for the British Colonial Forces in West Africa in the Nineteenth Century," *Odu* 10 (July 1974): 79–97.

163. Quoted in S.C. Ukpabi "British Colonial Wars in West Africa: Image and Reality," *Civilizations* 20 no. 3 (1970): 384.

164. Ukpabi, "British Colonial," 386.

165. Ibid., 387–88.

166. Ibid., 394–95.

167. Ibid., 395.

168. Howard Ernest Mueller, *Formation of a Mission Church in an African Culture: The United Brethren in Sierra Leone* (Diss. Northwestern Univ., 1973), 79.

169. Ibid., 81.

170. Ibid., 90.

171. Ibid., 91.

172. Ibid.

173. OFME, 43–44.

174. OFME, 73.

CHAPTER THREE

A United Brethren Missionary in Sierra Leone 1922 – 24

Education and Career (1896–1921)

Lloyd Burdette Mignerey was born in 1896 in Mowrystown, Ohio. He grew up in the Church of the United Brethren in Christ and felt called to some sort of religious vocation from a very early age. His autobiographical notes indicate that he "converted" in 1908 (age 12), and became a lay preacher with limited license to preach in 1912 (age 16), and an "annual conference license to preach" in 1915. In 1913 he entered Otterbein College at Westerville, Ohio, and graduated in 1917. Otterbein was the oldest and most highly regarded of his denomination's six colleges. He supported himself for the first three years of college by preaching at a small church in Peachblow, about twelve miles away. After graduation he served in the U.S. Army Medical Corps in France, traveled with speakers for the Temperance movement until the passage of the eighteenth amendment in 1919, and taught high school before his appointment as a missionary to Sierra Leone in 1921. He was stationed there from January 1922 to May 1924.

Mignerey had been keeping diaries since early adolescence. In later life he carefully preserved all of his writings from his college years onward, so that a record of his personal development is now available from that time through his early post-missionary years as a minister in Ohio. Near the end of his life, he donated his papers to Otterbein College. I found his diaries in a box in the crowded archive room on the third floor of the Otterbein College library. They are handwritten in a series of composition books. He later meticulously created a table of contents for each booklet, giving each entry a title on the last page. In

November of 1921, during the hiatus between his appointment as a missionary in June and his departure in December, he self-consciously began a new writing project which he titled "African Notes." The first part of this project is retrospective. He clearly sees his experience so far as forming part of a coherent story. The diary begins with a scene from his high school days which he titles "Children's' Prattle":

> Two youngsters, one of them in knee-trousers, came down the steps of the church (United Brethren) at Mowrystown. The lights were blinking out behind them as the janitor turned off the gas from the carbide tank with a long pole divided at the far end.
>
> Long ago the stars were out, and the street leading away from the village church down to the broad valley of the Whiteoak [River], stretched away like a ribbon in the moonlight.
>
> The two youngsters were among the last to leave the church. They walked away with the glow of new plans and purposes burning on their faces.
>
> Aimlessly they wandered down the street toward the valley of the Whiteoak. Their talk was low and tense.
>
> Hours later the two youngsters came strolling back, and turned southward toward the town square. The streets were deserted. Only here and there a window dully aglow by some light keeping an all-night vigil.
>
> "... And after that," the youngster in long-trousers was saying, "I want to go to college."
>
> "So would I," returned the youngster in short-trousers. "But it seems too far off to think about."
>
> "Don't you think it! You'll be out of High School in two more years. If I go on next year and get acquainted at College, we'll room together when you come. I believe, Lloyd, that we ought to get the very best training possible. A preacher has the biggest job in the world. He ought to be the best-trained man in the world."
>
> "And if that's true with a preacher, how much more that's true of a missionary," commented the younger of the two. After a brief silence broken only by the tramp, tramp of shoes on the pavement, the older boy began earnestly, "You know that 'Foreign Missionary Enterprise' book we've been studying? Well—"
>
> The talk drifted off in low and confidential murmurs.
>
> "There is where the greatest need is!" said the big boy, Glen.
>
> Some sleepless citizen of the town pulled aside the curtains of his bedroom and peered out.
>
> "Hm! Children's prattle! Better be home in bed," he growled, hearing only the low talk of the two boys, and then dropped the curtains again.

Lloyd Mignerey and Glen Rosselot did go on to attend Otterbein College together, and their dreams of missionary service came to fruition. As things turned out, both served in Sierra Leone, Mignerey from 1922–24, and Rosselot from 1920–1939. The volume which had been such an inspiration to the boys is *Our Foreign Missionary Enterprise*, published in 1908 by the United Brethren Publishing House as part of the United Brethren Mission Study Course. It contains chapters on each of the lands where the United Brethren had established missions: Sierra Leone, China, Japan, Puerto Rico, and the Philippines.[1] (Rev. W.R. Funk, who headed the United Brethren Publishing House, wrote the chapter on

Sierra Leone, partly on the basis of a brief visit there.)[2] This volume is evidently the primary document through which the United Brethren attempted to educate young people about its missions and about the societies in the midst of which those missions had been established. In this book the boys read that the Africans in Sierra Leone are "very decidedly the children of nature, and live in squalid habitations."[3] "Since the houses are entirely lacking in conveniences, of course the women are poor housekeepers." The African, we learn, "is not naturally an energetic person. Nature has been so kind to him in the abundant supply of food...he has not felt the need of being industrious in order to obtain a livelih-ood."[4] The African is religious but "nearly all the pagan's gods are de-mons....The cruel barbarities of the pagan do not necessarily spring from an in-born brutality of nature, but from his ideas of gods and religion."[5] "It is hard to make comparisons between those who are in the darkness of sin, especially when living under the different forms of paganism; but it does seem reasonable to suppose that the mind that finds its satisfaction in the worship of evil sprits only, is in the greatest need and deepest gloom."[6] As the older boy exclaimed to the younger "That is where the greatest need is!"

In his "African notes," Mignerey then skips over three crucial experiences in his life, for two of which he kept and preserved extensive diaries. His series *Crumbs from the Table of Life* chronicles in detail his intellectual and spiritual growth while a student at Otterbein College from 1913 to 1917, his experiences in France after the end of the war, and his subsequent work with the temperance movement. From the papers he has left us, a clear picture of Mignerey's reli-gious and intellectual orientation gradually emerges. His ardent desire to be-come a missionary grew out of a very specific interpretation of Christianity.

Lloyd Mignerey during WWI

His writings while at Otterbein trace his struggle to define his own Christian outlook. At Otterbein, the two intellectual movements that had the most decisive impact on his life commitments were liberal protestant theology and the social gospel. The liberal theology of Ritschl, Harnack, and Rauschenbusch did in fact have many adherents in the United Brethren Church at the time, and especially at Otterbein College, even though the predominant orientation in the denomination was more conservative. He was challenged to work out his position not only in the classroom, but through his weekly preaching at Peachblow. Mignerey recorded his intellectual and spiritual struggles in his college diary. The outcome of those struggles was an enthusiastic embrace of the most liberal version of the liberal Protestant theology of the time

In his college diary, Mignerey also records extensively his ardent commitment to pacifism and the dilemma it posed in the years leading up to World War One. He notes with distress the tone of war hysteria and jingoism emerging in public discourse as well as in everyday life. He even feels himself getting caught up in the hatred for the Kaiser being fomented in the press. "I—even I, pacifist that I am—sometimes feel that I could draw a gun on that man and shoot him down in cold blood with as little compunction as if I was putting an end to a copperhead."[7] He clearly recognizes that he faces a very painful moral choice, for it seems to him that his convictions obligate him to refuse military service.

After graduating in 1917, with a major in education and philosophy, he began work for the Anti-Saloon League of America (whose headquarters was in Westerville), traveling to Virginia, Georgia, and North Carolina. The selective service act of 1917 made it possible for conscientious objectors to serve in non-combatant roles. This evidently made it possible for Mignerey to resolve his dilemma. In April of 1918, he enlisted to serve in the U.S. Army Medical Corps. He served in this capacity in France. He has nothing to say about his experience of the war itself. After the end of hostilities, while still in the army, he spent five months studying at the Sorbonne. Toward the end of this time, in June of 1919, he revisited the battlefields at Verdun and the Argonne near where he had served. He drove an auto from Reims to the ruins of Fort Pompelle, and from a prominence surveyed the devastation, still evident seven months after the armistice:

> Good view from the top shows the surrounding battlefield at its very worst. Seeing a tank not far down the valley near the road where I had left the auto I started across the "field" to get a picture.—Again words fail. The lines of trenches and wire! Fragments of shells! Piles of grenades! Unexploded shells! (One monster shell was about ten inches in diameter and four feet in length.) My friend and I remark about the uncanny odor. *Something* is dead! He had a piece of candle in his pocket, and we carefully went down into a dugout. The depth almost unbelievable. The narrow stairway made two turns downward, into a long narrow room for about a dozen bunks. At the farther end I found a bayonet on the floor under one of the wire beds. Carefully examined it for wires, etc. (in case of trap) and, seeing none, I picked it up and carried it up to light, thirty feet above. Further examination showed it to be a German saw-tooth bayonet in a leather scabbard. An immense clot of blood on one side of the wooden handle. Brought it along as a souvenir.

Farther along, climbed out of the trench to get our "directions," and headed down again in the direction of the tank.

My friend suddenly yells out "Here's a dead German!"

Sure enough, in the grass at our feet is a black, twisted mass of gray uniform, boots and bones—and rotting flesh. The stench was not unlike that of a dead horse that I had seen above Verdun. I could scarcely believe that that bit of filth there was once a *man*. It is scarcely believable that one year after the fighting there, less than seven miles from Reims, there are bodies yet unburied. I say "bodies" because before we reached the tank we came upon two other similar corpses. (From *Crumbs*)

He had followed the developments in Europe closely before and after the war, and he was pessimistic about the future at the time of the signing of the treaty of Versailles.

"Civilization" is not saved. All that might have been won for civilization by an allied victory may be lost by our own hands. It appears as if we have lost sight of the realities. With the failure of the present regime to arrive at anything but a peace of revenge, "civilization" is less near salvation than ever. It seems folly to "foresee" a state of middle-age barbarism and superstition established in the entire world in the near future—but I fear that very thing. (From *Crumbs*)

Mignerey was honorably discharged in July 1919, and returned to the U.S., where he again took up work for the Anti-Saloon League of America in New York as a secretary and advance man for temperance speakers. In this capacity he traveled to Washington, Oregon, Kansas, California and Virginia, still maintaining his extensive diaries.

But the career path that had most deeply inspired him since his high school days had been that of a missionary. By the time of his return from the temperance campaign the eighteenth amendment had already been ratified, so he sought out the opportunity to do foreign mission work. Since none was forthcoming, he accepted a position teaching French and English in Mowrystown in September, 1920 (at age 25). In June of 1921 a mission opportunity opened up in Rotifunk, a town about 45 miles from the capital of the British Colony of Sierra Leone, Freetown. Mignerey resigned his teaching position to pursue this opportunity. He served as a missionary in Sierra Leone for approximately two years, first as head of the United Brethren mission station in Rotifunk (January 1922–April 1923), and then as principal of the Albert Academy, the United Brethren secondary school in Freetown (April 1923–May 1924).

In his college years, Mignerey had come to firmly embrace Walter Rauschenbusch's ethical interpretation of liberal theology according to which Christ's love commandment applies as much to the relationships between society and the individual as it does to the relations between individuals. In Mignerey's mind, capitalist society is itself a field in need of conversion. The gloom of its adherence to greedy self-interest has been penetrated by the light of Christ's example only very imperfectly. So Mignerey, like the missionary leadership of his time, did not view his "civilization" as some sort of inherently "Christian" blessing to be bestowed wholesale upon Africa. World War One and the Treaty of Versailles had caused Mignerey to question whether the Western world even deserved to be called "civilized," and in fact he foresaw his world descending even further into barbarism. Yet for Mignerey and even his liberal fellows, the unchristian gloom of Africa appeared incomparably darker than the unchristian gloom of Western culture. As he will write in his diary at the moment he sees Africa's coastline coming into view:

> Africa—the darkest of them all! For years you have been a great, unconquered continent. A country that has been sleeping, sleeping, just as it is now! Is it not awakening? Many have gone before us with the Good News to that great continent—and many shall come after us. But until our work is done we shall give our best to the Master's service among those whom He loves, and who know it not.

For to their eyes Africa apparently lacked anything like Christ's shining example of love. And without that example, the social reform that Africa needed as much as the West would be impossible—and in the West it was a challenge daunting enough. But in terms of social reform, a liberal missionary like Mignerey saw his task as being very much like his task in the U.S. In Western countries, the focus of liberal reform movements was on: fair labor practices; the abolition of the sale of alcohol; women's suffrage and women's rights, all with an emphasis on the significance of education. For Africa, a liberal like Mignerey desired to accomplish similar social reforms: the abolition of slavery (the extreme of unfair labor practice); the abolition of polygamy (seen as oppressing women); alcohol prohibition; and with a corresponding emphasis on the importance of education. Mignerey saw the imposition of colonial rule as something positive, since it abolished, as he was inaccurately taught, the cruel and destructive wars of the nineteenth century. Despite his impassioned criticism of capitalism, he saw the development of commerce with Western countries in Africa as contributing, at least partially, to progress. But genuine progress was contingent upon the spreading of the gospel of Christian love, upon which such progress depends both for its justification and for its motivating spirit.

Mignerey places at the very beginning of his diary a clear summation of the aim and motive for the great undertaking in which he is now to be engaged:

> "I am the Way, and the Truth, and the Life."

> He is the Way to the Father. He teaches us how a loving Father is yearning that His children might know Him. Thru Him we know God as Creator of the Universe, the answer to evolution, the explanation of science—and the Father of us all.

> He is the Truth—and He has said that "the Truth shall make you free." To know this Truth is to be free in every sense of the word. The body of humankind is freed from poverty, famine, pestilence and war. The mind is turned loose alike among the stars and among the lowly dust of the earth to explore the infinite wonders of creation. The soul is freed from ignorance, fear and superstition to walk with Him in daily communion, to learn His will and to follow Him, even to the far corners of the earth in obedience to His loving commands.

> He is, in truth, the Life! Without Him life has no meaning, death no promise but despair. With Him there is no death. With us in Him there is no death.

> He is savior of the world because he is Love, and love is the Life of the world.

To Him all men are brothers. And the stronger of His brothers must help the weaker of His brothers to know the Way, and the Truth, and the Life.

Africa for Jesus!

This statement does encapsulate his entire outlook: the essence of Christianity as 'the fatherhood of God and the brotherhood of man'; the essence of salvation as love with no mention of atonement; the placement of modern science and scholarship in a theistic context; the social gospel which concerns itself with the material conditions of human life as well as its spiritual depths; and finally the idea that within the brotherhood of man, Africans somehow represent the weaker brothers, and missionaries the stronger ones.

Mignerey had met Bishop Alfred T. Howard, Acting Secretary of Foreign Missions, in 1919, not too long after he had returned from France. Bishop Howard had asked him whether he would be interested in working in "one of our foreign mission schools." Mignerey was overjoyed by this turn of events, eagerly giving Howard his name and address. However, "many months" had passed with no word from Bishop Howard, and he had accepted a position teaching English and French at Mowrystown High School in September, 1920. He evidently taught in Mowrystown (which is near Cincinnati) for the 1920–21 school year, but found a position in Portsmouth, Ohio to begin in September 1921. He moved in order to be closer to Ruth Philips, whom he had known since his freshman year in college. Their acquaintance had been renewed early in 1920, they had fallen in love, and by mid-year were making plans for marriage in June 1922. However, in June 1921 Mignerey had finally gotten the word from Howard of the church's offer of missionary work in Rotifunk. Ruth enthusiastically agreed to accompany Lloyd to Sierra Leone. They were married in September, and departed for Africa in December.

Rotifunk, January 1922–April 1923:
"A Complexity of Life That Baffles Analysis"

Mignerey was unable to make any diary entries during his first eight months in Sierra Leone. When he finally returns to his diary, he writes that "many incidents that have impressed themselves in this time must go unrecorded, for the simple reason that they have accumulated more rapidly than I have had time or disposition to write." However, during that time he applied a great deal of effort to writing a series of eleven letters to churches back home, describing the various aspects of the conditions he encountered. Among the most interesting are his portrait of Rotifunk, and his discussion of "secret societies."

Rotifunk, located about 45 miles from Freetown, was the most important town in Bumpe chiefdom, and a major center of trade between upcountry and coastal areas. Connected to the coast by the Bumpe river, its status as a trading center was enhanced by the arrival of the railway to Freetown in 1900.[8] The name "Ro-tifunk," which means "at the barn" is in fact Temne. The Sherbro are

Lloyd and Ruth Mignerey in Rotifunk

the largest ethnic group in the Bumpe chiefdom, but there were also a number of significant immigrant groups including the Kuranko and the Lokko, and the area around Rotifunk was apparently predominantly Temne. Rotifunk was in fact a center of Lokko settlement, and it was the Lokko chief Sorie Kessebeh who gave land for the founding of the mission in 1878.[9] Kessebeh's son Santigi Bundu was the local chief of Rotifunk at the time Mignerey arrived. ("Santigi" is the Temne word for "section chief," but in this case, "Santigi" is apparently also a given name.) The Sherbro Paramount Chief of Bumpe, A.G. Caulker, also resided at Rotifunk at that time. Rotifunk itself is located very near the predominantly Temne region and the villages around Rotifunk were apparently Temne speaking. There was also a significant number of Krios at Rotifunk, and, at the time of Mignerey's service, four families of Lebanese traders. From 1900–1934 subscribers to the Rotifunk church included Krios (ca. 37%), Temne (ca. 13%), Lokko (ca. 6%), and Sherbro (ca. 5%).[10]

The mission station to which Mignerey was assigned consisted of a church, a school, and a dispensary. The typical station would have a church and a school, but when Mignerey arrived, only Rotifunk and Jaiama had dispensaries. (An additional dispensary was opened at the Taiama station in 1926.) Mignerey, his wife, Nora Vesper, and Maud Hoyle (who did not stay the whole year) were the only missionaries at the station—all of the teachers as well as the pastor were African. Between 1904 and 1924, school attendance at Rotifunk varied between 55 and 98 pupils, and church membership between 67 and 113.[11]

Mignerey's letter introducing Rotifunk to the congregations back home in fact contains many detailed and careful observations of that town including its physical layout, its economy, and its customs. The following excerpt from that letter has been edited to focus on Mignerey's more objective observations, which probably give us a fairly accurate picture of what Rotifunk was like in 1922:

> Come, walk with us through the town of many languages and many peoples. We pass along a road that winds with calf-path crookedness among native houses. At first all buildings look alike. They have low mud walls, few or no windows, and long slanting roofs the color of old straw. With the new arrival it is actually a case of not being able to see the town for the houses.....
>
> Most of the people wear the minimum of clothing—usually a cloth about the waist. Many wear the long flowing gowns common to Eastern countries. In this attire they resemble closely the people in the pictures of Bible times. Then there

are a very few others who manage somehow to perspire their way through life wearing tight-fitting clothing of European fashion....

If you walk with us to the eastern side of the town toward the compound of the Paramount Chief, we pass down the sloping side of a wide valley to the Bompeh River. On the left is a clump of bananas twenty-five feet high. Down the river to the right about one hundred feet is the town wharf, crowded with large and small canoes, some on the bank, some in the water.

We approach the river near the bananas. At this point it is spanned by a narrow footbridge of stone and cement. Here the river is a mere trickling brooklet, when the tide is out. The boats at the wharf rest on the bottom of the river. Twice each day the tide comes up the river from the coast, about forty miles away, making it possible for heavy boats to make their way from the coast to Rotifunk. When the tide comes in, the trickling stream grows into a deep-channeled river.

To the left of us, above the footbridge, is a pool which is perhaps thirty feet in diameter and three feet deep. Three or four men and women are standing amidstream, bathing. Half a dozen children splash and paddle back and forth across the pool laughing and shouting in glee. Near the bridge several women are dipping some country cloths into the water and pounding them upon some large stones. Still others come with big gourds or pails of tin. They walk in among the bathers and the washer-women and dip these containers full of the day's supply of drinking water. These they place upon their heads and "tote" away with the water dripping across their faces.

Across the railway beyond the river, near a Mohammedan mosque, is the Compound of the Paramount Chief [A.G. Caulker].... He comes from his house to greet us quietly in English.... [Mignerey here describes a brief visit with Paramount Chief Caulker].

We return along the same road to the town. We are now sufficiently well-acquainted with the strange, drab-looking houses of mud and grass to notice that, after all, they are not all exactly alike. The fronts of some of them have been made into little shops and stores. Most of them are hung with brightly colored cloths for sale....

In one house near the mission one man is bent over a tiny anvil. In his hand is a small pair of pincers. He is making a bracelet of African gold. We stop for a moment to compliment him for the fine workmanship, and to chat with him. We learn that he has the honest pride of an artisan in his work.

Across from the church is the town market. This is an old, open-air barri with high thatched roof above low walls of mud. It is about thirty feet long by twenty feet wide. Here native traders, mostly women, come from the bush, where they have bought wholesale from the country people. They have such familiar articles as rice, peppers, fish, bananas, pineapples, oranges, peanuts, coconuts, beans, guinea corn, plantain and kola nuts. Then they have a variety of less familiar native products such as "koos-koos," "foo-foo," "agidi," and "tubo-knuket." Usually once each week beef is on sale here....

There is much that we do not see behind closed doors and deep in the bush. The night, especially in time of moonlight, becomes alive with unknown sounds. Along the moonlit roads and bush paths tramp many weird processions that the uninitiated, even missionaries, are not supposed to see.... The [secret] societies are active mostly at night. During the brilliant moonlight of the dry season the towns and the bush are alive with the songs, and shouts, and calls of the societies. Africa seems to awaken when the sun goes down.

Mignerey evidently paid careful attention to his new environment. He has an eye for detail and his introductory observations survey the town as a whole in terms of its material, economic, social, political, and religious life. Mignerey is also clearly interested in reflecting upon the limitations of his own perspective—the shops look different when he looks more closely. His description of meeting the goldsmith betrays an ambiguous tone—is it respect, or condescension?

In his descriptions of Rotifunk and of "secret societies," it becomes clear that he made an effort to learn as much as he could about the customs of the people amongst whom he was living. And it is clear that his interactions with those around him were extensive: "With the people of the town we are thrown in daily contact. Aside from the routine work of the mission station, perhaps our greatest opportunity lies just here." The specific observations he makes about the Poro and Bondo societies are mostly very accurate, and he clearly grasped the central role they play. And instead of dismissing them wholesale, he is clearly aware that there may be much of importance he is simply in no position to know:

> I almost hesitate to write anything about these secret societies because what I know is mostly from hearsay. I have been able actually to observe first-hand only small and relatively unimportant details. And yet these societies cannot be ignored in any activity whatsoever that may be undertaken here. I think that there is little doubt that the secret society life is the one big absorbing interest of the native African. If there is any one thing that he lives for it is that.

But his observations also clearly show that he very much sees Africa from the point of view of the books, published by the United Brethren, which he must have read in preparation for his work—which themselves contain a good deal of accurate information, despite their prejudice against African culture. He clearly has thought seriously about how the "secret societies" relate to Christianity, and despite his self-critical attitude when it comes to observation, firmly puts them in the place he had been taught they belong:

> The head teacher in our school here is an active member of the Porro [sic]. He is cautious about giving any information, but he says that the society has been undergoing a gradual change for the better in the past ten years. It is said, further, by some natives that there is nothing anti-Christian about it. Because of the extreme difficulty of securing first-hand information I can only take their word for this. On the other hand, some of the things that are sometimes called Christian here are rather shocking to the missionary. More of the "African mind" at work. So it is practically impossible to pass judgment upon the Porro. So far as my knowledge goes this society has not directly injured the work of this station since our coming here. What other silent influences may be at work, however, I do not know. But it is a safe conclusion that the less time the people give to these secret societies and the more they give to the church the better it will be for them. The gospel has done more in fifty years to improve the black man than had his fear-compelling secret societies in fifty centuries.

Mignerey did not adopt an attitude as sneering as that of D.K. Flickinger, according to whom Africans "are emphatically devil worshipers; they are most profoundly selfish in their worship, as in most other things. We must not forget, however, that in their present condition they are not capable of exercising other than selfish motives."[12] He seems more in accord with J.S. Mills, for whom

> paganism is the cry for light of a soul groping in the dark; it is the tendrils of the heart, designed to cling to that which would lift man up into the sunlight, now binding him face downward to the earth; it is the perversion and abuse of man's religious nature, thereby bringing his whole nature into bondage to evil.[13]

However, Mills could also claim, somewhat contradictorily that

> there is no difference between natural virtue and Christian virtue....all goodness is a beam of that light, and is therefore essentially Christian....In the old world and the modern heathen world, in their systems of morality, religion, and philosophy are found many gleams of this true light, a sort of unconscious Christian faith in the better things to come."[14]

Mignerey, like Mills, was an individual of intelligence, inquisitiveness, and honesty. These qualities brought both of them to the verge of recognizing that the cultures they encountered had their own ethical systems, social bonds, and sense of the sacred. However, these observations that they willingly make are in dissonance with the pattern according to which they understand other cultures, in which all that is not Christian is either evil, or if good, only good in a rudimentary and feeble way. (And Mills certainly did not find in African culture any ethical tradition remotely approaching the quasi-Christian glimmerings he found in Confucius or Lao-Tzu.) The juxtaposition of clear observation with prejudiced interpretation in Mignerey's letters suggests a certain unbalanced state of mind of a kind inevitable in the initial experience of direct and engaged encounter with a radically different culture.

Mignerey contributes a number of factual observations of some interest, which are either first hand or the result of conversation. He describes the "very familiar" call of the Poro "devil" as "a sort of wheezy sound like a man blowing a horn with his nose," and explains that "a Porro man plays upon a native instrument and the 'devil' is supposed to be inside making the sound." He observes that when the Poro spirit enters a town, "all women and others who are uninitiated must rush into their houses, close the doors and stay out of sight until the 'devil' has passed." He notes that the Bundu (Bondo)[15] society too "has its 'devils' who occasionally parade in fantastic garb." On one occasion he had the opportunity to see "seven young women of the Bundu society"—evidently initiates—"accompanied by three of their 'devils'" enter the town, where they danced before the chief's compound "by the hour" to the accompaniment of constant drumming. That he observed the dance with a careful, and indeed self-critical, eye, and conversed with those around him is evident in the following observation: "One of the mission boys told me that one number of the performance represented the bees gathering honey. It was an interpretative performance kept well to the theme. They danced singly, never in pairs. I have never been able to observe the sex idea in their dances, as is the case with our more refined savagery at home."

The mission boys, none of whom had "ever actually seen" the Poro devil, could "tell some weird tales of his wonderful pranks," including the following:

A white man once induced the "devil" to go into a strong box. He closed and locked the lid and held a running conversation with his captive. He set out for England with the box. In mid-ocean the devil came out of the box in spite of locks and keys and returned to the African bush. This story is probably the reflection of the white man's historic inability to penetrate the secrets of the Porro society.

A tale which is also a telling commentary on the ambitions of some missionaries to eliminate Poro!

Mignerey did in fact have some grasp of the specific function of Poro and Bundu (Bondo), which he understood correctly to be "the one big absorbing interest of the native African." He has either heard, or possibly read, that "the Porro is the chief law enforcement body among native peoples, since the chiefs are the responsible heads of it, and often use it to compel obedience thru fear."[16] He has also been informed that in the Bundu (Bondo) society "there is a carefully designed system of degrees and titles and classes and ranks," and he speculates that "in this society the women find relief from the servitude that is their lot at home. Perhaps this accounts in a measure for the great hold of the Bundu upon the African womanhood." He also knows quite a bit about the educational function of the societies:

> The secret society bush is the only thing approximating a native school. Children are carried into the bush at an early age. It is not certain as to what is taught them during these months of initiation. At the very least, circumcision is practiced, new names are given the candidates, native dances and the use of certain native medicines are taught, and the fantastic markings of the society are cut or burned deep into the skin of the face, arms, chest, and back.

He has also heard that anyone who has not been initiated after a certain age is liable to be abducted to the Poro bush. Most of the mission "boys" had been initiated before entering the mission, but one uninitiated "boy" had been in the mission six years. This boy is terrified of the Poro "devil"—and tells Mignerey at one point that the cries of the spirit are the sound of him eating a man. (The "boy" says, however, that the Poro "devil" cannot enter the mission—and Mignerey reports that an agreement had been reached to this effect.) Mignerey did not know that the initiates were always spoken of as having been "eaten" by the Poro or Bundu (Bondo) spirit. It strikes Mignerey that even his six years at the mission has failed to free him from this "superstition." And yet at the same time he is well aware that when the "boys" who have been initiated hear the sound of the Poro spirit, it has "no terrors for them." Rather, "they seem to respect it highly."

He is also aware of the sacred status of the space in the bush devoted to Poro and Bundu (Bondo):

> Each society has its respective meeting place near some town. This is a high thick bush preserved as sacred. Entrances are few and are protected by powerful "medicines." I have it on good authority that the interior of this bush has cleared

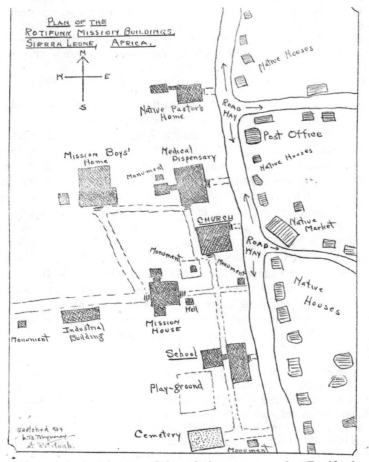

Mignerey's sketch map of the mission compound at Rotifunk

spaces connected by an intricate network of paths. In these rooms the various rites and ceremonies take place. Many times I have passed the Porro bush near Rotifunk, and once I actually penetrated a Bundu bush, without knowing it at the time…. [Mignerey, Rosselot, and mission "boys" had stumbled upon the Bundu bush while monkey-hunting.] The boys had gone on ahead and were within a few feet of the two animals. We were slowly breaking our way after them thru bush higher than our heads when we were arrested by a shrill chanted shout of women's voices from the bush directly ahead of us. The boys lost little time in beating a hasty retreat, saying all the while, "A-Bundu o yi ri! A-Bundu o yi ri!" (The Bundu is there.) Nothing could induce them to go for our game. Rosselot and I did not wish to violate the "sacred" bush and so left it.

The head woman of the Bundu followed us to the adjoining village, however, and seemed to be very much vexed with us. She jabbered loudly in a native tongue we could not understand. Several men of the town, including the head man, assembled and the woman retold the story with many gestures to them. For the most part they seemed to treat it as a huge joke, which did not seem to pacify the woman very much. One of the men fortunately spoke some Creole-English and we explained thru him that our trespassing was altogether unintentional, and that as soon as we had been warned we had left the bush. The woman was plainly displeased at first, but when we added to these arguments two brassy, West African shillings (worth about 50 cents), she seemed to be convinced—and satisfied.

Mignerey was an intelligent, observant, and self-critical individual, caught up in the demands of new employment in a culturally—not to mention climatically—alien environment, pursuing ideals to which he clung with ardent enthusiasm. It is hardly surprising that he expresses contradictory attitudes toward the culture he encounters, nor that he should at first be oblivious to those contradictions. More surprising is that he had the time, presence of mind, and energy to leave behind such a clear record of his thoughts and observations. It is clear on one level he was aware that he had entered a different cultural world (though of course he didn't call it that); that he attempted to carefully observe the life around him; that he asked questions and had open-ended conversations. And, aware of how limited his experience is, he shows an appropriate willingness to suspend judgment. He speaks of encountering "a complexity of life that baffles analysis." And yet despite this awareness of his limitations in the face of complexity, he still can confidently assert that "back of all this native life is a strange and almost impenetrable mixture of fear and superstition." And he concludes his introduction of Rotifunk with a cry of frustration whose tone hovers strangely between marvel and disgust:

> Our town is a town of vibrant, terrific, mysterious, active life. You may judge from some of the incidents mentioned in these letters how easy it is for the missionary at times to feel that he is helpless in the face of this vast accumulation of savagery. Again and again we are driven back upon our faith! Thank God, He, the author of our Faith is always there, smiling, and saying softly, "Have patience, my children. My love is at work in the world and in the hearts of men."

Of course, Mignerey, like his fellow missionaries, saw as his purpose doing battle with that "vast accumulation of savagery," by spreading the gospel. As a liberal, his focus on social reform was even more central than it was for conservatives. He saw the *essential* meaning of the gospel in the reformation of personal life and of society in accordance with love. And liberals and conservatives agreed that the central purpose of missions was to spread Christian belief. In the familiar cartoon image of how this was to be accomplished, a self-righteous white man stands declaiming before a crowd of uncomprehending native villagers. The practice of traveling to various locations and speaking before the unconverted—known as "itineration" —was indeed carried out, but was by no means the major occupation of the United Brethren missionaries. The explicit objectives of the United Brethren missions, first formulated in 1854, included not only itineration but also the establishment of schools. The original educational aim was relatively limited however, and involved instruction in the indigenous languages rather than English. The failure of direct itineration to win converts, and the conviction that both indigenous customs and languages were

obstacles to the gospel lead to a policy which laid much more stress on education. Specifically the boarding school was developed with the aim of raising
children in an environment at a distance from indigenous influences.[17] From the
reports of former students, it is clear that the missionaries did succeed at least in
endowing the schools with a pervasive Christian atmosphere—not limited to
starting and ending each day with prayer.[18] Itineration played a distinctly secondary role. The duty of the missionary-in-charge was to manage the entire station with its church, boarding school, and dispensary, and Mignerey was only
able to itinerate on weekends. The mission employed only one African worker
whose job carried the title of "itinerant." Not only pastors but also teachers were
required to itinerate. The reports on itineration they were required to submit to
the missionary leadership formed an important part of their performance evaluation, and this did lead to a certain amount of cheating and exaggeration—among
both teachers and pastors.[19]

Mignerey himself was critical of what he saw as an over-emphasis on numbers in the mission's itineration policy. But he by no means rejected the practice
of itineration, and in fact devotes to that topic one of the letters meant for congregations back home. A sketch map he included with the letter shows ten
towns, within about ten miles of Rotifunk, reached by itineration. (The towns
range in size from five to 50 houses. The two largest are Yenkissa, with 50
houses, and Mokabi, with 35. Mignerey counts the number of houses in Rotifunk as 100.) He first describes his activities at Ronietta, which consisted of
"forty-five minutes of story-telling, simple exposition, and exhortation" before
85 people, focused on "the story of Jesus healing and forgiving the sick man let
down through the house-top by his four friends." The sermon was briefly interrupted by a passing Poro procession. It is significant that Mignerey apparently
let the procession pass by without comment instead of using it as an occasion to
condemn heathenism. The letter then continues with an extended description of
his approach at three other towns and villages:

> I want to tell you of services similar to this which I held last Sunday. With
> two mission boys, and a Christian interpreter I walked out to a town about six
> miles west of Rotifunk. It was a large town by the name of Mokabi [Mignerey
> counts 35 houses there]. No services had been held there since 1917, five years
> ago. My boys were not anxious to go there because the people were not friendly,
> they said, but scoffed and ridiculed. One of them suggested that we avoid the
> town, that we bear to the north and return to Rotifunk by another way.
>
> We went on to Mokabi, however, after stopping by the way at two small vil-
> lages by the names of Kangama and Fulawahun, for services. These towns num-
> ber about five houses each. In these villages the system of itinerating was as fol-
> lows: we began by asking some man, usually the chief, for the use of his front
> porch for the services. Then we went about the village and invited the people
> from their homes and from their work to attend the services.
>
> We returned to the place of meeting and sang several songs in Temne. This
> hastened the arrival of the people. They sat about on the ground, in hammocks of
> grass rope, or in crude, triangular native chairs.
>
> After the singing my interpreter prayed in Temne. Then I spoke to the people.
> I had with me a big colored picture from an old picture chart illustrating the Sun-

day School lessons. A roll of these pictures, with the small cards accompanying them, comes to the Rotifunk Sunday School every quarter.

This large picture was held by one of the mission boys. I told the story of the picture. I spoke a phrase or a sentence in English and paused until my interpreter repeated it in Temne. This is a style of oratory that is entirely new to me. It is not altogether satisfactory because, just as one is moved by a succession of soaring thoughts, he is brought suddenly to earth by the necessity of stopping short until his interpreter can speak.

In the itinerating services of last Sunday I began by asking the people gathered about us to tell me something they recognized in the picture. The one which I used showed Elijah sitting among barren rocks by a brook, with barren hills in the background, a clear sky and several birds overhead.

In all three of these towns the only thing which the people identified positively was the image of a man. They recognized neither the stream, the hills, nor the birds. I then explained these details and told the story of God caring for Elijah by the brook Cherith. I tried as best I could to adapt all references to concrete things to the native life about me. The "bread and flesh" of the brookside menu became "rice and fish" in our story. Likewise, the "handful of meal" and the "little oil in a cruse" of the widow became rice and palm-oil in my version of the story. These changes were more intelligible to the people because, as I have said, their bread is rice, their flesh is fish, and their oil is palm-oil.

I illustrated God's care of us by the growth of their rice.

"You plant your rice," I said. "Can you make it grow?"

They shook their heads and replied by a series of grunts that meant "no."

"Then who does make it grow?"

Several of them were quick to reply, "Kuru! Kuru!" (God!)

I told them further that they would please God by telling this story of His care to the other people of the village who were not at the meeting. Then I passed out a number of the small picture cards illustrating the lesson. At one place the head man, an old man with white hair, eagerly took one of the cards and began to go over the lesson which I had just finished. I was very much surprised to see with what faithfulness he kept to every detail. I complimented him warmly.

Near the close of my lesson in each of these towns I told the people that someday I hoped to be able to speak to them in their native language; and that I wanted them to teach [me] how to say the text of the lesson in Temne, "God cares for you."

They seemed very much pleased and entered into this teaching process with great interest. Perhaps it was a new thing for them, perhaps not. But I knew that in teaching me a few words of their language they themselves were learning one of the fundamental truths of our Christian faith.

Many times they said, "*Kuru au bumar nu. Kuru au bumar mu.*" (God cares for you.)

This I asked each person to change for himself to, "*Kuru au bumar mi.*" (God cares for *me*.)

I then prayed a blessing upon the people; thanked them for their good interest, for the way in which they had taken part in the lesson, and so the service was dismissed.

This same program I used in each of the three towns. At Mokabi, however, I announced at the beginning of the service that at the close I would present the big picture to the big Chief of the place, and would give other smaller pictures to the people. Even though they do not understand everything in them, the people are very eager to get these highly-colored pictures. And this was the dreaded town of Mokabi!

The Chief gave us the use of his front porch for the meeting. He himself sat in a hammock throughout the meeting. He sent some of his men to call the people. They responded by filling the porch of the Chief's house, by crowding into the street, and upon the porch of the house across the way.

There was no scoffing, no lack of interest. And when I was through with the service the Chief asked me to come again, and to send a boy to him on the day before my coming. He said that he would have all the people of the town out to the service.

The religious message Mignerey attempted to convey to his hearers is in line with his own convictions: God is a God of love, who heals, forgives, and provides for us. And his approach shows respect for his listeners: he first of all asks for permission to preach; in the course of his preaching he attempts to translate religious metaphors into terms that make sense in the present environment; and he also he attempts to begin a religious dialogue. He straightforwardly reports that his listeners firmly respond that Kuru—the Temne creator-god—is responsible for the growth of plants, despite the fact that he elsewhere expresses his belief that the people live in fear and experience as a novelty the idea that God loves them. But in contrast to these evident signs of respect, there remains a note of condescension in his remarking that "the people are very eager to get these highly-colored pictures."

Some time around the end of October (between October 24 and 26), if we are to judge by the violence of his written expression, Mignerey's frustrations with African culture reached a boiling point. The occasion was the "Bible Institute" he and Glen Rosselot held, with 97 people in attendance. The content of this "institute" was a series of "lessons and sermons," presented by the two men, and its overall intent was to "state clearly to the church the attitude of Christianity and of the U.B. Denomination upon the questions of slavery, polygamy, and sexual immorality, all of which are the curse of Africa." He and Rosselot saw very much eye to eye on these matters—and they were incensed by what they saw as the laxity not only of the "native" church, but of the mission itself.

Most of his observations about slavery and polygamy seem to be based on first hand experience. Mignerey joins these observations with expressions of his unqualified opposition to these customs, and frustration both with the British government and the mission for tolerating them to any degree:

> Glen is greatly depressed over the conditions of the native church here at Shenge. He says that the native pastor (A.J. Caulker) owns slaves, and that the slave "palaver" is on the increase here. He said that recently a native man laid claim to a whole town, with people and all their goods. These people have been living in what they thot was perfect freedom for forty years. Glen said that the British court here, thru the British District Commissioner, sustained the claim to ownership of the people, but not of their property!
>
> The "law" seems to be, that slaves can not be bought and sold, they can be held only until they can accumulate the sum of four pounds sterling to redeem themselves. This is almost an impossible task when the owner receives all the pay when his slaves are sent to work for other people.

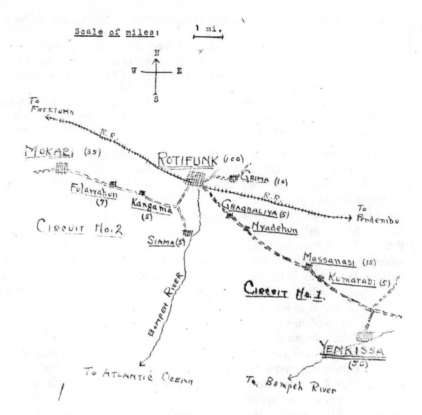

Mignerey's sketch map of Rotifunk and surrounding villages

If a man does not redeem himself from slavery, or if he is not redeemed, he is a natural and legal family legacy. This is the present attitude of the government. I met this man who claimed the town of slaves the other day. He is a plump, jolly, round-faced, old man who walks erect and briskly. He has a country cloth draped from his shoulders, carries a cane, is barefooted, and wears a black "plug" hat that came from goodness-knows-where.

We hear but little of the slave "palaver" at Rotifunk. This is perhaps because it is a more civilized center. The black population is largely of Creoles— the descendants of former slaves liberated on the West African Coast. I do not know of any of them holding slaves.

The problem of polygamy and its near neighbors— immorality and adultery— is common everywhere. It is stunning. It is very clear to us that polygamy is wrong, and is both un-Christian and anti-Christian, and should have no recognition by the Christian Church. But how to get the truth of this to native peoples is a very difficult matter.

I believe, with Glen, that the church here thru the missionaries, has evaded the question of instruction in sex-matters. We have been content with a statement or two in our printed handbooks, which nobody reads, to the effect that we can not recognize polygamy, and can not receive a polygamist into "full" membership. Then we have shut our mouths and proceeded to preach theology. I believe that the church should face this question, discuss it frankly and firmly, and show *why* it is wrong.

Mignerey's indignation intensifies as he continues to reflect upon the situation. He now describes polygamy as but one instance of a pervasive sexual immorality:

> Glen has had numerous "palavers" with church members in his district who disregard openly and unashamed the standards of the church regarding polygamy and personal purity. Men and women marry, separate, live with other men and women without marriage. The men have as many concubines as they can afford. The women of the household often ask their husband for other wives that their own work may be lightened. There seems to be no regret on the part of anyone. There seems to be no sense of wrong.

At this point his anger really does begin to cloud his judgment. In the following excerpt, for example, it is unclear where he could have obtained exact infant mortality figures—he must be just guessing—and his assertion that the undeniably high rate of infant mortality is primarily due to venereal disease is certainly groundless. But he is now sure that the sexual immorality he condemns has lead to disastrous rates of venereal disease and that venereal disease is in fact the root of all evil in Africa.

> The syphilis and the gonorrhea that is eating their life away they attribute to some tree or stone exerting an evil influence. They have absolutely no conscientious scruples against immorality in any of these forms. The train of evils following such conditions of life is appalling. The venereal disease is one of the blackest chapters of the gruesome story. Then there is the sterilization of the men and women from these diseases. I am told that most big chiefs have very few children who survive. At an early age they are absolutely senile, these men, because of excesses and disease. In every case the innocent children are the chief sufferers. Perhaps 65% of them die before one year old. Perhaps the percentage is higher. There is no way of telling. We know only that it is very, very high. It often occurs to me that this is nature's way of saving these children from a more horrible life as grown-ups. When the social standards of Africa make her worthy to have more children and better children, she will have them. The problem is to save the children, and to develop a civilization that creates a standard of living worth saving them for.
>
> Much of the intellectual and spiritual stupidity of the black race in Africa can be traced to the diseases and the excesses and the senility of its diabolical system of polygamy and immorality. The race here is above the animal world mostly in theory, and in the possibilities of improvement. This is the justification of Christian Missions. It is not to gain more adherents for the sake of numbers. Their lives and their collective standards of life must be reborn.
>
> But, oh, how slow the task is! It is still a matter for scientific investigation, as to how far the race as a whole is capable of developing in a given number of years. It seems that many of them take the first few steps easily. They can ask to be prayed for. They can learn to say prayers—some of them long and intricately theological, and that remind one of the older type of missionary whose chief concern was in getting them "to confess with their mouth the Lord Jesus," and thereby be saved. How dreadful is this mistake! Why have we not been able to

see that it is only a small, small beginning? The test comes in facing the old standards of heathen life, and the immoral practices with which they are familiar. The big task of the missionary is on the fields that have already been opened to the Gospel. On such fields he invariably runs into what is known as "arrested development." The ringing reports come from new fields. "One hundred stood up for Jesus in our revival meeting" said a recent letter from Jaiama, in the Kono country far to the east, and published recently in the "Telescope." It looks good in print. People who know the people here don't dare to [take] such statements seriously. "Standing up for Jesus" may mean much to the people at home, and very little indeed here. It may mean merely standing to please the white man who has come among them. It may mean an effort actually to follow his imperfectly understood request to "seek the Lord while he may be found." Or it may mean a sincere determination to accept Christianity with only faint glimpses of its real meaning when actually and practically applied in their daily relationships. The great task of the church among such peoples is to make sure the native Christian's "perseverance in the faith."

Mignerey's righteous indignation fixates upon polygamy as the root cause of "the intellectual and spiritual stupidity of the black race," a race which, it turns out, "is above the animal mostly in theory, and in possibilities for improvement." The bad habit of identifying races and assuming their inferiority and superiority, which Mignerey absorbed like almost everyone else in his cultural milieu, here finds a convenient rationalization. Mignerey grasps convulsively at the satisfying insight that the inferiority of the black race has a discernible cause —polygamy. And there is hope for the future, for Christian missions and Christian education are here to treat the disease. Unwavering opposition to polygamy was a core principle not only for Mignerey but for all the missionaries. But this is one issue for which there was almost no support among African Christians.

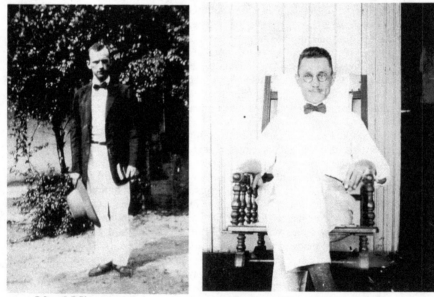

Lloyd Mignerey   **Glen Rosselot**

Even African pastors who also opposed polygamy were often appalled by the missionaries' failure to comprehend how deeply rooted the custom was in Africa. While the pastors often believed monogamy was preferable, they certainly did not share the perception that polygamy is somehow abominable or even the root of all evil. Mueller raised the question of polygamy with a farmer named Moses Barley who had attended the mission school in Rotifunk during the last decade of the nineteenth century, had spent his life there, and known the missionaries well. Barley was a life-long Christian who also had three wives. It is a measure of the African pastors' unwillingness to make too great of an issue of polygamy that Barley's wives, whom he always brought to church with him, were never refused communion. When Mueller asked him why he married more than one wife, Barley replied:

> It is not that the native man likes women. But economically you have to get two or three. If I put up a farm of about four acres my wife and I will not be able to work it alone. We have no mechanical machines to help us work. Everything must be done by manual labor. So you have to get two or three wives to help you economically or you are down. That is why the black man has so many wives.[20]

The disgust the missionaries felt for polygamy stems partly from their failure to understand a social system in which the household is the primary economic unit. Kenneth Little, in his study of the Mende, virtually paraphrases Barley's comment:

> As is the case in other African societies which carry on the cultivation of the soil by primitive methods, a plurality of wives is an agricultural asset. The work on the rice farm and in the palm kernel and oil industry is performed entirely by hand, and a large number of women attached permanently to the farming household makes it unnecessary to employ much wage labor.[21]

One factor in the missionaries' horror of polygamy may be the special identification in nineteenth century American Protestantism of the family as a sacred space requiring strict separation from the opposing secular space of the economic world. (For example, United Brethren bishop J.S. Mills' 1900 *A Manual of Family Worship With an Essay on the Christian Family* sounds this theme very clearly indeed.) In his loving description of the family hearth on the last night together with his new parents-in-law before leaving for Africa, Mignerey perhaps gives voice to this very notion: "For a long time, from our room adjoining, I could see the light play up and down, back and forth across the walls of the sitting room, outlining in lengthening shadows the chairs at which we had knelt. Was there ever a more sacred temple than that sitting room of our folks among the hills; or more holy altars than those chairs at which we knelt?"

Slavery was of course another social issue Mignerey took a strong stand on. The unbending firmness of the condemnation of what a missionary like Mignerey called slavery went hand in hand with a failure to comprehend the details of actual life. Moses Barley later argued with Walter Schutz about slavery, attempting to convey to him some of those very details. Schutz followed Mignerey at Rotifunk, where he served for 15 years. Schutz's attitude toward 'slavery' must have been similar to Mignerey's, although Barley never heard Schutz or any missionary speak out against slavery. (Mueller's informants report that it was in fact rare for a missionary to speak against slavery. Several remember Glen Rosselot as a notable exception.) Barley tried to explain to Schutz a particular form of domestic servitude in which an individual in effect becomes pawned:

> I remember [I] was telling Pa Schutz that if I am stranded and I have no money, the boy is my property so I can give him to another man for a few pounds until I can return it and get my boy back. He said that is slavery. I said, 'No, that is not slavery.' I can say, 'take my boy and give me so much.' When I get it back I can redeem him. That is the way people did it in those days. I can pledge my child and when I get money I can redeem him back. [22]

If 'slavery' is defined simply as an institution that reduces human beings to the status of a commodity, then the term 'slavery' is very misleading in the case of Sierra Leone, and West Africa generally.[23] The term 'slavery' has been used to refer to a whole range of situations in Africa of subservience and dependency. Some slaves lived as members of households, and others in separate slave villages, known in Krio as "fakai," associated with certain towns. In general, 'slavery' was a condition that could apply to members of a community who are not kin or are descended from slaves who are not kin. But slaves were not the only non-kin to be in a relation of subservience and dependence. A person who is not kin could also become a client of a household. Clients were granted land for a limited or an open ended period of time in return for the acceptance of certain obligations to the patron. Or, as Barley points out, a person, kin or not, could be "pawned" (by one's family, or one could even pawn oneself), that is, be placed in a condition of servitude in exchange for a loan, the labor performed functioning as interest on the loan. Such servitude ends as soon as the loan is repaid. In Mende society, for example, being a client, being a pawn, and being a slave represent progressively lower status in the household.[24] But even among slaves, there were gradations of status across a wide scale. The status of a slave can eventually approach that of kin, and as later generations of slaves often are kin, the distinction between kin or clients, and slaves, might easily become blurred.

The British government did not outlaw slavery in the Protectorate until 1927, although it did outlaw the slave trade at the time of the imposition of the Protectorate. During the nineteenth century, slavery and the slave trade had indeed been an important part of the economy of West Africa and specifically of the area that was to become the Protectorate. It is clear that in the nineteenth century, the slaves with the lowest status were war captives, and it is to their condition that the word 'slavery' most unambiguously applies. As Abraham points out, "the captives of war did the heavier farm work, and at first had few rights. They could be disposed of or used according to the behest of the master."[25] But their condition still differed from that of chattel slaves in the American South because of its potential for relative improvement. John J. Grace agrees with Abraham in his classification of the stages of potential improvement of status for a slave: The lowest stage is that of "trade slave," whom it is acceptable to sell. But slaves tended, after a "period of probation," to become part of households, and the longer a slave remained a part of a household the better his or her position might be. For example, while a family could possibly choose to sell a domestic slave, "customary law regarded the selling of a slave of long standing as shameful."[26] Second generation slaves were in an even more secure position, especially if they were the result of the marriage of a slave woman to a family member. Grace asserts that second generation slaves nevertheless retained a distinctly inferior status, while by the third or fourth generation, slave ancestry tended to be forgotten and the descendants of slaves might assume a status more like that of clients.[27]

Mignerey's outpouring of indignation occurs at a personal crisis point. He is coming to grips with his own reactions and embarking on a renewed questioning of his purpose in Africa. In his eyes, the alienness of the surrounding environment has taken on the countenance of moral degradation. But as his diatribe reaches fever pitch, it becomes clear that he does not wish merely to rant. His mind is casting about for a solution or at least a ray of hope. And he recalls that the solution lies in education, the enterprise to which he has pledged himself:

> The strong right arm of the Church is Christian education. This must include more than parrot repetitions of the catechism, of the Lord's prayer, and the Apostles' Creed. It must mean the Christian attitude toward every relationship in life. That is just as vital for the African—and more so in my judgment—as it is for our churches at home. Insofar as teaching the people these practical applications of Christian standards of life is concerned, our meetings of the past week were entirely worth while.

His entry immediately following, which he wrote no more than a day or two later, shows a marked change in tone. Having confronted the enormity of the forces that he believes a missionary must battle, he was close to despair over the possible success of his struggle. But it is as if he was asking himself—but what can I concretely *do*, here and now? For he emerges from his confrontation with despair by setting very specific, concrete goals. The title he gives to the entry is "My Task in Africa":

> Thru these past weeks, and especially during the past days of quiet meditation along the beach with the music of the sea in my ears, my own mission has taken on definite form. It is simply this: (1) to learn the native language; (2) to teach the people to read and write their own language; and, (3) to put Christian literature written in their own language, into their hands. Such is my task in Africa.

In June he had told an audience of Temne villagers that he hoped to learn their language, and by October he had completed the tenth lesson in A.T. Sumner's Temne textbook. He was impressed and inspired by his friend Rosselot who had "learned to use Sherbro more than any other missionary ever sent to Shenge." In October, having resolved upon the publication project, he got immediately to work. He begins teaching some of the mission boys how to read Temne, using the same textbook he was studying from. In November he begins discussing with the head teacher at Rotifunk the possibility of instruction in written Temne, and he reports that the government looks favorably on this proposal. By late November he begins daily lessons in Temne with one of the teachers at Rotifunk. By January, the Temne reader had been approved by the "general language committee and the conference," by the end of that month the text he had prepared was in the hands of the printer, and by the end of March, 100 copies of the reader had been produced by the Albert Academy Press, which were then distributed to missions in the Temne area to the north.

Though Mignerey resolved to focus his immediate energies on more modest aims, he certainly was far from abandoning his ideal of the complete transformation of African society. That ideal included the ending of polygamy, slavery, and the liquor trade. Through their church the missionaries were certainly in a position to exercise power over children in their schools and over mission workers, but they were in no position to simply dictate to society at large any program of reform. And yet, the mission church did have a certain degree of political influence. In attempting to pursue its program of social reform, the mission church had to work within a political framework that included a number of different contending forces, in the context of the imposition of the British colonial system of "indirect rule" over the Protectorate. This system placed the Protectorate under the control of its British governor, who served at the behest of the Colonial Office in Britain. The Protectorate was divided into districts, each governed by a British Commissioner. The District Commissioners each appointed a number of Paramount Chiefs to rule over the chiefdoms into which each district was divided.

The imposition of "indirect rule" disrupted the indigenous political system in two basic ways: First, it disregarded, and thereby dismantled, the several Mende, Temne, and Sherbro states that had emerged in the nineteenth century, each including a number of chiefdoms under a king. "Indirect rule" also disregarded, and thereby undermined, the more or less democratic and representative institutions on the local level such as the Poro society and chiefs' councils. The Mende Poro society, for example, was a center of power independent of the chief that the chief relied upon for support. Indirect rule, while on the whole drastically curtailing the powers of chiefs, at the same time increased the powers of chiefs over their own people, since the paramount chiefs had the backing of the British government, which disregarded indigenous democratic institutions that had in pre-colonial times acted as checks on the power of the chiefs. Many chiefs succumbed to the opportunities for corruption and oppression which this system introduced.

Mignerey was well aware of abuses of power among Paramount Chiefs. But he was of course unaware that the particular form such oppressiveness took was a result of the colonial situation itself, and not just another aspect of the "vast accumulation of savagery" he was sent to reform. So the conclusions and perceptions expressed in an entry which he titled "Chiefs oppress people" probably do have a basis in fact, despite the limitations of Mignerey's perspective:

> After the excitement of the monkey-hunt had passed the chief returned to his court and went on with his cases. As I passed thru a few moments later, a big man in blue country cloth was before the Chief [A.G. Caulker] on his knees begging for dear life. I do not know his offense. I do know that these chiefs are as cruel and heartless as sin when it comes to lording it over their people. In most instances that I have observed and have heard about the object of each chief seems

to be to fill his own pocket with money wrung from the people, and to render them as poor and helpless and harmless as possible. The government has made some effort to eliminate the excessive graft on the part of the chiefs, but with what success I do not know. There is certainly much of it yet.

Our native teacher at Yenkissa, [Mrs. Sarah] Roberts, for fifteen years at the service of our mission, tells me that there is much discontent in that section with the present Paramount Chief Caulker residing here at Rotifunk. She said that not long ago he demanded 3 pounds of the people, thru the local Chief Fosana, to defray expenses of a trip on government business to establish a boundary between two other chiefdoms not in this district. Then later he sent for another 3 pounds. Recently he has demanded a payment of 8 pounds by the Yenkissa Chief.

They say that these sums are extortionate, are far beyond what has ever been asked of them before, and are more than they are able to pay in connection with the government house tax and the local farm tax. (The government tax now on each farm is said to be 2/- [2 shillings] and one bushel of rice. This goes to the local chief, or Santigee, as rent of the land, all of which he "owns" within his district). Mrs. Roberts said yesterday that there was great dissatisfaction with the present chief on these grounds. The Frenchman Gasser brot the same news from Mokabi.

In each of these towns, however, the local chiefs were aspirants for the Paramount Chieftaincy before the appointment of the present Chief Caulker. The Chief at Yenkissa, Fosana, by name, is also a staunch Mohammedan. Chief Caulker is an openly professing Christian— his open polygamy does not seem to disturb him in this! All of these things may also account for the prevailing discontent.

At any rate it would be a great shame for Chief Caulker to fail in his reign, since it would be a set-back at least for "nominal" and "official" Christianity in these parts. Even that would not greatly disturb me, tho, as this sort of Christianity is not of the highest type anyway. Although native chiefs who are friendly to our work can do much to help the people, I often doubt if the masses of the people will ever have their hearts touched and their inner lives changed by this "official" Christianity, unless it is thru their children and their children's children, who may or may not be kept in the mission schools because of the influence of the Christian chiefs.

The Paramount Chief of Bumpe Chiefdom, A.G. (Albert George) Caulker, belonged to a Sherbro family that had been prominent and powerful for generations. The Sherbro had a longer history of interaction with Europeans than any other group in Sierra Leone. The Caulkers are descendants of the union of the European Thomas Corker, who was in Sierra Leone for a few years around 1684, and Seniora Doll, a Sherbro from another family already politically powerful. The Caulkers had been chiefs of the Bumpe region since 1820, when A.G.'s ancestor Thomas Stephen (Kon Tham) Caulker moved to Bumpe town on the Bumpe river from the offshore Banana islands. Once at Bumpe Town, Thomas Stephen (Kon Tham) Caulker married the daughter of a Sherbro "queen" known as the Kong Charma, thereby establishing a claim to authority in the larger Sherbro area.[28] The basis of the Caulker family's wealth and power had been the slave trade, which continued as their primary economic activity until 1820, when they turned to the trade in timber.[29] Over the course of the nineteenth century and through the 1920s, some members of the family were Christians, some Muslims, and some appear to have had some allegiance to both religions. A Caulker founded a C.M.S. School on the Plantain Islands as early as 1820—evidently while still engaged in the slave trade.

A.G. Caulker's father, James Canraybah Caulker, was a Christian literate in English, and had been Paramount Chief of Bumpe chiefdom from 1898–1903,[30] the critical postwar period that saw the reestablishment of the missions. His support for the United Brethren mission was evident in a speech given at the dedication of the Martyr's Memorial Church in Rotifunk: "'He pointed out to them the way in which the country is changing, and urged them to send their children to the school provided for them, that they may be able to take their places in the development of the country.'"[31] In line with his own recommendation, he sent A.G. to the United Brethren School at Shenge (Rufus Clark and Wife Training School) as a child, then the Wesleyan boys High School. One of A.G.'s widows reports that this education was a major factor in his selection as chief, and that he often said that the missionaries influenced him highly.[32]

A.G. Caulker became a leader who clearly threw in his lot with the government and mission. One expression of this orientation was A.G.'s refusal, on his

The "Native Chief" at the center of this photograph published in *Our Foreign Missionary Enterprise* (1908) is probably James Canraybah Caulker, father of A.G. Caulker. J.C.B. Caulker was appointed Paramount chief of Bumpe Chiefdom in 1898 and supported the United Brethren missions, working closely with J.R. King. He ruled until his death in 1903.

accession as chief, to submit to the traditional period of seclusion known as *an-kantha*[33] (or *kantar*) in Temne or *kungk* in Sherbro.[34] *An-kantha* is in fact a Temne custom which had evidently spread among the Sherbro since the majority of the local chiefs in Bumpe expected A.G. to follow it.[35] The period of seclusion is a sign of continuity with the past, since originally accession of a new chief followed the death of the old, and the Temne myth interprets the period of the new chief's seclusion as being merely the temporary absence of the old chief. *An-kantha* also at least symbolically involves a restraint on the chief's power, since it includes both ritual prohibitions and instruction in duties and traditions. But when Caulker became Paramount Chief in 1921, he chose to be consecrated as chief not through *an-kantha,* but in a Christian ceremony by the Pastor of the United Brethren church in Rotifunk, John Karefa-Smart. Mignerey participated in this ceremony.[36] According to Darrell Reeck, "Caulker objected to *kantar* because he felt that chiefs who participated in *kantar* lost their autonomy of office and ac-tion by binding themselves too closely to tribal authorities."[37] It is precisely this sought-after "autonomy" that lay at the root of chiefly corruption—by finding sources of legitimation in the colonial government and the mission, outside of traditional institutions, chiefs such as Caulker freed themselves from traditional democratic restraints upon their power.

The United Brethren missions clearly did have a certain amount of political and social influence. But they were only one institution among several others, no one of which had absolute control of society. Chiefs on the one hand had a cer-tain degree of traditional authority. The system of indirect rule in theory res-pected that authority. The British government's knowledge of traditional sys-tems was limited—although the government did make some effort to understand the traditional systems.[38] While the system of indirect rule did not live up to its putative respect for traditional society, standing in traditional society remained one effective basis for the gaining of power in the new order. The new system somewhat hobbled the Poro society, but it was not the intention and by no means the effect of the new system to abolish the Poro. The missions entered this complex situation by the permission of the British government. But while the government for the most part cooperated with the missions and in certain situations exerted political pressure on their behalf, it was never the overt policy of the British Government to Christianize Africa. The annexation of the Protec-torate was not based on any clear cut plan—rather, the steps the government took during the nineteenth century which eventually lead to annexation were taken piecemeal, with no overall ideological justification or ideal. What this meant in the case of the founding of mission stations in the Protectorate was that stations could not be founded without the permission and support of chiefs. The stories of the relations of the United Brethren missionaries to chief Sorie Kesse-beh at Rotifunk and chief Foray Vong at Taiama show how this situation could differently play out.

Taiama, the capital of the Kpa-Mende Kingdom, was a fortified grouping of sixteen towns whose total population was about 10,000 in the late nineteenth century.[39] Between 1894–96, as the British Government was making plans for the imposition of the Protectorate, negotiations were conducted among the Unit-ed Brethren missionary I.N. Cain, the chief of Taiama Foray Vong, and the chief of Senehun Madam Yoko. Yoko, who had been installed by the British,[40] was influential in Kpa-Mende politics. Foray Vong had initially rejected Cain's re-quest to start the mission. Cain had then turned to the British government, and the governor sent letters both to Vong and Yoko pressuring them to accept the mission. Reeck sums up the outcome of this situation in a way that clearly spells out the power relations in a situation where the chiefs are at least formally taken into consideration and have the power to extract some concessions, but in which the Governor clearly has the last word:

> In objection, Foray expressed fears that the mission would threaten the existence of the customary activities of the people, and extracted an assurance from the Governor that the mission would not subvert country customs and traditional religious practices. On the basis of this concession, the chiefs notified Yoko that they would accept the mission—indeed, they felt they were forced to do so after reading the contents of the Governor's forceful letters. Mr. Cain revealed his attitude when he wrote to the constituents that the mission was to bring 'eternal warfare' to all the heathen societies, beside whose bush the mission had been granted land.[41]

Foray Vong was convicted at the close of the Hut Tax war by the British Government of ordering the murders of two missionaries at Taiama, the Rev. Lowry A. McGrew and his wife. He had "allowed them to be decapitated," after "promising protection."[42] I.N. Cain, along with his wife and five other missionaries, was also murdered during the uprising—not at Taiama, but at Rotifunk.[43] Vong was hanged by the British in October 1898, along with 96 others, including "the leading Bumpe chiefs...and the Rotifunk missionaries' murderers."[44] Also, in further retaliation, the British destroyed the entire city of Taiama. Governor Cardew "instructed that some towns destroyed by government forces not be rebuilt" including Bumpeh, Gbamgbaia, and Taiama. Only "pressure from the Colonial Office" forced him to allow Taiama to be rebuilt.[45] The Poro bush at Taiama apparently remained in its position adjoining the mission until the 1930s, when it was forcibly removed, probably at the instigation of Charles Leader, to the outskirts of Mokoli.[46] Reeck believes that, in the pre-war environment that saw the founding of the missions in Taiama and Rotifunk, politics was the decisive factor motivating the Taiama chiefs to oppose the mission while Kessebeh embraced it: "Compared with Sorie Kessebeh, the chiefs of Taiama found little blocking their route to status achievement in the traditional structure on the one hand, and perhaps little opening or need for status achievement in the new framework on the other."[47]

Sorie Kessebeh was the leader of a group of Lokko who had migrated to the Bumpe country from the north. He probably engaged in the timber trade, but the Caulkers called upon him as a warrior for defense against Mende invaders. He was eventually rewarded by being allowed to settle at Rotifunk, where he became the local chief for the entire town (and not just the Lokko immigrants).[48] In 1890 he underwent a rather dramatic public conversion to Christianity at a United Brethren revival meeting, and in 1875 he willingly contributed land and even his own labor to the construction of the mission at Rotifunk.[49] Reeck notes that, despite holding traditional office in Rotifunk, he had never been granted land by the Caulkers,[50] and "aside from any purely spiritual benefits, the presence of the mission in Rotifunk contributed to Sorie's status and prestige, and these factors may in part account for his positive response. Sorie...was a stranger to Bumpe country and needed the security and importance that the presence of a European house a white man could give him in Rotifunk."[51] Sorie Kessebeh's son Santigi [given name] Bundu was the local chief of Rotifunk at the time of Mignerey's service there. Extant reports about Santigi Bundu are rather puzzling, taken as a whole. He had been tried for the murder of the missionaries in 1898 and acquitted, but was later convicted of plundering the mission and sentenced to 14 years.[52] One of Reeck's informants reports that during the Anti-Lebanese riots of 1919, "Santigi Bundu marshaled all the young men of the town and set them against anybody who came to pillage the Syrians." [53] Mignerey describes him in these terms: "Type of New Pagan—Opposes new P.C. Prison Record—Evade debts—English expert—polygamy—unreliable." In any event, Bundu evidently did not align himself closely with the mission and the government as his father had.

Mignerey classified the chiefs he had contact with into four types including the "New Pagan"—Bundu, and the "New Christian"—Caulker. He describes a sub-chief Charlie of Mokabi (a town of 35 houses) as an "Old Pagan," and Ali- mamy Fosana of Yenkissa (a town of 50 houses) as a "New Moslem." Mignerey observes that Chief Charlie, Alimamy Fosana, and A.G. Caulker had competed for the Paramount Chieftaincy of Bumpe, and he notes that Chief Charlie con- tinues to intrigue against the Paramount Chief and the Government. Fosana was the leader of a group of Kuranko who had originally immigrated to Bumpe sometime in the nineteenth century. By Fosana's time his people had become Sherbro speaking, but evidently still considered themselves to be ethnically Ku- ranko. His son, Alimamy Fosana II, told Reeck that a direct Fosana ancestor married the first daughter of the Kong Charma, while Thomas Stephen (Kon Tham) Caulker married her second daughter, and that only later. This estab- lished, in the eyes of the Fosana's, a strong claim to the Paramount Chieftain- cy.[54] Alimamy Fosana I persisted in making his claim to the Paramount Chief- taincy right up until his death in 1924, but the Government consistently backed A.G. Caulker.[55] Fosana, unlike the other three chiefs, seems to have made a very good impression upon Mignerey. Though Fosana is a "staunch Mohammedan," he apparently invited the United Brethren to start a school in Yenkissa and made contributions to the Red Cross. Mignerey also praises Yenkissa for its cleanli- ness and sanitation.

The striking fact about the whole socio-political situation in Bumpe chief- dom in the 1920s is that it was in no way monolithic. While the chiefdom was predominantly Sherbro, the area around Rotifunk was evidently Temne, and there was a significant presence of Lokko, Kuranko, Mende, and Krio. Promi- nent leaders included individuals from the Kuranko and the Lokko as well as the Sherbro ethnic groups. Cultural institutions such as the Poro and Bondo cut across ethnic differences. Temne institutions such as *an-kantha* had been adopted by Sherbro leaders. The Sherbro Caulkers, who owed some of their power to a more than century-long association with the Western world, had to contend with the more traditional Lokko, Kuranko, Temne, and Mende. The British Colonial Government had consistently been appointing Caulkers as Pa- ramount Chiefs, but the Poro society, though weakened, was far from destroyed.

In any particular area, there was a network of political power relations engaging several groups: the Colonial Government, the missions, powerful families, and traditional social organizations such as the Poro. The colonial Government was represented by the District Commissioner; the mission was represented not only by Western missionaries but also by African pastors and teachers; the powerful families were represented by chiefs and sub-chiefs. Mueller's interviews with African teachers and pastors who served in the 1920s and 1930s provide interesting insights into the power relations among these individuals.[56] It is hardly surprising that the missionaries were viewed as being allied with the District Commissioners—who did in fact at times intervene politically on the missionaries' behalf. This perception made the chiefs disinclined to interfere with the missions.

Not only the missionaries, but the African pastors as well, were highly respected among the people of their towns and villages. Africans involved with missions played an indispensable role in the relations between the Colonial Government and the people, since the Government needed to deal with people who could read and write and speak English, and the missions were the primary providers of Western education. African pastors, respected both by the Government and by their own people, had an especially important role in this regard. The African pastors were taken very seriously by the District Commissioners

Martyrs' Memorial Church, Rotifunk

and the government. For example, a District Commissioner, in a court investigation, was willing to accept the testimony of an African pastor as conclusive proof,[57] and, in one case, a District Commissioner was even dismissed because of a bad report from an African pastor.[58] Missions could be founded either through the enthusiastic support of a local chief, as at Rotifunk, or through the reluctant support of chiefs pressured by the Colonial Government at the request of the Western missionaries, as at Taiama. There were also tense power relations among missions of different Christian denominations: Once the United Brethren missions had been established at Shenge, Rotifunk, and Taiama, efforts began to establish Roman Catholic missions in those towns, but the United Brethren missionaries successfully intervened with the chiefs and the Government to stymie those efforts.[59]

Shortly after his arrival in Rotifunk, Mignerey participated in the consecration of A.G. Caulker as Paramount Chief of Bumpe Chiefdom. The consecration was held at the Rotifunk United Brethren Church, known as the "Martyrs' Memorial Church." Caulker expressed his alliance with mission interests through at least two official actions as Paramount Chief—the prohibition of labor and public works on Sundays, and the prohibition of alcohol. Mignerey's account of what he calls "a palm wine palaver" is interesting for the light it sheds on the role a missionary could play in the enforcement of alcohol prohibition. It is evident that the head missionary becomes in effect an arm of the chief's government in the enforcement of a decree that emerged from the alliance between the chief and the mission. At this point (December 8, 1923), Mignerey had been missionary-in-charge for almost a year. In this incident, Mignerey ends up in fact playing the role not merely of a concerned citizen reporting an infraction, but in fact, of a policeman. He takes it upon himself, apparently with the approval of the Paramount Chief, to interrogate and admonish the offender, and he consults with the chief afterwards concerning the best course of legal action:

> This morning saw an unusual palaver arise and pass into history. It began several weeks ago when the Paramount Chief here made a law prohibiting the making or selling of palm wine in his Chiefdom. The Chief tells me that he has a long letter from the government backing him in this law. He promised to let me see it, but he has forgotten to send it over today.
>
> About two weeks ago Miss Vesper noticed a man bringing a jug of palm wine to the house of a Creole man named John across from the dispensary. There has been much fighting and general brawling in the John household by day and by night. Miss Vesper reported the matter to the Chief. He asked her to keep on the lookout and report immediately any other violation.
>
> This morning Alfred Keister came running over to me to say that Miss Vesper and he had seen a man bring palm wine to John's place, and that John had taken it across the center of his little shop and had put it in a side room. I sent a note at once to the Chief. He sent a young man from his family and one of his court officers to me asking me to identify the man who had brought the wine. His officer was under orders to seize him and carry him to the court.
>
> I went over to John's place and asked him about the man who had been seen there shortly before. He said that he had gone back to a small "faki", north of town. When questioned concerning the palm wine which the man had brought he was confused at first, but finally explained that the man had carried it away. His wife joined in and told a conflicting story to the effect that their own boy had brought some wine that morning.
>
> John became very abusive towards me. He accused me of complicity in this because I was white and he black.

This is something that I have noticed several times during the short experience here: the blacks are always the first and the quickest to draw the "colorline" argument whenever they are crossed in anything right or wrong. This is a common experience of the other missionaries. A few years ago, Mr. Musselman[60] tells me, when the Marcus Garvey fever had taken hold of these people some of our own native workers, like Mr. Manley, head teacher at Shenge, wrote most abusive letters to the mission management accusing of race prejudice and discrimination, oppression and abuse.

This morning these accusations from John passed me without ruffling me in the least. Some days I can be calm and self-possessed in the midst of almost any disturbance. This was one of them. I told John simply and kindly that he was mistaken in this; that if I had any color feeling I would not be in Africa—I would have stayed at home among my own people; and that I was doing this by the Chief's request.

He refused to allow the Chief's men to search his house. The Chief then asked us all to come over to his place. With this order I knew that there was no further hope of securing evidence on John's premises. Already a very strong smell of palm wine came out of the little room to the right. I suspect Mrs. John of pouring it out while John was palavering with the Chief's men in front of the shop. At any rate, there would be no hope of getting it, once we had left the house.

The chief questioned us concerning the happenings of the morning. John admitted that he liked palm-wine very much. He told conflicting stories which were corrected by the Chief's men. But in the absence of positive evidence the Chief did nothing but reprimand John severely. He also talked with him kindly concerning the reason for the anti-liquor law. He said that most trouble in his court had been because of palm-wine palaver. He said that before he made the law, as many as ten cases a day came to him for settlement. Now there is only an occasional palaver. The murder which stirred the town a little more than a year ago—and for which the murderer paid his life to the government—was caused by drinking. The Chief said that Rotifunk today would not recognize Rotifunk of the old days, when the streets were shaken with drunken brawls. The Chief very cleverly solicited John's cooperation in keeping Rotifunk sober, and gave him authority to apprehend any vendor of liquors who might come into his shop.

I had a long talk with the Chief after John had been dismissed. He said that he was sure John was guilty, but that he did not care to prosecute him without positive and unmistakable evidence, for the reason that John is a Creole man—Sierra Leonean, he calls himself, as do all the Creoles,—and that Creoles feel themselves far above the native people. They resent being brought to a native chief for trial, and usually carry every case on to the government's district commissioner. While they are obliged to observe all the native laws, under penalty, in case of persistent violation, of banishment from the Chiefdom, they feel themselves to be under the special dispensation of the government as distinguished from native law. I know this to be true from other sources, as well. At the dispensary it is notorious that the Creoles want to push in ahead of all other natives waiting in line for medicine. They positively do not wish to take their turn because it means allowing native people whom they consider their inferior to be served before them.

The Chief says that he will not hesitate to prosecute the Creoles, even if they do carry the case to the "D.C.", but he wishes to be very sure of his case before doing so. I believe that he is right in this attitude.

This evening John hung up a sign roughly printed on cardboard outside his shop. It was intended for Miss Vesper. It read: "England expects everyone to attend to his own business." Miss Vesper was slightly nearsighted and could not read it. She asked Frances what it was. But Frances couldn't read it. "It's the A-B-C's Mr. John put there to teach his little girl to read," she said.

And thus closed the palm-wine palaver- excepting that the Chief plans to have two of his court officers in plain clothes watch the place across from the dispensary.

In another incident from almost the same time (November 14), Mignerey deals with an individual who arrived in Rotifunk to sell traditional medicines. He approaches Mignerey ostensibly "to get a primer to learn to read," but turns out to be an illiterate Muslim from Lagos who has applied to several Paramount Chiefs with a written petition "for permission to open up a 'dispensary' to sell native medicines that are powerful 'for both Mohammedans and Christians who believe the ten commandments.'" He had at first met with the Paramount Chief, who "was taking his time to decide." He is evidently now applying to the missionary-in-charge as to a person he assumes has political influence. Mignerey sees no value whatsoever in traditional medicines, and when he talks the matter over with his wife and the dispensary nurse Nora Vesper, they agree "that the man was coming with no good purpose." In general, he complains, Africans place far too much confidence in, and spend far too much money on traditional medicine, only turning to the mission dispensary as a "last resort." He also assumes that "this Mohammedan would use his peculiar position as medicine man to work upon the people's fears and propagate his own religion, which is positively a great stumbling block to the spread of the Gospel here." Mignerey goes to discuss the matter with the chief, whose decision, it turns out, "had been delayed until he could talk the matter over with the missionaries." The chief evidently decides to refuse the man permission, since he does "not wish to permit any action that would do damage to the Mission medical work." The missionary-in-charge evidently does not by himself have the authority to exclude such an individual from Rotifunk, and yet the Paramount Chief is eager to cooperate with the interests of the mission as the missionaries define them.

While Mignerey certainly appreciated the strong support A.G. Caulker provided the mission, Caulker was not an individual who excited his admiration. Mignerey sums up his perception of Caulker in these terms:

At any rate it would be a great shame for Chief Caulker to fail in his reign, since it would be a set-back at least for "nominal" and "official" Christianity in these parts. Even that would not greatly disturb me, tho, as this sort of Christianity is not of the highest type anyway. Although native chiefs who are friendly to our work can do much to help the people, I often doubt if the masses of the people will ever have their hearts touched and their inner lives changed by this "official" Christianity, unless it is thru their children and their children's children, who may or may not be kept in the mission schools because of the influence of the Christian chiefs.

Mignerey evidently sees Caulker as an individual who supports only the externals of Christianity—the school, the church, the establishment of certain social policies like alcohol prohibition. He does not see Caulker as one of those whose hearts have been touched and whose lives have been changed. Mignerey offers a litany of complaints against chiefs in general—such as their support of slavery, and their financial exploitation of the people, including not only excessive taxation, but also, Mignerey claims, the use of wives to entice men who are then apprehended and forced to pay damages. He never suggests that Caulker is at all an exception in regard to such abuses—and he specifically complains about Caulker's excessive taxation and ownership of slaves. But what most shocks Mignerey is that Caulker, who grew up in mission schools and is the primary supporter of missions in Bumpe chiefdom, is also an open polygamist. "Chief Caulker is an openly professing Christian—his open polygamy does not seem to disturb him in this!" In this regard Caulker also was in fact by no means an exception even among Christian chiefs.

The ending of polygamy was the single social reform to which the United Brethren missionaries were most consistently and passionately committed. But it would have been inconceivable for a Paramount Chief, for example, to make the slightest effort to abolish or restrict polygamy in the chiefdom as a whole. The only individuals over whom the missionaries had any power whatsoever when it came to the question of banning polygamy were those in one way or another associated with the mission or the church. Mueller's interviews with pastors and teachers paint a clear picture of the very limited steps the United Brethren missionaries were able to take in pursuit of their most prized social reform. Christian chiefs were usually and perhaps always polygamous, but, at least on this issue, the missionaries found themselves unable to pressure, penalize, or exclude politically powerful members of the community upon whom the mission depended for support. The only means they had of pressuring regular African churchgoers was by excluding polygamists from participation in communion. In fact, two classes of churchgoers were established: "communicant members" and "seekers"—partly to provide a means for polygamous families to nevertheless have some degree of participation in church life. But while the missionaries did refuse communion to most polygamists, they made a very convenient exception in the case of the polygamous chiefs.

Another major obstacle to the realization of the missionaries' dream of the abolition of polygamy was that the African pastors did not share it. Even when the pastors were opposed to polygamy they had a much better understanding of the socio-economic situation of which polygamy was a part, and much more sympathy for the dilemmas polygamous Christians faced. For example, polygamous converts to Christianity had to ask: does becoming a Christian require the abandonment of part of one's family, a family to whom one has made promises and has all sorts of obligations? Can this be the way Christ would have a husband treat a wife, a father his children? African pastors consistently served communion to polygamous Christians—and not only chiefs, but those of humble status as well. And some among the missionaries, including Musselman (the General Superintendent), were willing to "let sleeping dogs lie," as Rev. David Shodeke put it, and not interfere with the African pastors' tolerant policy. [61] There was only one group upon which the missionaries could even attempt to work their will in this regard: the African teachers employed in mission schools.

Teachers were summarily fired when the missionaries found out they were po-lygamous. Polygamous teachers had to conceal their families from the missiona-ries—and many succeeded in keeping the secret. This was an issue that all the missionaries took seriously, but Charles Leader, missionary in charge at Taiama from 1925 until 1950, and later at Bo from 1951 until 1962, stands out in the memory of teachers and pastors for his approach to polygamy. While those who worked with him all praise his skill in building up the Taiama mission, the ma-jority nevertheless take a very dim view both of the zeal with which he hunted down polygamous mission workers, and his unjust handling of their cases, in which the presumption of guilt predominated. And Leader's seemingly prin-cipled stand appears in an even worse light when we learn that he too lacked the courage to refuse communion to polygamous chiefs. It is interesting that for all the violence of his hatred of polygamy, Mignerey does not appear to have taken any steps against polygamous mission workers—but this may be merely due to the fact that his term of service at Rotifunk was relatively brief.

As the missionary in charge of a major station in an important regional cen-ter, Mignerey occupied the position of a prominent and politically powerful member of the community, and this position required his engagement with that community in a number of ways. But much of his time and effort were absorbed by his management of the Rotifunk mission itself, and especially of the school. In 1882 the United Brethren mission had had approximately ten stations, with a total school enrollment of about 282,[62] and by the time of the war in 1898 the number of stations had grown to 20.[63] Despite the enormous setback of the war, by 1910 the United Brethren were operating 30 schools with a total enrollment of 833 boys and 303 girls.[64] Total United Brethren school attendance had grown steadily from 460 in 1900 to 925 in 1922, 928 in 1923, and 863 in 1924, and continued to grow in the ensuing decade, reaching 2437 in 1933.[65] The schools were linked together in a system whereby smaller village schools fed central primary schools in the towns of Rotifunk, Shenge, Bonthe, Taiama, and Jaiama, which in turn fed the Albert Academy, in Freetown.[66] (Harford School for Girls in Moyamba was not granted full secondary status until 1950.[67]) These schools were supported completely by contributions from the church in the United States, until a system of fees began to be introduced at the beginning of the cen-tury, and a system of partial government support in 1912 (which was contingent upon annual Government inspection of each school). But while government aid and fees both gradually increased until 1931, the largest source of funding re-mained the church.[68]

Chiefs supported the schools not only by granting land and labor but also by supporting and recruiting students. One of Reeck's informants states that "A.G. Caulker kept many children, both boys and girls, in his Rotifunk compound at his expense and sent them to the Rotifunk school." [69] Reeck found, from the informants' reports, that

> Chief A.G. Caulker of Bumpe Chiefdom worked hand in hand with Walter Schutz, missionary at Rotifunk [and Mignerey's successor], for the growth of school program and enrollment. Schutz would consult Caulker in regard to new plans, and Caulker sent his nephews and other boys to school and supported

them. Furthermore, after his election in 1921, Caulker suggested to the people of the chiefdom that they open a chiefdom school at Bumpe town. The school was built and placed under the UBC administration, but financed by the chiefdom. In 1938, when the chiefdom came under the Native Administration, Chief Caulker himself assumed support of the school out of his own funds at least until 1945, perhaps longer. [70]

In Taiama, however, the chief resorted to active conscription—conscription that was at times resisted by the families involved:

> In 1921, Chief Morlu Briwah of Kori Chiefdom, perhaps at the suggestion of Miss Eaton, and after consultation with his headmen, assigned quotas to each chiefdom section of a certain number of boys to be sent to the Taiama school. The result is reported to have been the conscription of about forty-five new scholars. The chiefdom provided their food. This arrangement was maintained until 1925. [71]

One of Mueller's informants from Taiama, Peter Pieh, also confirms this fact, relating the story of how he himself was conscripted against his parents' will. The Paramount Chief succeeded in conscripting four children including Pieh from Pieh's particular section of Kori Chiefdom by threatening to fine the village should it not produce them. Briwah supported the children he conscripted, but most of them dropped out after a few years. By the 1950s, Pieh had gone on to become a pastor, serving at Taiama and elsewhere, though he never attended Albert Academy. [72] Briwah's selection as Paramount chief at Taiama had been supported by the missionaries (Miss Eaton and Miss Aikin).

Reeck provides very concrete evidence for the socio-economic impact of the mission schools in Rotifunk and Taiama. The overall socio-economic situation was that of a traditional society in which the vast majority pursued subsistence agriculture, while a minority held high status positions as Paramount Chiefs, sub-chiefs, chiefdom speakers, or officials of societies such as the Poro or Njayei. [73] The colonial institutions were superimposed upon this traditional society. These institutions effected almost no change in the nature of the economic pursuits of the vast majority. But they did create a new status group consisting of those who were employed by missions, schools, and government in either a supervisory or laboring capacity. The mission schools were the primary means by which individuals were enabled to enter this new status group. Reeck tabulates statistics on the students at Rotifunk and Taiama between 1904 and 1934 according to the socio-economic status of their fathers or sponsors and the socioeconomic status they eventually attained. Forty-one percent of the students came from a "traditional" background, and 35% from a "modern" one (there being no data on the remaining 19%). By contrast, the eventual occupations of only 9% of the students were "traditional," while those of 65% were modern (there being no data on the remaining 26%). [74] More than half of the fathers or sponsors of the students from a "traditional" economic background were traditional office holders. While the background of 24 students was that of the traditional elite, only seven students became traditional office holders. Eighteen percent of the students came from a traditional farming background, while less than 3% are known to have become farmers. Also, between 1898 and 1940, school attendance at Rotifunk grew 400%, at Taiama, 1000%.[75] The growth in mission school enrollment upon the establishment of colonial rule clearly is a function of the need for access to new opportunities for employment in the colonial situation, and families within both the traditional elite as well as those already employed in the modern sector disproportionately took advantage of these new opportunities for the advancement of their children.

In a letter to a friend in October, 1922, Mignerey provides a succinct report on the Rotifunk boarding home:

> We have fifteen boarding pupils in the boys' home. They are in the grades in the day school but are from six to twenty-two years of age. This is because many children here do not go to school until they are fifteen or sixteen. Our boys are a fine bunch of normal boys. They pay about $30 a year and furnish their clothes and books. In addition, they work six hours a day on the mission compound. They do all our house work except the cooking. They also do the washing and ironing. During the dry season they gather wood to last during the rainy season. They keep our walks clean and the lawn cut.

The total enrollment at the school, which included day as well as boarding students, was 66 at the beginning of 1923. The boarding school boys had a full schedule each day: prayers from 6:00–6:15; work from 6:15-8:00; school from 9:00–2:30 with an hour recess; work 2:30–5:00; play and supper 5:00–7:00; study 7:00–8:30; lights out at 9:00.[76] Student records on twelve of the boarders show that five were sons of subchiefs and one of a chief. The fathers of five were Muslims. "Native" or "African" is listed as the religion of three of the fathers and eight of the mothers.

Mignerey includes a number of entries that record his attempts to solve various problems that arose with the mission "boys" (who ranged in age from 6 to 22). It becomes clear that he knew them well and devoted a great deal of personal attention to fostering their academic and moral development. One entry, while portraying a somewhat atypical situation, provides a very clear picture of Mignerey's basic attitude toward the students:

> One of the failures today was Joe Caulker, a mission boy. He is about 22 years old, has been in the mission about seven years, and is still in the Standard IV. Months ago I was convinced that Joe did not belong even in a standard as advanced as the fourth. His work all year has been poor, and his examination was no exception. He presents the curious problem of the subnormal mind. There are several of this type in the school, but I know Joe much better, because of daily contact with him as a mission boy. He is slow, but absolutely trustworthy, and he even tries earnestly in his school work. He is apparently dense. He simply lacks the capacity for further mental development along the lines generally marked out for schools.
>
> Joe feels his failure very keenly. He has not eaten, and this evening he absented himself from the big "Chop" which we gave the boys on tables on the mission house downstairs porch. Late this evening he was not in his room. Sam said that he was wandering among the mango trees below the Industrial Building.
>
> I called him to his room and had a long talk with him in as kindly and a fatherly way as I know how. I went over his papers to show wherein he had

failed. I made it clear to him that this did not say that he was not a good and trustworthy boy, but that on the other hand, we felt confidence in his truthfulness and his honesty.

It was our idea to allow him to go on in the studies which were of particular interest to him. When approached on this subject he decided that he liked grammar and arithmetic best of all. And these are the two things in which he is especially dense! I almost gave up hope of helping him to any further advancement in school. But on second thought I will try to get him into a few subjects that will interest him. One of them is composition—for he likes to tell yarns, and can keep the other mission boys—and missionaries, too,— spell-bound by the hour. Another subject is Temne since he is a Temne boy. I think he will be delighted with the work in reading and writing Temne which I hope to get going next year. I have promised all who complete the course satisfactorily a small Temne New Testament.

Joe dried his tears and seemed to take on new hope. To offset his disappointment further we plan to take him with us on our vacation to Mt. Leicester next week.

Mignerey clearly views Joe Caulker as an individual, and tries to promote his development in a way suited to his individual needs and abilities. He spends time talking things through with him, and comes up with a concrete plan for improvement. But Mignerey cannot help but view his situation through the lens of his education, an education hardly free from overt racism:

This has awakened me to the problem of the subnormal pupil in our school. I believe that were the subject investigated fully, it would be found that a large number of the older pupils in our day school come easily into this classification. It is a matter of common knowledge that the children of the first, second, and third standard, show a mental brilliance that begins to diminish rapidly with the fourth standard, and in many cases, is entirely extinguished before the sixth standard is reached or completed. It is said by learned men who write the big, red-backed books that this early retarded development is especially characteristic of the black race. I do not wish to take their word for it so much as to make actual, scientific observation of it for myself, with a view of adapting the school curriculum to the needs of the abnormal child.

Mignerey can hardly be blamed for taking seriously what had been presented to him as possessing the prestige of science, and it is notable that he still maintains a critical distance toward the "learned men" and their "big, red-backed books."

Students at Rotifunk (Mignerey's photographs)

The dispensary at Rotifunk attracted patients from a very wide area, and the fact that 10,771 medical treatments were administered there in 1929 gives some idea of its impact.[77] Mignerey reports that he occasionally was called to assist at the dispensary—his service in World War One having given him some medical qualification. One has the impression that Nora Vesper ran the dispensary with a very high level of competence. Mignerey reports no problems with the dispensary or conflicts with her of any sort. He seems to trust her implicitly. One incident he recorded sheds particular light on Vesper's dedication, the nature and quality of the medical care the dispensary offered, and on the personal connection that grew between Mignerey and the Africans with whom he worked. On January 22, 1923, the child of a mission worker had become gravely ill. Mignerey evidently made notes on the situation several times over the course of the following two days:

Today about noon, while we were eating "breakfast," a native woman came running into the dining room crying frantically, "Zeno da die!"

It was difficult for the moment to realize that this woman was Mrs. Sarah Zizer, a good friend of ours and the mission, and for many years an assistant of Dr. Zenora Griggs at our dispensary. For several weeks she had been staying at the dispensary with her three little children, Laura, Rosa, and Zeno, named from Dr. Griggs. Zeno especially had been a close playmate of Ellen, Miss Vesper's little Loko girl of three years. Both were about the same age, and both imitative and playful. One night not long ago we were all over at the dispensary, and were called in by Miss Vesper to see a "church service" being held by these two tots. It was highly amusing. They prayed, sang, preached, and discussed the "service" for our benefit, giggling and twittering as girls will the world over.

Only day before yesterday Sarah took the children to her husband's home down the river fifteen miles to Bompeh. Little Zeno marched into the mission house and said goodbye to Ruth as big as you please.

Only last night, Sarah says, Zeno awakened about one, crying with a pain in the abdomen. She gave the pickin' [Krio for 'child'] three drops of worm medicine and later the child went limp in her arms. About eight this morning with Zeno still unconscious Sarah got in a canoe with several strong men to paddle, and came as quickly as possible to the Mission here. She was frantic when she rushed into our dining room. All she could say was that Zeno was dying.

We all rushed over to the dispensary, to find the baby in the midst of the perspiring boatmen. Miss Vesper and Miss Hoyle made a hurried examination and gave an enema to clear the bowels. Neither knew what the exact nature of the trouble was, but both declared that it must have been some sort of poisoning aside from the worm medicine. It was possible that the child had eaten something poisonous on the preceding day.

They are still working with her at the dispensary. Miss Vesper was in a few moments ago and requested me to write Mr. Musselman telling him that she would not be down to Freetown tomorrow unless there was a change in Zeno's condition. She had been scheduled to go on her three weeks vacation tomorrow at Bethany Cottage on Mt. Leicester. Because of Sarah's close connection with the mission in the past, and because of her personal faith in Miss Vesper, she feels that she should not desert Sarah in this hour. She is wise and good to do this.

If Zeno is no better in the morning they will send for the doctor at Moyamba to come on the one o'clock train.

Sarah was over again this evening. She is completely upset. She is fearful that her husband's people will accuse her of killing the child with the worm medicine. I talked with her as best I could, and she very readily knelt and prayed with me, after I had read her the lesson of Jesus about the Father's care for his children.

How helpless I felt in the face of this near calamity to a mother's heart and a mother's love! How best to point her, to lead her to Him who drives all care away? The little that I could do seemed so insignificant for this heart torn between grief and fear.

The following evening at 8:15 P.M. he has worse news to report:

> The worst has happened to little Zeno. Many of Sarah's husband's people came and were humbugging her about Zeno until her mind was hardly her own. They are a loud-talking, meddlesome lot of uncivilized old women who have urged that Zeno be taken to the "bush" for native medicine. Sarah opposed all yesterday and last night.
>
> Miss Hoyle and Miss Vesper stayed up most of the night with Zeno, whose condition grew worse and worse. She did not regain consciousness. Sometime in the night she had a convulsion which Sarah happened to witness, and herself fell into a fainting fit which turned out to be the miscarriage of a child about two months old. Poor suffering woman! She was at the end of her strength. Her meddlesome relatives had their way. Early this morning Zeno was carried from the dispensary to a native house.
>
> The baby was dying when they did it. It was no surprise to learn of her death a short time later. They carried the body down to the house of Santigee Bundu, where they are preparing for a funeral tomorrow morning. Ruth and I were down there this evening. She and Miss Hoyle are making a little dress for Zeno, as requested by Sarah.
>
> When they carried the baby from the dispensary this morning Miss Vesper's connection with the case was finished. She could do no more, and so left for Freetown on the train this afternoon, as she had planned.

Mignerey is in fact somewhat surprised by how much Zeno's death has affected him.

> The death of this little black pickin' comes nearer to us than ever I imagined could be possible. Babies are babies and children are children. They laugh and cry, and romp and play, and worm themselves into your affections in spite of yourself. Thus came little Zeno. Her sudden death has given us all an aching heart.

That "children are children," he almost admits to himself, is something he has still to learn. Inevitably, African customs become an issue as Zeno's extended family becomes involved. Customs and attitudes are involved which Mignerey finds exasperating:

> The saddest and the most aggravating aspect of the whole affair, however, is the meddling of the husband's relatives. In this case it seems that a woman is not the owner of her own children. I know of other cases of a similar aspect. Older relatives practically dictate what is to be done to the child, often in spite of a mother's protest, and when they have never before taken any interest in the youngster.
>
> This dictatorship of the aged often constitutes a stumbling-block to the new generation of Christians, as is the case today with Sarah. In standing for the new Faith they more often than not must contend against the old order as it seeks to lay hold upon them thru older relatives. Few of them stand out against it, even as long as did Sarah.
>
> "How long, oh Lord, how long?"

Although Zeno's extended family has had some say in what has been done, she does have a Christian funeral the next day:

A brief funeral ceremony was held over the body of little Zeno at eight o'clock this morning. A carpenter had made a little coffin which was neatly covered with white. Sarah was unable to come, and the father (drunken renegade that he is!) did not stay for the burial, but went down to Bompeh last night. His brother—a very decent man—alone represented the family at the church. A small crowd attended. Rev. Smart read the simple ceremony, I lead in prayer and the service was dismissed. The child was buried, not in the mission cemetery, but on the site of an old house down near Santigee Bundu's compound. I do not know who selected this pagan resting place. Very likely the meddlesome relatives.

That the child is nevertheless not buried in the mission cemetery may reflect a conflict between Sarah Zizer and her non-Christian relatives which has resulted in a compromise.

The majority of Mignerey's entries concerning students deal with cases of boys stealing—and mostly from each other. He mentions three by name. After having dealt with a number of such cases, Mignerey is moved to confide that: "Sometimes, in moments of depression, I think that thieving is in the black man's blood, and is bound to come out sooner or later. That is rather a gloomy view to take of the race, but it seems to be pretty well grounded in facts." But despite the racist undertone of his attitude toward the mission boys, his frustration never finds an outlet as anger toward them. His wrath is reserved for the social conditions of polygamy and superstition which he believes have held Africa back. He endeavors to be patient and compassionate in all situations. And while it does not appear that he would necessarily rule out corporal punishment in every possible case under present conditions, he does firmly believe that it is practiced in the mission far too harshly and extensively—and wants the practice to eventually be eliminated. He reports several cases where he has the opportunity to flog a boy—where it is even expected—but refuses to do so. This position evidently placed him in conflict with some teachers and some missionaries. He had continuing problems with one teacher in particular, who, Mignerey believed, was at times simply out of control when it came to the use of corporal punishment:

> Monday evening I had another complaint about flogging in the school. A native woman with only a dirty blue cotton cloth twisted about her waist and hanging to her knees, brot her little girl to show me a small raw place on the child's back on which were a few drops of blood. Teacher Hallowell was the accused. The mother was very much "vexed" over the injury, but after she had gone over her complaint she felt much better. Ruth and I brot the girl to the Mission House and applied some lysol salve. I wanted to mention the matter to Hallowell yesterday but was taken sick before I thot of it. This is the upteenth complaint that has come of this teacher's brutality. I had a big palaver with him about it once, and he promised to be more careful in the future. He has been doing better, I think, until this recent relapse. The girl's alleged offense was talking in school. Someday I hope to see this middle-aged paganism removed from our Christian schools, even tho some of our own white missionaries do flog to the extent of forty-five cuts for taking a piece of crochet work into the yard without permission. Miss Gibson exultantly recited this tale to us from Moyamba, where she herself administered this punishment to a girl in school there.

It emerges here as elsewhere that Mignerey is well able to see that his own culture is just as much in need of reform—in some ways just as "pagan" and indeed as contemptible—as he considers the "pagan" culture of Africa to be.

Mignerey, his wife, nurse Nora Vesper and her assistant Maud Hoyle were the only missionaries at the Rotifunk Station. The African staff during the year of 1922 included the pastor John Karefa-Smart, teachers D.B. Hallowell, Paul Keister, Johnathan Weaver and Jacob Massaley as well as the head teacher Ross Lohr. Changes in staff required the action of the mission board, and at its meeting in January 1923, Mignerey's recommendation that Jacob Masseley be removed for "immorality" was accepted. In addition, Jonathan Weaver was transferred to a different station, and Elma Hedd and Elizabeth Kamara, graduates of the Harford School for Girls in Moyamba, were taken on as teachers for beginning students. Mignerey recommended Weaver's transfer to break up what he saw as a disruptive rivalry with Hallowell, but recommended retaining Hallowell as well as Lohr. All in all, the station employed six African workers at this time, in addition to the four missionaries. This proportion of African workers to missionaries was fairly typical for large stations like Rotifunk and Taiama: between 1900 and 1935 the number of missionaries at Rotifunk was usually about 3 while the number of African workers grew from about 4 or 5 to 12; at Taiama the number of missionaries mostly ranged from 2 to 4 while the number of African workers grew steadily from one to nine.[78] All United Brethren missionaries were appointed by the Board of Missions in the United States, which was elected by the General Conference of the Church and consisted entirely of Americans. As Mueller explains,

> The members of the Board...formulated general mission policy for the six widely separated foreign conferences and then left the implementation of it to the missionaries in each field. As well as appointing missionaries and selecting one of them as superintendent, it determined the amount of money each field received from the total funds the General Church designated for mission activity.[79]

The layers of the overall hierarchy for the Sierra Leone mission were therefore, from top to bottom: the Board of Missions in the United States, the General Superintendent in Sierra Leone (John F. Musselman), the rest of the missionaries, the African pastors, and the African teachers.[80]

Mignerey had high regard both for Lohr, the head teacher, and Karefa-Smart, the pastor. However, he complains that generally the African workers, including Lohr, are frequently very late in returning from vacations, and he dislikes the traditional mission policy of overlooking such absences when it comes to the question of wages. But he does not appear to have made an issue of this with Lohr. He also complains to Musselman that Pastor Smart has been away from Rotifunk for half of the Sundays in a six-month period—but he did not raise this issue with Smart either. Mignerey also complains in his diary that the teacher Weaver does not respect his authority. For example, he objects when Weaver pulls Paul Keister away from his itinerating work and into the classroom without consulting the missionary-in-charge. "Weaver has been impudent to me for a long time, but I have over-looked most of his 'color' insinuations, and his know-it-all attitude toward every school question." On the whole, Mignerey was extremely dissatisfied with the way the Sierra Leone mission was being administered. He concludes his entry on his conflict with Weaver with these general observations:

> The present difficulties of school management are largely the outcome of a lack of supervision in the past, as well as an absence of any system worthy the name of a school organization. My present hope of improving the school here is not with the old teachers, but with the new. It is a great trial of one's patience to have some half-civilized bushman with a fifth standard schooling get egoistic over his "education" and obnoxiously impose his "superiority," his "knowledge," and his "experience" as a barrier to every practical improvement in the school. Things move very slowly in Africa, if indeed they move at all! Improvements seem to be spasmodic with each new generation. It seems well-nigh impossible to change a habit after it has been initiated from someone else for five or ten years, to say nothing of a whole life-time.

All of Mignerey's frustrations came to a head in the case of Hallowell's excessive flogging of students. Mignerey had an interchange of letters with Musselman on this issue over a time of several months. He explained to Musselman in great detail his complaints against Hallowell, and also against the way Musselman was running the whole mission system. Musselman apparently attended carefully to Mignerey's concerns and responded in as conciliatory a way as possible. Musselman, who had earlier served as missionary-in-charge at Rotifunk, was aware that Hallowell was difficult to manage. Early in 1922, he wrote to Mignerey with regard to "the proposed transfer of Hallowell to Moyamba" that "the missionaries there do not want him there under any circumstances" and that it appears that Rotifunk is the only station at which he can be placed, despite the fact that Musselman "would like very much to get him away from Rotifunk for your sake for I do not want that he should treat a new man as he has been treating Mr. Richter and myself."[81]

In May Mignerey writes to Musselman explaining the efforts he has made to reign in Hallowell's habit of flogging. He requires Hallowell to keep a record book for his floggings. Hallowell promptly loses the record. When Mignerey

sends him a new one, he overtly ignores it. Mignerey finally directly confronts him over his persistent disobedience. Hallowell responds by directly challenging his authority: "In this interview he attempted to deny everything that had occurred. He said that I should have to deal with him thru Mr. Lohr and not directly with him personally. He said

John F. Musselman served in Sierra Leone from 1909 to 1947. He began at the Shenge, Mofuss, and Rotifunk stations, and from 1922 until his retirement in 1947 was General Superintendent.[82]

further that the official board was managing the school and not myself." Mignerey tells him that if he does not start to keep the record he will will be suspended
from work, with a recommendation to the board for his permanent removal. This
option finally motivates Hallowell to cooperate.

Mignerey puts the question directly to Musselman: "Now, I would like you
to tell me just what are the limits of my authority in the school here. It seems
that the pastor is under the impression that he is the manager of the school. Must
every instruction of mine be taken up thru the official board of the church?"[83]
Musselman evidently responded in person to his question at the Mission Council
meeting of July—defining the position of the missionary-in-charge as essentially
that of an "advisor." The prompts Mignerey to write in September with his "resignation as local manager of the day school," since the role of "advisor" does
not carry "sufficient authority"[84] Musselman writes back on the same day that
"there was never any thought to minimize your authority in the least or to make
it any less than that of any other missionary in the field." But he also points out
that "when a mission begins to operate in a certain district it has absolute authority over what is being done, but as that mission turns to the development of a
native church and a native pastorate the work of the missionaries become more
and more of an advisory nature [sic]". Musselman points out that Smart and
Lohr are the two highest paid African workers, and that

> Mr. Smart is considered one of the best native preachers we have and Mr. Lohr
> is one of our best teachers. It seems to me you men ought to get on well together,
> and I think you will when you understand each other better. The men have a feel-
> ing that much of your dealings with them is along the line of criticism and it
> makes them feel discouraged when they have tried to do their best. Being an Eng-
> lish colony we must follow English customs to a certain degree. The fact that the
> Rotifunk school was pronounced the best school in the Protectorate last year
> leads Mr. Lohr to believe he is working along right lines. Much of the work done
> in any line here is far below the average work done at home and we are very of-
> ten surprised that results are forthcoming.

Musselman continues to define the authority of the missionary-in-charge as
"very largely advisory," and he also specifies quite clearly the channels through
which the missionary needs to move in order to make various kinds of policy
and staffing changes.[85]

Mignerey responds five days later that "your information regarding the position of the Local Manager here is enlightening. It is definite information, and
clears some doubts in my own mind, especially regarding the administrative
responsibilities that I had feared were placed upon the Local Manager by the
government. This person is evidently a manager who isn't supposed to manage!
Which confirms my conviction that my relation to the Rotifunk Day school is
more theoretical than practical." He maintains to Musselman that the missionary-in-charge as manager of the day school should at least have the power to
suspend teachers until the mission board can take action. Musselman's response
almost two weeks later sheds a great deal of light, I think, upon the problem that
Mignerey is experiencing. Mignerey had little respect for Musselman. In the

diary he describes him as lacking in principle and as evasive in regard to the issues that are put to him—a perception shared by his friend Glen Rosselot. But in this letter Musselman clearly states that it is within the authority of the missionary in charge to suspend a teacher pending action by the mission board (as Mignerey had done in Hallowell's case). And it seems to me that Musselman may have an appreciation of the complexity and difficulty of the missionaries' situation that is lost on novices like Mignerey and Rosselot:

> I re-read your letter of Sept. 19th several times and am of the opinion that I failed in making some things plain. The term missionary-in-charge, is a local one and conveys to the minds of the people, the one in charge of all the work of a station. In the minds of the people head-teacher or local manager does not measure up either in standing or authority.
>
> The missionary-in-charge of a station does have the authority to suspend a worker, if he wishes to do so. The people all know he does and nobody knows it better than the workers. The workers also know that you have authority to call them any hour of the day or night you wish.
>
> As missionary-in-charge of Rotifunk you have oversight of the work at the dispensary, church, school, and home. Miss Vesper has charge of the work at the dispensary and I am sure you would not go to the dispensary for medicine for your boys without consulting her. Much the same is true of the church and the school.
>
> It is very hard to make a change anywhere in Africa for what they have, satisfies them, and a new method will not be welcome in a school or church until it can be proved that the new method is really an improvement over the old one . . . .
>
> You will doubtless never know, or appreciate how near to a crush the school was the day I came from Moyamba. The teachers were in a bad frame of mind. I never felt that the time spent in talking over the things that led up to the palaver was wasted. If I could always feel that my time was spent to as good advantage as it was then I would feel well repaid.
>
> No matter how small a palaver is here, one must give those who are out of sorts a sympathetic hearing, otherwise to the African mind there is no satisfaction. If I would have cut that palaver the way we settle disputes at home, I am sure things would have happened for which we all would have been sorry.
>
> I am sorry you feel that Mr. Lohr is the "Big Chief" for he is not. There is a vast difference in the minds of the people between missionary-in-charge and head-teacher. Mr. Lohr is more keen than some others to adopt new methods and I am sure when he sees plainly the need of changes you wish to make he will fall in line and help carry them out.[86]

Musselman with pastors A.T. Sumner and C.A.E. Campbell

This interchange between Mignerey and Musselman is interesting for a number of reasons. The missionary-in-charge was seen by the people as a figure of authority—some of Mueller's informants confirm that the missionaries were seen almost as District Commissioners. But despite that authority, they were in a very ambiguous position. Mignerey's difficulty may have lain in that ambiguity itself rather than in what he saw as Musselman's lack of principle and decisiveness. Musselman and Mignerey agree that the goal of the mission is in fact to make itself unnecessary, that the goal is to get a "native" church up and running on its own. And yet, in the present situation, they do have final authority when it comes to the governance of the church. And, whether they liked it or not, the mission was a center of political power, and the political power it possessed represented and was derived from the power of British occupation. The very existence of something like a mission "station" reflects this reality. A town in an uncolonized country like the United States has churches, and schools, and hospitals, and the schools and hospitals are in fact sometimes associated with churches. But the churches and schools and hospitals are not cordoned off into a special "station" to which has been assigned a "missionary-in-charge." (The United Brethren Stations were in fact surrounded by barbed-wire fences, and could be entered only with permission.[87]) Why in fact did there need to be such a person as a missionary-in-charge in addition to the principal of the school, the pastor of the church, and the manager of the hospital? Clearly, the role of the missionary-in-charge is to make sure that the church, school, and hospital are run in the way that the churches at home, who at this point still supply most of the funding, want them to be run. So the missionary in this role is at the central nexus of the contest for power occasioned by colonial conquest. And the colonial situation had put churches in a position of rulership which they could not officially endorse, and about which many representatives of those churches had ambivalent feelings. Hallowell does a good job of playing upon the weaknesses in Mignerey's position: "He said that I should have to deal with him thru Mr. Lohr and not directly with him personally. He said further that the official board was managing the school and not myself." Mignerey is subordinate to a mission board which in fact wants to build a church and school system that can run itself.

Musselman implicitly criticizes Mignerey for supposing that he could settle disputes in Africa in the same way one might do so in the United States, and he evidently recommends that in Africa more than in the United States, it is essential to spend a great deal of time achieving consensus, and that unilateral imposition of decisions by a lone authority figure is much less acceptable in Africa than in it is in the United States. "No matter how small a palaver is here," Musselman points out, "one must give those who are out of sorts a sympathetic hearing, otherwise to the African mind there is no satisfaction. If I would have cut that palaver the way we settle disputes at home, I am sure things would have happened for which we all would have been sorry." Musselman may be here showing an appreciation for two essential aspects of his situation in Africa toward which Mignerey is probably still relatively oblivious. First, American individualism often takes the form of an individualistic authoritarianism—whether it is the authoritarianism of the innovative business leader, or the authoritarianism of the crusading reformer. But Africa generally represents a social setting in which authority rests much more upon group consensus and tradition than it does in the United States. Musselman probably has, through long experience, gained a much better appreciation of how human relations differently play out in Africa. Second, Musselman is probably right that the missionary-in-charge, in the minds of perhaps the majority of the people, was a figure of authority, and that the people had accepted that authority, having in fact by this point accepted the authority of British colonial power. And he probably also appreciates better that beneath the acceptance by the people of the authority of the mission, there is an undercurrent of resentment, and that the missionaries had better acknowledge this before embarking full-speed-ahead on a self-righteous crusade for social betterment.

The African pastors and teachers Mueller interviewed who served in the 20s and 30s again and again express a distinctly ambivalent attitude toward the missionaries. Their very real respect, gratitude, and even affection for the missionaries exists side by side with resentment and anger over both the subordinate position assigned to Africans in the mission hierarchy and the unmistakably racist attitudes the missionaries more often than not were guilty of holding. The attitude of racial superiority was reflected even in overt policies: all mission compounds were surrounded by barbed wire fences and no one could enter without permission; no Blacks were allowed in Hill Station in Freetown; at least through the 1920s no Blacks were allowed onto the second floor of the Mission House in Freetown; no African ever stayed in the Mission House lodgings; missionaries rarely stayed in the houses of African pastors; in church certain pews were reserved for missionaries.[88] Such habits and rules were the expression of a deep seated attitude of paternalistic condescension that found expression both in personal relations and policies of church governance.

Rev. S.M. Renner,[89] in a conversation with Mueller, recounts an incident which defines particularly clearly the prevalent attitude of paternalism:

> I think in the first conversation we had I did mention the American-Negro relationship did have much to do with 'coloring' the thinking of the missionaries. Never mind that they were missionaries; they were Americans and they had an idea of the Negro as not quite ready to take on responsibility. I will give you an illustration. I was elected secretary of the Conference and suggested to the superintendent that I should prepare the manuscript and edit the minutes for publication, for printing the Conference minutes. He did not think I could do it. Well, somehow, either he fell ill or there was a sort of rupture at the mission house, and it was getting late to print the minutes. Dr. Weidler, the principal, said to me 'take the responsibility. Go ahead, edit the minutes, and print them.' So I edited the first set of minutes edited by a Sierra Leonean. I can't recall the year, but I think it may have been 1918 or 1921. And being in charge of the press I printed the minutes. I recall the look on the face of the superintendent when he came back to find out that the minutes were almost ready for publication. He wanted me to send copies of what had been printed. I did send copies down (to the mission house). He said, 'Certainly you did not do this alone; Dr. Weidler must have

helped you.' I said, 'Well, ask Dr. Weidler.' Dr. Weidler believed in African leadership. And he was surprised that I edited the minutes. And later on I was told that the missionaries commented that these minutes were done better than you did. But it is the belief that the African is not developed to take on the responsibility. And the responsibility that some of us took on were wrestled from them in a way.[90]

Both Mueller and Reeck became acquainted with and interviewed Moses Barley of Rotifunk, who had attended the United Brethren school in the 1890s, but had gone on to become a farmer. Through Barley we can get a glimpse of how the missionaries were perceived by individuals who did not join the modern sector:

> *Mueller:* Did the missionaries treat Africans as their equal?
> *Barley:* We looked upon them as superior people. There was that complex upon the white man. So the white man does not keep very close to the black man. The missionary—they are good to people. They teach them. They do good to them. But they live up in the mission house. And seldom people go to him. It is only the teachers and mission workers that sometimes speak unto them with their complaints. They did not treat the black man as their equal, despite their coming with the Bible. Because I was talking to Pa Schutz one day. He told me that he knew the black man. I said, 'Dr. Schutz, you don't know the black man. It is only the black man that can tell me that he knows the white man. And it is for this reason. You come here and go to your mission house there. All you know is what you are told. You do not go to the farms. You do not go to people when they are dancing. You do not go to their houses; you stay at home. But when the black man goes to America, no sooner he landed than he began to live like the white man. He knows the white man.'
> *Mueller:* What did Pa Schutz say?
> *Barley:* He said, 'it is true.'

While the official policy of the church and the mission was the eventual establishment of a self-governing church, the reluctance of the missionaries to cede authority to Africans in the 1920s and 30s was motivated at least in part by their racism. An African pastor recalls a remark by Charles Leader which strikingly reveals one missionary's aversion to the very idea of an African having authority: "He said that whenever he saw an African pastor in a preacher's gown it took the spirit from him."[91] African pastors and teachers did have a place in the United Brethren hierarchy—at the bottom. The broad outlines of mission policy were determined by the mission board in the U.S., but the application of those policies and administrative decisions were the responsibility of the missionaries in each location, who met as the Mission Council. But the Mission Council had to present its recommendations for ratification by the church Conference, and this latter included the African pastors and a small number of African laymen. In meetings of the Conference, Africans and missionaries always sat apart.[92] In the 1920s the Conference usually approved the council's recommendations without opposition. But in the 1930s, the number of Africans in the Conference grew to equal the number of missionaries, and the "pastors began to challenge certain policies." The pastors were also cognizant of the clear disagreement among missionaries, even as early as the 20s and 30s, over how much power and autonomy the African pastors should be granted. Musselman (along with H.H. Thomas) consistently supported steps toward a greater Africanization of the church—the policy Musselman explicitly reminds Mignerey of in his letter. Charles Leader, who became missionary-in-charge at Taiama in 1925 and Walter Schutz, who replaced Mignerey at Rotifunk, were consistently opposed to these steps. The difficulty with which even small steps toward greater African self-governance were taken between 1925 and 1930 represents another clear example of the missionaries' deep reluctance to cede any authority.

Through interviews and the perusal of church records, Mueller has carefully pieced together the history of an incident in 1930 in which this conflict came to a head. In 1925 the General Conference of the church in the U.S. provided for the creation of an "Administrative Committee" in each mission Conference. The majority of the members were to be appointed by the Mission Council (which is to say, by the missionaries), but a minority would be elected by the conference (which included Africans). The duties of the "administrative committee" would be "to interpret the needs of the field to the Board [i.e. The Board of Missions in the U.S.], and to administer the funds contributed by the Board."[93] In other words, there was now a possibility of the creation of a new committee with some real power, some of whose members would be elected by a conference which included some Africans. This provision was published in the book of rules and regulations known as the *Discipline*. The missionaries in Sierra Leone ignored even this limited proposal for five years. Finally, in 1930, the African pastors S.M. Renner and J.K. Ferguson interrupted the annual conference in a rather dramatic way, pointing out that the meeting was not being run according to the *Discipline*. As Renner later explained to Mueller:

> We didn't know of the *Discipline* until one or two of us found the *Discipline* on the missionaries' table. And we ordered them out and studied the *Discipline*. They didn't run this church in accordance with [the] *Discipline*. I recall the first time we quoted from the *Discipline*. The chairman said, "what book is that you are quoting from?" We said the *Discipline* of the UBC Church. And the missionaries all looked up like that.[94]

On another occasion Renner recalls the story a little differently: the pastors interrupted the meeting to point out that it was not being run according to the *Discipline*, and the superintendent (at the time, Charles Leader) did not even have a copy and had to send to the mission house to get one. But in any event, as a result, the administrative committee provided for in the *Discipline* was established.

Renner had been questioning the missionaries for some time, and had as a result been transferred to a less desirable post. According to Mueller, "many pastors, particularly the Creoles who were more aggressive on this issue, were appointed to less desirable stations as punishment for questioning the missionaries assumption of superiority. E.K. Ferguson remarked that missionaries attempted to make any pastor who opposed them 'unhappy in their work.' He continued, 'you were bound to agree with all they said and did. Woe to you if you did not!'" [95] Even though, by 1932, the African pastors were in a majority at the conference, they nevertheless took action to oppose the missionaries only rarely.

Mueller identifies several reasons for this reluctance, including: the possibility of reprisals from the missionaries (who still controlled all appointments) such as the ones taken against Renner; the fact that the church in Sierra Leone was still financially dependent on the church in the U.S.; and the fact that the pastors genuinely admired the missionaries and were grateful for the educational and financial support they had individually received. Most of all, the pastors had a sense of shared engagement in a common cause with the missionaries. That shared engagement, in the pastors' eyes, overshadowed the missionaries' prejudice and ignorance. As Rev. David Shodeke put it: "We felt we were doing God's work and the more we moved together the better we would be able to attain it. There was not this kind of feeling that people were against us."[96] When challenges were made, it was generally by the younger pastors, such as Shodeke. When older pastors chose to exercise a restraining influence they could count upon immediate acceptance, in accord with the African tradition of respect for elders. One such case occurred in the conference of 1932, at which the missionaries proposed a ten percent wage cut for mission personnel in the face of funding reductions due to the depression. The missionaries had privately decided to cut their own wages by only five percent. However, the African pastors had gotten wind of this decision and called the missionaries to account for it at the conference meeting, sparking an acrimonious debate. But the debate was brought to an abrupt end when an elder pastor (T.B. Williams), who had been sitting quietly until then, arose to say "hard times make men think," and concluded his speech with the admonition to "accept a ten percent reduction and go back to our stations and increase local support."[97] The pastors accepted the ten percent. The missionaries' eventual pay cut was never disclosed. But the pastors had succeeded in painfully embarrassing the missionaries—Shodeke recalls that Musselman had gotten red in the face.

Another unusual instance in which the African pastors took action against the missionaries occurred at the Annual Conference Meeting of 1935. Charles Leader had at this point been a missionary in Sierra Leone for ten years. The pastors' resentment especially of his readiness to summarily dismiss any teacher accused of polygamy had grown to the point that they could no longer abide the injustice. As David Shodeke explains,

> We were just tired of him. This man was so blind to native traditions, native customs, native life. He was a good organizer; we must give the devil his due. He wanted to build Taiama from the decadence of the 1898 war. And to say truth he really built up Taiama to what it is today. But in my opinion he just found pleasure in picking holes here and there. You just have to inform Mr. Leader of any misdemeanor of anybody. He didn't take time to investigate. He was prosecutor general! It came to the place where everybody got fed up with him.[98]

The pastors' retaliation was essentially symbolic, and its message made a painful emotional impact upon the missionaries. As Renner recalls:

> a few of us got together and decided to elect him secretary of the Conference. (laughter) I suppose he held it against me to the day of his death. (laughter) .... All along an African had been Conference Secretary. We decided to vote Dr. Leader as Secretary of the Conference. And almost unanimously the vote was for

Leader to be secretary. [At this point, Leader's wife burst into tears.] That took the missionaries. They almost resigned! They thought it was a humiliation of him to be elected as the Secretary of the Conference. (laughter) And when he read the minutes the next day, we almost took one hour to correct his minutes. (laughter) We almost took one hour to correct his minutes! We corrected his statements; we corrected his grammar. He almost resigned. So if you are talking about getting organized into a bloc that was one time when we felt that this man should feel that we too could take some action.[99]

But in considering this turn of events, we should bear in mind that the pastors' action was unusual, and that in their minds Leader was also unusual. On the whole, as Shodeke put it, "There was not this kind of feeling that people were against us." Leader's behavior, though in pursuit of explicit mission policy, was exceptional enough to drive a group of pastors strongly disinclined to rock the boat to publicly humiliate him.

Albert Academy, April 1923–May 1924: "If I Had Any Color Feeling I wouldn't Be in Africa"

Despite the difficulties Mignerey faced, he must have made a good impression upon the Sierra Leone U.B. mission hierarchy, for in March, 1923, he was appointed principal of the Albert Academy in Freetown, with his service to begin in April of that year. He served in that capacity until his term of foreign service ended in May, 1924. In retrospect, the Albert Academy might well be the most important single permanent contribution the United Brethren made to Sierra Leone. The United Brethren opened the Albert Academy in Freetown in 1905. The Albert Academy was only the sixth secondary school to be established anywhere in the Colony or the Protectorate, and it was the first United Brethren secondary school.[100] Enrollment started at 46, grew to a high of 173 in 1908, and fluctuated between a low of 63 and a high of 173 between then and 1924. In the subsequent decade enrollment fluctuated between a high of 134 and a low of 86.[101] In addition, only four students graduated in 1910. The fluctuating enrollment and initially low graduation rates were probably due to the fact that many of the boys left school early to find work .[102] But despite these difficulties, it is clear that from the beginning the Albert Academy set and adhered to a high standard, comparable to schools in Britain and the United States. The United Brethren administration established and adhered to a rigorous graded curriculum. Students were offered four courses of study: classical, scientific, biblical (for future preachers), and normal (for future teachers). At the time, "the courses listed for the other secondary schools were entirely classical and contained no science....The teaching of science was a complete innovation in Sierra Leone, and the Academy was a pioneer in this field."[103]

The early success of the Academy received official recognition from the Government. The Director of Education in 1919 was willing to make the following statement:

I wish to congratulate the School Authorities on the progress shown. Basing my hopes on what I have now seen I anticipate from the Albert Academy as high a standard as that set by our Secondary Schools in England and Scotland. I do not mention the U.S.A. as my knowledge of that great country is purely theoreti-cal.[104]

The Director's awkward aside about the United States is not surprising, given that there was a certain degree of tension between the United Brethren and British educational policies. This tension was even evident in the speech given by the Governor of Sierra Leone publicly opening the school in 1905. Sir Leslie Probyn openly expressed regret that Albert Academy had been established in Freetown rather than in the Protectorate. This embarrassing proclamation motivated J.R. King, the United Brethren Conference Superintendent, to respond with an extended defense of the Church's decision in *The Sierra Leone Weekly News*. King drew attention to the practical consideration of the central location of Freetown and the value of bringing boys from various ethnic groups together. In addition King insisted that

> we believe that our young men will be able to take in more culture by their contact with the civilization of Freetown. To be sure, some contend that there are phases of life here that are not desirable: but what city or country can boast that this is not true? Education is intended to lead the individual out of his own self to another and better self. Men travel to let the influence of a new environment broaden their lives.[105]

Albert Academy was set up as the capstone of an educational system whose feeder schools were in the Protectorate. But the Government was to a certain extent uncomfortable with the idea of the influence of a new environment broadening the lives of the Protectorate peoples. The issue of education illuminates one of the many contradictions in the British colonial policy of indirect rule. On the one hand the Government needed literate Africans who could participate in British institutions. But on the other, the British wished to preserve traditional African institutions and rule through them, and they disliked the way education tended to loosen the hold of traditional authority.

When the British set up their own secondary school at Bo in 1906, it was on a very different plan from that of Albert Academy. First of all the school was deliberately located in the Protectorate rather than in Freetown. Admission was reserved almost exclusively to sons of chiefs, and the school's official policy was to strengthen the ethnic identities of the boys rather than to forge national consciousness.[106] Corby clearly sums up the central aim of this policy: "Sir Leslie Probyn, governor from 1904–1911, was particularly eager to educate future chiefs who would effectively mesh themselves into the British administration's policies at the chiefdom level, thus providing for a continuity of the established elite."[107] The United Brethren had no particular interest in this aim. The goals of the church included training its own teachers and preachers as well as its idealistic goal of simply bringing what it regarded as the best of Christian civilization to Africans. Albert Academy also distinguished itself from other schools in the substantial program of manual training included in its curriculum. Even the government recognized the appropriateness of such a program especially in a predominantly agricultural country. But such was the hold of the traditional British system of classical education that these remained isolated efforts.

Laying of Cornerstone of Albert Academy: J.R. King is upper left next to Acting Governor G.B. Haddon-Smith in a top hat, Zella King is standing on the other side of Haddon-Smith; upper right are at least two pastors, T.B. Williams and A.T. Sumner; lower right and left are probably teachers

Over the course of the twentieth century, the Albert Academy played a crucial role in educating Sierra Leone's leaders. Rosselot sums up the impact of the academy had by 1935 upon a wide range of institutions, including the church itself:

> A study of the appointments of mission workers reported at the Conference of 1935 reveals the fact that of the 150 males assigned work, 80 teachers and 6 pastors were graduates of the Academy, and 8 other teachers had spent some time in the Academy. Thus out of a total of 150 male workers, 94, or approximately two-thirds, were furnished by this institution. But this is only a part of its contribution. Alumni of the school are to be found in medicine, law, science, education (the present African Assistant Director of Education of the Colony is a graduate of the Academy), colonial government service, both in Sierra Leone and other colonies, marine engineering, His Majesty's customs, Post Office, Medical Department, the Secretariat, Harbor Master's office, Government Treasury, Crown Law Office, Police Department, Public Works Department, and also in many of the European firms.[108]

A disproportionate number of the political leaders who emerged in Sierra Leone in the twentieth century had roots in the United Brethren Church and mission schools. The two most prominent graduates of the Academy are the first and third presidents of independent Sierra Leone: Milton Margai (1911-1914[109]) and Siaka Stevens (Jan. 1916-Dec. 1922[110]). Margai and Paramount Chief Julius Gulama (also an Albert Academy graduate), were the two most important leaders of the Protectorate Assembly which was formed in 1945.[111] Others include Doyle Sumner who became minister of education and John Karefa-Smart who was appointed minister of external affairs in 1960. The pastors and teachers I have quoted—David Shodeke, E.K. Ferguson, J.K. Ferguson, S.M. Renner— are all graduates of the Academy. Renner was Chief Gulama's pastor, close friend, and political as well as spiritual advisor, and Gulama was always a strong supporter of the United Brethren Church.[112] (Gulama was, by the way, certainly no exception when it came to polygamy. However, neither Renner nor Shodeke nor Musselman, nor, apparently, for that matter, any other minister ever refused him communion—even though Renner confronted him about his polygamy.) One of Mueller's informants suggested that one reason for the disproportionate representation of United Brethren in Sierra Leone's political leadership was that the Church in effect provided a space and a network for political activity not otherwise available. Rev. Eustace Renner reported that "the idea of the SLPP, of a united Sierra Leone, originated in the parsonage at Moyamba. It was the only neutral and unsuspected ground. This was true because Dr. Renner had rapport with all the leaders. And he was looked upon as spiritual advisor to these various leaders. So out of this came the Protectorate Assembly."[113] The Sierra Leone Peoples Party (SLPP) was founded in 1951, with Milton Margai as its leader.

Mignerey's role as principal of Albert Academy was a clearly defined and important one. As the chief administrator of a school which (in his assessment) was comparable to the best American high schools, he seems to have carried out his duties with a high degree of competence, fairness, energy, and imagination. In many ways, this was his first really professional job, and his diary presents an interesting picture of a highly motivated, idealistic and open minded individual gaining practical wisdom and learning from his mistakes in a position of responsibility. The only other missionaries at the Academy were A.S. Nichols, W.N. Martin, and G.M. Richter, all of whom evidently worked in the Academy shop, Martin serving as shop director. The academy employed nine African teachers (known as "tutors") who made up the rest of the academic staff. They included three Krios, two Sherbros, one Mende, and one Temne. Two weeks into his work at the Academy, Mignerey expresses a great deal of satisfaction at finally

Original Albert Academy Building

being given a job with substantial, clearly defined responsibilities and concrete goals:

> The work here is the thing. I have an office all my own, and regular office hours. I teach one class in English Junior. I keep about 150 accounts by the double entry system of book keeping. The Administrative work of a school system of this size is no small task, and makes no small demand upon wisdom and energy.
>
> But what of that? Altogether, this is a real job, and the most satisfactory that I have had out here. Perhaps two weeks is too early to form a right judgment, but I think not. I have had already some triumphs and some sorrows of the work. The first have been more or less accidental blunders, and the few sorrows have come from my ignorance of the system here in all of its details.

At the close of the term, he sums up his reflections on his new role as an administrator. While he clearly respects and relies upon the tutors, and is strongly committed to backing them up in conflicts with students, the note of paternalism does not fail to make itself heard again here just as so often before:

> My own energies have been directed largely toward management of men and boys here at the Academy. I have much to learn, and feel that I must be doubly alert because of a lack of any special training in business management. The greatest factor is undoubtedly the human factor. And the strength of the organization must depend upon the willing, enthusiastic support given the principal by the teaching staff and by the students. The Staff had been my first concern. I look upon them as the men upon whom I must depend for the carrying out of details of the school program. In time I expect to have their full confidence, and to have them well disciplined in working my program for the school. This, too, is a matter of personal contact, and cannot be attained merely by writing a circular letter. I am told that Embree sided generally with the students in disputes with the teachers. My own policy has been to stand by the tutors whenever they are right, and to expect every boy to obey without question. "Do what you are told, and talk about it later, if necessary," is the rule of discipline. The tutors have made blunders—they are like children themselves sometimes—but generally they deserve the backing of the principal. When students learn this there will be less palavering with the teachers. They will know that obedience is the first law of the school. I am a little old fashioned in this, perhaps, but it is a sound conviction. Willing obedience to the Higher Laws is a quality of character that might well prove one's salvation throughout life. I have no complaints against the tutors. Unwittingly they are teaching me how to manage them.

Mignerey was evidently much busier at Albert Academy than at Rotifunk, so his work-related diary entries are not as extensive. His new concerns included the birth of his first child (Elinor) on August 28, 1923: "We are three and our joy has trebled." Many pages follow on the experiences of a new father.

He does record however, one unusual incident regarding a mentally disturbed student:

> This case goes down in my mental notes as the case of William Lamin. Last night about midnight, Ruth and I were awakened by loud talking in the room above us—one of the dormitories for the boys. The voice was loud, guttural, des-

perate. There was a sound of scuffling, and a terrific smash, as of a window broken. Then a scramble of boys along the hall. More of the loud angry yelling.

I got into my bathrobe, lighted a lamp and hurried thru the classroom next our upstairs hall. I reached the school hallway on the second floor and mounted the steps to the third story. The dormitory room in question presented a wild scene. Tutors Daugherty and Williams were holding one of the boys tight to the bed. He was yelling, twisting and jerking to get up. His eyes were wild. Splintered glass was scattered over the floor. The boys said he had thrown a bottle against the wall.

The boy's convulsions soon ceased and he became limp as a rag. I then learned from the boys and the tutors that this boy had aroused them by his loud talking, as tho quarreling with someone. That he had seized the bottle and hurled it across the room against the wall. That he had climbed to the window and was going out on his head when the tutors arrived and caught him by the heels.

The boy's eyes opened presently and he seemed to be in a daze, but answered questions intelligently. He knew me. I thought he had had a bad nightmare and was over it, when suddenly his eyes popped open again, he yelled a hoarse unearthly yell and climbed over me to the window again. It was done like a flash. I couldn't stop him but I grabbed his legs with my arms and held tight. His head and arms were out over the window. The tutors pulled him back and he went on screaming disconnected words and phrases the drift of which seemed to be, "I'll not go with you! Let me alone! No! No! I will not!" And a great deal of unadulterated profanity.

We held him down again until he relaxed and quieted. Then the boys began to whisper strange things about this boy being "called" by a ghost. It seems that he had approached one of the boys on the evening before this, telling him that someone was down by one of the big cottonwood trees in the front yard calling and calling him. The two boys went down there but there was nothing there. All evening, it appears, this boy, William Lamin, had talked fearfully of hearing this calling down by the cottonwood.

Later in the night we moved him to another bed, away from the window. During one of his quiet spells, he related to us what had happened: "I came awake during the night," he said in substance, "and saw a little dog running around the room. I watched it come up to my bed—it was about this high. Then I looked up and saw a white woman there. She was vexed with me and asked me to give her a ring or one thousand pounds. I told her I would not and to get out. She said, 'All right if you don't, you'll go with me.' She came toward me with a chain and I picked up a big stone and threw it at her. It missed her, though, and she put the chain around my neck and dragged me through the window. I couldn't help it at all—she just pulled me along. I held back all my best but—Look there she is again!"

Crash! Lamin was out of bed and dashing for the window again. We stopped him and brought him back to bed where he went through another spasm.

There was more to this than a nightmare and so I sent for the school doctor. He had a maternity case and could not come. He sent two dope pills (I had written him the symptoms of the case) and we got these down Lamin during one of his quiet periods after I had tied him to the bed. Teacher Williams and I stayed with him until early this morning. He aroused from the dope sleep after Dr. Pratt had come and gone. The boy appeared not to have remembered a thing that had happened, neither the "calling" of the previous evening nor the struggle during the night. This morning he told me that he had had four such periods of sickness while in school at Cape Mount Liberia. Dr. Pratt told me the boy was mentally unbalanced and should be sent home at once. I made arrangements for him to go this afternoon.

This is a revelation to me of the native way of accounting for the actions of an insane person. With them, it is some mysterious, magical, ghostly influence from the spirit world. They see and believe the fancy caused by a wandering mind without recognizing the trouble that gives rise to the fancy. I see by the records, that Lamin is a new boy admitted during the last term by Mr. Embree. Yet this slight acquaintance with him made no difference to the boys. They accepted the "calling" story as gospel truth. In emergencies like this the "black" comes out, in spite of their years of Christian Schooling. They can not understand a religion without superstitions attached. This probably accounts for the early grafting of pagan superstitions to the teachings of the Master until they have been distorted far from their real meaning.

Mignerey also records some of the conflicts that arose in his relations with the missionary staff at the Academy. One of the problems he faced was a flaw in the Academy's administrative structure. The Director of Manual training (as Rosselot reports in his 1936 Master's Thesis in Education from the University of Chicago on UBC mission schools in Sierra Leone) "had practically complete control over his department," including control over a separate budget:

> The principal of the school has practically no authority over or responsibility for the department as the organization now stands. The Director sets the wages for the boys, completely controls them during the hours they are in his department, and his consent must be given before these self-help boys can leave for their vacation periods. This sets up a dual authority in the school which often creates difficult problems in administration, and which should be very carefully studied by the higher authorities of the mission.[114]

Rosselot himself served as principal from 1928–1934, and was clearly describing problems that both he and Mignerey had to grapple with. Mignerey records his successful resolution of a conflict with the shop personnel regarding boys who participated in the Academy's "self-help" scheme by working in the Academy shop to cover their school fees. They were not paid their first year, but their pay was increased each year as their skills improved.[115] These boys were required to work four hours a day and a conflict arose when the shop director required overtime work without notifying the principal. Mignerey worked out an agreement with Nichols and Richter that boys could be required to work overtime when needed in emergencies, but that the principal was to be notified on such occasions.

His work at the academy also brought him into contact with African pastors through the Ministerial Institute class the church conducted at the Academy during July. Participation in the institute was a requirement for ordination. Mignerey taught a class in psychology, using a text by Angell, to fourth year students in the institute. The participants included S.M. Renner and Max Gorvie, who were to go on to become prominent pastors in the United Brethren Church in Sierra Leone. Mignerey's description of the class is remarkably positive and fair minded, but again is not without its note of condescension:

Teaching the class was a pure delight and it was only with difficulty that we confined our class discussions to one hour's time. Rev. Syl M. Renner, and Rev. Max Gorvie were the best in the class and did remarkably well on the theme and examination work. Rev. Seymore Wilson came next. He was interested and worked faithfully but was an older man with less experience in school than the other two and did not grasp the material quite so readily. Rev. H.M. Kessebeh failed to do satisfactory work. His mind was elsewhere and he scratched through his work without preparation and by such attempts at bluffing and side-tracking the discussions that I had to adopt a policy of ignoring him. If a mature man did not care enough to work on his lessons, no amount of bull-dozing would have been in place. He failed and was sore about it. Many of them must learn yet to *work* for what they get.

The class, tho small, was different in no respect from a mature class at home.

Some bright, interested, laborious. Others dull, studious, plodding. Others lazy, bluffers, evaders, depending on their wits and favoritism for passing credits. Renner has told me since that our class discussions opened his eyes as nothing else ever had to the development of his own child. He says that he finds himself studying his child from a psychological standpoint— a thing he never did before.

In Rotifunk, Mignerey had been confronted with some accusations of racism. But he found those accusations easy to dismiss, coming as they did from an individual engaged in selling alcoholic beverages on the sly. The accusation of racism he finally faced in Freetown was a very public matter, displayed in the Freetown press. And while he found this accusation also easy to dismiss, it was most likely one which would later give him pause.

The story of this "palaver" began with the Academy's plans to sell some furniture built by students in the Academy shop. Nichols arranged for an exhibit of Academy work at a shop in Freetown, Patterson and Zachonis. The exhibit included "chairs, desks, tables, trays, and a cabinet victrola." Mignerey had already initiated a publication for the school which came to be called *The Academy News* and would include writing from English classes as well as news of the Academy. The Academy produced an issue devoted to Academy wood work, "and several hundred copies were taken over to the city several days before the exhibit." The exhibit was a resounding success. "He [Nichols] and the boys were there all day and crowds kept coming and going until evening." But Mignerey was surprised to discover that something about the special issue of the *Academy News* had stirred up controversy.

> One original feature of this edition was a half page cartoon. It showed a comic white man with cap on his head and pipe in his mouth asking a comic negro running at full speed where he was going. The reply was to the effect that he was going to the Albert Academy Exhibit at P.Z's. Nichols got up the picture and I stenciled it for the mimeograph. I ran off the cartoons on this machine and then had the sheets run thru the press in the Academy Print Shop for the regular reading matter. The result was enough to make them wonder how we were doing original cartooning up here. Some of the print shops haven't much love for the Academy Press because of our superior quality of work, and because the boys are taught the process of roller making. The other shops had been guarding this as a trade secret, and without the process a press can not operate for long. The rollers go bad in this climate very quickly.

The strange outcome of our innocent cartoon, however, was a palaver.

A one-sided palaver, because we refused to take part in it. A man by the name of Edmundson, principal of a so called technical school here, protested against the publication of the cartoon. He wrote to Musselman and broke into print in the local papers, saying that this cartoon was a slur on the black people, that it was making light of them, and holding them up to ridicule. Edmundson himself is a black man, but not a native of this country. He said that we missionaries, himself included, had come to help the black man, not to make him a laughing stock.

I can only surmise what his purposes were in launching this attack. I am of the opinion that it was to counteract the good impression made by the exhibit. The "technical" school attempts work of this sort, but can not come up to it in any way. He may have wished, too, to drag the Academy into one of these newspaper controversies with which the local press occupies itself most of the time. The contending parties compete in the use of vile adjectives regarding each other, they go on writing these mud-slinging letters to each other thru the papers, much to the amusement of the general public. It is better than a dog-fight. Usually the government or the editor or some friend with the proper pull has the controversy choked off. And the newspaper space is soon occupied with another one with variations to suit.

Time spent in such controversy is time worse than wasted. I calmed our own uneasy Academy staff by telling them that my policy in this case was not to stoop to such a palaver, but to ignore Edmundson entirely. The staff had passed upon the cartoon before it was printed, had laughed, and had declared it suitable—and they were all native Africans. Our motives in publishing the cartoon were without

SOURI GOES TO THE EXHIBIT.

Mignerey and Nichols' cartoon in the *Academy News*

blemish, and it was our policy to steer a straight course ahead. The fact that a man like Edmundson had taken up the matter was an evidence to me that there was something in the work of the Academy that aroused his jealousy. Let us pity him, work on as before, and let our work stand upon its own quality. The staff agreed and the matter ignored as far as the school was concerned. Mr. Renner told me that he knew of an article being submitted for publication that attacked the Academy bitterly, and that he himself had seen the editor and had the article suppressed.

It is an established fact that a certain element of blacks here want their own race to have the upper hand in everything African. This is true of government, education, and church. Marcus Garvey's influence is lurking beneath many a black heart here, even tho the government has suppressed his propaganda. This element here does not hesitate to attack the government. But the government does not worry. Not long ago they commenced an attack upon Mr. Denton, Secretary of the Church Missionary Society's activities here, a veteran Englishman, cultured and of long experience in affairs of the Colony. I learned from Musselman that they kept up such a barrage of mud-slinging that Mr. Denton's nerves were almost a wreck, when suddenly the whole thing stopped abruptly, and it leaked out that the Governor had put a stop to the whole mess.

Edmundson's letter was left with Mr. Richter who wrote a reply, pointing out that no harm was meant by the cartoon, that the black man in the picture was caricatured no more that the white man, and that Nichols and I, being new to the work in West Africa, did not anticipate the evil impression that this might make, etc., etc. I wished Richter had kept out of it. He cuts everybody the wrong way out here, missionaries and blacks alike, and I feared his reply would only encourage a continuation of the palaver. He sent me a copy of his letter, and I advised, after his explanation, a complete ignoring of Edmundson's attempts to get us away from our real work and entangled in controversy. That was the end of it. I do not feel that it was a coward's trick to handle it as we did. It was not a matter of running away from the issue. It was going ahead, with us, as though no attack had been made. It would have been easier to write some short snappy letters about Edmundson to the press. I can use some cutting adjectives if I choose. I can grow sarcastic to the extreme. But to what end? A handful of withered grass! A little publicity, to be sure, but of a sort that I do not care to stoop to do.

I have gone into detail because this incident strikes me as a revelation of this elusive thing called the 'African mind,' 'African psychology,' 'The African point of view.'

Toward the end of the school year of 1923, it became known, and Mignerey heard, that the British governor had been displeased with the past year's graduation ceremony. This set Mignerey thinking, and he woke up early the next morning and furiously wrote out his conception of an allegorical play to be enacted by the students in the coming graduation. When he typed up the first scene and circulated it among the African tutors at Albert Academy, he was quite surprised by their reaction:

The first scene, as originally written, caused a great deal of discussion among the tutors, to whom I submitted a copy for criticism. They were at first a little backward, but I encouraged them, that I might get the "African viewpoint," and so be able to change the pageant as much as possible to conform to it.

My idea had made the play African, with the thot of having it make a personal appeal to the black people. I showed the people in chains of superstition, suffering, and ignorance, until their release and freedom came thru Christian Education. It was the universal opinion of the teachers that the people would resent the scenes showing the people in a "bad light." The teachers themselves, of course, did not like it. They did not seem to be willing to admit—or even to recognize—the past and present condition of the masses of people. Some of them knew less of conditions fifty miles up-country than I! This was true especially of the Creole, Mr. Forde, B.A. I found them all ignorant of social conditions of Africa as a whole. I mean they knew even less than I about their own country, and I know little enough. From all of which it was easily seen that they were of the opinion that they were just as much civilized as any other people on earth.

I respected their feelings in the matter and deliberately set about to butcher this pet child of my brain. I was tempted at first to give up the whole idea of a pageant, but the teachers insisted on going on with it. They like the general idea, even tho it was a new one to them. Our cooperation was practically perfect, once I got them to discuss their own viewpoint candidly. I did this with them individually and in group staff meetings. I put the matter to them this way at one time in our discussions: We are showing two pictures. One of the people in chains. Another of the people freeing themselves by their own effort in Christian Education. This seems to me to be the highest compliment that can be paid to any people. Which impression do you think the people who attend the Commencement will carry away with them: Africa in chains, or Africa liberated?

The teachers agreed at once that the people would remember the Africa in chains and would deeply resent it, and that while in this mood, the scenes of liberation would make little or no impression for good.

The redraft of the first scene bears little resemblance to the original Mss., which I am keeping as material for a psychological study. The revised Mss. seemed to please them immensely, and I was satisfied that what would please them would please the people, too. In its final form, the local application was changed to a generalization: not Africa in chains of Ignorance, but the whole of Mankind, and Albert Academy doing her part with other Christian Schools of the world in freeing man from Ignorance.

He made some effort to feel out the reactions of the teachers, both individually and in groups. When he suggested giving up the idea of a pageant, the teachers insisted they liked the idea and wanted to go ahead with it. They worked closely together and produced a new version that was apparently satisfactory for all.

The original version of the first scene of the pageant presents a remarkable picture of the ethnocentric viewpoint Mignerey had absorbed through his American upbringing and education. The lines given the character "Ignorance" make it clear that ignorance is to be simply equated with indigenous African culture. The scene depicts the contention of "Ignorance" or "the spirit of Ignorance" with "Education" (also referred to as "the Spirit of Christian Education") for control of the destiny of "Africa" or "the Spirit of Africa." In passages which Mignerey has crossed out on the typescript, apparently in response to the criticism he received, Ignorance is given lines such as these:

> In years gone by I have told the people to fight and go to savage warfare. They steal through the bush. They mangle and torture and kill their own black brothers.

Some they eat. Some they bury head downward in the earth. I put a nameless fear in the hearts of the people. I bring horrible diseases to rot their bones and bring them down to early graves in pain and sorrow.

And then, specifically referring to practices in indigenous religion:

I have told them that some imp has brought these things upon them, and that they must wear some powerful charm to drive their pain away. They do not know that it is I myself, the Devil of Ignorance who brings these things upon them.

The above passages were completely cut. Mignerey made numerous smaller deletions—but the essential thing is that he changed the character "the Spirit of Africa" to "the Spirit of Man." Nevertheless, the near-final typescript and the printed version still bear traces of the original intent. "Ignorance" still is implicitly identified with traditional African religion:

AFRICA [*"MAN" substituted*]—But with all that he [i.e. Ignorance] does, he cannot blot out that knowledge of the divine with which I was born.
    IGNORANCE—I can distort it. Much of my wisdom is distorted truth. I can keep you from knowing more about this deity of whom you talk, as though he were more powerful than I. Have I not given you images of wood and stone? Have I not peopled this country with devils which I have taught your people to fear more than your deity Himself?[*replaced by: "Have I not taught your people to fear devils more than your deity Himself?"*] I have made you helpless. Your doom is sealed.

Mignerey also deleted the following line he gave to "Ignorance": "Remember that I have dulled their [i.e. the Africans'] minds by centuries of evil customs and vicious habits."

By changing the character "Africa" to the character "Man," Mignerey does completely change the significance of a passage such as the following:

EDUCATION—spirit of Africa[*Man*], how long have you been bound?
    AFRICA[*MAN*] —For thousands and thousands of years.
    EDUCATION—How came you to be bound?
    AFRICA[*MAN*]—I do not know. My bondage began in the long, long ago before men began to[*could*] reckon time. Once in the power of Ignorance, he locked these chains upon me. He dragged me from sight of my African[*the*] people, and to this day few of them know that I still live. Fewer of them have seen me. This lying villain has made them think that I am gone forever.

Mignerey's original version both portrays Africa in extremely negative terms, and also identifies traditional African culture with ignorance. Mostly by changing "Africa" to "Man" throughout the play, Mignerey ostensibly eliminates the implicit theme that Africa has a special problem with ignorance not shared by the rest of mankind, and that Western civilization in the form of Christian Education represents its only salvation. In a later portion of the printed version of the play, (which came to be titled *Progress*) the following lines appear, further working against any implicit identification of Africa with ignorance and Western civilization with its opposite:

IGNORANCE— (*Slowly and Impressively*) —the poison in this knife is discord, jealousy, suspicion and hate. I have caused even so-called Christian nations to forget their Christian principles. I have easily lead them into wars that have shaken the foundations of the earth and left ten million men bleeding and dying in the field of battle. What have you to say to that?
(EDUCATION HANGS HIS HEAD AND IS SILENT)
You are silent?
EDUCATION—For shame! This once you speak the truth. You have brought untold misery in the world with your poison jealousy and suspicion.
IGNORANCE—I have even injured you.
EDUCATION—You have.

It is worth recalling that Mignerey had direct personal experience of trench warfare in France in World War One. This was certainly an experience that lead him and many others of his time to deeply question the satisfaction that the older generation took in the glorious destiny of Western civilization. Perhaps the shame that "Education" expresses in this passage reflects a little of the experience Mignerey had of the teachers' reaction to his original play. Perhaps he is beginning to question the unqualified right Western nations assumed they had to be the reformers of Africa.

Mignerey threw himself into the planning of the pageant in the closing days of the term—putting himself under a tremendous strain, since his responsibilities as principal were very substantial, and even more so at the end of the academic year.

This work of writing, typing, discussing, redrafting, retyping has taken my time and energy to an alarming extent during the last few weeks. It has meant much working at night. I have managed to keep one scene ahead of them. As they committed and rehearsed one scene, I prepared the next. I made six copies of the typewritten Mss. One copy each for myself and the four leading characters, and one copy to be cut for the minor characters.

Except for the four leading parts the lines are few for the other characters, and have been committed over night. The most difficult part of all, the Demon of Ignorance, I gave to Tutor Lewis-Taylor. It demands more real acting than the others. The Spirit of Christian Education I gave to Tutor [A.T.] Sumner. The spirit of Mankind I gave to one of the Senior Boys, Thomas Milton, and the part of Every student to another Senior Boy, A.R. King. I coached the rehearsals, and organized the teachers as assistants: Mr. Williams for the music, Mr. Kandeh for prompting and care of costumes, Mr. Daugherty and Mr. Forde in charge of the audience, and of the boys outside the building. We have rehearsed once a day, after 3:30 in the evening. The shop boys have come down at 4:00. All seem to be laboring with the impression that this is an experiment, something new under the Sierra Leone sun, and something that is likely to create a great deal of interest on the part of the people who attend Commencement.

In spite of the rush, as the year drew to an end, he took the time to invite the tutors and senior students to dinner with his family:

This last week of school we are having the teachers and the senior boys take dinner with us. We have invited them in by twos. I am wondering now why we have not done more of this sort of thing. It is a contact with them that is far more intimate and personal than any official relation in the school. It is in such unguarded moments as this that they see and learn some of the higher Christian standards of family life, and of a happy orderly home, one man and one woman.

The dress rehearsal, which had him quite worried, went off splendidly:

This evening (Wednesday) I arranged for the dress rehearsal of the Pageant. We invited the Mission House people up for the occasion and for chop after- wards. The Nichols were down, too.

Several friends of the tutors and of Mr. Renner were also in for the perform- ance which began shortly after four-thirty. I sat with the Richters and timed the play. I interrupted only a few times where necessary. I was interested more in the way in which the performance was received by the audience. All of our Mission people were warm in their appreciation, and seemed genuinely surprised at the extent of the play. The tutors seem delighted with it. I am satisfied, if they put the thing on as well next Friday as they did today. But I have my gravest fears. They are so unreliable that I half expect one or more of our important characters to turn up missing on Commencement day. This thought is enough to drive me mad, if I entertain it for long. I told Ruth the other day that I would not be greatly surprised if Tutor Lewis, in the part of Ignorance, should have a temperamental fit of some sort and fail to go on with the part. In that case I am prepared to don his costume and go on with the part. I have read and acted it on several occasions already, as I have the other leading parts, to show something of the way in which they should be interpreted.

In the dress rehearsal of today, however, Lewis did well. He made such an ef- fort to be dramatic that he over-emphasized his words. Many of them sounded "chewed," and altogether undistinguishable. I called him after the performance and coached him as diplomatically as I could on this point. Especially his pro- nunciation of the words defining his "poison knife" on which much of the story centers: "The poison in this knife is discord, envy, hate, jealousy, suspicion." He seemed to take my suggestions in a good spirit, and I am only trusting that he may put himself faithfully into it on Commencement Day.

The suspense is awful, and I have attempted to let everyone know how much I am depending on them to do their very best.

Mignerey was absolutely exhausted by the end of the term, and looked for- ward to a well-deserved rest:

It seems too that everything is piling up at the last minute these days. The fi- nal examinations have been in progress this week and the recording of grades, the making out of grade cards, honor certificates, and the settling of credit-palavers is in order. Occasionally I make a mistake in entering the credits, but more fre- quently the boys forget how many credits they had at the last term exams, and how many they have worked out in Backwork exams. And this means going mi- nutely into the records. I have had much of this to do and will have more before school is out.

I have scarcely had time to think of it, but I shall certainly welcome the relief that will come with a little rest after Commencement. I have tried to imagine this place quiet, and it seems too good to be true. To have it quiet, with no interruptions, no pa- lavers, no worries of boarding students by night or of day students by day. Just plain, pure, unadulterated silence! A few days more and I hope we shall have it!

The last entry for a long time in his diary expresses his relief over the success of the commencement program, the successful conclusion of the term, and at last a chance to rest:

> Welcome rest!
> Peace!
> Quiet!
> Solitude!
> What a flood of delight to possess them all, for a season at least!
> Commencement is gone these two days. Again the last wandering footsteps have departed on the long year end vacation in the native towns and villages.
> The great day and the great experiment of the Pageant came to a head about as planned. I tried to secure flags for decoration of the Assembly room. After trying the British military hospital and the Ordinance Department at the barracks on Tower Hill, I was finally directed to the Colonial Treasuries office, and wound up in the Assistant Colonial Secretary's office. This agreeable gentleman secured several large flags for me from the harbor master. The fact that the Governor was to be present at the Academy opened numerous doors that otherwise would have been closed.
> Tutors and boys spent Friday morning in scrubbing the hall, and decorating it beautifully with flags, bunting, palm leaves and flowers. The room was crowded with seats from the class rooms.

Mignerey remained principal at Albert Academy until May, when he returned to the United States, on what he thought would be a furlough. He had in fact become extremely ill. Doctors had recommended his return already in December. The last entries in the diary are a "postscript" and an epilogue, evidently made much later, perhaps at the time of his departure for home.

Postscript
> Diary ends at this break-off point. The tension at the Academy Commencement and the subsequent responsibilities postponed writing of further "notes"—until they were never written!
> The "new" commencement program was well received by all, warmly welcomed by some.
> Members of the Governor's staff who were present were: His Excellency, Alexander Remeford Slater, C.M.G., C.B.E. Governor of Sierra Leone; Mrs. Slater; Rt. Rev. G.W. Wright, D.D., bishop of Sierra Leone; Mr. V. Booevi, Print Secretary and A.D.C. to His Excellency; Mr. J.T. Finley, Colonial Secretary; Mr. F.C. Marriott, Director of Education; Mr. C. Mary, Mayor of Freetown; and others attending the annual Commencement Exercises of Albert Academy, Freetown, Sierra Leone, British West Africa.

Immediately following, Mignerey inserts an epilogue, in the form of a quotation from Rudyard Kipling. (The source is an operetta by Kipling and Wolcott Balestier called *The Naulahka: A Story of West and East*.) The stanza Mignerey quotes strikes a surprising note which is in marked contrast to the enthusiastic cry of "Africa for Jesus!" with which he began his endeavor:

Epilogue
> Now it's not good for the Christian's health

To hustle the Aryan Brown,
For the Christian riles and the Aryan smiles,
And he weareth the Christian down;
And the end of that fight is a tombstone white
With the name of the late deceased,
And the epitaph drear: "a fool lies here
Who tried to hustle the East."
                    —Kipling

Mignerey Reader of Blyden:
"Clearer Glimpses of Our Own Inconsistencies"

One of the most fascinating things about Mignerey's diary is that within his thinking, alongside the racist and ethnocentric view of Africa he seems to firmly hold, there are many signs of a very different view, or at least of the beginnings of a very different view. This different view is evident at times especially in some of the conclusions he reached in retrospect. He apparently planned to write a book about Africa that would draw upon his diary. And a very detailed outline of that book, followed by a short introduction, is among his papers. Also, the final chapter of the diary is a long, carefully prepared essay entitled "Does It Pay?" in which he makes a well-researched examination of what he considers to be the benefits of missions—and of British rule—to Sierra Leone. His conclusion that colonialism is an overall benefit is based upon: the unquestioned assumption that Africans do not have the resources to solve their own problems; the inaccurate and prejudiced understanding of African culture he gained in America, to which was possibly added a distorted understanding based on hearsay in Sierra Leone; and finally a questionable perception of the history of the interior of Sierra Leone in the nineteenth century.[116] This is what he has to say about the latter, in defense of British colonialism: "The political conditions among the tribes of Sierra Leone seventy-five years ago or less, are now a matter of history, the country then was in a continual uproar from tribal dispute.... The masses lived in terror and were helpless." But again, this acceptance of colonialism contrasts with, and perhaps even contradicts a number of other statements that he makes.

One of the most striking facts to emerge from Mignerey's book outline is his very high regard for Edward W. Blyden. Blyden was the most well known African-American spokesman of the late nineteenth and very early twentieth century. He was born in 1832 in St. Thomas, Virgin Islands. In 1847 he went to New York to enter college but was rejected because of his race. He emigrated to Liberia in 1850. He eventually became president of Liberia College and held various high posts in the Liberian government. He became internationally known both through diplomatic activities and through the publication of a great number of scholarly and informative articles about Africa. He traveled widely, but resided in Liberia until his death in 1912.

Blyden agreed with the race theory of the time to the extent that he believed that the races were essentially different. But he was one of the few voices strenuously insisting that the races are nevertheless equal, and that it is absurd to try to rank them. He believed that each race had its own unique contribution to make. His experience in Liberia convinced him that an African country could not be governed according to Western principles. He in effect asserted that Africans have   their own culture that in many ways is even superior to Western culture. He is also extremely unusual in that, while remaining a strongly convinced Christian, he developed a very deep appreciation and understanding of the Islamic faith. He learned Arabic, and became well versed in the Qur'an and other Arabic literature. In fact, he became at least as well known and respected in the Islamic world as he was in the Western world.

Blyden's evaluation of indigenous African culture was also unusual for his time. In his earlier essays, published in *Christianity, Islam, and the Negro Race* (1888), he had tended to disparage "pagan" African culture in favor of Islamic African culture and Christianity. However, in two later works, *African Life and Customs* (1908) and *The Three Needs of Liberia* (1908), he seems to value indigenous African culture more highly. In those works, he explicitly defends the Poro and Bondo societies, communal ownership of land, and polygamy.[117] In *The Three Needs of Liberia* he asserts that the communal nature of African society makes impossible the extremes of wealth and poverty that industrial capitalism has created in the Western world, and that the communalism of traditional, indigenous African culture is in fact closer to the ideal of Jesus than Western capitalism is:

> White men tell us of the necessity and the importance of there being class distinctions—rich men and poor men—princes and beggars—in every community, but this was not Christ's idea, and it is not the African's idea. The African idea is the idea of the first Christian church—"One for all and all for one."[118]

Blyden's observations reveal an obvious affinity for the social gospel. But Blyden's views represent a Christian assessment of racial issues and of indigenous African culture that radically contradicts what Mignerey had been taught by church and missionary authorities in the U.S. Blyden's assessment of the state of things in precolonial Africa also clearly contradicts the picture of chaos and barbarity that Mignerey had accepted as a justification for British colonialism.

Mignerey lists both *Christianity, Islam, and the Negro Race* and *The Three Needs of Liberia* in the bibliography he appends to his book outline. The outline includes six specific page references to Blyden's works. He cites the following quote *four* times, once copying it out verbatim:

> And then in the campaign which they [the Christian churches] are attempting to carry into the Soudan they raise the war cry, "Christ or Mohammed." But it is not Christ or Mohammed; it is the white man or Mohammed; and in such a contest Mohammed will be the victor every time. His methods are so different. He is an oriental and can obey literally the command to go without purse or script. The Arab and the indigenous missionary in the heart of Africa confront the European missionary empty handed, and success is not with the man armed and equipped. His *impedimenta* are a burden as well as an obstruction. His individualistic methods make him inaccessible to the masses. If they would come to Christ they must go upstairs.
>
> The only impression made upon the nobler spirits by this display of material superiority and the condescending patronage it suggests is that stated by Dante, that no

food is so bitter as the bread of dependence and no ascent so painful as the staircase of a patron, and they shrink from the proffered coddling.

> Thou shalt have proof how savoreth of salt
> The bread of others, and how hard a road,
> The going down and up another's stairs.

On the contrary, Christ ordered his apostles to abide in the houses of the people whom they desired to evangelize and eat *their* bread.[119]

Presumably, Blyden's analysis here struck Mignerey as an apt diagnosis of the problems of the Christian missionary in Africa—problems Mignerey himself faced. And Blyden is here saying that the Christian missionary is failing because he brings with him racist and ethnocentric attitudes. Along with Christianity, the missionary brings the baggage of the assumption that the white race and Western culture are superior to the Black race and African culture. Only a few pages further, Blyden also had this to say:

> The great European powers, who, since the memorable and disreputable scramble five-and-twenty years ago, have been trying to govern the natives according to the laws of Europe, have found out their mistake, chiefly through the information imparted to them by their own travelers.... They have now understood that Africa has a social, industrial, and religious system, and they are making strenuous and praiseworthy efforts to study it.... The failure of their former methods—the dislocations, disintegrations and exterminations resulting from them—show that they were wrong; that where they did not produce corpses they created apes and criminals.[120]

In this passage, Blyden clearly condemns both the massive European conquest of Africa that began in the 1880s, against which the 1898 rebellion in Sierra Leone was a reaction, and also the attempt to abolish African culture in favor of Western culture in Africa. Mignerey, in the section of his outline sketching the role of the missionary, includes notes that quite possibly arose from reflection on the above passage of Blyden. First, Mignerey appears to recognize the harmful effects of the imposition of an alien culture: "When native superstitious checks are removed by the introduction of Western ideas what can be done to supply an equally strong motive for morality?" And despite his defense of colonialism and support of the British government, he notes that the role of the missionary includes "Checking injustice of foreign governments and foreign representatives in *land robbery* and *labor exploitation.*" In the first section of the outline, entitled "The Masses," Mignerey first presents, under the heading "*National Characteristics* (Negative?)," the following list, which reflects much of what he had already had to say about Africans in the diary:

1. Dishonesty, thieving, lying
2. Immorality
3. Irresponsibility (laziness) with work, copper [i.e. money], property
4. Superstition
5. Arrested Intelligence
6. Cruelty
7. General Mental Inertia
8. Palavering

Needless to say, much of this negative evaluation stems from his lack of understanding of African culture and the prejudices he had been taught in the U.S. Non-Christian religion is automatically labeled "superstition," a tradition of communal social organization is interpreted as "irresponsibility" where "property" is concerned, a set of traditions regarding sexual conduct and marriage that differs from American traditions is automatically labeled "immorality," etc.

But, immediately following, Mignerey adds, under the heading "Conclusion," the following observations, which, while probably falling short of rejecting colonialism and missionary activity outright, include clear criticism of the way both British colonial power and Christian missionary influence are often exerted. This criticism indicates that, whatever problems Africa may have, the influence of Western society is not necessarily beneficial. Mignerey's observations here sound in some ways very much like a direct reflection of Blyden's views:

> 1. Such people a prey to stronger nations. Ex[ample] the Historic Partition of Africa.
> 2. Many *bleed* the people and contribute nothing to their development in self-respect.
> 3. Many with the professional position of "helpers."
> 4. Contact of great *institutions* of government, *commerce, education, religion,* with these masses. What is prevailing motive of these institutions?
> (a) the contact a personal one thru *people* representing these institutions. — what are the *personal* motives of these representatives?
> 5. Out of these conditions arise the constant struggles between personal forces—a *struggle of ideas*.
> (a) Out of this struggle the New Africa is emerging.
> (b) What shall it be?

But then, the final entry on the list reads: "6. What do the people want? (Food, Clothing, Shelter, Medicine, Enjoyment.—*Lack of Aim*.)," with the implication that the Africans are possibly not capable of dealing with the struggle on their own. But Mignerey was far from thinking that the label "civilized" could be applied to the Western world in unambiguous contrast to "uncivilized" Africa. He had experienced the horror of trench warfare in World War One, and was sharply critical of Western capitalism and the liquor trade. In the final section of the outline, entitled "The Old and the New," under the heading "IV.— *Counterpart of African Evils in Modern-Christian-White Civilization*" he lists the following:

> 1. White Men & Black Women
> 2. White Man's liquor
> 3. Foreign Cruelty to Blacks
> 4. Poverty—
> 5. Race Hatred and Race Problems.
> 6. Superstition: See ads, etc of [illegible].
> 7. Dishonesty: Ex[ample] Conviction of Asst. D.C. [District Commissioner] by Ross.

Elsewhere in the section titled "The Old and the New" Mignerey includes these observations on Africa and the African:

> *Possibility of developing 'his own life'* by rejecting the worst of his own and foreign characteristics, and cleaving to the *best* of his own and foreign civilizations.
> —No "African" or "foreign," no "white" or "black"—only "good" and "bad"—
> Neither African nor foreign represents the whole of either good or bad.

Mignerey comes close to repudiating standard ethnocentric thinking—but, from the following sentence, it appears that Mignerey may feel the African lacks the ability to distinguish good and bad: "—For this is needed a training in *judgment* and *discrimination*." Presumably the necessary training must be provided by Christian missions. But in the outline, he himself also includes the question: "Who is to decide what is 'good' or 'bad' for the African?"

In *The Three Needs of Liberia* Blyden does not only criticize Christian missionaries, but also clearly rejects the idea that missionaries are needed to reform the customs of Africans. Mignerey must certainly have read the entire text of *The Three Needs* (a pamphlet of only 36 pages), and one wonders how he felt about an attack as direct as the following:

> Africa, therefore, has a right to demand of Europe, in reply to its indiscriminate appeals for the demolition among us of immemorial customs, an answer to the following question: "If we abolished customs known and tried and helpful to us, and adopted yours, what shall we do with our submerged tenth, our thieves, and prostitutes?" ... Then Africa must say to our would-be benefactors on these subjects: "Great and good friends, *you* grapple with *your* domestic and social problems and leave us to grapple with *ours*. In political, military, material and financial problems we need and solicit your guidance and help, but as to the subtle problems which involve the physical, physiological and spiritual or psychological well-being of the people, we deprecate your benevolent but dislocating interference. As to your marriage laws, we beseech you to believe that for Africa you are mistaken—fatally mistaken."[121]

In his diary, Mignerey lays particular emphasis, for example, upon the abolition of polygamy, and criticizes the missions for being too willing to look the other way. Did he later reconsider views such as this?

The writing he did in Africa includes several indications that he already recognized his lack of understanding of African culture. For example, one of the letters he sent to the home churches describing customs in Rotifunk includes the comment that "I have scarcely penetrated the surface of things as they are. There is certainly a complexity of life that baffles analysis." But there are no references in any of his diaries or letters to Blyden, while in the book outline, as I have pointed out, the influence of Blyden is extensive. I think it likely that Mignerey acquired copies of Blyden's works while in Sierra Leone, and read them upon his return, or possibly during the long voyage back to the U.S. As Mignerey looked back over his experience, reading Blyden may have prompted him to alter his views. He certainly did not have much opportunity for quiet reflection during his time in Africa. At Rotifunk, while he apparently functioned effectively in his position, he was also somewhat overwhelmed and at times depressed by his new environment. During his time in Freetown, he was extremely busy, and shows very definite signs of stress toward the end of the school year. It is remarkable that he was able to produce the informative, well written, and perceptive record he in fact left behind. If, as seems likely, he had never been exposed to ideas such as Blyden's prior to his arrival in Africa, the book outline indicates that his understanding of Africa and its relation to the West had begun to change significantly as he reflected at home upon his previous two years' experience. Blyden was in fact arguing, as we would say today, that African *culture* is distinctly different from European culture, and that this difference should be taken seriously. Blyden's was of course very much a voice crying in the wilderness of his time. But one of Mignerey's remarks indicates that the significance of the idea of the cultural is beginning to dawn on him. In outline form he comes to a conclusion:

> 3. *African is Oriental at heart.*
>   a. you cannot "hustle the east." (see Kipling's poem)
>   ....
> 5. The great need of scholarly research into the working of the African Mind, his native customs, folklore, —Intelligence tests.

He must have noticed that Blyden at one point describes the African as "an oriental." And Kipling's image of the fool who tried to hustle the east is one that really hit home. In today's society, phrases like "cultural diversity" or "multiculturalism" are so much a part of everyday discourse as to have become almost banal. Calling the African "oriental" may be Mignerey's awkward way of beginning to express a genuine insight into the reality of cultural difference in a context that lacks any kind of standard vocabulary for such notions.

Another example that reflects the presence of contradictory, or at least dissonant, ways of thinking, is the negative attitude toward Marcus Garvey that Mignerey expresses in the diary, in contrast to his positive attitude toward Edward Blyden in the book outline. Since he mentions Blyden only in the outline, written as he later reflected back upon his experience in Africa, this contrast may reflect a distinct change in his way of thinking.

There are two references in the diary to Garvey. In both cases, Mignerey refers to Garvey in response to accusations of racism. In the first case, recorded at Rotifunk, this is what Mignerey has to say:

> This is something that I have noticed several times during the short experience here: the blacks are always the first and the quickest to draw the "color-line" argument whenever they are crossed in anything right or wrong. This is a common experience of other missionaries. A few years ago, Mr. Musselman tells me, when the Marcus Garvey fever had taken hold of the people some of our own native workers, like Mr. Manley, head teacher at Shenge, wrote most abusive letters to the mission management accusing of race prejudice and discrimination, oppression and abuse.

In response to another incident, in Freetown, in which Mignerey was accused of racism, Mignerey refers to Marcus Garvey in these terms:

It is an established fact that a certain element of blacks here want their own race to have the upper hand in everything African. This is true of government, education, and church. Marcus Garvey's influence is lurking beneath many a black heart here, even tho the government has suppressed his propaganda. This element does not hesitate to attack the government. But the government does not worry.

Insofar as Mignerey sees in Garvey's viewpoint the assertion that Blacks should "have the upper hand in everything African," his perception of Garvey's viewpoint is accurate. However, Blyden expresses exactly the same idea in the essay Mignerey apparently admired so much, *The Three Needs of Liberia.*

While Garvey and Blyden were certainly two very different men, with two very different careers, they share many similarities. Their viewpoint about the destiny of the Black race, and the relationship among African Americans, Africa, and white America, is basically the same. Both believed that, as things stood, African-Americans had no chance of achieving equality by fighting for it America. Both believed that only if strong, independent, Black nations in Africa were created would African-Americans begin to gain any respect in America. Therefore, both supported the idea that the emigration of African-Americans to Liberia was of paramount importance. The idea behind such emigration was not the wholesale departure of Blacks from America, but rather that the creation of strong Black African nations would enhance the status of Blacks in America, and that the American immigrants could aid in this process.[122] Garvey and Blyden shared the idea that African culture had its own greatness and integrity, and did not need to be improved by Western culture. Finally, they were both supporters of the independence of Africans from colonial rule.[123]

Both Garvey and Blyden were natives of the Caribbean, Garvey having been born in Jamaica in 1887 (making him 55 years younger than Blyden and 11 years older than Mignerey). From early on, he displayed outstanding rhetorical skills and a unique talent for the grass-roots organization of social protest. By 1920 he had developed the first truly mass movement among African-Americans, the Universal Negro Improvement Association, whose keynotes were Black pride, self-help, and entrepreneurship as well as the cause of Liberia and emigration. He attracted a high level of attention all around the world. He was rejected by other African American leaders, such as W.E.B. Dubois of the N.A.A.C.P., but was an inspiration to millions of ordinary African-Americans as well as Africans chafing under the oppression of colonial rule. Garvey called unambiguously for an immediate end to colonialism. For example, in 1923 he suggested to England and France that they simply "pack up their baggage and clear out of Africa."[124] Garvey was popular in Freetown among followers of Blyden, and there is evidence that a branch of the U.N.I.A. was active there in 1920. The *Sierra Leone Weekly News* at first welcomed Garvey's ideas, but soon recoiled at his talk of ending colonial rule.[125] By 1920, Garvey's newspaper, *Negro World*, had been "banned in most of Black Africa and colonial authorities were keeping a close watch for U.N.I.A. organizers."[126] The "Marcus Garvey fever" and the influence of Marcus Garvey "lurking beneath many a black heart" that Mignerey refers to in fact simply represent agitation for the end of colonial rule. Blyden was certainly not prone to Garvey's flights of rhetoric, and he certainly wasn't the leader of a mass movement. He was a careful and scholarly thinker who expressed his convictions in a subtle and precise prose style, and who had a long career as a diplomat, government official, and college president. He had nothing like Garvey's penchant for provocation and confrontation. And yet, the convictions of the two men were basically the same. Why did Mignerey think of Garvey with such suspicion and contempt, and Blyden with such respect? The particular point that Mignerey objects to is the demand for an immediate end to colonization. While Blyden did not agitate for decolonization, he did unambiguously condemn the scramble for Africa, which he personally witnessed from beginning to end.

Further evidence that Mignerey became increasingly aware of and increasingly critical of the inconsistencies and contradictions in attitudes toward Africans and Africa he had held as a missionary comes in an article he wrote in *The Religious Telescope* in July 1933. *The Religious Telescope* was the primary publication of the United Brethren Church. Mignerey wrote a weekly column for the *Telescope*, addressed to young people, during the early 'thirties. The column in question was titled "Friendship With Other Races." While he here uses the word "we" in a way that might simply suggest "most people," I think he clearly intends "we" to include himself:

> Relationship of white people with other racial groups here at home is always hanging in a delicate balance. Negroes, we say, are a "problem." So are Japanese and Chinese. Our racial prejudice pictures them all as low-down, tricky trash. This, of course, is no more true of them than it is of us. Our attitudes of helpfulness, nevertheless, have been marked too often by a spirit of thinly-disguised condescension. Beneath the surface we have assumed that the cream of the earth is undoubtedly white.
>
> Other forces have been at work in recent years to challenge this attitude. Leaders of other races have been bold to question the grounds of our assumed superiority. We ourselves have caught clearer glimpses of our own inconsistencies. The trend in many quarters is unmistakably toward a common level of appreciation, understanding, and helpfulness.
>
> We are convinced that the moving force behind this trend is the spirit of Jesus, one of whose basic attitudes in all his dealings with people was his appreciation of the supreme worth of [human] personality....
>
> It seems that we are now in the painful process of cleansing ourselves from some of the smug hypocrisies by which we have violated this principle of Christian fellowship in other years.[127]

Mignerey clearly sees that racism is not necessarily a matter of of hatred, but can often be found hiding behind the apparently well-intentioned actions and benevolent feelings of those who do not at all think of themselves as racists. He will soon make it clear that when he refers to "our attitudes of helpfulness," he means to include the missionaries' attitudes. But first, under the heading of "Facing Ourselves in the United States of America," he proceeds to recount some "specific examples taken from the sample case of personal experience." It is remarkable that Mignerey confronts head on in these examples a racism that is by no means subtle, but is of the most overt and ugliest sort. At the head of the list is the following incident which evidently took place in a small Ohio town, which he satirically renames for the sake of its anonymity:

A returned missionary from Africa once mentioned casually to a group in the local church in Buzzard's Glory, United States of America, that he and his wife occasionally had the native teachers in their home for dinner. Whereupon one of the
listening group said emphatically, "You don't think that Jesus would eat at the
same table with a Nigger, do you?"

Also, the town of "Monkeyville," which "points with pride to the fact that no
black people are allowed within its corporate limits," still has "three foreign
missionary societies...going through the usual motions of helping black people
in far, far-away tropic isles of the sea." And in the town of "Baloneyburg...the
growth of a community of black people in the neighborhood of one our churches
brought consternation to the saints—white saints of course. White people left the
community," and those who didn't move "transferred to other churches....The
conference...sold the building—at a loss—to the incoming black people, and
hurried away to more congenial fields where the white saints could be spared the
dreadful annoyance of black saints, and sinners clamoring for spiritual attention
at their cathedral door!" It took remarkable courage to speak with such honesty
and bluntness of the sin of racism infecting Mignerey's own church and community. One wonders what sort of response this article created—it is the only
one dealing with race in the entire series of articles he wrote for *The Religious
Telescope*.

Mignerey makes it clear that it is not only his own community and his own
church, but also his church's missionaries in Africa, and indeed he himself, who
have been guilty of racism. After all, weren't the teachers at Albert Academy, in
their reaction to the original version of his play, trying to get the message across
that his "attitude of helpfulness" was "marked by thinly disguised condescension," and that "beneath the surface" he was assuming that "the cream of the
earth is undoubtedly white"? Didn't many of Mignerey's comments in the diary
and the outline reflect a perception of Africans as "low-down, tricky trash"? The
following is the explicit judgment he makes about white missionaries in the article:

> Such attitudes [of racial prejudice] are tragic enough here at home. They become
> fatal if perchance they reach the fields of our foreign missions. Consider a com-
> ment made some years ago by Doctor Blyden, a scholarly black man in Africa,
> writing concerning the white missionary in his book, "Three Needs of Liberia."

And here Mignerey reproduces the same passage—in which Blyden criticizes the Christian missionary—that he had earlier copied into the book outline
he had prepared:

> His individualistic methods make him inaccessible to the masses. If they would
> come to Christ they must go upstairs. The only impression made upon the nobler
> spirits by this display of material superiority and the condescending patronage
> which it suggests is that stated by Dante, that no food is so bitter as the bread of
> dependence and no ascent so painful as the staircase of a patron, and they shrink
> from the proffered coddling.

"The Closing of the Mission Door"

During the years 1924 to 1942, Mignerey worked as a pastor at a whole series of United Brethren churches in the South East Ohio Conference. In 1935, at the age of 39, he wrote up an autobiographical outline, detailing his accomplishments year by year. Reflecting upon his life so far, he also drew up a list of the five greatest "Challenges to my faith," evidently in the order he had faced them:

1. College—Sophomore
2. World War
3. Closing of Mission Door
4. Corruption among the Ministry—(c.f. Apathy of, to Moral Questions)
5. Treachery Among the Laity of the Church

From his return home in April, 1924, until August 1926, Mignerey made persistent and repeated efforts to arrange for his return to Sierra Leone. The Mission Board, in effect, refused to send him back, even though he was technically only on furlough. Mignerey carefully preserved the detailed correspondence related to this effort. Those involved in the decision were Samuel Ziegler (General Secretary of the U.B. Foreign Missionary Society), Alfred T. Howard (President of the Executive Committee of the U.B. Foreign Missionary Society), and A.S. Nichols, who had worked with Mignerey as head of the shop at Albert Academy, and was now also on furlough in the U.S.

Mignerey had become quite ill in Freetown by December 1923. He was still not well by the time of their departure in May of 1924, and was vomiting blood on the ship. His daughter told me (in 1995) that he had probably developed tuberculosis. We learn from his wife's diary that in August 1925, the mission doctor still advised against his return for at least 6 to 8 months, because "there has been something at the top of his lungs." Yet in May 1925 his wife understood that "Dr. Ziegler expects our return to Africa June 1926."

In a letter to Ziegler of January 5, 1926, Mignerey begins his earnest entreaties that he be allowed to return to the mission field[128]:

> With all of this, though, our thoughts revert to the work which we have left behind in Africa. It seems that we started something for our Lord there which we have never finished. Our call to that work was so certain! Our agreement with the board was for at least two terms. The call to that work is even more insistent now than it was then. Our moral obligation to the church to complete the term of service there seems all the more binding. We are sure that one does not really have a fair chance at the work until after the first term of service. Health problems and relations with co-workers are better understood and can be better managed. After a period of study at home native African ability and native aspirations loom up in a new light. After all, to work with the people then, to help them, to inspire them to Christian faith and Christian living seems to be about the greatest sort of work we can do.
>
> We are still at your service. Is the way not open?

Ziegler replies on January 30th that "our appropriation to Africa does not allow the sending out of an extra family unless it becomes absolutely necessary." He also mentions that Nichols had requested to be sent back to Albert Academy with Mignerey. Ziegler also reports that he will now be leaving on a six month trip to the Orient, and that Howard will be handling this matter in his absence.

What follows is a very tangled tale of bureaucratic infighting and clumsiness. It is true that Mignerey's liberal theological views were unpopular. And his return to the U.S. does coincide eerily with the Scopes trial in Tennessee. However, all in all, it does appear that the essential reason behind the Board's refusal was probably simply that Howard did not like him—although of course this never comes out in the open in the correspondence. But Howard's personal disinclination to return Mignerey to the field does not seem to arise from any sort of hostility to Mignerey's theological position. In his writings in the *Telescope* and in his correspondence Howard comes across as a folksy, genial individual who dislikes open conflict. And Mignerey comes across as a very blunt, forthright individual who believes it his duty to confront problems and disagreements as directly and honestly as possible.

The bureaucratic snafu was this: The Board had not clearly delineated the boundaries of the authority of the principal of Albert Academy and of the Academy Shop director. Mignerey and Nichols had worked this out between themselves, and Nichols then insisted that the U.S. Mission Board ratify this arrangement. He understood from Ziegler that the new rules had been ratified. But Howard then wanted H.H. Thomas to temporarily leave Jaiama (which had additional missionary staff), in order to step in for Martin as principal of the Albert Academy, since Martin was due a furlough. However, Thomas was dead set against the new rules, and Nichols absolutely refused to return unless the new rules were put into place. So Howard told Thomas that he would not have to follow the new rules at the Albert Academy, and hired a new missionary, Tozier, to take Nichols' place as shop director. Mignerey stood by Nichols unwaveringly. The Board could have otherwise solved the problem by taking on the "extra" expense of sending Mignerey back, instead of reducing the previous staff levels at Jaiama. Mignerey's strong suspicion was that the main reason this did not happen was Howard's covert antipathy for Mignerey—and my guess is that Mignerey was probably right. (It may in fact be that the Board wanted to reduce expenses—assuming that Martin on furlough would not continue to be paid any more than Mignerey on furlough.) Another detail that casts some suspicion on the Board's financial explanation of their denial of Mignerey's request is that a new missionary (and wife) had been suddenly recruited in 1925, to be sent to Sierra Leone immediately. The new missionary was Charles Leader.[129]

However, it does not seem to be the case that the Board excluded Mignerey either because of his liberal theological views, or because of his enlightened views about Africa. And H.H. Thomas, the man Howard wanted to install at Albert Academy instead of Mignerey, is remembered by African pastors as the single the most enlightened missionary in their experience. Musselman and Thomas were the advocates of greater African autonomy, while Schutz and Leader, who arrived in 1923 and 1925, were to emerge as the opponents of greater autonomy. Yet Schutz recommended to Howard that the way to solve the conflict would be to return Mignerey and Nichols to the Academy together.

One reason I have explored the annoying intricacies of this situation is to demonstrate that a mission board's decisions were not likely to be determined strictly by some sort of ideological criterion. If they had wanted an ideological target, Mignerey would have been perfect. His liberalism may have been a factor, but so also his outspoken personality. And being a theological liberal did not necessarily imply an enlightened view on racial and cultural issues. The situation seems essentially to have been this: that under a limited budget, and given the fact that Howard was simply not enthusiastic about Mignerey, Howard engaged in a game of juggling personnel in a way that would result in a net reduction in personnel for a given time in Sierra Leone, as well as the exclusion of Mignerey from the field. The antipathy between Mignerey and Howard was likely much more one of temperament and personality than of ideology.

Notes

1. The extent of both its missionary and educational endeavor is remarkable for what was a relatively small church. Membership was: 25,000 in 1841; 94,453 in 1861; 204, 492 in 1889; 370,000 in 1921. J. Bruce Behney and Paul H. Eller, *The History of the Evangelical United Brethren Church* (Nashville: Abington, 1979), 155, 230, 255.

2. J.S. Mills, W. R. Funk, and S. S. Hough, *Our Foreign Missionary Enterprise* (Dayton, Oh.: United Brethren Publishing House, 1908), 45 (hereafter OFME).

3. OFME, 3.

4. OFME, 4–5.

5. OFME, 8.

6. OFME, 10.

7. *Crumbs* [Otterbein], February 3, 1917, p. 160.

8. Darrell Reeck, *A Socio-Historical Analysis of Modernization and Related Mission Influences in Two Chiefdoms in West Africa, 1895–1940* (Diss. Boston Univ., 1970), 206.

9. Ibid., 56–66.

10. Ibid., 241.

11. Ibid., 227.

12. D.K. Flickinger, *Ethiopia: Or Twenty Six Years of Missionary Life in Western Africa* (Dayton, Ohio: United Brethren Publishing House, 1882), 79.

13. J.S. Mills *Mission Work in Sierra Leone, West Africa* (Dayton, Ohio, United Brethren Publishing House, 1898), 30.

14. From Mills' address, "The Kingdom of God, the True Socialism" in William R. Funk, *Life of Bishop J.S. Mills, D.D.* (Dayton, Ohio: Otterbein Press, 1913), 211.

15. While the most common spelling is "Bundu," Lamp shows that "Bondo" more accurately reflects the actual pronunciation of the word not only in Temne, but also in the Mende, Limba, Bullom, and Gola languages. See Frederick Lamp, *Temne Rounds: The Arts as Spatial and Temporal Indicators in a West African Society* (Ph.D. Dissertation, Yale Univ., 1982), 281.

16. In this, Mignerey got the wrong impression—in neither the case of the Mende nor the Temne was the chief the head of the Poro society. See the first section of chapter 5, "Mende and Temne Sociopolitical Systems and the Poro society."

17. Howard Ernest Mueller, *Formation of a Mission Church in an African Culture: The United Brethren in Sierra Leone* (Ph.D. Dissertation in Religion, Northwestern University, 1973), 45–49.

18. See ibid., 103.

19. Ibid., 129–30.

20. Howard Ernest Mueller, "Oral Data on the Development of the United Brethren in Sierra Leone, Gathered 1971–72," 379 (hereafter MOD).

21. Kenneth Little, *The Mende of Sierra Leone: A West African People in Transition* (London: Routledge, 1951), 141.

22. MOD, 385.

23. See Igor Kopytoff and Suzanne Meiers, "African 'Slavery' as an Institution of Marginality" in *Slavery in Africa*, edited by Suzanne Meiers and Igor Kopytoff, 3–84 (Madison: Univ. of Wisconsin Press, 1977), esp. 7–12, 22–24.

24. John J.Grace, "Slavery and Emancipation among the Mende in Sierra Leone," in *Slavery in Africa* by Suzanne Meiers and Igor Kopytoff (Madison: Univ. of Wisconsin Press, 1977), 418.

25. Arthur Abraham, *Mende Government and Politics Under Colonial Rule* (Freetown: Sierra Leone Univ. Press, 1978), 22.

26. John J. Grace, *Domestic Slavery in West Africa, with Particular Reference to the Sierra Leone Protectorate, 1896–1927* (New York: Barnes and Noble, 1975), 8; Abraham, *Mende Government*, 22.

27. Grace, *Domestic Slavery*, 8. One case the District Commissioner Stanley of the Sherbro District handled is particularly interesting for the light it sheds on the complexity of the issue. The redemption of slaves had been a precolonial tradition, and the 1896 Protectorate ordinance approved this practice. The colonial government started issuing redemption certificates in 1905—which meant that District Commissioners had the responsibility of the determining the validity of redemptions (Grace, *Domestic Slavery*, 192–96). The case involved a woman, Banja, and her eight children, who had lived with a Madam Kunna for many years previously, but in the immediately prior year had lived with a Mrs. Williams. Madam Kunna then claimed them as slaves. Mrs. Williams tried to redeem them for £30. But Stanley refused to recognize the redemption. Madam Kunna was in fact an elderly woman who was married to a slave who was also Banja's father and the children's grandfather. Also, Stanley judged that Mrs. Williams had "enticed the slaves away from Madam Kunna," (ibid., 224) and that "the slaves had been working as domestics" for her and that "one of the women had been used for immoral purposes" (ibid., 225). In addition, Mrs. Williams had never before claimed relationship with Banja, and only attempted redemption when Banja and her children were returned to Madam Kunna. It would doubtless provoke the ire of missionaries like Mignerey to learn that a British District Commissioner had refused to accept a redemption. But this case illustrates well the complexity and ambiguity of the actual situation. In a society in which elders retain authority over the members of their households even when those members are adult, and in which intermarriage between slave and free is commonplace, there can be a genuine blurring of the distinction (that outsiders would make) between the authority of parents and "ownership." Banja's story is as much a case of a family dispute about where children and grandchildren should reside as it is about slave ownership. And what is called by the name of "redemption" in this case in fact seems suspiciously close to "purchase"!

28. Reeck, *A Socio-Historical Analysis*, 59; Christopher Fyfe, *A History of Sierra Leone* (Oxford: Oxford Univ. Press, 1962), 10 (hereafter HSL); Christopher Fyfe, *A Short History of Sierra Leone* (London: Longmans, 1962), 23 (hereafter SHSL).

29. Reeck, *A Socio-Historical Analysis*, 61.

30. Ibid., appendix 2, 297; J.R. King, "The Death of Chief Caulker," *Women's Evangel* 22 no. 11, Nov. 1903, 169; Zella King, "Martyr's Memorial Church," *Women's Evangel* 23 no. 12, Dec., 1904, 179–80.

31. "For instance, J.C.B. Caulker...A.G. Caulker's father and Paramount Chief of Bumpe Chiefdom in 1901 to 1905 [sic], spoke at the dedication of the Martyr's Memorial Church in Rotifunk in 1904 to the following effect: 'He pointed out to them the way in which the country is changing, and urged them to send their children to the school provided for them, that they may be able to take their places in the development of the country.'" Reeck, *A Socio-Historical Analysis,* 234–35. Reeck's source is Zella B. King, "Martyr's Memorial Church," *Women's Evangel* 23 no. 12 (December, 1904), 179.

32. Darrell Reeck, "Oral Data Regarding the History of the Process of Modernization and Related Mission Influences in Sierra Leone (1968–69)," interview #14.

33. the prefix *an-* is the form of the definite article in Temne.

34. Reeck, *A Socio-Historical Analysis*, 255.

35. One of Reeck's informants also reports that "kantar" was an originally Temne custom which some Sherbro had come to adopt ("Oral Data," interview #148).

36. Lloyd Mignerey, "Some First Impressions," *Sierra Leone Outlook* (March 1922), 5–7; Reeck, *A Socio-Historical Analysis*, 255.

37. Reeck, *A Socio-Historical Analysis*, 255.

38. See, for example, the 1901 account of the Sherbro by District Commissioner T.J. Alldridge, or the account of the "Temne and other tribes" in *Anthropological Report on Sierra Leone* by the Government Anthropologist Northcote W. Thomas.

39. Adu Boahen, *Topics in West African History* (Essex: Longman, 1986), 98.

40. Abraham, *Mende Government,* 137.

41. Reeck, *A Socio-Historical Analysis,* 127–28.

42. Arthur Abraham, *An Introduction to the Pre-colonial History of the Mende of Sierra Leone* (Lewiston, New York: Mellen, 2003), 193.

43. Mills, *Mission Work,* 187.

44. HSL, 589; Abraham, *Introduction,* 194.

45. Abraham, *Introduction,* 162.

46. Reeck, *A Socio-Historical Analysis,* 251; "Oral Data," interviews #89, #93.

47. Reeck, *A Socio-Historical Analysis,* 147.

48. Reeck, *A Socio-historical Analysis* 64, "Oral Data," interview #20.

49. Ellen Groenendyke , "Three Early African Experiences" *The Evangel* 40, nos. 7–8 (July–August, 1921), 201–202; HSL, 420; OFME, 60–64; Reeck, *A Socio-Historical Analysis,* 122.

50. Reeck *A Socio-Historical Analysis,* 142.

51. Ibid., 121–22.

52. Ibid., 177.

53. Reeck, "Oral Data" interview #140.

54. Reeck, "Oral Data," interview #135.

55. Reeck, *A Socio-Historical Analysis,* 218–19.

56. See MOD, interviews especially with Shodeke, Eustace Renner, Saboleh, Gbundema.

57. Reeck, *A Socio-Historical Analysis,* 218–19.

58. MOD, 112 (Shodeke).

59. Reeck, "Oral Data," interviews with Barley, Pieh, Ellen Caulker.

60. John F. Musselman was General Superintendent of the the mission from 1922–1947.

61. MOD, 176 (Shodeke). Shodeke graduated from Albert Academy in 1928, was ordained a United Brethren minister in 1931, and served various stations until 1945. Before ordination he had been a teacher and itinerant at Rotifunk. He resigned from the UBC in 1945, and became a minister in the independent West African Methodist Church. Shodeke is one of the most insightful, frank, and forthcoming of all of Mueller's informants.

62. Glen Rosselot, *The Origin, Growth, and Development of the United Brethren in Christ Mission Schools in Sierra Leone, West Africa* (M.A. Thesis in Education, University of Chicago, 1936), 19–20.

63. Ibid., 41.

64. Ibid., 51.

65. Ibid., table 1, 117–118.

66. Ibid., 51–52.

67. http://www.harfordschool.org/history/HSGhistory.html

68. "One of the first considerations of the Conference at the beginning of the present century was the matter of school fees as a means of developing self-support. The home Boards had paid heavily toward the support of the schools but gradually the people assumed more and more responsibility as school fees were imposed. In 1914 the amount of fees collected reached £48–5–4. Two years previously the eligible schools had been placed under government inspection, and the grant received in 1914 was £200–11–0. This was approximately five times as much as the school fees but only about one-fifteenth of the total expenditure for the schools. In 1924 the school fees increased almost three-fold over those of the previous year, rising from £99–12–1 in 1923 to £268–0–7 the following year. The government grant-in-aid the same year was £450–0–0, having increased gradually from year to year since 1912. The school fees reached their maximum, £625–13–0, in 1931, and the government grant-in-aid that year was reported as £968–5–0—107–08….Considering the government grants-in-aid as earnings of the schools together with their school fees, it will be readily admitted that commendable progress has been made toward self-support, although the Mission Board still bears by far the major share of their cost" (Rosselot, *Origin*, 108).

69. Reeck, "Oral Data," Interview #15.

70. Reeck, *A Socio-Historical Analysis,* 233.

71. Ibid., 233.

72. MOD, 351 (Pieh).

73. Reeck also mentions "persons identifieable as members of a ruling house" as a status group (Reeck, *A Socio-Historical Analysis*, 199). In Bumpe, the Sherbro Caulker family certainly had long standing wealth and political predominance, even to the extent that it might be termed a "ruling house," but kingship and chiefship among the Mende and the Temne were clearly not hereditary, as Abraham (*Mende*, 35) and Ijagbemi ("Rothoron," 2–3) have demonstrated (see also Dorjahn, "Changing," 165).

74. Reeck, *A Socio-Historical Analysis*, 201.

75. Ibid., 226.

76. Mignerey letter to Alonzo Marion, Oct. 9, 1922; Mignerey Collection, Otterbein University Archives.

77. Reeck, *A Socio-Historical Analysis*, 246.

78. Ibid., 215.

79. Mueller, *Formation,* 138.

80. Mueller, *Formation,* 138–142.

81. Musselman letter to Mignerey, Feb. 9, 1922, Mignerey Collection, Otterbein University Archives.

82. Walter Schutz, "Memorial Service—Dr. J.F. Musselman and Rev. S.B. Caulker," *Sierra Leone Outlook* 38 no. 5 (Sept.–Oct. 1947), 5. Musselman had retired in July of 1947 and returned to the U.S. He died suddenly and unexpectedly two months later. In the same issue of S.L.O., Nora Vesper wrote "A Tribute to Dr. Musselman" (13). She had worked closely with Musselman at Rotifunk from 1916–1922. "The people of Rotifunk were like a big family to him, and he did a lot of visiting in the homes. Some times when he was late for dinner we found out that he had eaten with some one in town. The people knew that he liked native foods and few days went by that something was not sent to him. He was at home with Syrians, Creoles, Mendes, Temnes, and Sherbros alike.... Some years ago he made the statement that he made it the aim and purpose of his life to speak to some one every day regarding their soul's salvation."

83. Mignerey letter to Musselman, May 25, 1922, Mignerey Collection, Otterbein University Archives.

84. Mignerey letter to Musselman, Sept. 14, 1922, Mignerey Collection, Otterbein University Archives.

85. Musselman letter to Mignerey, Sept. 14, 1922, Mignerey Collection, Otterbein University Archives.

86. Musselman letter to Mignerey, Sept. 26, 1922, Mignerey Collection, Otterbein University Archives.

87. See MOD, 141 (Renner).

88. MOD, 140–141 (Renner), 170 (Fitzjohn).

89. Syl M. Renner started at Albert Academy in 1913, and worked as the printer there until 1923, when he was ordained. He subsequently served as a pastor in Freetown and Moyamba. When the superintendency of the mission passed into African hands in 1951, Renner became superintendent of one of the two districts into which the mission was then divided. He participated in the Ministerial Institute class that Mignerey conducted in July 1923.

90. MOD, 145.

91. MOD, 147 (Renner).

92. MOD, 63 (Renner).

93. Mueller, *Formation*, 143.

94. MOD, 66 (Renner).

95. Mueller, *Formation*, 110.

96. MOD, 114.

97. Mueller, *Formation*, 146–47.

98. MOD, 178 (Shodeke).

99. MOD, 147 (Renner); see also 178 (Shodeke), and Mueller, *Formation*, 147–49.

100. OFME, 55–59; Earl D.Baker, *The Development of Secondary Schools in Sierra Leone* (Ph.D. Thesis, University of Michigan, 1963), 45; Rosselot, *Origin*, 51.

101. Rosselot, *Origin*, table 1, 117–118.

102. L.O.G. Lisk, *The History of the Albert Academy and its Contribution to the Development of Sierra Leone* (Diploma in Education Thesis, Fourah Bay College, 1965), 14.

103. Rosselot, *Origin*, 78–79.

104. Quoted in Lisk, *History*, 23.

105. Quoted in Rosselot, *Origin*, 77–78.

106. Richard Corby, "Bo School and its Graduates in Sierra Leone," *Canadian Journal of African Studies* 15, no. 2 (1981), 330, 325.

107. Ibid., 324.

108. Rosselot, *Origin*, 85–86.

109. See Lisk, *History*, 75.

110. Siaka Stevens, *What Life has Taught Me* (Abbottsbrook, Eng.: Kensal Press, 1984), 33–54.

111. Martin Kilson, *Political change in a West African State: A Study of the Modernization Process in Sierra Leone* (New York: Athenaeum, 1969), 154–58.

112. MOD, 176–80 (Shodeke), 325 (Renner).

113. MOD, 117 (Eustace Renner).

114. Rosselot, *Origin*, 84–85.

115. Ibid., 83–84.

116. For my account of this historical issue, see the section on "Warfare and Trade in the Nineteenth Century" in Chapter Two.

117. Edward Wilmot Blyden, *African Life and Customs* (Chesapeake, N.Y.: ECA Associates, rpt. 1990), chaps. 2 and 3; *Three Needs of Liberia* (London: Phillips, 1908), 8–9.

118. Blyden, *Three Needs,* 19–20.

119. Ibid., 22–23. The quote is from Dante's *Paradise*, Canto 17.

120. Ibid., 29–30.

121. Ibid., 8–9.

122. See Edward Wilmot Blyden, *Black Spokesman: Selected Published Writings of Edward Wilmot Blyden,* edited by Hollis R. Lynch (London: Cass, 1971), 18–19; 28–29; E. David Cronon, *Black Moses: the Story of Marcus Garvey and the Universal Negro Improvement Association* (Madison, Wis.: Univ. of Wisconsin Press, 1969), 83–85; Marcus Garvey, *Philosophy and Opinions of Marcus Garvey*, edited by Amy Jacques-Garvey (New York: Atheneum, 1992), 52–53: "As four hundred million men, women and children, worthy of the existence given us by the Divine Creator, we are determined to solve our own problem, by redeeming our Motherland Africa from the hands of alien exploiters and found there a government, a nation of our own, *strong enough to lend protection to the members of our race scattered all over the world*, and to compel the respect of the nations and races of the earth" [emphasis mine].

123. See, e.g. Garvey, *Philosophy*, 59.

124. Garvey, *Philosophy*, 40–41.

125. R.L. Okonkwo, "The Garvey Movement in West Africa," *The Journal of African History* 21, issue 1 (1980): 106–107.

126. Cronon, *Black Moses*, 9.

127. Lloyd Mignerey, "Friendship with Other Races," *Religious Telescope* (July 22, 1933), 22.

128. Mignerey carefully preserved the correspondence quoted here, and it was left to the Center for Evangelical United Brethren Heritage at Union Theological Seminary

129. Darrell Reeck, "Oral Data Regarding the History of the Process of Modernization and Related Mission Influences in Sierra Leone (1968–69)," interview #6.

CHAPTER FOUR

Traditional African Religion and Society in Sierra Leone

Mignerey was a man who thought about things, and took very seriously his responsibility to follow his thoughts wherever they might lead, regardless of the consequences. As I have shown, his outlook, while very much his own, was also one more or less shared by a liberal minority in his predominantly conservative denomination. But his spiritual journey out of racism led him to take risks that few others dared. He was also probably fairly unusual in his ability and willingness to empathize with what he called "the African point of view." He recognized the limitations of his understanding, but he did come to understand quite a bit even in the short time he was allowed to serve. I have so far focused mostly on his story and the story of his denomination. That story provides a perspective that has drawn us into the world of Protestant Christianity in the United States in the first two decades of the twentieth century, and then into the world of Sierra Leone in the 1920s. But at this point the question arises of the viewpoint of those cultures with which he came into contact. How did the world appear from *their* perspective? What was that "African point of view" he more and more seriously struggled to grasp? To answer this question I must now leave Mignerey and his struggles behind. In this chapter I focus on the religious beliefs and practices of the two largest ethnic groups in Sierra Leone, the Mende and the Temne. I endeavor to gather together as much evidence as possible in order to clearly define the nature of those beliefs and practices. But my aim is not merely definition and the tabulation of evidence. My aim is to understand those beliefs and practices, to understand them empathetically as well as intellectually, to make sense of them personally as much as to explain them objectively. To do this I need to work out a basic understanding of the nature of religious experience as such. I introduce this chapter with an outline of this basic understanding. I carry out my subsequent discussion of Mende and Temne religion in terms of the understanding I have developed. The discussion of traditional African religion in this chapter also lays the groundwork for my discussion in Chapter Five of the way African traditions interacted with Christianity.

James and Niebuhr:
A Definition of Religious Experience

The missionaries from the United States and Britain who were sent to Africa brought a set of religious beliefs and practices that differed in many respects radically from traditional African ones. In attempting to understand what happened when this confrontation took place and some Africans accepted the new beliefs and practices, very basic questions about religion and human nature inevitably arise. Is there even any common context within which the differing religions may be understood? Does it even make sense to talk of a single essence, "religion," in both cases? The widespread attack on "essentialism" in contemporary intellectual circles tends to deny that there is any set of terms that can define an essence of religion or human nature that all cultures and humans share. I believe this wholesale rejection of any and all "essences," typical of the contemporary "postmodern" movement, is ill-founded. The refutation of radical anti-essentialism is not within the scope of the present study.[1] What I would like to do is to outline a set of assumptions about religion and human nature which may help to make sense of the confrontation of traditional African culture and Christianity in the early twentieth century.

There is an essence of human nature which is closely tied to the essence of religion. This essence is not identical to what any objective expression conveys. Examples of what I mean by 'objective expression' include philosophical or scientific statements about human nature, religious creeds, and cultural symbols such as ceremonies and artworks. The essence of human nature is prior to all of these, and is their foundation. William James, in *Varieties of Religious Experience*, provides one of the best expressions of the sense of 'prior essence' I am getting at: "That unsharable feeling which each one of us has of the pinch of his individual destiny as he privately feels it rolling out on fortune's wheel."[2] James is well aware that the "feeling" of the "pinch of one's individual destiny" is something frequently dismissed in intellectual circles. That feeling "may be disparaged for its egotism, may be sneered at as unscientific, but it is the one thing that fills up the measure of our concrete actuality, and any would-be existent that should lack such a feeling, or its analogue, would be a piece of reality only half made up."[3] The essence of human nature is the experience of being an "I," from the perspective of "I." This is *not* to say that the essence of human nature is individuality in isolation from community, or of individual moral autonomy, or even to have a unique individual personality with special personal traits. "The perspective of 'I'" does not mean a set of beliefs about individual personality in its relationship to the world and to others. The point that James is making is much more fundamental. All human beings experience life as "I am here, I am here with others like me, these things are happening to me, I need to do something." This is not to say that all humans make these, or any other, particular assertions. But these assertions point to the primordial essence of human life.

Michel Henry has recently elaborated this basic point in great detail. What Henry calls attention to about "the pinch of one's individual destiny" is that such a feeling is prior not only to judgments made about it but to reflection itself. This feeling is our very being, and our very being is our very living. The human mind is constantly engaged in acts it lives through. For example, we can look around us and see things. The things we see are the objects of our seeing. But how do we experience our very living? For example, how do we experience our seeing before we reflect upon our seeing? According to Henry, we experience our act of seeing within that very act of seeing itself. We experience living through living, and not first by reflecting on living, making it into an object, and making judgments about it. Such objectification, while inevitable, also inevitably, for Henry, involves a kind of distortion and alienation. But lived-through experience, as lived through, is also that which gives objectification the only meaning it has. Henry's contribution is to have shown in detail the essential role of the non-objective and non-objectifiable in human life.

James makes certain claims about what the fundamental experience of the "pinch of individual destiny" is like. Within the experience of "I" there is a sense of higher and lower. The sense of higher and lower is a lived reality prior to explicit moral and religious thinking. Words that may grow out of the sense of lower include "despair," and "guilt." Words that may grow out of the sense of the higher include "hope" and "redemption." In *Varieties of Religious Experience*, James surveys a wide range of personal religious testimonies, and one common factor he discovers relates to this experience of the higher. Again and again, within the religious experiences James surveys, the individual "becomes conscious that this higher part is conterminous and continuous with a MORE of the same quality, which is operative in the universe outside of him, and which he can keep in working touch with, and in a fashion get on board of and save himself when all his lower being has gone to pieces in the wreck."[4] Our experience of "I" shades off into a feeling of "more," and our experience of this more can undergo a transformation. The transformation which brings the "more" to life overcomes despair and draws into one's life renewed energy and hope. The "more" that James is referring to is usually connected with some explicit set of beliefs. But James is calling attention to the reality of feeling which is the prior foundation of those beliefs. The experience of "more" is at the primordial level of our "I" experience—and as such is prior to explicit expressions and formulations.

James points out that another name given to the "more" is the subconscious mind. As such, it is not an experience that only occurs sometimes to certain people, but rather is a permanent dimension of all experience. I think there is a distinction implicit in this dimension. The experience of the "more" must, first of all, be the experience of *realizing* that something or someone *matters for its, her, or his own sake.* And secondly, this realization is one that effectively motivates one to act or indeed to live for the sake of that value. The universal essence of human nature is not simply the experience of "I" from the perspective of "I," but also the experience of people and things *mattering*, from the perspective of "I." By this I do not mean the experience of things mattering for my sake, but rather, *my* real experience of what matters, in contrast to what I might merely *tell* myself I should or do feel, and with what others *tell* me I should do or feel.

Everyone knows that one can be well acquainted on an objective level with what is going on in a certain situation, and even of why one should care about what is going in, while still not caring at all, while still not realizing for oneself that the situation and its participants *matter*. The difference between reciting the reasons why one should care, and actually caring, is not an objectively specifiable difference. And again, one may indeed care about the value in question, and desire to devote oneself to it, but fear that one lacks whatever it takes to continue to care and to struggle in the face of opposition or adversity. James by no means claims that the experience of spiritual rebirth he describes is entirely passive. He assumes that the person "whose lower being has gone to pieces" is in fact quite aware of this situation and is struggling mightily against it. The sense that there is a power one can "get on board of" does not arise because we will it to, but arises nevertheless only at the end of a long struggle when we begin to despair of our own powers. It is a feeling that wells up inside of us and gives us motivation we did not know we could have. But it nevertheless essentially requires our active, voluntary response.

If "the more" characterizes "the experience of things mattering as such," not only our experience of "I" but also our experience of the world and of beings in the world are characterized by the "more." This experience is a *personal* experiencing. It is inseparable from personal feeling. Indeed I am claiming that the "personal feeling" we have for things and people in the world is in fact our experience of the "more" at the heart of each as an individual being. That the meaning of anything always involves "more" in this sense means not that anything particular always implies and leads to more of what is particular, but that the meaning of anything in particular has within itself that which is in principle unspecifiable.

Michael Polanyi has explored in detail the role of such personal feeling even in the objective understanding of the world to which natural science aspires. One issue he explores that is especially—though perhaps unexpectedly—pertinent to the present context is the relevance of taxonomy to biology. Polanyi shows how the scientific study of living things, which aspires to a description of living things in exclusively chemical terms, in fact cannot sever its ties to the act simply of looking at living things and recognizing one as being a living thing of a particular kind, such as "bird" or "Prothonatary Warbler (*Protonotaria citrea*)." Polanyi shows how there can be no set of rules to follow, or absolutely determinate set of defined features, which will enable us to recognize and classify living beings. Such recognition and classification can only be learned through personal knowing—it cannot be reduced to a set of impersonal criteria: "Taxonomy is based on connoisseurship."[5] There is literally no substitute for the personal experience of simply looking at living beings and gradually sensing which ones belong to which species. What one learns through such looking cannot be reduced to a set of rules that another person could mechanically follow and arrive at the same recognitions. Contemporary science, Polanyi wrote, devalues such knowing. He finds in our culture "a steadily mounting distaste for certain forms of knowing and being; a growing reluctance to credit ourselves with the capacity for personal knowing, and a corresponding unwillingness to recognize the reality of the unspecifiable entities established by such knowing."[6] Such unspecifiable entities include species of plants and animals.

And Polanyi makes it clear that not only the recognition of species, but the recognition of life, is a matter of recognizing that which is unspecifiable: "the insights by which we recognize life in individual plants and animals, and distinguish their several kinds…reveal a reality to which we have access by no other channels."[7] Inherent in the personal recognition of a particular kind of living thing is necessarily the personal recognition of a living thing as such, and of life as such. Out of the heart of any recognition of individual life grows the sense of mattering, that this individual life is something that matters, that is worth caring about. The unspecifiable background of experience out of which arises our recognition of individual beings as living, and each as of a certain kind, and as mattering, is another example of our experience of the "more." In making this claim, I am of course applying the notion of the "more" to a realm beyond that to which James originally applied it. I am claiming that the "more" suffuses or underlies not only self-experience, but also objects in the world as experienced. One might call this an "objective more"—not in the sense that its meaning is objective or objectifiable, but rather in the sense that everything objective, as experienced, bears within itself an unobjectifiable dimension of meaning.

As is very well known, ever since Descartes, philosophers have pursued the question of how it is possible for an individual consciousness to know real objects other than itself. Within this question, a series of further questions emerges: How can I know any object? How can I know the real existence of objects in the spatial world? How can I recognize anything as anything? How can I recognize life? How can I know other "I"'s, which, though embodied, do not exist in space like physical objects do? There is no adequate answer to any of these questions. But from the perspective of James and Polanyi, I would like to suggest that each level of knowledge and recognition is inescapably personal, and essentially involves a fundamental level of feeling which cannot be made entirely objective and whose meaning essentially involves that which cannot be objectively specified. This founding level of feeling is essential to our perception both of being and of value.

I am at this point of course providing a very summary treatment of an enormously complex realm of philosophical issues and ideas. The philosophical traditions I am drawing upon in shaping an approach to these issues have been relatively unpopular among the intellectual elites of the latter half of the twentieth century in England, the United States, and even Europe: the philosophies of

William James, of Edmund Husserl, of Alfred North Whitehead, of Louis La-velle, of Maurice Merleau-Ponty, and of Michel Henry. But the consensus—whether it be that of positivism or of postmodernism—that dominates those elites has nevertheless been unable to relegate these movements to the status of outcastes.

In broad terms, what philosophers as disparate as James, Husserl, White-head, Merleau-Ponty, Lavelle, and Henry share is the fundamental notion that consciousness and being are not limited to what is objectively graspable and propositionally definable, and that feeling is the fundamental dimension of hu-man consciousness out of which the objective dimensions arise. Of course with-in this group there is much disagreement as to what "feeling" is, and in what way and to what extent the concept of feeling can help us understand human existence and human knowledge. For example, Henry makes claims for feeling that Husserl would most likely call extravagant. But one of Husserl's crucially important contributions to this discussion is his phenomenological demonstra-tion that our knowledge of other human beings, of "other minds," cannot be an inference. Even though, in a sense, nothing is more transcendent to one "I" than another "I," nevertheless our knowledge of the existence of other "I"'s is, and can be, nothing like a hypothesis we somehow create to explain a set of data consisting of the observed motions of living bodies. In a sense, our knowledge of others, of "other minds" must be a matter of direct perception, although the definition of this sense presents insuperable difficulties. The term Husserl uses for such perception is "empathy." And Husserl's insistence that empathy is not a matter of inference is in a sense an extension of his more basic insight that the perception of spatial objects is not a matter of image or picture consciousness. Appearances are not additional objects that double and represent real objects. Rather, appearances are that *through which* the objects themselves appear to us. (If, in seeing an object, what I see were directly something like a picture, the question would remain of how I then know what it is a picture of. That know-ledge would also have, however, to be only knowledge of a picture—leading to an infinite regress.)

Drawing on the work of Whitehead, Henry and especially Lavelle, I suggest that the fundamental dimension of our experience of other beings is that of *par-ticipation* in their life. Such participation is prior to judgments I make about them, and even prior to our knowledge of them as objects over against me. I recognize the life of beings around me by participating in that life, and the self-consciousness of other beings by participating in that self-consciousness. By 'participating' I do not merely mean doing things together—I mean that the primal original starting point of my encounter with them is already a kind of participation. Knowing is always a kind of empathy. In everyday terms, I am calling attention to the fact that there is always available to us the sense of the life of the living beings around us *from within*. If we let ourselves, we can feel what they feel from their perspective.

The difficulty this view faces is, of course, that *what* we know by participat-ing in the life of others is precisely that it *is* other in the most radical sense. But while I can never *be* another "I," there is no limit to the involvement of my life with the life of other I's, and of my life with theirs. Our experience of others is of an involvement that reaches without limit into the depths of one's own self experience, coupled with a distinction which makes each I irreplaceable and unrepeatable in its perspective and inviolable in its agency. The meaning of caring about others is inseparable both from the reliving of their experience and participating in their being, and from the recognition that the experience and being of others is in the most fundamental sense absolutely independent and distinct.   The reason I am willing to introduce such a radically paradoxical idea into the present discussion is that I find that it does more justice to the experience of human existence than any other: and specifically to the experience of human beings in their social, ethical, and religious life. Our non-objective experience of the "more" is at the heart of not only our self-experience but our experience of the spatial world, the living world, and of other selves. And this affective experience is in some sense the experience of a unity of self and other, self and object, that is both prior to their distinction and the foundation of that distinction. To acknowledge the inescapable significance of this experience does not necessarily imply having attained a clear vision in which its paradoxes are somehow mystically resolved.

The fundamental human experiences to which the notion of participation does justice are those of love, of beauty, and of community. In personal and communal relationships people again and again have the sense of sharing in a common life, of participating in one another's lives, of being caught up into something that is both beyond the self and yet seems to well up from within the self. And the experience of beauty again and again has the character of feelings being somehow inherent in the appearance of things, and of the enjoyment of those appearances through a kind of sharing in those feelings. I somehow sense, perhaps through a ritual, that I am participating in the common life of a community, or I somehow experience the pain or the joy of a loved one "as if" it were my own.

What is the relationship between my experience of a common life, and my experience of another person's pain or joy, and the actual inner lives of others? Is my sense of a common life, or my sense of another's pain or joy, just some sort of copy or image of the experience of others? Is it something merely within me, which then somehow corresponds to that which is in others? But—and this is a conclusion Husserl himself does not draw—this would be but a form of the theory of perception as picture consciousness. Do I then experience directly the inner lives of others after all, but merely as objects, and not in their very inwardness? But in fact I do not do this. I experience the inner life of others *in its subjectivity, in its very inwardness.* If I merely experienced it objectively, the question would remain, how do I know it *as it is*, namely *as* subjectivity, as non-objective self-experience? For its very subjectivity, its very inwardness, its very non-objectivity, is precisely what I must know, if I am to know another "I" at all. Despite the insuperable paradoxes that ensue, there seems to be no alternative but to conclude that my own non-objective self-experience participates directly in the self-experience of others. And again, this is also not merely an abstruse speculation or esoteric mystical utterance. People in general are quite willing to describe at least certain very moving life experiences in very similar terms.[8]

The notion of participation I am defending has affinities to Whitehead's view, but is most explicit in the work of Lavelle and Henry. For both, one's knowledge of others is only made possible through the participation of one's own consciousness in a common life. For Henry, that life in which I participate is the same life that I live—it is my own non-objective self awareness as such. I am myself, as non-objectively self-aware, only through my participation in that life, and through that same participation, I also am in community with others.

> If one must speak of the experience of others, how do the members of the community relate to one another in life, in a way prior to their being together in a world? In this primordial experience, which can hardly even be thought—since it does evade all thought—the living being is not for himself, nor for another. He is nothing but pure experience, without subject, without horizon, without signification, without object. What he experiences is identically: himself; the wellspring of life; and the other insofar as the other is also this wellspring.... Community is like a subterranean water table of affectivity and each person drinks the same water from this well and this source which, at the same time is none other than himself.[9]

Lavelle describes the participation through which we encounter "other minds" or better, simply "other human beings," in these terms:

> It would be an error to think that it is through phenomena, which is to say, through expression, that one's communication with other consciousnesses is accomplished. Rather, this communication itself presupposes a *strictly ontological communion* which only arises within an existence out of which all the consciousnesses arise, from which they draw their participating activity, and by which they are capable of entering into unity, one with another.[10]

It is through our participation in the same Being, the same Life, that we participate in the lives of others. For Lavelle this participation is inseparable from expression: the human face, human gestures, human language. But such objective expression is not a medium on the basis of which we somehow infer the existence of others. Even though there is no communion without bodily expression, communion is existentially prior to expression; communion is the foundation of expression and not vice versa. The feeling we have of the life of others from within is not a "projection" but is in fact the source from which even the mere fact of our recognition of them as other living beings arises. Without this primordial feeling there would not even be anything there for us to project anything onto. Life is shared and we can share in the life of others. The real being of others is present to us, and *in* us, through such sharing.

Lavelle makes an explicit connection between his philosophy of participation and Levy-Bruhl's anthropological concept of participation. An oversimplified understanding of such participation would have the "primitive" constantly absorbed in some kind of mystical trance in which the difference between self and others disappears. But Lavelle insists that participation in the being of others is simply human affectivity as the fundamental nature of human perception and human existence. According to Lavelle:

The primitives are the metaphysicians of pure affectivity.... That which distinguishes modern science is the isolation of matter, the recognition of mechanisms in matter which we can bring under our control and make use of to meet our needs.... But nature is infinitely more rich and subtle than the abstract representation of it provided by science; science leaves nothing but the skeleton of nature; science withdraws all color and life. For nature does not nourish our intelligence alone, it also nourishes our power to feel and to love. Our consciousness as a whole finds in nature a resonance. This resonance exists between things, between spirits and things, and among spirits themselves.[11]

Lavelle does not mean here to be describing only "primitive mentality." He is describing human existence as such. Levy-Bruhl works with essentially the same concept of affectivity—and Levy-Bruhl as well denies that "participation" is a mode of feeling confined to "primitives." Lavelle quotes Levy-Bruhl to the effect that "were the primitive mentality to disappear, with it would possibly also disappear poetry, art, inventiveness in the sciences, in short everything that makes for greatness and beauty in human life."[12] Levy-Bruhl's reflections on the notion of participation, recorded in the *Notebooks* he kept during the last year of his life, are particularly relevant here. By the end of his career, Levy-Bruhl had not abandoned the notion of participation, but he had revised his understanding of its relationship to logical, conceptual thought. Participation is an affective, emotional experience that is primary. For example, through participation, one experiences one's identity with ones appurtenances—with one's hands and limbs. But one also experiences one's identity, for example, with a totemic animal, in a sense like that of one's identity with one's appurtenances. Levy-Bruhl realized that identity with a totemic animal is not a violation of the logical law of contradiction, but only of physical possibility. And Levy-Bruhl also affirmed that participation is not a peculiar feature of "primitive peoples," but is in fact a universal dimension of human consciousness. "I understand the facts better today, and I have recognized, first that participation did not belong exclusively to the primitive mentality but held also a place in our own, or, if one prefers, that the primitive mentality is in reality an aspect, a condition (Maritain) of human mentality in general."[13] And participation, in Levy-Bruhl's final view, is by no means something in the human condition that is somehow ancillary, supplemental, or to be superseded. Participation is necessary and essential. "This mentality we constantly find around us, and even in us....represents something fundamental and indestructible in the nature of man."[14] "In this way, participation is not 'explained'—it cannot be and ought not to be, it has no need of legitimation; but one sees its necessary place in the human mind—and as a result its role in religion, in metaphysics, in art and even in the conception of the whole of nature."[15]

Our awareness of beings is our awareness of beings as values, and the very sense of "being as a value" itself represents an unspecifiable context. Not the context of other, additional beings, which might give a being value, but the inner context of each being which is its being-a-value. My point is that this is something we *feel*, and this inner context is our most primordial feeling. James claims that religious experience has two stages: "the unease" and "the solution." The unease is a sense of despair which drains away the feeling that life is worth living, or that one has the inner strength to sustain the effort to pursue, create, or be true to the values one cares about. The "solution" James describes as "the getting on board of" one's higher self and "sav[ing] [one]self when all [one's] lower being has gone to pieces in the wreck." The "more" as "solution" is on the one hand a powerful feeling. But that very feeling both inspires and requires a deliberate, active response. James describes not only a relatively passive sense of a powerful "more," but also an active "getting on board of" that more.

The Protestant theologian H. Richard Niebuhr begins his analysis of the meaning of faith with considerations that really constitute a philosophy of religion rather than merely a segment of theology. These considerations, I think, provide a clearer picture of what James' "getting on board of" involves. According to Niebuhr, faith is a universal human reality. Humans simply do not live without faith. By this he does not mean that all humans are implicitly Christians or share any particular set of beliefs. Rather he means that to be human is to live in a universe of values that are capable of inspiring our allegiance. We experience the values around us not as inert and static—but rather as powers. Our allegiance to those powers is not a matter of having beliefs *about* them, and not even fundamentally a matter of believing *that* they exist, but rather, believing *in* them. To believe *in* a value is to rely upon it as a power one can trust to make life worth living—and not only in a spiritual sense, but also in the sense of providing for one's physical needs. Along with the act of trust goes the act of loyalty—of commitment to the value which involves obligations for specific actions. Niebuhr claims that, to live, simply *means* to relate to values in this way.

Niebuhr includes an extensive discussion of the specifically social values. Various kinds of groups to which people belong are always among the most prominent and potent values in their lives—one need only think of the family, the school, the nation, the church, the business organization. One inevitably relies upon one's society for physical sustenance as well as for a sense that one has a meaningful place in the world. And societies are clearly objects of loyalty, making demands upon their members and inspiring active allegiance. Of course all values are not specifically social—there are truth, moral standards, beauty, and pleasure as well. But Niebuhr's perspective on values continually brings out the social character of even the ones not explicitly social.

In short, through James and Niebuhr (as well as Polanyi, Henry, and Lavelle), I am bringing to the discussion of religious interaction a certain perspective on the nature of religion and its relation to human nature. The primary assumption is that humans live in what is primordially a universe of values. What is universal in human nature is personal experience and personal knowing. Personal knowing is the knowing of the world as a world of values. The meaning of knowing a being as a value is the experience of "more." Personal knowing is not primarily an objective knowing but rather a participation. The individual, in knowing the world personally, is participating in the life of the surrounding beings. In caring about the surrounding beings, the individual is naturally led to care about their origin and destiny. The arising of the sense of value, participation, origin, and destiny *as* vital issues is the experience of the "more." The vital awakening of the sense of "more" is in a sense passive—it is not something we can seek out but rather can only be open to. Faith as loyalty and trust is the active response to our spontaneous experience of values with their inherent sense of "more." On the whole, Niebuhr's discussion of religious experience slights the passive origins that James so clearly focuses on. Niebuhr, in his emphasis on faith as active, neglects the passive dimension of experience—which is really the imaginative dimension—upon which the active dimension of faith itself relies. The two thinkers together present a more complete account of religious experience.

James's notion of the "more," and Lavelle's notion of affectivity and participation, both represent the *passive* dimension of experience, and are terms of phenomenological descriptions, and not values to which anyone pledges allegiance. Reflection on this dimension may well lead the development of concepts such as "Life" or "Existence" or "Being" or "God." But the concepts of the "more," of "participation," and of "affectivity" are meant first of all as merely descriptive, in answer to the question of what the experience is like through which we know the reality of values, of others, and of the question of our origin and destiny. The fact that human experience universally has these characteristics does not mean that all humans implicitly believe in Life, Being, or God, or even that anyone has ever thought specifically in terms of these phenomenological abstractions. To live through an experience of communion which brings a particular value (such as "my family," "my nation," "honesty," or "the class of 2006") to life is simply not the same as to commit oneself to and trust in an explicit value called "Life" or "the spirit of Life" or "the spirit of Nature" or "God, the Origin of Life."

I am claiming that the universal religious experience is that of the "more," of participation, and of loyalty to and trust in values. But there is a further dimension, which is simply that of our human capability for explicitly recognizing that we share a common human situation, and for reflecting upon and raising questions about that situation. Those questions include questions about our origin and destiny. In recognizing that we share a common human situation, who we are, as such, and the world as a totality, as such, becomes an issue for us. These questions, I claim, do not represent merely the pursuit of abstract speculation. They arise from a person's actual encounter with his or her own being in the world confronting other beings and persons. The questions are inspired by the sense of "more" at the heart of my experience of values and of concrete existence itself as a value. Such questions have of course been posed in countless different ways, and been given countless different answers. The whole of human philosophy, religious thought, and "mythology" comes to mind.

Niebuhr, as a Christian theologian and not just a philosopher of religion, advocates a certain way of posing and of answering these questions. The questions for Niebuhr are: Why do I exist? Why do humans exist? Why does the world exist? Why do values exist? Why are all the values to which humans devote themselves doomed to frustration? Niebuhr's answers are: Humans and the world exist because they were meant to exist. God created them because he values them. God created humans, time, and space. He is that upon which all depends. God at the same time is the enemy of what we value, since all that he created is limited and doomed to die. Through faith, nevertheless, we are capable of trusting in God as the ultimate and absolute value and power which gives meaning to life in spite of its inexplicable tragedy. Our relationship to God, in faith, is one of "friendship."

In James's terms, the "unease" for Niebuhr is a matter of passing through the despairing recognition of the finitude and mortality of all we value, and the "solution" is the inner power of meaning we gain through trust in God, which is at the same time a deliberate act and a gift. Our experience of the "more" involves: a sense of the values around us and of the value inherent in our own existence; a sense of mystery which suggests the question of origin and destiny; and a sense of power which seems at once to well up from inside of us and to have its origin beyond us. For Niebuhr, the "solution" comes through communion with our origin. But both James and Niebuhr insist that the question of religious experience as such is simply a different matter than the question of which "solution," or which object of faith, persons or groups may adopt. Taking James and Niebuhr together, we may say that the "more," "loyalty," and "trust," simply define us as humans. How we respond to and interpret the "more," what we are loyal to and trust in, is infinitely various. Even questions and beliefs about origin and destiny cannot be said to define religious experience or religious life as such, although the consistency is striking with which such questions are raised and such beliefs appear across time and across cultures.

African Religions and Religious Experience

Religious experience is the experience of the world as a world of values and living powers; it is the experience of vital participation in the surrounding world and in one's society, including one's attitude of active allegiance; and it may be concern about one's origin and about one's connection to one's origin. Traditional African religions encompass all these dimensions of religious experience.

In the balance of this chapter I will be applying the understanding of religious experience just sketched out to traditional African religion, specifically Mende and Temne religion, with some reference to related traditions, such as the Kpelle. I will employ the notions of the "more," of loyalty, and of trust to interpret the experience of ancestors, God, magic, spirits, and the human community. The human community, in traditional African religion generally, encompasses both the living and the living dead or ancestors. I will claim that these three dimensions—loyalty, trust, and the "more"—together constitute the experience of "communion." I will argue that the typical locus of religious experience for these groups in fact lies in communion with the human community of the living and the dead. Generally, both pragmatic reliance on magic and spiritual reliance on God are, in different ways, ancillary to this central experience of communion with human community.

Reliance on Ancestors and God

Traditional African religions include perhaps universally the assumption that one's dead ancestors are still alive as spirits, and still exert an active influence upon goings-on in the world. The sense of the presence and activity of the ancestors is the most immediate expression of engagement with one's origins. The ancestors represent one's origin most obviously in that they first of all are, or will be, one's parents. But the transformation into ancestorhood involves more than death and afterlife—reaching ancestorhood means assuming the role of watching over the social group of one's living descendants and enforcing traditional moral regulations. The loyalty toward and trust in one's social group among the living extends to loyalty toward and trust in the ancestors. If people believe in the ancestors as much as, or even more than, they believe in their parents, their relation to their ancestors will be one of love and loyalty and not merely fear.

Concern for the question of origins in African religions has also given rise ideas about God. Most traditional African cultures include the belief that a single God created everything in the world, including the earth, nature spirits, human beings, and according to some cultures, subordinate divinities.[16] What might constitute an accurate generalization about the *attitude* of most African cultures toward the creator-God is a matter of dispute among those who have thoroughly surveyed the available evidence. Is "worship" of God an important part of most African traditional religions? John Mbiti, in just such an attempt to reach accurate conclusions about African traditional religions in general, claims that "the majority of prayers and invocations are addressed to God, and some to the living dead or other spiritual beings many of whom serve as intermediaries."[17] Harry Sawyerr, in his study of the Mende, Akan, and Yoruba, concludes that "one cannot but be impressed by the fact that among all the tribes which have been studied, there is always some reference to God as the center of the supreme Authority which controls the world."[18] However, Sawyerr continues, "he is also believed to be remotely situated from the everyday events of human life" and "God is...never worshiped," except as in the case of the Akan."[19] Sawyerr concludes, for example, from his extensive study of Mende religion, that it does not include the direct worship of this ultimate creator God—devotion and prayer is focused upon the ancestors. The ancestors do, however function as intermediaries between the living and God, and God is recognized as the final power beyond, and underlying, the power of the ancestors. From this it may be concluded that, even though the traditional Mende may not directly *worship* God, they do *believe in* God in Niebuhr's sense, since their loyalty and trust in the ancestors assumes the dependence of everything and everyone on God, and includes the sense that the ancestors are closer to God than the living are. The term that E. Bolaji Idowu assigns to this kind of belief is "diffuse monotheism" or "implicit monotheism." Idowu chooses these terms "because here we have a monotheism in which there exist other powers which derive from Deity such being and authority that they can be treated, for practical purposes, almost as ends in themselves."[20]

Robin Horton, who is extremely critical of the way he claims scholars like Mbiti and Idowu view African religions through "Judeo-Christian spectacles," acknowledges that most traditional African religions do include the notion of a creator God. But Horton is close to Sawyerr in asserting that the attitude toward such a God is not one of worship. Horton defines religion as the "extension of the field of people's social relationships beyond the confines of purely human society."[21] And, Horton claims, both human relationships with humans and with non-humans such as gods or spirits can be located on a continuum depending on their purpose. At one end of the continuum lies communion. Relationships of communion are valued for their own sake. At the other end lies the purpose of prediction and control of events. Relationships with humans, gods, spirits, ancestors, or God can be experienced as mere means to the attainment of ends other than the relationship itself.[22] Horton claims that all religions involve both dimensions, but differ in their relative emphasis on communion versus prediction and control. Horton claims traditional African religions are focused on the prediction and control of events in this world, and in them, "the quest for communion takes a definite second place."[23]

Horton's pointing out of the many analogies between traditional—especially magical—practices and Western science is extremely illuminating. Horton may be right that communion with God, gods, or spirits is relatively attenuated in, and not at the center of, traditional African religious experience. The perspective I have developed from James and Niebuhr constitutes a specific definition of what we might mean by "communion," which is the dimension of religion that exceeds the prediction and control of events: the "more" as the experience of value and the attitude of loyalty and trust which humans take toward values. Myth and ritual do express feelings and attitudes beyond a desire for physical well being and the determination to achieve it, including a sense of wonder over the question of one's origin and destiny, a sense of being at home in a world teeming with spiritual beings like oneself, and an attitude of loyalty toward and trust in other spiritual beings.

However, it may well be that God and creation myths involving God never lay at the center of traditional African religious concerns. And it is certainly true that a great deal of emphasis was placed upon the prediction and control of events through communication with ancestors and spirits, and that the most immediate object of concern and appeal was most likely to be the ancestors, and that in turn concern with the ancestors had a great deal to do with the prediction and control of events, such as disease. But what of one's relationship to one's human community? Horton simply defines religion in such a way as to exclude that relationship. I define religion otherwise, regarding the most essential feature of religion as relationship to values—including one's living community—rather than relationship to the supernatural. The question of human community in fact creates something of a problem for Horton's limitation of religion to supernatural concerns. Horton's conclusion from his survey of ethnographic work on attitudes toward the ancestors is that "the central features of emotional and relational commitment with the ancestors are continuous with the central features of commitment to living elders."[24] This continuity challenges Horton's arbitrary exclusion of relationships with living humans from the realm of religious experience. If Africans experience their personal relationships with their elders as intrinsically valuable, does this valued communion then vanish when their elders die and become ancestors? The case of ancestors thus also calls into question

Horton's central claim about the centrality of prediction and control, and the secondary role of communion in traditional African religious experience.

Sjoerd Hofstra, in an early study of the Mende, describes a scene of ritualized mourning he witnessed:

> One of the first times, however, when I witnessed a wailing, I could not help feeling sympathy with the group of women whose husband had just died and who now were loudly lamenting and crying. I concluded that their sorrow must be very great, and I said so to one of my informants who was walking with me. His answer, however, cooled down my feelings to some degree. "We Mendi wait. After three months you can see which of the women is feeling real grief. The wives who loved their husband, will then still show their grief. The others, however, will be glad, because they will then get another husband."....After the wailing for Maama [a young woman who had died suddenly and unexpectedly] which I briefly described, I heard my informants making remarks about the affected way in which one of the women praised the beauty of the dead. They thought also that she had been too hasty in asking to give messages to the ancestors. On the other hand, the mother of Maama was unable to cry. At first we heard her announce in bewilderment to some people whom it concerned: 'Life is not in Maama!' or 'Life is not in my child!' But later on, when the people were wailing, she stood at some distance from her house, leaning against a wall; she was evidently overwhelmed by grief and unable to say a word. This was clearly understood by the people, as could be noticed from their respectful and sympathizing attitude. Such and other ways in which the personality can express itself are possible within the framework of ceremonial behavior.[25]

Beliefs about the presence of the ancestors, unsurprisingly, do not make grief any less real than it is for human beings everywhere. But if another expression of sentiment Hofstra encountered is at all typical, a real sense of communion with ancestors is very much a part of Mende beliefs about the living dead: "In a talk which I had with a group of Mendi friends about these problems of death, one of them remarked: 'We Mendi have a saying: If I die, it cannot be helped. I am not going the way of a stranger. I shall meet my family there.'"

[margin note:] mende belief

Regarding the relative importance of communion vs. prediction and control, Horton writes:

> From all this, one answer to our question about the loadings of communion and manipulation in religion seems to be that those religions with a highly manipulative emphasis are found in conjunction with human social systems whose communion aspects are 'balanced' in the sense sketched above; whilst those religions with a very strong element of communion occur where there is a similarly strong imbalance in the human social system.[26]

[margin note:] imbalance

The point Horton seems to be making is that modern societies, with their greater mobility and impersonality, are unbalanced due to their lack of intimate and stable communities, and religions such as Christianity, with their emphasis on personal communion with the deity, are in a sense compensations for this imbalance. More traditional societies involving more stable and intimate communal life, by contrast, are 'balanced' in the sense that intimate communion with one's community is a living, daily reality, and as a consequence, personal communion with gods or spirits is unnecessary. One striking fact that provides

(margin note: Communion of one's social group.)

some support for this interpretation is that it does seem that the most intimate experiences of communion in Mende religion are heightened experiences of communion with one's social group, as in the Poro and Sande initiations. But it seems likely that this sense of social communion shades off into veneration of ancestors. Horton's analyses on the whole point to the conclusion not that communion is a secondary element in African religions, but rather that it is at least as important as prediction and control, but is centered upon communion with one's immediate human community rather than with God. Horton does define religion as the "extension of the field of people's social relationships beyond the confines of purely human society."[27] But the foregoing discussion raises the question of why purely human social relationships should not just as well fall within the field of religion. My definition of religion as the experience of value encompasses both.

Reliance on Magic and Spirits

(margin note: magic and medicine)

A third extremely widespread aspect of traditional African cultures is magic and 'medicine'. Magic and 'medicine' represent the dimension of traditional (and not only African) cultures that is perhaps the most difficult for members of modern Westernized societies to comprehend. The basic belief underlying reliance upon 'medicine' and magic is that there are forces in the world, really effective in determining the course of events, which are subject to human control. Of course, this assumption is identical to the basic assumption behind modern Western physical science. According to Western physical science, force in nature obeys certain laws which follow mathematical pattern. Knowledge of these laws is useful in the application of physical force through human action, for example, to make bridges, steam engines, antibiotics, or atomic bombs. In traditional societies, the idea of force does include what everyone would recognize as physical force (for example, a tree falling on someone, or a person picking something up). But the "force" that is in the world is not limited to physical force in this sense. There is a force which can respond to what we say to it, and agree to physically perform what we ask of it, as long as we know the right way of speaking. This force may be thought of as relatively personal, or relatively impersonal. "Magic" is the communication and negotiation with this force, or with exemplars of this force, that may inhabit, for example, certain kinds of plants. A 'medicine' may be a physical object, composed of, perhaps, the leaves of certain plants whose mystical force has been enlisted to accomplish certain goals by a person schooled in the effective means of communication with such forces.

The use of magic to prepare 'medicine' has the specific goal of the control of events and of human behavior. 'Medicines' are prepared to, for example, ward off disease and prevent accidents. They may also be used to bring illness to those who disobey societal regulations, for example, against stealing. If religious experience is our experience of the world as a world of intrinsic values, and is a matter of how we relate to those values as values, then magic in this sense is not a part of religion. For clearly the function of magic in traditional societies is analogous to the function of physical science, technology, and perhaps something like "organizational psychology" or "public relations" in modern Westernized societies. 'Medicine' is clearly a tool, an instrumental value.

But if we consider the wider context of the experience of the world from which beliefs about magic emerge, a clear connection to religion becomes apparent. This experience is of a world "swarming with souls," as Harry Sawyer puts it. Every relationship is a relationship of living intersubjectivity—not just relationships with the living individuals around one, but also relationships with the dead, relationships with the spirit of one's society, relationships with animals and plants, and with the spiritual forces inhabiting them, and relationships with spirits inhabiting the bush. For example, dreams of one's dead relations are not experienced and remembered as "mere imagination," but as actual contact and communication with the living dead. Certain kinds of plants are not experienced as mere physical objects, but as the habitation of the spirit of that kind of plant, with whom one can and does communicate and make agreements.

A member of a modern Westernized society, reading and hearing reports of these experiences, may perhaps do so with some discomfort—or perhaps respond with laughter, or even scorn. The missionary literature is certainly replete with the latter. I do not personally believe that it is possible to actually communicate and make agreements with the spirit of any species of plant. But one fact often overlooked is that Western physical science, which assumes only the existence of blind physical force and material particles, has succeeded only in making certain accurate predictions. The accuracy of those specific predictions simply has not proven that only physical forces and material particles exist. And in fact all of us have immediate, absolute evidence in our own conscious and embodied existence that consciousness is real and that events do occur—i.e. the movements of our own bodies—that are in fact due to conscious decisions and not simply to the blind operation of physical forces. And yet this simple idea meets with widespread condemnation in contemporary Western culture. From a comparative cultural perspective that is interested in evaluating as well as describing culture, it seems to me that if anything deserves the pejorative epithet "superstition" it is the set of unquestioned materialistic assumptions that has invaded so much of Western culture especially in the past two centuries.

The assumption that the world consists only of physical forces and material particles also flies in the face of our experience of life. When we recognize a living being, we are encountering something that the assumptions of physical science cannot begin to explain or account for. Life does appear as a power and a force. The growth of a plant from a seed *looks like* an instance of effort being made to reach a beautiful and satisfying goal. Even the life of plants appears to us as akin to our own life, and life appears to us as something akin to consciousness. We experience that life through participation, which is prior to any objectification. The belief that one can communicate with the spirit of a plant has its natural origin, I suggest, in the encounter with that plant as a living being. The appearance of any living being is such as to suggest that this is a being one might talk to. It is a measure of the pervasiveness of the materialist superstition in our society that a statement such as this is likely to be greeted with laughter, scorn, and sneering dismissal. The reality is that we know life, but we do not know what it is, we cannot explain what it is, and we do not know what it might be.

The feeling that surrounds our experience of life suggests that there is *more* to it than meets the eye. According to the materialist view, our perception of the life and beauty in things—of the feeling of vitality in a tree or a bird, or even a sunrise—is merely an epiphenomenon, merely the effect of material causes. I am suggesting to the contrary that our experience of life and beauty is *truthful*—the *origin* of the experience is in fact the very life and beauty the experience seems to perceive. This does not mean, however, that reliance upon magic and spirits implies a reliance upon some sort of unitary spirit of life or nature. Spirit beliefs do not amount to some kind of romantic nature-worship. I merely mean to suggest that spirit beliefs are rooted in the real appearances of things, and even if not literally true, are nevertheless not mere illusions or arbitrary concoctions.

Bonds of Social Loyalty and Trust

A fourth dimension of religious experience is the individual's relationship to the social group to which he or she belongs. The importance of one's relationship to one's group, and the intimacy and strength of the bond between individual and group, is much greater in Africa than in modern Westernized societies. The group is a powerful reality one confronts in every aspect of life, and the words 'loyalty' and 'trust' that Niebuhr uses aptly define what we mean by such 'bonds.' Michael Jackson, in his study of the Kuranko (an ethnic group in Sierra Leone that occupies an area to the north of the Mende and just to the east of the Temne) provides one of the clearest discussions available of the meaning of group solidarity in Africa. Jackson points out that, in contrast to Western cultures, what is primary is not the isolated, autonomous individual, but being together with others: "The most fundamental postulate in the Kuranko world view is that persons exist only in relation to one another."[28] Jackson is not saying that there are no individuals in African culture, or that there is no fundamental I-experience. Rather, he affirms such I-experience as universal: "In Kuranko the word *morgo* denotes the living person. In this sense *morgo* refers to the particular man, the empirical subject of speech, thought, and will, which is recognized in all societies."[29] The difference in relation to Western cultures is evident in the Kuranko word *morgoye*, or 'personhood':

> *Morgoye* is quite unlike the English word *personality*, which connotes personal identity, a 'distinctive moral character especially when of a marked kind' (OED). *Morgoye* refers to moral qualities which ideally characterize social relationships. While *personality* implies an individual who stands out against his or her social background, *morgoye* connotes abstract qualities of social relations. In particular, *morgoye* denotes altruism and magnanimity, virtues which the Kuranko set at the foundation of the social order. Of a generous person, mindful of others, who gives without ulterior motive, it is said *ke morgo* ('this is a person').[30]

Jackson describes a particularly striking image the Kuranko use to express their understanding of social relations, and of the relation of the individual to the group:

> The interdependence of members of the community or of a family may be expressed in terms of the network of ropes which are tied over the rice farms when the crop is nearing maturity. One end of the rope is always tied to the foot of the bird-scaring platform where the children sit with slingshots and keep birds from scavenging the rice. When this main rope is tugged, all the tributary ropes shake. This scares away birds. It is sometimes said that 'one's birth is like the bird-scaring rope' (*soron i le ko yagbyile*), or '<u>one's birth is like a chain</u>' (*soron i la ko yolke*) because <u>one's fate is always inextricably tied to the fate of others</u>. In the case of the family group it is said that the main rope is like the father where it is secured to the bird-scaring platform, and like the mother at the free end; the children are the tributary strands. These images, borrowed from the fields of farming and gift-exchange, at once indicate that Kuranko ideology reflects a mode of production, distribution, and exchange in which community relationships are central.[31]

family bond

And Jackson also points out that society, in the Kuranko world view, is not limited to a group of living human beings:

> The ontological priority of the group as a network of interdependent parts, and the absence of the idea of the individual as an autonomous moral being, help us understand several aspects of Kuranko thought which at first glance might seem bizarre. From the Kuranko point of view the field of social relationships may include totemic animals, ancestors, bush spirits, a divine creator, fetishes, as well as man. In other words, Being is not necessarily limited to human being. *Morgoye* may be found in relations between man and ancestor, man and totemic animal, man and God, and so on.[32]

Bond of

<u>Bonds of loyalty and trust unite not only living humans, but also the living</u> with the dead. Even magic involves bonds of loyalty and trust. One relies upon the spirit of the plants with whom one has made an agreement. And one's relation to that spirit may not be merely personal—rather, there often exists a traditional relationship between certain spirits and certain societies that possess the knowledge of certain medicines. *Morgoye*, which we might even translate as 'loyalty and trust,' binds spirits, living humans, and departed humans together into a single society.

loyalty and Trust

Ancestors and God in Mende Religion

The source of the most extensive information on Mende religion is the book *The Springs of Mende Belief and Conduct.*[33] This volume is based on the notes of the British Methodist missionary W.T. Harris who worked in the Segbwema circuit in the Mende area of Sierra Leone from 1930-1957. Harris seems to have been genuinely interested in the religion and life of the people among whom he worked, and his observations are clear, thorough, and unprejudiced. (I can't help but wonder if, had Lloyd Mignerey been given the opportunity to work in Sierra Leone for seventeen years instead of two, he might have left behind a comparable set of papers.) The edition we have of Harris's papers was prepared by the Sierra Leonean theologian Harry Sawyerr, after Harris's death in 1959. "Edition" is not really an accurate term for this volume, since approximately half of the text was inserted by Sawyerr.[34] The volume is really a kind of collaborative effort. Harry Sawyerr (1909-87) grew up in the Mende area of Sierra Leone, as the son of a Krio mission worker and minister. Sawyerr became an Anglican priest in 1943, and was Professor of Education and Theology, and Principal, at Fourah Bay College.[35] Sawyerr is skeptical of suggestions (including Idowu's) that traditional African religions constitute an original revelation that has somehow prepared the way for Christianity. But his attitude toward those religions, and especially the Mende religion, is one of sustained interest and respect.[36]

The picture of Mende belief that emerges from the available sources is this: The world of social relationships includes the living, the living dead (ancestors), non-ancestral spirits, and Ngewo[37] (God). Everyone in this web of relationships is completely dependent upon Ngewo. Ngewo may act directly upon humans, but most often his action is indirect, through ancestral spirits. Also, Ngewo may receive requests directly from humans, but most often, such requests are made through ancestors as intermediaries. Also, all of the members of the social web, including ancestors and certainly non-ancestral spirits, have a certain freedom of action. Ngewo is the creator, and he helps every living being to be what it is[38] even when that being's aims are anti-social,[39] but Ngewo is ultimately on the side of justice and social cohesion.

Harris records two Mende creation myths. Sawyerr identifies one as expressing the idea of a kind of "call into existence." The myth may be summarized as follows: Ngewo was originally a huge spirit who lived in a cave. He had no one to talk to or play with. Going to the entrance to the cave, he expressed his desire for companions, and pairs of each kind of animal, including humans, entered the cave. The implication seems to be not that there already were creatures outside of the cave, but that the cave entrance itself represents a kind of gateway to existence. Life inside of the cave at this point was a kind of paradise—everyone was happy, and everyone could find plenty of food to eat. But Ngewo made a strict rule that his own food was not to be touched by any of the creatures. One day one animal did eat some of that food. In fact, each kind of animal, including the humans, eventually ate some of that food. Whenever that happened, Ngewo threw the creature out of the cave, and in doing so, also gave the creature its name. Now Ngewo "has gone up far above men," and "all the animals and men are still wandering around in the world looking for this sweet-smelling food."[40] This myth is clearly concerned with the question of origins—the entrance to the cave expresses the sense of the mystery of beginnings, since it is apparently an entrance *from nowhere*. The cave is a symbol of an original paradisiacal totality—the myth also mentions that Ngewo could make the cave as large as he wished. It expresses the feeling that nowadays all creatures are constantly longing and searching for a way to return to an original closeness to Ngewo.

A second creation myth Harris records also evokes this sense of a primal separation. Sawyerr notes that this story expresses the idea of "creation by making" rather than by a "call into existence":

Long ago, *ngewo* made the earth and all things and finished by making a man and a woman. These two people did not know *ngewo*'s name; they only referred to him as '*Maada-le*' ['he is grandfather']...One day *ngewo* addressed them saying, 'Everything you ask me for, if you want it, you shall have it.' .... When they began to come to Him very often, He said to Himself, 'If I stay near these people they will wear Me with their requests; I will make another living place for Myself far above them.' [One night] the people went to sleep. When they woke up next morning, they looked about, but could not see Him. They lifted up their heads and saw Him... spread out very big...From the place where He stayed, He made two living things, one for the man and one for the woman, which he named *fowl*. When He handed them over, He said, 'Whenever one of you does wrong to his companion you must call Me, and when I come you must give Me back my fowl.' They agreed. He then returned to His own town. When anyone did wrong to his companion, he always said '*ngewo yei-O ngi bi le ve*' ('O God, come down, I wish to give you your fowl').....One day, *ngewo* came down to them and said 'Farewell.' He then exhorted them, saying, 'See, I have made an agreement with you, concerning your dealings with one another; therefore do not have a bad heart (bear malice) towards one another.' They replied, 'Yes.' Then He went to his own place. From that time they called him *leve* ['Up,' 'High'].[41]

Sawyerr identifies certain themes about God in this myth which he finds confirmed by other aspects of Mende culture: God as "Creator-Father, Chief-Judge, and Protector." Although God is rarely called "father" explicitly, people do refer to themselves as his "children," and in the story he is called "grandfather."[42] The story also includes the theme, echoed in the other creation story[43] that humans were originally close to God who immediately provided for all their needs, but that this closeness has been lost. But God established a definite connection to each human being that bridges the gap. The words "'*ngewo yei-O ngi bi le ve*' ('O God, come down, I wish to give you your fowl')" are in fact the expression uttered when invoking a formal curse upon someone for a wrong they have done.[44] Curses are believed to be effective, by the power of Ngewo, in causing sickness for wrongdoers until the wrong has been confessed and restitution made. All this does imply that Ngewo is intimately concerned with the affairs of each individual person, and that Ngewo's concern is moral. In this sense God is the ultimate judge and protector. But Ngewo's status as strictly moral is qualified by the belief that God cares for all of his children—even when they do wrong: "it is often thought that a habitual criminal is at first protected by Ngewo from being caught by his victims, and only when he persists in doing wrong does God give him up, and then, he is caught." And Sawyerr asserts that "one has to recognize the fact that the Mende strongly believe that justice will be maintained on the earth, that truth will triumph over falsehood and right over wrong because, as it is firmly believed, *ngewo* is just."[45]

Even though Ngewo is believed to take a direct interest in the affairs of humans, appeals to the ancestors are more common than direct appeals to Ngewo. "In the general run of things, the ancestors are the true exemplars of the spirit world....Indeed, prayers to *ngewo* are generally channeled through the ancestors." But direct appeals to Ngewo do occur. The phrase *Ngewo jahun*, which means "under God's protection, may it be so," or "God willing," concludes every prayer, and also every curse.[46] Very short prayers for protection or deliverance (especially in times of emergency) and prayers invoking blessing are addressed directly to Ngewo, with the expectation that they will be heard.[47] The rite invoking a curse by asking Ngewo to come and take back his chicken is a direct appeal. And the taking of an oath involves laying one's hands on the ground and swearing to *Maa ndoo*, the earth, who is considered to be Ngewo's wife, and is also known as *Maa Ngewo* "Mrs. God or Mother-God."[48] (In fact Sawyerr, noting the similarity of the word *Ngewo* to the word *ngawu* [moon or egg] speculates that the original Mende religion may have been a form of moon worship which was also a fertility cult.[49]) But Harris and Sawyerr agree that "in spite of the accepted ultimate authority of *ngewo*, no temples or shrines are erected for Him and no sacrifices are offered to Him."[50]

According to Sawyerr, in the view of the Mende, humans are made of *nga-fa* (spirit) and *nduwui* (all the components of the body). The *nga-fa* comes from Ngewo through the mother, and returns to Ngewo at death.[51] The funeral rituals include the *kpila-gbualei*[52] ceremony. With the body lying at the graveside, each member of the family "recounts the bad things done to them by the deceased. When they have mentioned all the offences, they forgive him by adding, 'since he is dead now, we have no grievance again. May the avenging spirit of frustration and failure let loose against him for his faults be stayed.'"[53] Then the spleen is removed from the body and dropped into a special solution. If the spleen sinks, the individual is proven to be a witch; there is then "no dancing at the funeral and people laugh at the mourners."[54] The *nga-fa* of a witch does not return to Ngewo.[55] On the third day after burial in the case of a woman, and the fourth day in the case of a man, the *tewenjamei*,[56] or water-crossing ceremony, takes place. On that day, the *nga-fa* is believed to have reached the river it must cross in order to join the ancestors. Without the performance of this ceremony, the departed person will be unable to cross the river, and will return to cause trouble for the living.[57]

Even the religions of cultures that include an intellectual elite capable of imposing explicit doctrines on society at large are never completely consistent or monolithic. It should hardly be surprising that religions without written records or the tradition of explicit doctrine might contain a variety of beliefs and practices which do not form a consistent harmonious whole. I think the inconsistencies within and among the available reports of Mende religion are probably due at least in part to just this reality of variety, and not to any failure to uncover the "true essence" of Mende religion. Kenneth Little states that conceptions of the afterlife are generally vague "though it is pictured sometimes as a clean town, with white sand."[58] Harris and Sawyerr report that the good are separated from the evil after they all cross the river, the good being sent to "*dada-gole hun* (the city of the white sand), where all are happy" and the evil to "*ngombi-me-hun* (the place of eating knees)" where they "suffer extreme hunger."[59] Hofstra reports that all the dead are waiting, with their chins on their knees, for the living to feed them.[60] Harris and Sawyerr also report that "there is no clear-cut idea as to who are the bad people." The group of bad people would mainly include witches, but, they suggest, could also include anyone who has violated important societal regulations.[61]

Other sources call into question the idea that, in Mende belief, those who simply do bad things are sent to a kind of hell. Either Harris and Sawyerr have misinterpreted what they heard, or there is present a variety of viewpoints. Hofstra reports the case of the death of a section chief "who had been rather a wicked man" and violated many taboos. A rite had been performed to purify him of the violation that had brought about his sickness, which had proved fatal anyway. Hofstra was told that the rite had not been in vain, for without it, the ancestors would not have let the chief cross the river.[62] This suggests that what is decisive is the absolution, performed by the living, for the evil done by the departed person, and not a judgment upon the person's deeds rendered after death. According to one of Howard Mueller's Mende informants, Rev. Isaac Ndanema, "Somebody with a questionable character...at the time of death will be absolved completely."[63] This would imply that the *kpila-gbualei* ceremony accomplishes this absolution. The only exception would be that "the community law says that a witch is not a person and thus is not given funeral rites in the village."[64] And in fact, the spleen of each dead person is tested to discover if that person was a witch. According to Ndanema, a witch "is not buried; and he goes to a place where God is not."[65] Ndanema insists that "the attitude towards judgment [of] the main revealed religions has never occurred to the native person."[66] "There is no stage of being unaccepted or accepted once they have entered the world of the ancestors."[67] "The idea of suffering in the next world is not a native idea. The idea which is native is the idea of a witch, who is cut off from the ancestral community."[68]

Both Hofstra's and Ndanema's sources tend to contradict the view Harris and Sawyerr report, that after the crossing of the river there is a judgment on each person sending him or her to a heaven or a hell. And none of the sources suggests that Ngewo directly passes judgment on anyone. Ndanema's and Hofstra's information, which is very consistent with most of what Harris and Sawyerr report, suggests that the decisive moment is the absolution given by the living at the time of death, and the witch-test that the living perform, and not any subsequent judgment either by God or the community of ancestors. Another of Mueller's informants, Rev. David Shodeke, tends to confirm Ndanema's observation:

> We find ourselves bound to our families, our communities, and our societies even unto death. And this is why our death ceremonies mean so much. Friends and relatives travel long distances [to attend the ceremonies]. This is an attempt to make a way in terms of what we know. The African believes that whether you are good or bad there is that period of cleansing. And these ceremonies help to pay for the cleansing of sin that you have done.[69]

Perhaps Harris and Sawyerr's version reflects a greater influence of Islam or Christianity on the community Harris studied. Little, in commenting on the vagueness he found in the Mende conceptions of the afterlife, was of the opinion that "ideas which are more specific are obviously influenced by the teaching of local Moslem preachers."[70]

Again, somewhat contrary to the notion that the good ancestors are in a kind of heaven, both Little and Hofstra report that the way of life of the ancestors is in many ways just a continuation of their life as it was among the living.[71] But all the sources, in effect, agree that in one important respect the existence of the departed is transformed upon death—they now have the role of guardians of the morality of the community of the living, meting out corrective punishment to those who violate societal regulations and to those who fail to remember, honor, and sacrifice to (i.e. feed) the ancestors.[72] The role of ancestors as guardians of morality implies a significant transformation. As Ndanema puts it, "once a member of a family has joined a group of ancestors...their action is always just."[73] Also, despite the fact that the ancestors have "crossed a river," they are also felt to be intimately aware of, concerned about, and active in the affairs of their living descendants.[74] Those more directly and intimately concerned with the living are the recently departed, including all of those within living memory, known as the *kekeni*.[75] But the acknowledged ancestors also include those beyond living memory, known as the *ndeblaa*. The *ndeblaa* are closer to Ngewo, "and are often referred to as being in the arms of *ngewo*."[76]

The ancestors are regularly appealed to, for example, to ensure a good harvest and a successful hunt. Such a ceremony is practiced in some areas at the beginning of each harvest at the base of a hill, and involves offerings or sacrifices of a portion of the rice harvest, and of animals.[77] Also, through recourse to a diviner, it may be discovered that a particular illness has come about as a result of neglect of an ancestor, or the violation of some societal regulation or taboo. In such a case a ceremony is performed at the ancestor's grave, involving the offering of food, the confession of wrongdoing, and the request for forgiveness.[78] Prayers often suggest connections among the *kekeni*,[79] *ndeblaa*, and Ngewo. Sawyerr records a typical prayer to ancestors: "O God (*ngewo*) let it (our prayers) reach you, kenei Momo; let it reach Nduawo; let it reach all our forefathers (*ndeblaa*) who are in your bosom (i.e. by your side)."[80] Harris and Sawyerr record another prayer, made at a riverside ceremony honoring heroic ancestors who died in battle: after the names of the *kekeni* have been called "the *hemoi* [prayer-specialist] prays, 'O ancestors, you of old who prayed in this place, through you we go to the *ndeblaa*. The rain has not yet come, let the rain come in abundance...Let everything be done to help the children."[81]

Unsurprisingly, Mende culture apparently does not contain any single universally agreed upon doctrine regarding the relationship between the ancestors and Ngewo. When Harris inquired whether or not the ancestors act on their own, he got three different kinds of responses: 1) "Ancestors can answer in their own power, up to a point"; 2) "ancestors can answer a prayer, 'if God is willing,'"; and 3) "the prayers are conveyed through the succession of ancestors and finally presented to *ngewo* himself."[82] Prayers clearly are directed both to ancestors and to Ngewo, and some prayers do suggest a kind of succession, passing from *kekeni* to *ndeblaa* and finally to Ngewo. Sawyerr concludes from the form of prayers such as these, and the attitudes they convey, that it is in fact appropriate to say that the Mende do worship their ancestors, and that their attitude towards, and feeling for, the *ndeblaa* is scarcely distinguishable from their attitude toward Ngewo.[83] Indeed, the idea of "distant ancestor" can easily shade off into "Great Ancestor" and from there to "Creator God."[84] And what is a father or a mother but one's closest ancestor? The blending of the idea of ancestor and God that occurs in this form of "ancestor worship" is scarcely distinguishable from the blending of meanings that occurs in the metaphor "God is our father." But all this also calls into question Sawyerr's claim that the Mende do not worship Ngewo.[85] Apparently it is true that the Mende do not have shrines or highly developed ceremonies that focus specifically on Ngewo, so if worship is defined in that sense, Sawyerr is right. If worship is defined in Niebuhr's sense of "believe in," it is clear that the Mende believe in Ngewo. Even though Ngewo may not be the primary focus of religious attention, many prayers and practices convey the feeling of dependence upon Ngewo. Traditional Mende culture clearly does *include* the "diffuse monotheism" that Idowu describes.

Mende Ethics

In attempting to form a clear picture of Mende ethics, it is useful to recall the image that Jackson learned from the Kuranko:

> The interdependence of members of the community or of a family may be expressed in terms of the network of ropes which are tied over the rice farms when the crop is nearing maturity. One end of the rope is always tied to the foot of the bird-scaring platform where the children sit with slingshots and keep birds from scavenging the rice. When this main rope is tugged, all the tributary ropes shake. This scares away birds. It is sometimes said that 'one's birth is like the bird-scaring rope' (*soron i le ko yagbyile*), or 'one's birth is like a chain' (*soron i la ko yolke*) because one's fate always inextricably tied to the fate of others.[86]

The central positive value in Mende ethics as well is that of harmony among members of a community whose lives are lived within a web of relationships of loyalty and trust, like the web of strings connected to the bird-scaring platform. The kinds of Mende 'sins' that Harris and Sawyerr identify all involve some kind of breaking or twisting or perversion of the strands of the web that connect one individual to others. These kinds of 'sins' are considered not only to be types of actions but also conditions into which a person brings him or herself through such violation.

Kaye literally means 'rust,' so that 'sinfulness' or 'immorality' is expressed through the image of 'being covered with rust.'[87] Examples of *kaye* include a son leaving home without his father's permission and a nephew refusing to help his maternal uncle.[88] *Kaye* also includes violations of certain detailed formal regulations, such as those associated with Poro and Sande and *simongama* (incest) regulations.[89] According to the *simongama* regulations, a man is prohibited from sexual relations not only with his own mother and sister, but also with his wife's sister, his wife's mother, and any descendant of his wife's sister or brother. Even shaking hands with one's mother-in-law, sleeping with one's wife on one's mother-in-law's bed, or striking one's wife in the presence of one's mother-in-law are classified as *simongama* or incest.[90] Underlying these regulations seems to be the notion of the sacredness of motherhood.[91]

Kava means 'cheating,' and immorality of this kind involves taking advantage of or harming a person who is helpless, such as a child, or a blind or handicapped person.[92] Other specific instances include stealing game from another person's trap, or palm wine from another person's tap.[93] The extreme form of this kind of immorality, represented by, for example, poisoning a child, is known as *kpegbeli.*[94]

Koto means 'to fold up' and immorality of this kind involves a bending or twisting or distortion of specific ties one has with others.[95] *Koto* means being untrue to the responsibility one has either to those in authority over one (such as parents), or those over whom one has authority. Examples include a son actively undermining the interests of his father; a chief not giving a defendant a fair hearing in a court case; a family member failing to participate in a relative's funeral rites.[96] The extreme form of this kind of immorality, represented by, for example, a disobedient son, is known as *hake.*[97]

The terms *kaye, kava, koto,* etc. obviously do not constitute a systematic classification, but the unifying theme is clear: moral behavior is a matter of being true to the obligations defined by one's position in a web of human relationships. Notably missing are certain other themes prominent in Western cultures: the notion of independent self-development as a moral ideal; the notion of self-reliance as the highest value; the notion of individual personal achievement or of the accumulation of personal wealth as a worthy goal; the notion of life as a competition whose inspiring aim is to win out over others. African tradition differs even from the Western tradition introduced by the missionaries on the issue of moral responsibility being a strictly individual matter.[98]

Mende society includes definite sanctions that can effectively prevent the social disruption of *kaye, kava,* and *koto,* as well as restore harmony when disruption has occurred. Indeed, the maintenance of social harmony appears to be closer to the true aim of these sanctions than any kind of retributive justice. These sanctions include punishments imposed by the ancestors, curses invoked by the living, and illness as an effect of the 'medicine' of the *humoi* and other societies. Each kind of sanction involves the effect, or threat, of physical illness or death, and with each sanction goes also the possibility of a formal confession followed by the revocation of the sanction. The *humoi* society specializes in violations of sex regulations, including the prohibition of incest (*simongama*), of sexual activity on farm land, and of sexual activity during the day.[99] Either curses by the living or sanctions by the ancestors may be the consequence of various forms of each of the three kinds violations: *kaye, kava,* and *koto.* For example, ancestors will take the part of a helpless person who has been cheated or harmed in a case of *kava,*[100] and may visit illness on a person who neglects his ancestors in a case of *koto.*[101] A disobedient son may be cursed by his father or a nephew may be cursed by the maternal uncle he ignores (cases of *kaye*).[102] A person may invoke a curse on someone who has abused his position of authority, in the case of *koto* or *hake.*[103]

The invocation of a curse involves several formal stages. First, God's permission is sought. According to Ndanema, "it seems to be assumed that God is invited to adjudicate between the persons concerned."[104] A 'medicine' is purchased, and is considered to be what directly produces the desired effect.[105] The intent to invoke the curse is publicly announced a few days in advance, and the entire village is invited. If no one publicly confesses, a formal ceremony is conducted, which begins by calling to Ngewo and asking to return his chicken. Ndanema points out that an actual chicken is not used at this point; the call invokes God's attention, referring to his promised concern for humans.[106] Sawyerr points out that there is never any reference to the ancestors in invoking a curse.[107]

Sawyerr, in an article on "Psyche in Conflict," explores the real psychological efficacy of curses; of the subsequent confession they elicit; and of the ceremony formally withdrawing the curse.[108] Behind these traditions lies the insight that privately nursing a grudge or resentment, and also a private knowledge of one's own guilt not publicly admitted, are psychologically unhealthy, and may even lead to physical illness. The traditions include the very public announcement of a curse, preceded by an ample opportunity for the guilty party to confess and promise to amend his or her ways and/or make restitution, upon which both parties know the curse will be revoked and the matter not spoken of again.[109] These traditions clearly serve the purpose of maintaining both social harmony and psychological and physical well-being. Sawyerr points out that curses and, for example, thief-catching medicines really do make people sick. It is a reality that being cursed by a parent or other close relative may be psychologically debilitating, perhaps inducing depression or panic, which can indeed lead to physical illness. Also, for a person who has grown up as a member of a community, that community is a real power in which he or she participates and which he or she really confronts—even though that power is not something physical. The power is something internalized, that has become part of the psychological makeup of the individual. The guilt of the thief may well come back to haunt him psychologically, until a public confession is made.

Some of the details of the reconciliation ceremonies in which curses are revoked are especially interesting in view of analogies to baptism African Christians came to perceive. According to Sawyerr, "All cases of curses being revoked include some action which symbolizes an absolution from the guilt of the crime or offense. Usually the offender takes a ritual bath."[110] In the formal ceremony in which a maternal uncle revokes a curse against his nephew, *all* of his sister's children "lie flat on their stomachs and hold the uncle's feet with both hands."[111] The uncle, calling upon Ngewo, formally revokes the curse. The mother (the uncle's sister) brings a bowl of water; the uncle blows some of the water over the children's heads, pours the rest on the ground, and smears some of the mixture on the forehead of each nephew and niece. It is notable that the neglectful behavior of one nephew results in a curse reaching all of his brothers and sisters. The children holding their uncle's feet is an effective symbol of their collective guilt and obligation, the use of water symbolizes the washing away of the curse and the letting go of ill feeling—collectively by spraying, individually by anointing the forehead of each niece and nephew. At the conclusion of the ceremony, everyone cries out together "*Ngewo jahun!*"—"by the power of God, let it be!"

The Mende and Kpelle Ideas of 'Medicine'

Harris and Sawyerr fully describe the role of 'medicine' in the invoking of curses. And they also describe the shrines that the *humoi* society erects to enforce sexual regulations. These shrines apparently contain the power to cause illness in offenders. Rites of absolution include public washing and whipping by the *mee-nde* (an elderly *humoi* priestess), and may include a ceremony at the shrine.[112] But Harris and Sawyerr do not describe how the shrines or the medicines originally become invested with magical efficacy, or *hale*. Sawyerr is apparently right to emphasize the real psychological efficacy of curses. But the traditional Mende do not themselves describe what is happening in that way. The traditional belief is that there is a power inhabiting the 'medicine' itself which causes the offender to get sick.

It is difficult to find a clear definition of *hale*. M.C. Jedrej does clearly outline the three ways the word is *used* in Mende: 1) to mean a medication very much in the sense of that word in the English of the modern world—either obtained from a government hospital or prepared from a traditional formula; 2) to refer to an object prepared for use in swearing or cursing, or an object (known as *to hale*, 'standing *hale*') prepared to be placed, for example on a farm to cause illness in thieves; 3) to refer to a "secret society"—the expressions in Mende for 'Poro society' and Sande society' are simply *polei hale* and *sande hale*.[113] Jedrej is primarily interested in defining the function of *hale* within the totality of Mende culture, and does not define *hale* itself. Nor does he report how objects originally become invested with *hale*. Little, in his definition of *hale*, points out that *hale* is not so much the object itself as "a special kind of supernatural power or quality which becomes attached to the object through the influence of Ngewo."[114] But it is unclear from what Little reports whether *hale* is a neutral force pervading everything, created by Ngewo, which can be used for good or evil, or whether Ngewo has to specifically sanction its use, or whether it is a force possessed by spirits who have to be invoked. Perhaps all of these different notions of *hale* are widespread.

The single most illuminating discussion of *hale* or 'medicine,' is provided by Beryl Bellman in his study of the Kpelle, a group in Liberia geographically and, in many ways, culturally close to the Mende. Bellman's primary goal was to hear how the Kpelle themselves describe their own beliefs and practices. To that end he pursued the anthropological ideal of 'participant observer' to a point few other investigators have attempted. Bellman reports:

> I joined secret societies and participated in as many local activities as I was able. Although it may appear curious that a Western social scientist was permitted entry into African secret societies, the ability to join is based more on the ability to find a sponsor in the societies and a willingness to undergo the risks of the initiation rituals [which include extensive scarification] than on any other factor.... After joining the Snake Society, the Zo of other secret societies became interested in my joining their associations.[115]

Bellman himself became an expert in the preparation of Kpelle 'medicine'—
to the point of being often consulted by the Kpelle themselves. "The medicine
categories I obtained from Kpelle speakers were elicited in both formal and in-
formal situations. In the latter I learned medicines as a member of two different
societies (the Kali Sale and Gbo Gbling) and from various Zo with whom I established both long and short term apprentice relations."[116]

Bellman has first-hand knowledge of how 'medicines,' or *sale* in Kpelle, are
prepared. (This dimension appears to be missing from all the other sources.)
Bellman is committed to basing his work upon the descriptions that arise within
the context of actual practice from the viewpoint of the person involved. Here is
the description one of Bellman's Kpelle friends gave of how to prepare *sale*. The
crucial point seems to be communication with the "spirit of the medicine":

> Before any medicine can work the leaves must know you....The Zo [expert in
> medicine] talks to the spirit of the medicine and tells it that you are now the
> owner and so the leaves should work for you. Once the spirit of the medicine
> knows you then you can make the medicine. So you see it is impossible for a man
> to steal a medicine.[117]

A *Zo* Bellman studied with explained that "'the spirit of the medicine'...was
the same spirit he talked to whenever picking leaves in the bush to be prepared
later into some medicine."[118] When Bellman asked for further explanation, he
continued:

> When you learn the medicines so well that you know them and have no doubts
> about them, that is what I mean by the spirit of the medicine. And then sometimes
> in your dreams a person will come to you and show you some medicines. That is
> the spirit of the medicine also. You can never see that spirit on this side, only in
> your dreams.[119]

Bellman then asked directly what the "spirit of the medicine" was. The *Zo*
replied:

> Everything has a spirit. When you call upon a medicine to help you it is that spirit
> that helps you. You cannot see this spirit in man, nor can you see it in leaves. The
> person who comes to you in your dreams is really a *jina* that you yourself call the
> spirit of the medicine. Each leaf has one spirit. It is like a person who is tapped on
> the shoulder. When you are tapped you turn to that side and listen to all what the
> person has to say. Then if someone taps you on the other side you turn in that di-
> rection to listen. Or if you are tapped from above you turn your head up and ask
> what is it that the person wants. The same is with the medicines. You call or tap
> the medicine in one way by saying, *"Baga hey hey mensia, hayet may kasia bo,"*
> and the leaf turns to you as a member of the *Kali Sale*; or if you call the medicine
> by saying, '*Zinc ka zinc, kanbe ka kanbe,*' the spirit of the medicine will turn to
> you as a member of the Gbo Gbling society.[120]

Bellman finds in the *Zo*'s description the assumption that "the spirit of the
medicine is the living force that exists within the leaves." According the Bellman, the Kpelle idea of such a spirit is not of an invisible individual who happens to be somehow perching in a particular plant, but "the spirit within each
species of leaves [my emphasis]."[121] And the spirits of various species associate

themselves with various human societies such as the *Gbo Gbling* or the *Kali*. One approaches the spirits of the plants as a member of a particular society, which the spirit also belongs to. Humans and plant spirits have a definite set of mutual obligations as members of these societies. The power of the 'medicines' is simply the power of these spirits to accomplish certain objectives, such as healing, or causing illness or death, and humans can make agreements with these spirits to use their power upon specific people or places.

African Magic, The Magic of the Church, and Protestant Magic

Communication with ancestors, the dead punishing the living for their immoral behavior, the efficacy of curses, species of plants joining societies and agreeing to follow human instructions, are all factors taken for granted in African cultures, which may appear quite alien to members of modern Westernized societies. But it would be inaccurate to classify these social phenomena as simply "non-Western." Keith Thomas, in *Religion and the Decline of Magic*, through the study of the historical record both of official theology and popular belief, has shown exhaustively that beliefs very similar to the African ones listed above were pervasive in England from the medieval period through the seventeenth century, and were explicitly sanctioned by Christian churches, both Catholic and Protestant.

The cult of saints in medieval Catholicism, which persisted until the fifteenth century, was very similar to the African cult of ancestors. Saints were believed to have the power not only to cure, but also to inflict, disease.[122] The official position of the church was that in the case of petitionary prayer directed to the saints, "the saints were only intercessors whose entreaties might go unheeded," but it did not object to the many prayers offered "on more optimistic assumptions."—i.e. that the saints themselves could work miracles.[123] Petitionary prayer—i.e. requests for specific outcomes, like the healing of disease or the success of an endeavor—was officially supported throughout the period by both the Catholic and the Protestant churches. The attitude behind a petitionary prayer directed, for example, to the *ndeblaa*, is indeed scarcely distinguishable from a prayer to a saint, and a similar ambiguity exists in popular belief as to whether the ancestor/saint acts directly or only carries the request up to Ngewo/God. The powers of the saints were just one example of the supernatural power that the "medieval church...claimed to be able to exercise."[124] Blessings upon all kinds of mundane objects, like houses or armor, were regarded by theologians as "possessing a power which was more than merely spiritual or symbolic."[125] The "orthodox view" on the use of holy water to cure illness or increase the fertility of fields "was that there was nothing improper about such actions, provided they were performed out of genuine Christian faith."[126] Just as the Kpelle speak to the spirit of the leaves they gather, "the church itself recommended the use of prayers when healing the sick or gathering medicinal herbs."[127] Just as the Mende have participants in a court case swear on a 'medicine' which will bring disease or death upon them if they lie, "the standard method [in the middle ages] of inducing a witness to give honest testimony was to require him to swear a solemn oath as to the truth of this evidence. The assumption behind this procedure was that perjury would call forth the vengeance of God, certainly in the next world and quite possibly in this one."[128]

Of course the Protestant Reformation attacked all of these practices (except petitionary prayer itself), labeling them 'superstition.' But Thomas shows how magical beliefs were suppressed by Protestants in some forms only to return in another form—beliefs about Providence. The traditional African belief is that disease or death is never by accident, but can always be explained by reference either to the ancestors' disapproval of one's actions, a curse, or witchcraft. The Reformation brought a new emphasis upon the idea that nothing happens without God's permission, and nothing happens by chance. This theme of Providence is a pervasive one among reformation theologians.[129] Natural disasters, plagues, diseases, failures, were again and again attributed to the wrath of God punishing the sins of those who were struck down. The theologians and religious writers did not promise that all good behavior would be rewarded, but, as Thomas puts it

> by the end of the seventeenth century, and in many cases long afterwards, the overwhelming majority of clerical writers and pious laymen sincerely believed that there is a link between a man's moral behavior and his fortune in this world, whether in bodily health or professional success. It was impossible to reiterate the view that sin was the most probable cause of misfortune without conveying the implication that godliness was somehow linked with prosperity. Of course, the preachers would have explained that it was only spiritual prosperity with which they were concerned, and that God's promises related solely to the life to come. But their flock only too often took a cruder view, and so on occasions did the clergy themselves.[130]

Thomas further suggests that "it is possible that the notion of a random distribution or worldly reward and punishments enjoyed greater currency before the Reformation than it did for sometime afterwards."[131] Harry Sawyerr, as a relatively conservative Sierra Leonean Christian theologian, draws critical attention to the fact that such Protestant theodicy represents in a way the same attitude toward good and bad fortune as that embodied in African tradition:

> One also comes across statements, chiefly from overseas Protestants, to the effect that, for example, a child meets with an accident and dies because God wishes to demonstrate to the parents that He loves him better than they do. Any like comments merely add force to the pagan attitude that such a death is due to some superior hostile external agency. In place of such a fatalistic attitude Christians should seek to cultivate an attitude which accepts that death is an inevitable consequence of birth and it overtakes different individuals differently and at different stages of their life. But, whatever the circumstances, direct responsibility for a death must not be laid at God's door.[132]

While the Reformation ferociously attacked many of the "superstitions" of the Catholic church, its emphasis on Providence may have been moving Christianity even closer to the traditional African world view. Of course one dimension of the Protestant doctrine of Providence is alien to the African view—what

Max Weber defined as "the spirit of capitalism." In effect, according to Weber, Calvinism fostered the belief that a life of hard work, systematically planned, aiming at the highest productivity possible, with no limit set to the extent of that productivity, and resulting in the acquisition of the highest level possible of personal wealth, represented the working of Providence. Providence rewards those who lead such a life with the wealth they acquire, and God rewards them with eternal salvation. And the emphasis is on the moral rectitude—in terms of rule following and honest pursuit of gain—of the individual life before God.[133] The idea of limitless pursuit of gain, and the relative isolation of the individual from the community central to this Protestant mentality are of course alien to the ethical world view of the African groups I have been discussing.

Ancestors, God, and Spirits in Temne Religion

The impact of the 18th century Futa Jallon jihad upon the Temne was much greater than upon the Mende. Muslim traders and Islamic education were welcomed and some Temne leaders became Muslim. But Islam otherwise did not have a great impact on the majority of people.[134] There is nevertheless, in the case of the Temne, much clearer evidence of the influence of Islamic religious concepts than in the case of the Mende. The Temne probably began with an idea of a creator god named Kuru. According to Turay, that term "also means 'sky,' but has the literal meaning of 'the abode of God.'" Kuru is also referred to as *Kurumasaba*. The suffix "*masaba*," according to Turay, derives from "the Mandingo *mangsa-ba* (the big king)," and is the term used by Muslims, presumably following the usage of Mandinka (Mandingo) immigrants.[135] According to Frederik J. Lamp, Kuru is probably not considered either to be an ancestor or to be part of *ro-soki* (the spirit world). But he "is worshiped in sacrifice and his name is invoked in oaths," though "he has no shrines to his name."[136]

The Temne term for ancestors is *wunifi,* and for spirits is *kerfi.*[137] Traditional Temne experience the ancestors as abiding in a place somehow continuous with the everyday world, from which they can keep an eye on the living. The name for the place of the ancestors is (confusingly) *ro-kerfi,* and the name for the place of the spirits (*kerfi*) is not *ro-kerfi* but *ro-soki.*[138] According to Lamp, *ro-soki* as the place of spirits is "tripartite," inhabited by: 1) "non-ancestral spiritual beings" (*an-kerfi*); 2) "evildoers" (*an-ser,* singular *o-ser*) in *ro-seron*[139]; and 3) the living dead (*am-baki or a-fam a-fi*) in *ro-kerfi.*[140] Turay speculates that originally the *kerfi* were in fact the ancestors who later came to be worshiped. There is some further evidence for this. For example, stones representing *kerfi* are taken from the graves of ancestors.[141] But by the nineteenth century, *kerfi* came to unambiguously denote spirits rather than ancestors. The *kerfi,* though created by Kuru, act independently of him, and can be good or evil, and can serve the good or evil ends of humans, for a price. Regarding the fate of the dead, it is unclear whether there is one place for them all (*ro-kerfi*), or whether the good are rewarded in heaven and the evil punished in hell. Most likely, in pre-Islamic Temne belief *ro-kerfi* is the same for all. According to Lamp, "it is described as both below the earth where the sun dies at sunset and across a river which the dead must traverse."[142] The Temne words for heaven (*ro-riyana*) and hell (*ro-yahanama*) are of Arabic origin.[143] It seems likely that the two views of the afterlife have simply been superimposed rather than integrated.[144] The Temne also owe to Islam the concept of *Sethani,* an evil force, in conflict with Kuru, and the concept of *melakas* (angels) who are Kuru's servants.[145]

Schlenker (a nineteenth century German missionary to the Temne) quotes and translates a brief Temne creation story.

> Our fathers did not tell us much about the creation of the world, they only told us that when God [Kuru] made the world, he put it on the head of a giant....This person carries the world on [his] head. They told us that all the trees, and all the grass, and all things which grow on this earth are the hair of the head of this giant; and all living creatures are the lice of his head. He, on whose head the world was put before, has died, and another man carries this world again on his head. When they put the world on him, he was in a sitting posture, and turned toward the East [*ro-toron*]. They told us that this person turns himself, but that he turns softly, so that the people cannot know it; except that time when he turns toward the West, then men know it; because at that time there arises an earthquake, so that houses and trees fall down. At that time when this person falls down, and dies, the whole world is at an end, and every thing in this world will perish. After a long time God [Kuru] will take this world away, that he may put again a new world.[146]

The story Schlenker quotes proceeds to describe the events of creation in a little more detail. Kuru added the first man and the first woman to the completed world, evidently at the same time. The man and woman were at first completely ignorant. They asked for something to eat. Kuru first gave them rice, and explained how to prepare it and eat it. They ate only rice for a year and then asked if there was any other food. Kuru then showed them animals, and separated out those which were to be eaten and those which were not. Then Kuru showed them medicines, and farming tools, and fire. But the man and woman still did not know how to reproduce, and asked Kuru how they were to do so. God therefore gave them pills to eat which created sexual desire.[147]

Originally there was no death. Rather, people lived from six to eight hundred years, and then, "they did not die, God came to fetch them." However there came a time when a man was born who was "wicked" and "violent." "He had plenty of money, and many slaves, and plenty of cattle." He "did not care for any one, and did just as he pleased, and troubled all his people." Yet Kuru had given him "great power, he was a warrior, and he was a gentleman." Kuru's servant finally came to fetch the man, but he refused: "I will not, I do not go: I am still a young man," he said. The servant kept returning for many years, but still the violent man refused. Kuru sent many more servants, but the man beat them, and they returned to Kuru. Finally Kuru sent two more servants. The first was "Mr. Sickness [*Pa-Ratru*]." "Go," said Kuru to Mr. Sickness, "take hold of him, go thou before, thy companion will meet thee." No one could see Mr. Sickness, but the violent man could not refuse this guest. And the next morning, the companion too arrived. His companion, Mr. Death [*Pa-Rafi*] was a young man. The people could not see Mr. Sickness and his companion, but they could hear them. Mr. Death [*Pa-Rafi*] told Mr. Sickness that the man would not live long, and that he "would have no pity on him." Then "he took away the breath (*an-nesam*) of the man, and he died." "After this God [Kuru] gave power to Sickness and Death, that they might walk all about in the whole world; lest some time another person arise, and act as this one did before."[148]

This Temne creation story is strikingly different from the Mende creation stories reported by Harris and Sawyerr. Yet there is also the obvious common concern about the origin of the world and humankind, and about their separation from the creator. While one Mende story places the original creation in a cave, the Temne story attends in more detail to the created world, likening it to, or identifying it with, the head of a "giant" or "great person." In both cases, the "fall"—separation from the creator or the advent of death—results from humans making excessive demands, though only in the Temne story are those demands explicitly associated with evil. Frederick Lamp, in his extraordinarily detailed study of the Temne religious sensibility in relation to artistic imagery and cultural practice, reports that Schlenker's 1861 account "is the only indigenous Temne account of the creation of man…Neither I nor any other researcher since then has been able to find anyone who remembers the account, but Schlenker recorded several versions and seems to have verified it with at least three informants."[149] Whether or not the creation story was still known in 1922, it may be of some significance that when Mignerey asked Temne villagers the question "then who does make [the rice] grow?" some immediately responded "Kuru! Kuru!"

James Littlejohn and Frederick Lamp have made very interesting studies of the way Temne experience space in terms of their notions of creation, ancestors, spirits, and witches. They have shown that while the Temne creation story may have passed out of living memory, the spiritual meaning of east and west, and the sense of the earth as a living power evident in that story, along with a number of other analogies, remain evident in the Temne experience of space. Space is not the uniform, neutral, quantitatively measurable continuum of science, but is characterized throughout by felt qualities. The felt experience of space is especially evident in Temne notions about East, West, North, and South. According to Littlejohn, for the Temne, the East is of primary importance, and appears not simply as a direction but a kind of place (*ro-toron*[150]):

> Their cardinal points contain meanings which qualify activities and events in various ways. This is indicated in their account of the creation of the world by Kuru. After the world was put on his head the giant turned East. When the giant turns West there follow earthquakes and destruction. East and West are not only opposite directions in an operation of the intellect but existential contraries with East the life-sustaining direction, West the destructive one. East is singled out above the other directions, literally. "We think of East as rising up like a hill, of everything going up to the East," Temne say. The adverb for "up" (*rokom*) is often used in place of the word for East (*ro-toron*), and correspondingly the word for West (*ropil*) is frequently used for "down," both in the sense of down a slope and in the social sense of "down town." Among the reasons they give for the pre-eminence of the East is that the ancestors came from there and still are there. Hence all sacrifices and prayers to them have to be done facing East "otherwise your prayer won't be answered." If the sacrifice is an animal or bird its throat

must point East so that blood flows towards there, blood being the ancestors' share of the offering on which they live. Conversely it is through the ancestors that the Temne live in the mode in which they do. "We owe everything to the ancestors, land, blood, houses." Each living Temne is a re-incarnation of a grandfather, not in the sense of a re-instatement of the complete person of a grandfather but in that conception occurs only by the instigation of one, whose name the individual bears and whose body he reproduces. Each Temne has 'come from' the East.[151]

In addition, the Poro bush is located to the West of the village. The entering of the camp is experienced as the death of the initiates, and their return, seen as rebirth, is from the east.[152] Also, when a chief dies, it is said that he has only journeyed to *ro-toron*, and the installation of the new chief is seen as simply the return of the old.[153]

While *ro-toron* is both heterogeneous and distant, *no-ru, ro-kerfi, ro-soki*, and *ro-seron*[154] are heterogeneous and near at hand. *No-ru* is the space of everyday life. Since *no* means "here" and *ru*, "to plait" Littlejohn suggests that "the name seems to indicate that the giant's hair has been combed and wrought," rather in the sense that the Greek *kosmos* suggests both order and beauty. *Ro* means "there," "to," "at," "from" and "as a frequent prefix in place names, indicate[s] a 'place of.'"[155] *Ro-kerfi* is the place of ancestors (but literally the place of spirits), *ro-soki* is the place of spirits (though literally the place of vision), and *ro-seron* is the place of witches. Witches, spirits, and ancestors can have effects on *no-ru*—such as accidents or disease—and the first two can themselves enter *no-ru*. The places of witches, spirits and ancestors are not really elsewhere, but rather in a sense, all around us in *no-ru*. As Shaw explains,

> These non-human regions are said to be like large towns and to be spatially contiguous with *no-ru*, although some describe the place of the ancestors as being in the east (see Littlejohn 1963). They are "here" and all around us, but as it is usually expressed in Temne, there is a "darkness" (*an-sum*) which hides them from us; their inhabitants can see us, but we cannot see them.
>
> In some contexts, however, this "darkness" is not merely a visual barrier between us and the non-human worlds, but can be entered by those who mediate between them. Certain categories of people can penetrate the darkness and can see and participate in these worlds by virtue of possessing "four-eyed" vision, in which the two visible eyes of ordinary people are supplemented by two invisible eyes. Such people are termed *an-soki*.[156]

While diviners are considered to be able to see into what for others is the darkness of the heterogeneous regions, everyone can have some sense of their presence. Littlejohn observes that

> some changes in bodily tonality indicate to Temne that ancestors are present. One verb indicating this is *ninsne*, 'to apprehend the presence of the ancestors,' for which there is no English equivalent. To come to or wake up from a dream is *nisne*, to feel someone touching one without being able to see the person is *tilne*;

ninsne is somewhere in between. Asked to describe *ninsne* Temne say, 'you just feel it in your body.'"[157]

In addition, people encounter *ro-soki, ro-seron,* and *ro-kerfi.* Encounters with spirits, witches, and ancestors in dreams are not thought of as mere imagination, but are considered to be real encounters with those beings in the heterogeneous spaces they inhabit.[158]

No-ru is also internally differentiated in terms of its relationship to *ro-soki* and *ro-seron.* Certain *no-ru* spaces are *an-kantha*[159] or ritually "closed," i.e. closed off from the places of witches and spirits. All homes, most farms, and the human body are *an-kantha.* The closure is effected through a variety of specially prepared objects. In addition, the meeting places of "secret" societies are closed both against evil influences and non-members, and the seclusion imposed on new chiefs as part of their installation is also regarded as *an-kantha.*[160]

I would like to place Littlejohn's and Lamp's discussions in the context of the phenomenological ideas to which they relate. Littlejohn points out that traditional cultures like the Temne do not possess the same notion of space that Western culture does. But what do we mean by "the idea of space in Western culture"? Specifically, ancient Greek mathematics and geometry introduced the notion of idealized shapes, to which visible shapes correspond, and the notion of measuring those shapes in terms of identical abstract units; Descartes introduced the notion of space as a continuum, every point on which may be located through three coordinates on vertical and horizontal axes. Even though the majority of Western people have little if any understanding of Euclidian geometry and Cartesian analytic geometry, the notion of space as an infinitely extended, uniform, and precisely measurable continuum is widely familiar, and has had a significant impact on the way people in general experience the world. Now these notions only exist where and when they have been introduced and adopted. The question then is, how do people experience space without the "benefit" of these notions? Traditional cultures lack them.

Edmund Husserl, in *Crisis of the European Sciences* argues that in perceiving the world as an abstractly measurable continuum, we have overlaid our experience with a "garb of ideas." Our ability to perceive the shapes and sizes of objects is prior to our interpretation of shape and size in terms of ideal shape and exact unit. Husserl in fact denies that objects have exact shapes and sizes. Rather, the "objective reality" of objects consists in their infinite determinability. Objects give themselves to us as that which can be more and more precisely measured, without limit. So Husserl accepts the idea of "objective reality" but precisely in the sense of an infinite ideal. That the measuring units and notions of the marketplace or everyday life are far too imprecise for science does not mean that those of the market place are false and only those of science represent objective reality. The ideal shapes and units of geometry represent simply the idea of carrying to infinity the process of ever more precise measurement. Husserl vehemently denies that the mathematized world of scientific theory is the true, objective world, and the world of everyday experience is somehow mere appearance.[161]

The widely accepted notion of objective space includes the idea that the shapes, sizes, and locations of objects are independent of any observer. "Up," "down," "right," and "left," have no objective meaning, but merely relate to the observer's viewpoint. Pushing the idea of objective space just a little farther, this notion also includes the idea that objects don't "really" have colors. In "reality" there are only light waves, which cause the experience of color. So when we see the blue sky above us, we are only seeing light waves, and the sky is not really there. Husserl rejects this widely accepted notion. Our experience "I am here, and there are objects around me," is inseparable from our embodiment. We can only experience objects from a particular embodied perspective—which is to say from a perspective for which there is an up, a down, a right, and a left. And we can only experience a shape as that which appears through a potentially infinite multiplicity of perspectives. Husserl holds that it pertains to the very being of objects to be knowable and perceivable. And the very meaning of being perceived is to appear through perspectives to an embodied consciousness with its own "here," "up," "down," "right," and "left." Natural science conceives a mathematized world of ideal shapes from which embodied perceivers and their sensuous experience have been eliminated. For Husserl, this mathematized world is simply not to be identified with objective reality, but is merely an abstraction which helps us to predict and control events. Husserl does not say that the world is merely an experience. But he does hold that it pertains to being to be experienceable. Perception is the actualization of this potential, and is hence not merely a type of event in nature.

Another way of making this point is to note that the idealized objective space of science with no color, no "here," no "up" or "down," etc., is simply not the world we live in. And it would in fact be impossible to live in such a world. Husserl of course goes even farther—such a "world" would be for him, not only impossible to live in, but radically inconceivable as a world at all. Science's abstract model of the world is just that—an abstraction which owes its meaning to the concrete reality it abstracts from. The notion that objective reality is simply to be identified with the abstraction posited by physical science richly deserves the pejorative designation, "superstition."

The world we live in, or, as Husserl puts it, the life-world (*Lebenswelt*) is universal, constituting the very meaning of the world as experienced by embodied consciousness. The import of physical science has been widely misunderstood in a way that blinds us to the foundational centrality of embodied, individual, conscious existence. So while Littlejohn is right that science has influenced and altered the way "Western" or "Westernized" people experience space, he overlooks the fact that a fundamental contradiction lies at the heart of this "Westernized" experience. Our standard misinterpretation of the meaning of physical science contradicts the inescapable reality of the life world—and this contradiction is one we rarely even acknowledge. According to the standard misinterpretation, the life world itself is a primitive mode of experience which the civilized advances of physics have decisively superseded. But in attempting to persuade us that there is no up and down, that colors are illusions, and that there is no real "here," the standard misinterpretation hollows out human existence and undermines the only source from which can arise our sense of dignity, meaning, and purpose.

One dimension of the life world which Husserl never extensively investigated is that of the expressive qualities of appearances. Twentieth century psychology has investigated this dimension, which it has termed "physiognomic perception." There is even experimental verification that humans reliably associate certain shapes with certain feelings—for example "lines sloping downward from left to right to express the words 'sad' and 'sorrowful' and lines sloping upward from left to right as expressions of 'joyous' and 'strong.'"[162] The empiricist tradition, of course, interprets this phenomenon as merely one of "association." This tradition misunderstands consciousness as somehow composed of units. One unit, a perceived shape, causes the emergence of another unit, a feeling of sadness. But psychologists working from a number of perspectives challenge this interpretation. For example, Heinz Werner, who finds physiognomic perception especially typical of children, notes that this experience is simply not a matter of the association of units originally distinct.

> During the physiognomic period of childhood…it is the very absence of polarity and high degree of fusion between person and thing, subject and object, which are characteristic. The average adult has a physiognomic experience only in his perception of other human beings, their faces and bodies. The child, on the other hand, frequently sees physiognomic qualities in all objects, animate or inanimate.[163]

Werner attempts to explain physiognomic perception as characteristic of a kind of primitive or embryonic early stage of mental development, in which subject and object are relatively indistinct. And yet, he notes that physiognomic perception is also characteristic of artists, with no suggestion that art itself is some kind of primitive activity.[164] But he shares with Gestalt psychologists the rejection of an associationist explanation.[165] The feeling is not distinct from, along side of, externally connected with the shape. Rather, the feeling seems to be inherent in, to live in, to be one with the shape. An expressive symbol like a falling line or the mask of the blinded Oedipus does not lead us to confuse our own feelings with the ones we find in the symbol. And yet, within the distinction, we do affectively participate in the very feeling inherent in the appearance. Empathy is emotional involvement and not detached observation. And it is simply an accurate description of the experience of empathy and the experience of expressive symbols to say that it feels like a merging within a distinction, a deep participation in that which is insurmountably separate.

Littlejohn makes use of Werner's discussion of physiognomic perception to interpret the traditional Temne experience of space. Physiognomic perception needs to be seen, I have been arguing, the context of the life world of which it is a dimension. Littlejohn describes the kinds of significance that the East, or *rotoron,* has for traditional Temne, in a way that suggests the origin of that significance in physiognomic perception: East is the origin of life and the home we are destined to return to. East is the home of the ancestors, to whom prayers are directed. West is the region of death to which the world may potentially turn.

The enlightened common sense of Western culture may tell us that there is really no such thing as up and down and above and below and East and West and blue and red and yellow. But in the world we live in, the blue sky is above us, the sun rises up in the east, moves across the sky, and then sinks down in the west. Physiognomically, light expresses life and hope, and darkness death and despair. The rising sun expresses the feeling of a hopeful beginning, the setting sun the feeling of an ending. The blue sky above us expresses the feeling of something higher and better to which we aspire or of which we dream. Such observations may appear banal, but they nevertheless represent the substance of our daily experience of the visible earth. To be deprived of these splendors, as more and more people are in crowded, polluted cities across the world, is to be drained of something essential to life. And this basic, daily, experience has been an inspiration for the religious thought and stories of the millennia: the early Greek view in Hesiod makes the sky a male deity (*ouranos*) and earth a female one (*gaia*); the ancient Egyptians, rather an exception to the rule, reversed the genders; and in the medieval European view, the sky was literally heaven. (C.S. Lewis gives a remarkable account of the Western medieval view in *The Discarded Image*.)

I hold that the origin of these notions lies in the felt experience of the earth below, the blue sky above, the sunrise in the East and the sunset in the West. They are "beautiful," we say. I hold that their beauty is inseparable from the feeling they express through our physiognomic perception of them. That feeling is a feeling of life which includes a sense of "more." The "more" suggests an origin in more life beyond itself. William James, discussing the felt sense of "more" in mystical experiences, remarks that it is simply a matter of accuracy to describe that experience as the sense of an origin beyond the individual's consciousness which is felt to flow into that consciousness. How to accurately describe the experience is one question, he notes. The question of whether that origin really exists, is another. Likewise, I am suggesting that religious ideas can grow out of certain kinds of experiences. The beauty of the sunrise and of the sky seems to have and to express an origin beyond itself. Ideas such as *ouranos*, heaven, and *ro-toron* have grown out of this impression of origin. Whether there really is such an origin is simply another question. If this sense of origin is after all truthful, then that the sky is a god, or that the sky is heaven, or that the East is, is not a mere illusion.

While the earth, sky, and sun are undeniably physiognomic, the physiognomic nature of the perception of space as, for example, *ro-soki* or as *an-kantha* is ambiguous. *Ro-soki*, *ro-kerfi*, and *ro-seron*, while very much 'right here' are at the same time shrouded in darkness to normal vision. Physiognomic qualities do very likely contribute to certain places being regarded as the haunts of spirits: As Littlejohn observes:

> Not only are the main features of the landscape linked with demons of different quality, but signs and reminders of their presence are everywhere. Bush demons inhabit ant-hills, caves, huge trees which remain from the primary forest: a clump of bush definitely known to belong to one has the special name of *e-kinga* and is avoided.[166]

And the sense of being surrounded by *ro-kerfi*, for example, is reported as a bodily feeling.[167] Yet Temne experience the space they live in as being at the same time the invisible space of spirits, witches, and ancestors, and they perceive certain areas as having been closed off from (*an-kantha*) the invisible space of witches and spirits. Especially the perception of space as *an-kantha* must involve more than physiognomic perception. It is through an explicit interpretation of what one sees that a home, for example, is seen as closed off from evil spirits and witches. In general it is true that how an object appears depends not just on its inherent physiognomic qualities, but also upon what one interprets the object to be. For example, when I see my house and recognize it as my home, the inherent quality of what I see is no different than if this particular house happened not to be my home. But my perception of it as my home is not simply a matter of associating a judgment or a feeling with what I see. It is inherent in what I see itself. How I interpret what I see affects how it looks to me, even though it has no effect on any objective quality. So for traditional Temne, a house being *an-kantha* affects the appearance of the house and how it feels to approach and enter its space; and this is all bound up with the interpretation of surrounding space as *ro-soki* and *ro-seron*.

On the basis of three years of fieldwork, Lamp presents an extremely detailed discussion of the Temne notion of *an-kantha,* its practice, and its relation to the Temne world view as a whole. This discussion is relevant to question of spirits in Temne belief, and of how Temne experience the presence of spirits—both ancestral and non-ancestral. According to Lamp, "closing a space by means of *an-kantha* relegates that space to the spiritual world, *ro-soki.... An-kantha* places the space within the realm of the cooperative spirits of either *ro-soki* or the subdivision of the ancestors, *ro-kerfi*.... It closes the space, however, against the intrusion of the evil world, *ro-seron*."[168] Lamp describes in great detail the different kinds of "constructions" which mark space as "closed." There are two broad categories of constructions: those whose function is the "repelling of evil," and those which accomplish the "attraction and containment of beneficial spiritual forces."[169] Lamp shows that within each of these two categories, the Temne recognize several distinct kinds. For example *am-bempa, an-wanka,* and *an-sena*[170] have a thief-catching function much like the Mende *to hale. An-bempa* and *an-wanka* in particular are used to enclose farms, *an-sena* to trap thieves on the road.

There is evidently a commonly accepted vocabulary of elements used in constructions. Various natural and cultural objects—such as stones, shells, mortars, fishing nets—are used to build each one. Lamp views construction as involving something like a language:

> The construction is said by the Temne to work as a total statement. Individual elements are senseless apart from the whole, just as words or phrases taken out their structural context lose their meaning. It was difficult to elicit specific information about the efficacy of the elements because the informants felt that it was the construction that had power and not the individual parts. Nevertheless it was apparent that each element has significance in itself contributing to a complex whole.[171]

Lamp gives numerous illustrations of how constructions are put together and are perceived to function. For example, one *an-sena*, or "trap" was put together like this:

> They first erected a tripod of sticks. Near the top they suspended four pieces of firewood horizontally. These represented the thieves to be caught. A palm branch was attached to the top of the tripod, at the side facing north. Directly underneath the tripod a miniature grave was dug and covered over with a mound of earth. This was the prospective grave of the guilty party. On top of it was laid a small piece of white cloth of the type used to wrap a corpse. The grave was aligned with the road, East and West. At either end of the grave an anthill was placed: a small one toward the East, and a large one toward the West. These were said to represent twins. Twins have power beyond ordinary people and have access to the spiritual world. The title of the element is *a nar na*, "they will help them." On top of the anthills were placed *e-thof,* the circular supporting pads of twisted grass used to carry loads. The heavy load of spirituality that twins carry on their heads would "shout" and jump on the thieves and attack them.[172]

The construction just described includes a representation of a grave and a shroud, and this representation is perceived to have a role in the causal efficacy of the construction as a whole. The representation of a grave is perceived as somehow having a role in possibly killing someone. The orientation toward east and west and the anthills represent twins and a connection to the world of spirits. In other constructions, for example the *an-wanka*, vines can be used, "'to make it [*an-wanka*] look awful' informants say.... it is said to catch the victim by the neck and strangle him."[173] White thread, "representing the spider's web, is often wound round and through the supports of the scaffolding. The web is considered the medium of support for supernatural beings."[174] The *an-thof*, in its everyday use, is a pad placed on the head when loads are borne on the head. In a construction, "the hole in the middle of the *an-thof* represents a medium of communication between *no-ru* and *ro-soki*."[175] Constructions involve both meanings rooted in physiognomic perception (e.g. the awfulness of the look of the vines, the relationship to the East) and explicit interpretation (the grave and the shroud as involved in causing death, the *an-thof* and the thread as an opening for and support for spirits). But it is clear that the Temne do not simply assume that every time something has a certain look or a certain meaning, it automatically has the power to make things happen. First of all, the elements must be brought together into a statement. And elements are often chosen or created on the basis of features that set them off from an ordinary context (e.g. they are "miniaturized" or "broken or worn beyond use"). Being used in a representation, or fashioned as a representation, in itself sets them off from the everyday context of use and nature. These features—being no longer useful, being in a representation—function as signs that these objects have an extraordinary meaning. And Lamp also points out that they are "set apart from ordinary use in an extraordinary context."[176] But what is that extraordinary meaning and that extraordinary context that these features signify? As Lamp puts it "the ritual construction acquires spiritual efficacy because its elements are transferred from *no-ru* to *ro-soki*."[177] But *ro-soki* is simply the realm of spirits. I think that the understanding of these "constructions" as involving a kind of lexicon and syntax may be slightly misleading. The constructions are more than elements combined into a structure. In the experience of those who build the constructions, the causal efficacy is not a simple, direct result of the creation of a structured meaning. A review of Lamp's description of the various kinds of constructions shows that in almost every case, not just the combining of elements, but also the invocation of spirits, is involved. In fact, it may be that the very meaning of the structure is precisely the invocation of spirits. For *an-wanka*, "*an-kerfi* are invoked."[178] *An-sena* " invokes the power of both the ancestors and the *an-kerfi*" and "is itself considered a spirit, *o-kerfi*."[179] *An-kantha* is "a specific application of the larger context of 'closing.' Generally its purpose is to close a space against spiritual evil and to place it within the realm of spiritual good.... It is usually applied to towns and houses.... [It] is placed only by a religious specialist."[180] *An-sathka* or "sacrifice," "involves the invocation to the ancestors, and through them, to God, Kuru."[181]

The physiognomic and interpretive meanings the construction evokes appear as the manifestation of the presence and power of the spirits invoked.[182] For example, the vines both look awful and are something that could be used to strangle someone. Both together give the vines a threatening look. But it is not that Temne simply confuse the power of that threatening look with the presence of spirits. The spirits also have to be invoked. The origin of the very idea of spirits may indeed lie, as I have argued, in the objective "more," which is a felt dimension even of visual perception. But the perception of an object as a construction such as *an-wanka*, *an-sena*, or *an-kantha* still depends upon an explicit interpretation. In *this* feeling of awfulness and threat seen in *this* object recognized as, e.g. *an-wanka*, the real presence of a spirit is felt. One may believe or disbelieve that such deliberate constructions of signs, symbols, and representations can actually embody the real presence of spirits who have the power to make things physically happen, and can be called upon to excercise that power. But the belief that a deliberate symbolic construction embodies the real presence of a spirit is hardly limited to traditional African religion. One need only think of the Christian tradition of the Eucharist.

Within this cultural context, everyone knows that we are surrounded by the space of spirits, ancestors, and witches. But certain people are regarded as being able to see into this invisible space. They are called *an-soki*.[183] According to Shaw, the word *sok*, common to *an-soki* and *ro-soki*, "is associated with vision and visibility as well as knowledge and comprehension."[184] Diviners represent one kind of *an-soki*, "their power to divine deriving from their relationship with either a patron spirit or a recent diviner-ancestor who gives them revelations of hidden knowledge, initially through an initiatory dream."[185] Shaw has studied in detail the practice of a particular Temne diviner. A private divination session proceeds as follows:

> A client consulting Pa Biyare first gave a small quantity of money as a "shakehand" and then explained the problem. Pa Biyare, seated on a Muslim prayer mat on the floor, rubbed the pebbles with his hands and spoke the Muslim prayer, *Bismillahi Rahmani Rahim*, under his breath. He then instructed the pebbles to

reveal (*tori*) truly, softly repeated the client's question to them and cast the pebbles.[186]

The casting of the pebbles is a complicated procedure, following rules for generating a pattern of pebbles arranged on the ground. The rules provide for both an element of randomness and an element of choice—the diviner has the discretion to arrange the pattern differently depending upon the kind of situation his client is consulting him about. Each pattern is a generalized symbol of a possible range of human situations, and includes suggestions as to possible ritual responses. But the pattern may be interpreted very differently depending on the situation, and the diviner clearly has a great deal of leeway in his particular interpretation. In other words, while the patterns are generally suggestive, there is clearly no set of definite rules used to reliably deduce definite interpretations. The interpretation, we would say, is always "inspired." The diviners view this inspiration as coming from the spirits: "Pa Biyare said that his knowledge of how to interpret the patterns came from the spirits, and other *an-bere* diviners sometimes gaze into a small mirror in which they see spirits (especially their patron spirit) as an additional source of inspiration."[187] The diviner arrives at and shares an interpretation of the situation at issue, and makes a specific recommendation for action. But in private divination, the expression of the interpretation remains somewhat oblique:

> Rather than making specific accusations, private diviners use euphemistic language and veiled innuendoes. If a diviner "sees" that a woman client's co-wife is a witch who is attacking her children, for instance, she may be told that "in your house, there is a woman who is a bad person," "bad person" ... being a euphemism for "witch." She will usually be told to make a sacrifice which will cause the witch's *an-hake* to fall upon her, bringing her witchcraft into the open, by for example, making her spontaneously confess her hidden deeds. [*An-hake* is "an Islamic-derived concept denoting an external force sent by God (Kuru or Allah) which will sooner or later bring about the exposure of the miscreant's wrongdoings."][188]

Whatever else it may mean for the diviner, "seeing" into *ro-soki* clearly means receiving inspired interpretations. The sense that ideas somehow "come to" us, the experience of suddenly seeing a solution to a problem after one had given up straining for it, the feeling that it is through something other than or more than our own agency that we make progress in understanding anything, such experiences are hardly confined to diviners or shamans, but are simply characteristic of human consciousness as such. Human consciousness is always surrounded by an indefinite background, and new thoughts, ideas, understandings, interpretations, solutions seem to emerge out of that background. The "more" at the heart of human consciousness suggests the presence of an origin within ourselves that is yet beyond ourselves. We may assign different interpretations to that sense of origin, referring it to the unconscious, or to brain activity, or to God or of course also, to spirits. Here again, whether any of those interpretations are true is just a different question from that of the accuracy of the description of human consciousness as such in terms of James's notion of "the more."

Men's and Women's Religious Associations or "Secret Societies"

The term "secret society," used for the men's and women's associations that are at the heart of the traditional social organization in large parts of Sierra Leone, Liberia, Guinea, and the Ivory coast, is extremely misleading.[189] For these associations are completely public—indeed they could be said to define "the public" and its functioning in these cultures. All adult men belong to the men's societies, and all adult women belong to the women's societies. One's entrance into these societies is simply what defines one as being a full, adult member of the community. The initiation of children and adolescents into these societies ritually marks the transition from childhood to adulthood. Initiation also involves spending a period of time—which in an earlier era might be several years but today may be a much shorter period—in an area adjacent to but separated from the village, undergoing training and education in the skills and knowledge needed for adulthood. Those skills and knowledge include the practical (such as farming and hunting), the aesthetic (including dancing), and the religious. While the men's societies include all adult males, they do involve an internal hierarchy. The position of chief does not coincide with leadership of the men's society, and the chief can only act with the cooperation of the men's society membership.

My discussion of the men's and women's associations will focus on the Mende, but will also make reference to the Temne and Kono groups in Sierra Leone, the Gola and Kpelle in Liberia, and the Mandinka in Guinea. The region these groups cover—with the Temne and Kono to the north, the Mende immediately south, and the Gola to the southeast between the Kpelle and the Mende—represents the geographical core of this cultural tradition. The word *Poro* is used to denote the men's associations of the Mende, Gola, Kpelle, and Temne. The Temne also have the male *Rabai* association.[190] The women's associations are usually known as *Sande* by the Mende, Kono, Gola, and Kpelle, but as *Bondo* by the Temne.[191] The process of initiation has the ethical and religious significance of making present to the initiates the ideals and requirements of their society as a whole, and indeed of making present the sense of that society as as a spirit demanding their loyalty and inspiring their trust. In Mende, the words for men's association and women's association are *Polei hale* and *Sande hale* respectively.[192] The word *hale* can denote the "supernatural" or "mystical" power which can be activated in certain material objects, such as preparations of leaves, and which is able to have physical effects such as illness or death. Whether *hale* is a neutral, impersonal, force or the force possessed by a spirit, in effect *hale* is amenable to persuasion if one knows the right way to approach it. The Mende believe that Poro and Sande are each represented by a specific spirit (*nga-fa*), named *gbeni* and *sowei* respectively, and this spirit is made present through a masquerade.[193] The spirit of Poro and Sande has the power to enforce Poro and Sande regulations through the infliction of disease and death.

Map showing relative location of the Temne, Mende, Gola, Kpelle, Kono, and Kuranko. Shaded area represents the range of the Poro/Sande-Bondo tradition. (Map by permission of Frederick John Lamp.)

If the origin of the idea of *hale* lies in our experience of living beings as values and powers we confront and with whom we experience intersubjective communion, it does indeed make sense that people experience their own society as *hale*. The group to which one belongs is in a sense a living being—it is a being whose power one confronts and in whose life one participates. If the fundamental fact of life is the primal participation of each individual life in the lives of others, the very being of a group is the co-participation of its members in the act of identifying themselves as members of that group. Particular groups are the kind of thing that exist simply because people think and feel they do. As Durkheim puts it: "there is a realm of nature in which the formula of idealism is almost literally applicable; that is the social realm. There, far more than anywhere else, the idea creates the reality."[194] A group I belong to is not simply an object I am aware of. It is a being that exists only through each individual's subjective sharing in the act of the group's self-definition. Membership in a group involves an attitude of loyalty to the group and trust in its support for the individual. But the power underlying those bonds is the primal participation in the life of others and of the group.[195] That the Mende refer to Poro and Sande as *hale* means that they experience the group to which they belong as a power.

Durkheim regards the experience that individuals have of the group to which they belong as the origin and foundation of all religious experience. He attempts to describe the experience of Australian aborigines, whose participation in exuberant, physically demanding, and finally frenzied communal rituals for weeks on end, he infers, must result in an altered state of consciousness:

> Once the individuals are gathered together, a sort of electricity is generated from their closeness and quickly launches them to an extraordinary height of exaltation. Every emotion expressed resonates without interference in consciousnesses that are wide open to external impressions, each one echoing the others.[196]

Durkheim's word for the heightened state of awareness arising through ritual activity in a group is "effervescence." Durkheim claims that "it is in these effervescent social mileux, and indeed from that very effervescence, that the religious idea seems to have been born."[197] Durkheim is describing the very kind of heightened consciousness through which one's co-participation in the life of a group is made present and comes alive. Durkheim's idea seems to be that this is in fact the essence of ritual.

The members of the group, in their ritual exaltation, experience "impressions of dependence and heightened energy," but these feelings "become more closely attached to the idea of the totem than to that of the clan." Durkheim claims that "religious force is none other than the collective and anonymous force of the clan" and that "because that force can only be conceived in the form of the totem, the totemic emblem is, so to speak, the visible body of the god."[198] The totem is the symbol of the clan or group—the members experience it as an object, but the depth of feeling that lends the object its significance is the heightened experience of the reality of one's living participation in the group. Durkheim insists that this feeling, and the totemic beliefs it gives rise to, are fundamentally not an illusion, but actually a kind of truth:

> Indeed, we can say that the faithful are not mistaken when they believe in the existence of a moral power to which they are subject and from which they receive what is best in themselves. That power exists, and it is society. When the Australian is carried above himself, feeling inside a life overflowing with an intensity that surprises him, he is not the dupe of an illusion. That exaltation is real and really is the product of forces outside of and superior to the individual.[199]

Of course, from the Jamesian standpoint I have adopted, the origin of the experience of power in religious life is not limited to society and our experience of society. But Durkheim is in fact describing the way society is experienced as a power we participate in and depend upon. I would like to focus especially on the qualities of heightened awareness and emotional intensity that Durkheim refers to. Human beings are always depending upon the society and groups to which they belong, and they are always experiencing their participation, dependence and allegiance to those groups. But a heightened, intense, exalted experience of this participation is not an everyday matter. I contend that the function of ritual is precisely to bring to life one's feeling of the significance, of the mattering, of values to which one has, or may have allegiance (including the group one belongs to). Niebuhr's exploration of loyalty and trust as the essence of social faith neglects precisely the dimension that Durkheim so clearly focuses on: the arising of the experience of one's group as a value to which one *may* be committed, the experience of *mattering* that opens up and motivates the possibility of active allegiance.

The Poro *gbeni* spirit and the Sande *sowei* spirit both play an essential role in the initiation process through their performance by masked dancers. As such they may be considered to be objectifications of the power of the group. But the symbols inherent in ritual are not only objects one may see, but also actions that one does and suffers—one does not merely look at the symbol, one lives through it. Poro and Sande initiation and training involve a series of ritual dramas in which the initiates participate, and the whole process may be considered an extended ritual drama. The drama as symbol does not merely express a meaning, it also impresses a meaning: in living through the symbol, the participant brings alive the mattering of the values to which participation expresses his or her commitment. The concept of symbol and metaphor I am working with here denies that symbol and metaphor can be reduced to the interrelationships among objective statements or meanings (such as similarity, analogy, or whole-part). The essence of symbol and metaphor lies in the power of language and action to bring to life the experience of values as mattering, an experience that is prior to objective expression. I believe this experience is exactly what Durkheim was really getting at in his discussion of "effervescence."

The Guinean writer Camara Laye, in his famous memoir *L'Enfant noir* (translated as *The Dark Child*) records his experience of undergoing an initiation similar to that of the Mende Poro. His account of that initiation and its significance agrees with that of anthropologists who have studied the men's associations of the region. He points out specifically that in the view of his society, initiation represents "the beginning of a new life." Circumcision is a test of manhood he is determined to face bravely The initiation process is not just an ordeal for the boys to endure, but is a festival which the whole community takes very seriously, and participates in with enthusiasm and joy.[200] Camara's description of the celebrations that build up to the circumcision ritual evokes precisely the experience of "effervescence":

> We would dance until we were out of breath; but we were not the only ones dancing: the whole town danced with us! They came in throngs to watch. The whole town came, because the test, so very important to us, was equally important to all. No one could be indifferent to the fact that this second birth, our real birth, would increase the population of the town by a new group of citizens. In our country, all dances have a cumulative tendency, because each beat of the tom tom has an almost irresistible appeal. Soon, those who were just spectators would dance too. They would crowd into the open space, and, though they did not mix with our group, they would take an intimate part in our revels, rivaling us in their frenzy, men as well as women, women as well as girls, though the women and girls danced apart from us.[201]

Camara also describes his feelings about facing circumcision in a way that makes clear the commitment to certain values that the ritual involves:

But, however great the anxiety, however certain the pain, no one would have dreamed of running away from the ordeal...and I, for my own part, never entertained such thoughts. I wanted to be born, to be born again. I knew perfectly well that I was going to be hurt, but I wanted to be a man, and it seemed to me that nothing could be too painful if, by enduring it, I was to come to man's estate. My companions felt the same. Like me, they were prepared to pay for it with their blood. Our elders before us had paid for it thus; those who were born after us would pay for it in their turn. Why should we be spared? Life itself would spring from the shedding of our blood.[202]

Initiation includes practical instruction, but it also represents the continuing creation of a social group and the creation of a social meaning. The initiation of children into adulthood (an act in which the whole community participates) *is* the act of collective self-definition that creates the social meaning "our group." But what is the group to which the initiated belong? In contrast to the self-definitions prevalent in many Western societies, the collective self-definitions that occur among groups such as the Mende and Temne do not appear to be specifically *"ethnic."* The identity individuals assume is named "Poro member" or "Sande member," rather than, "Mende" or "Temne." The initiated belong to Poro or Sande. And Poro and Sande cross ethnic boundaries. This does not mean that there is a single Poro and Sande organization that unites the different ethnic groups possessing this tradition. The organization of the Poro and Sande is essentially local, although there are many shared traditions. There are recognized commonalities and recognized differences between the Poro organizations in different areas. Membership in these associations does not seem to imply the creation of a clear cut sense of "insiders" and "outsiders," as does membership in certain exclusivistic Western Christian churches does. There is a clear cut division between children and adults, and between men and women, but in an important sense children, Poro, and Sande are experienced as belonging together and as interdependent. The Poro and Sande spirits can indeed be understood as personifications of the spirit of "our society," or "our group." But membership in Poro and Sande do not seem to necessarily involve the spirit of defensiveness toward, or of "ethnocentric" prejudice against other groups.

The act of self-definition proceeds according to the three stages identified by Van Gennep of separation, transition, and incorporation. In the case of the men's associations, the first stage involves the gathering of the boys from their homes, their transfer to a cleared area of bush near the ground sacred to Poro, and circumcision. In the cases of the Mende, Temne, and Kpelle, the transfer involves a more or less public ceremony. For the Kpelle, the initiates are gathered by a *Zo* official, and engage the Poro spirit or *ngamu* in a mock battle outside of the fence of the village.[203] For the Mende, the Poro spirit, *gbeni,* enters the town and his followers collect the boys from their homes. The spirit is heard throughout the town "making harsh nasal sounds, like someone groaning"[204]—but evidently not seen, since the sight of *gbeni* is forbidden to non-members of Poro.[205] The Temne *Rabai* initiation begins with an all night community celebration which culminates before dawn in the boys moving to the camp. The Temne boys are then shaved bald and washed.[206] Circumcision takes place immediately for all three groups. (However, Bellman makes no mention of circumcision among the

Kpelle.) At this stage, marks are then cut into the backs of the Mende boys,[207] and into the necks, chests, and backs of the Kpelle boys.[208] Both the Mende and the Kpelle refer to these marks as the teeth marks of the Poro spirit. Entering the initiation process is spoken of as 'being eaten by the Poro spirit.' The boys are spoken of as 'dead' from that point until they return to the village. That return is spoken of as, and acted out as, their rebirth from the belly of the Poro spirit or his wife (Kpelle).[209] The Temne do not make use of this death and rebirth metaphor, but the initiation is said by them "to resemble the death of the boys."[210]

Little describes the Mende transitional period of training as quite harsh: "They sleep at night on a bed of sticks under covering clothes which have been soaked in water, and they remain out of doors, if it rains. The singing and drumming lasts until one or two o'clock in the morning and the boys are awakened again at dawn."[211] However, Little had only second hand acquaintance with the initiation. One of Bellman's Kpelle informants describes the Poro camp in very different terms: "It is a large town. It is very enjoyable. Most of them don't even want to come out."[212]

For all the groups, the actual training the boys undergo is not esoteric, but includes every kind of practical preparation for their lives as adults: hunting, agriculture, crafts, some 'medicine.' Their preparation is also religious and aesthetic. Little somewhat slights the aesthetic aspect: "On the social side, the boys learn drumming and to sing the special Poro songs. They practice somersaults and acrobatics."[213] But Lamp has a much clearer appreciation of the significance of the aesthetic dimension:

> During Rabai the strictest attention is given to discipline—self-regulated, peer-group sanctioned, as well as supervised. Through music and dance in which Katumla [the *Rabai* spirit] is catalyst, the initiate is made to understand the beauty of coordinated effort, of the strength of interlocked parts, and of a total chord in which each tone is vitally important but indistinguishable when performed correctly."[214]

The Mende refer to the completion of the Poro initiation, with the incorporation of the initiates back into the community, as the 'pulling' of the Poro, or *Kpia*. The *Kpia* involves a four day ritual in which, again, the whole community is involved. The boys are made to stay awake all night—they are told it would be fatal if they sleep and dream of the Poro spirit. Just before dawn, the Poro spirit enters town, moaning as if in labor before the assembled community, which is in a celebratory mood. "The women clap their hands and the men reproach him for detaining their children for so long." Then the spirit flees, not to return until next year.[215]

The symbolism of the final ceremony before the Mende boys return to the village is particularly striking:

> The boys are lined up in a semi-circle at the stones of the *palihun* (the deepest part of the bush) round the *Sowa*, or head official and the *Mabole*.[216] (The *Mabole* is the only woman official of the Poro and serves the boys as a matron.) Moss and thread are wound round the boys' toes, so that they are all tied together in a continuous chain. On their heads they wear caps of moss and leaves of the umbrella tree....The *Mabole* stands in the middle, facing the sacred stones. She

invokes the spirits of the society on their behalf, and prays that each new member may be as strongly attached to the society as the thread and moss which now bind them together.[217]

The moss and thread are a clear symbol of the web of human relationships, related to the Kuranko image of the ropes attached to the bird scaring platform, and the Mende absolution ritual in which nieces and nephews all lie on the ground grasping their maternal uncle's ankles. Next the *Mabole* calls upon the spirits of the society and finally upon God, here referred to by the old name *Leve*:

> Father Siaffa, let it reach you; let it reach to Kanga; let it reach (lit. 'be laid down') to the head, the great one (i.e. God). This is what *Leve* brought down (showed us to do) long ago. These children, whom we are "pulling" from the Poro today, let nothing harm them; let them not fall from palm trees; make their bodies strong; give them wisdom to look after their children; let them hold themselves in a good way; let them show themselves to be men![218]

This prayer confirms that the Mende believe that the Poro and its accompanying traditions were instituted by God and that Poro is overseen also by the ancestors. The prayer is petitionary in asking for protection, but it also reveals something about the human qualities the Mende value. The motivation for Poro initiation is the concern of parents for their children, and the ideals Poro stands for are strength, wise parenting, upright behavior, and courage.

When this step is completed, the boys are taken to a stream and in the presence of their fathers, a ceremony remarkably similar to baptism occurs. Each boy is lowered into the water and kept there until his father produces a fowl; this is repeated four times for each initiate. The boys are then dressed and prepared for their triumphant return to the village. Four days of feasting and celebration follow.

The corresponding incorporation ritual for the Temne *Rabai* initiation is known as *kakus*. This celebration lasts from evening till dawn, and involves the entire community. The boys begin by practicing the pattern of singing and dancing they will perform as they re-enter the village at midnight. The dance involves the rhythmic pounding of the *katak* staff (pl. *tatak*) given to each boy on the completion of his training. The staff is a sign of "achievement and certification" and is carried throughout these final ceremonies.[219] At the top of the staff is an individually carved figure which can take various forms. Having been carved "by one who works with the supernatural" *tatak* are presumably invested with power.[220] Lamp's description of the scene at midnight suggests the celebration's quality of "effervescence":

> The Rabai assembly enters the village and is joined by the women and children. The *angbethi* [initiates] continue their dance encouraged and accompanied by a crushing crowd of villagers singing in unison and moving as particles attracted to a swirling mass. Total participation is mandatory. Energy rises in intensity. I once saw a passive spectator summarily ordered to withdraw: "You're not singing; you're not dancing—it's better you go to bed and sleep!"[221]

The Gola are a group in Liberia geographically located directly between the Mende and the Kpelle. D'Azevedo, in his discussion of the relationship between Poro and Sande among the Gola, points out that "it is commonly acknowledged among surrounding peoples that the Gola have retained the most conservative and exemplary traditions with regard to the structure and content of those two associations."[222] And among the Gola, the Poro and Sande exist in a state of *balanced interdependence*, both in theory and practice. This interdependence is expressed in the myth of the origin of Poro and Sande that the Gola embrace. According to this story, Sande was the first organization, and the Gola were originally ruled by women. In response to warfare around them, the men began a new association, with its own powerful spirit. With this spirit behind them, the men negotiated a deal. The men would rule the country for four years, then the women for three, and so on forever. This pattern is even now followed for alternating Poro and Sande initiation sessions.

Carol MacCormack, in her study of the Sande among the Sherbro and Mende, has a similar emphasis upon the balanced interdependence between Poro and Sande. The dual institution of Poro and Sande maintains a distinction between gender roles in society that reserves definite powers for women and insists upon mutual respect between genders within the established framework. MacCormack points out that while women do go to live in the compounds of their husbands, they then join the local Sande chapter, but also return home to their mother's chapter to give birth. The married woman is not isolated but always enjoys the support of a women's organization. The Sande chapters have an internal hierarchy composed exclusively of women, and of course women rise to positions of authority within that hierarchy.[223] The authority of Sande includes the enforcement of Sande regulations—which apply both to men and to women. "Sande laws make explicit the respect that should be shown to all women. The laws are carefully observed by both men and women, being reinforced by supernatural sanctions and by pragmatic political action on the part of women locally organized into a hierarchy of offices."[224]

MacCormack points out that men are often required to, in effect, provide major financial support for the Sande organization, through the very custom of "bride price." The initiation fees for Sande are very high, and the family of a girl's husband to be is "expected to help with initiation fees, often contributing the major portion together with bride wealth."[225] Little reports that in 1901, the Sande initiation fee included "a bushel of rice, a fowl, a gallon of palm oil, a barrel of rum, and a 'head' of money at 3 pounds."[226] This suggests that even if the family of the prospective husband does not directly contribute to Sande, bridewealth compensates the girl's family for the very high Sande fees—so that Sande is perhaps in effect supported primarily by the families of prospective husbands.

The initiation and training of new Sande members is of course within the direct control of Sande itself. MacCormack notes that the head (known as *majo*) of the Sande chapter "is ultimately responsible for the quality of such initiate's training for womanhood. She passes on strong, positive definitions of womanhood in the imagery of oral tradition, art, and practical skills. She, or some other

The woman to the Bondo spirit's left seems to share the same expression of composure and concentration as the mask; in fact, everyone does, even the nursing mother and the little girl. Lamp argues for the following suggestions about the mask's symbolism: The neck rings on the mask represent not plumpness (as is commonly asserted by Western interpreters) but rather the water out of which the Bondo spirit has arisen. The crests on the mask represent not female labia (as is also commonly asserted) but rather the sprouting of plants. The whole mask may represent the form of a chrysalis, consonant with its theme of fertility.[227] (Photo by permission of Frederick John Lamp)

senior official, is also midwife and adviser on all gynecological matters."[228] Just as in Poro, the Sande initiation includes training in all the practical skills needed in adulthood: "farming, spinning, childcare, diagnosing illness, compounding and administering medicines, singing, and dancing." And the girls develop not only skills, but also attitudes and values. For example, "in the evenings the initiates and elders gather about the fire, singing, dancing, talking, and telling stories. The stories end in a moral or a dilemma which is debated long into the night, encouraging a more mature exploration of the human condition."[229]

According to Ruth Phillips, the masked *sowei* spirit, or *ndoli jowei*, embodies and expresses the ideal of womanhood that Sande inculcates. The usually stylized face expresses an "inner spiritual concentration" that Sande women seek to emulate.[230] Phillips' definitive volume on Mende Sande masquerades, and an article by Lamp on the Temne Bondo mask contain several photographs that strikingly illustrate the intimate tie between the mask's expression and the consciousness of the Sande women. Phillips includes one photograph of a woman, standing next to *ndoli jowei*, whose bearing and facial expression clearly echo the mask's—and Phillips herself points out this connection.[231] Lamp includes a similar photograph, though he does not explicitly point this out.[232] Phillips quotes Sylvia Boone's description of the ideal that the Sande mask represents: "The eye blinks in dazzled acknowledgement of what one should and could be: intelligent, capable, authoritative, adaptable, courageous, patient, honest, persevering, strong, and 'straight.'"[233] Boone's explanation of the expressive power of *ndoli jowei* continues as follows:

> Sowo, and other Mende masked figures, remind us that human beings experience a twofold existence: one in the world of the concrete—flesh, matter, things; the other in the world of the spirit—dreams, aspirations, reason, imagination, faith. The masks of the spirit are, in effect, fabrications of this spiritual reality. In the form of emissaries from an "outer space," they dance into sight, and as Incarnations they mingle with us mortals in the human arena. Mende elders have helped me see that the masks are the collective Mind of the community…. They are materializations of Mende aesthetic canons and moral ideals; they are role models shaping the character of the Mende, influencing their feelings, thoughts, and actions.[234]

Phillips identifies Boone's approach as one with "deep roots in the idealist metaphysics" according to which artworks "are actual embodiments of a metaphysical Thesis or Idea."[235] Phillips appears to be critical of such an approach. But Phillips apparently also sees the *Sowei* mask as embodying an idea or ideal, for example, of "inner spiritual concentration." Based on specific observation of Mende reactions to *sowei* appearances, including the names that the masks are given, Phillips appears to draw conclusions that are actually quite close to Boone's: "The *ndoli jowei*, whether in a humorous, irate, or troublesome mood, is a strong and compelling presence." "A human being in her vicinity has no choice but to abandon mundane pursuits and pay homage in the form of undivided attention." "The interpretation of mask names shows us that the Mende understand physical beauty as an active quality which enhances a masker's—or a woman's—forcefulness and personality, enabling her to capture public attention, accumulate wealth, and influence other people."[236]

I suggest that the masks, and indeed artworks in general, need not embody *explicit* ideas, but rather communicate or powerfully project a conscious sense of the importance of certain values. The experience of confronting the mask, indeed the experience of confronting an artwork generally, is one that may give rise to verbal interpretations, but is fundamentally prior to verbal interpretation.[237] The masks and ritual dramas of African tradition are an intimate part of the fabric of actual living—they exist not for the sake of creating an aesthetic impression for a detached observer in a museum, but rather in order to call forth a living sense of values in a context that requires a participant to make an active commitment to those values.

Sande or Bondo mask from the collection of Otterbein University. On this mask, the entwined serpents seem like extensions of the rings, so that the rings could represent either water or the serpents themselves. According to Lamp, "the serpent seems to refer on the masks to the descent from the spiritual world above bringing a renewal of life to the physical."[238] Above the face, three different cross-hatch patterns represent plaited hair, which suggests the cultivation of plants as well as refinement.[239] It is as if the Bondo spirit inspires cultivation which leads to new life. Yet Lamp also notes there is "some evidence" that the Temne think of conception "in terms of the descent of the fetal spirit from above, and the spiritual conception of the child in the head, the seat of spiritual receptivity."[240] (The markings beneath the eyes identify the mask as probably Kpa-Mende.)

Bellman provides a perspective on the significance of symbol, metaphor and ritual different from the one I have been advocating. He closely associates the phenomenon of "secrecy" with that of metaphor—and, in the process, clarifies exactly what "secrecy" in the so-called "secret societies" actually involves. Secrecy in this context is not fundamentally a matter of hidden information. The actual hidden information that Poro involves is minimal. Most of what goes on in the Poro and Sande camps is well known by everyone. "Secrecy" has more to do with the rights that various categories of people have to mention certain things, and the different ways different groups of people are required to refer to certain things if they can mention them at all.

> For instance, a member of the Poro may refer to the place where the novices re-side as *weiawoli* (the "little forest") or euphemistically as Nairobi, after the capi-tal of Kenya, which is popular in Liberia because of Highlife recordings. The women, however, must openly maintain that the boys are dead and living in the *ngamu ko su* ("inside the devil's stomach").[241]

Of course everyone knows the boys are not really dead. The required use of the metaphor 'inside the devil's stomach,' Bellman argues, has the primary function of distinguishing Poro members (males) from non-Poro members (fe-males). The use of the metaphor expresses recognition of and respect for the social reality of Poro, and of the different roles each gender is assigned. Secrecy in this sense is, according to Bellman, "a fundamental organizing principle in [Kpelle] political, economic, social, religious, and interpersonal behaviors."[242] Bellman carefully shows how ritual metaphors do represent this kind of "secret," and do have this social function.

I am emphasizing that the ritual metaphors also express certain intrinsic val-ues. The metaphor of death and rebirth, in which initiates ritually participate, expresses, or rather impresses, the feeling that the painful transitions in life are worthwhile, that transition, frightening as it really is, has a purposive and inspir-ing direction. In fact, I would like to propose that initiation rituals are close to the center of African religious experience. It is precisely here that James's dra-ma of the "unease" and its "solution" is most clearly evident. The ritual separa-tion from the community—whose meaning is inseparable from the loss of child-hood—is the unease. And the solution is re-incorporation into the community. The unease is also the ordeal, and the solution is the withstanding of the ordeal. On the personal, spiritual level, the meaning of the whole lived-out ritual drama is precisely in the inner strength, self-motivation, and sense of worthwhileness gained by proving oneself a match for the ordeal to the rejoicing of one's whole community. Joseph Campbell has been guilty of many oversimplifications, but his fundamental insight is correct: "It has always been the prime function of mythology and rite to supply the symbols that carry the human spirit forward, in counteraction to those other constant human fantasies that tend to tie it back."[243] To claim that 'to carry the human spirit forward has *always* been the *prime* func-tion of mythology and rite' is an exaggeration. But Campbell is not mistaken in finding such a function in mythology and rite. This is a fundamental dimension of symbol and ritual that Bellman passes over in silence.

Phillips, pointing out that appearances of *ndoli jowei* in the initiation rituals and celebrations vary in different areas of Mendeland, describes the particular schedule in one chiefdom. *Ndoli jowei* appears in the village two or three days after the girls have entered the Sande camp and undergone circumcision, to announce that initiation has begun. Two weeks later *ndoli jowei* appears again to announce that the girls are to arrive home again the following day; she celebrates by dancing all night, and herself brings the girls to the village. After this point the girls spend their days in the village but their nights in the Sande camp, and wear white clay on their faces. The last appearance of *ndoli jowei* marks the conclusion of the whole initiation. The girls are collected from their homes, covered with white clay, lead by *ndoli jowei* to a river where they are ritually washed, marking their final release from the initiation session. Then "the Sande graduates are seated in state and are feasted and made much of for several days."[244]

Lamp writes that the form of the Temne Bondo mask "varies little from one ethnic group to the next, individualized mainly by incidental details."[245] The Mende and Temne artistic and ritual traditions are indeed close. The Temne name for the spirit is *Nowo*.[246] The Bondo official who performs *Nowo* is called *Na-soko*.[247] The *Na-soko* does not simply choose to perform Nowo—rather, *Nowo* comes to her from "beyond the water" which is "not the water of this world." This experience may occur in a dream.[248] The Bondo initiates first encounter *Nowo* at the time of circumcision "when her overwhelming presence is said to mesmerize them and relieve the pain." She is involved throughout the initiation process. She "dances with the girls, inspiring awe and trepidation" and she also acts as a judge in matters of Bondo law, "execut[ing] punishment when it is required, either on delinquent initiates or on men who violate the sanctions of Bondo."[249] Lamp also agrees that the mask embodies an ideal: "The chief formal characteristic of the mask" is "the sacred function of female grooming and its metaphorical connection to spiritual righteousness as a fundamental virtue of civilizing female force....The delicate coiffure of women stands as a symbol of human refinement, both male and female."[250]

Fuambai Ahmadu is an anthropologist whose family is Kono and who grew up both in Freetown and in Washington DC. In 1991, her final year at a university in Washington, she chose to return to the area where her family originated in the Kono region in order to undergo Bondo initiation, including circumcision. There has been a longstanding campaign in Western countries against the practice of female circumcision. Ahmadu's research, which incorporates her personal experience, is dedicated to understanding the role that initiation plays in Kono culture and in the lives of Kono women. Ahmadu herself says she neither supports nor opposes the practice of circumcision, but she is critical of much of the campaign against it. She provides a clear discussion of the issues surrounding the practice, and of the significance of the Bondo association, attending to the viewpoints of Kono women themselves. Her description of her experience is compelling, providing, by the way, an "insider" perspective on the experience of social "effervescence" at the heart of this ritual:

Social Coercion and pressure to conform, however, do not explain the *eagerness* and *excitement* felt by vast numbers of participants (residents in Kono as well as outside) in initiation ceremonies, including mothers of initiates, even if these same mothers also experience anxiety over the safety of their daughters. It is difficult for me—considering the number of these ceremonies I have observed, including my own—to accept that what appear to be expressions of joy and ecstatic celebrations of womanhood in actuality disguise hidden experiences of coercion and subjugation. Instead, I offer that most Kono women who uphold these rituals do so because they *want* to—they relish the supernatural powers of their ritual leaders over against men in society, and they embrace the legitimacy of female authority and, particularly, the authority of their mothers and grandmothers. Also, they maintain their cultural superiority over uninitiated/uncircumcised women.[251]

Ahmadu's account also includes a concise summary of the ideals that Sande inculcates. In a society in which women are in many respects in a subordinate position, Sande or Bondo is an institution which nevertheless empowers women within that context. Ahmadu's description clearly delineates what independence and strength can mean in such a situation:

> Vis a vis their husbands and their male (and female) lineage representatives, young novices are taught to *feign* subservience—in verbal communication, body language and gestures, and the performance of domestic duties—in order to live harmoniously with their affines. But ritual leaders do not only teach subservience. They themselves are examples of ultimate female authority: wise, unyielding, and unsentimental. It is the *soko*'s responsibility to see to it that novices are inculcated with the ideals of femininity as laid down by previous ancestresses: stoicism, which must be displayed during excision; tenacity and endurance, which are achieved through the many other ordeals a novice must undergo; and most important, 'dry-eye,' that is, daring, bravery, fearlessness, and audacity— qualities that will enable young women to stand their ground as adults in their households and within the greater community. [252]

I have attempted to present a fairly comprehensive account of traditional African religion in Sierra Leone. My primary focus has been on the Mende and the Temne. I have considered traditional religion in terms of several dimensions: God, ancestors, magic, spirits, ethics, and "secret" societies. Robin Horton claims that religion has two dimensions, that of "communion" and that of prediction and control of events. He also claims that in traditional African religion, "communion" plays at most a secondary role. From the perspective of this survey, it becomes possible to begin to evaluate Robin Horton's claim that "communion" is secondary in traditional African religion. (A conclusive evaluation of that claim, if even possible, would obviously involve a massive review of research. My aim here is simply to relate that claim to the available material on traditional religion in Sierra Leone.) I think it is indisputable that a great deal of what falls under the category of beliefs and practices relating to magic, spirits, and even ancestors has at least the primary function of prediction and control of events. As Horton himself points out, an emphasis on prediction and control is hardly alien to Western religion, and is especially prominent in the medieval period. But is Horton justified in claiming that "communion" is only secondary in traditional African religions? He acknowledges the presence of beliefs and stories about God in religions such as that of the Mende. But, he claims, "communion" with God is not the central focus of such religions. This does seem accurate in the case in the religions I have considered. However, I argue that the Mende creation stories are not merely instrumental values, but do evoke and express a sense of wonder over the mystery of our origin and destiny. So while religious feelings such as communion with God may be secondary, there is definite evidence that such feelings do have a role to play (which Horton does not exactly deny).

But there is one dimension of the religions I have considered which challenges Horton's contention that "communion" as such, is secondary. The central focus of these religions is in fact on communion—not with God, but with one's human community. This is evident most strikingly in the accounts of initiation rituals I have considered. What Durkheim describes as "effervescence," I have argued, is very much an experience of communion or participation in a common life *for its own sake*. And clearly, Poro and Sande training aims at the inculcation of character traits which have intrinsic value. And what is at stake in formalized rituals for the laying and the withdrawing of curses is clearly the maintenance of harmonious relations among members of a community. Are we to believe that such harmonious relations are a merely instrumental value, and that moral violations, repentance, and forgiveness have no personal, emotional, and spiritual significance? Clearly such ceremonies exist for the sake of the intrinsic value of interpersonal communion. Horton's view avoids self-contradiction only by excluding by definition the experience of living community from religious experience

The case of ancestors, on the basis of the material I have considered, is harder to assess. Clearly, the displeasure of ancestors is often invoked as an explanation for accident and disease. But ancestors also have the social function of enforcing moral rules by punishing the living. Are we to believe that it is mere fear of punishment, and not also reverence and respect for ancestors, which motivates obedience to moral rules and social regulations? To the extent that reverence and respect for ancestors may indeed underlie such obedience, communion with ancestors must form an important dimension of traditional African religions. It is relevant here that the spirits of the Poro and the Sande/Bondo societies are also *ancestral* spirits. The communion with one's living community in the initiation celebrations clearly has a dimension of communion with ancestors. And at least in the case of the Temne, as Lamp points out, "the aged are considered closest to the recently deceased and the fact that both are called by the same term, *am-baki*, 'the old ones,' implies that they are virtually one and the same."[253] There is clearly a strong sense of continuity between the community of the living and of the living dead.

On the other hand, some of the material on Mende funeral ceremonies suggests a relatively greater focus upon the importance of the living community. While the ancestors do have the role of enforcing moral regulations, it is the living who absolve the dead person of guilt and, through ritual, open the way to join the ancestors, provided that person has not been revealed to be a witch. The final restoration of harmonious communion would seem to take place through this specific ceremony. On the whole it seems that the living and the dead form a single community, and communion with that community is the central focus of religious life. Jackson calls attention to the Kuranko notion of *morgoye*, which "connotes altruism and magnanimity, virtues which the Kuranko set at the foundation of the social order."[254] And he goes on to point out that the social order is not limited to that of living humans: *"morgoye* may be found in relations between man and ancestor, man and totemic animal, man and God, and so on."[255] If Jackson's observations are at all an accurate clue to the nature of traditional African religious experience, while it may be true that the focus of communion is on one's immediate, human community, the scope of that communion is nevertheless far more encompassing.

Notes

1. The detailed reasons for my rejection of such "anti-essentialism" are to be found in my article "Husserl, Hegel, Derrida, and the Notion of Time," *International Philosophical Quarterly* 36 no. 3 (Sept. 1996): 287–302.

2. William James, *The Varieties of Religious Experience* (New York: New American Library, 1958), 377.

3. Ibid.

4. Ibid., 384.

5. Michael Polanyi, *Personal Knowledge* (New York: Harper, 1964), 351.

6. Ibid., 350.

7. Ibid., 359.

8. For a Husserlian discussion of these issues that lays out the alternatives and comes to a somewhat different conclusion, see James Hart, *The Person and the Common Life* (Dordrecht: Kluwer, 1992), 175–205.

9. Michel Henry, *Phénoménologie matérielle* (Paris: Presses Universitaires de France, 1990), 178, my translation.

10. Louis Lavelle, *De l'âme humaine* (Paris: Aubier, 1951), 400, my translation.

11. Louis Lavelle, "La crainte du surnaturel" in *Psychologie et spiritualité* (Paris: Albin Michel, 1967), 192. Michel Henry also incorporates the idea of "resonances" between mind and nature, via Kandinsky's aesthetic theory. See my "Michel Henry's Phenomenology of Aesthetic Experience and Husserlian Intentionality," *International Journal of Philosophical Studies* 14.2 (April 2005): 191–219.

12. Lavelle, "La crainte,"193. I have not been able to find the source of Lavelle's quote of Levy-Bruhl. But it does reflect what Lucien Levy-Bruhl says elsewhere, for example in *The Notebooks on Primitive Mentality,* trans. Peter Rivière (Oxford, UK: Basil, 1975): "In this way, participation is not 'explained'—it cannot be and ought not to be, it has no need of legitimation; but one sees its necessary place in the human mind—and as a result its role in religion, in metaphysics, in art and even in the conception of the whole of nature" (180).

13. Levy-Bruhl, *Notebooks,* 104.

14. Ibid., 142.

15. Ibid., 180.

16. See E. Bolaji Idowu, *African Traditional Religion: A Definition* (Maryknoll, New York: Orbis, 1975), esp. 140–65; see also John Mbiti, *Concepts of God in Africa* (New York: Praeger, 1970), and *African Religions and Philosophy* (New York: Praeger, 1969).

17. Mbiti, *African Religions,* 61.

18. Harry Sawyerr, *God: Ancestor or Creator? Aspects of Traditional Belief in Ghana, Nigeria, and Sierra Leone* (Harlow: Longmans, 1970), 3.

19. Ibid., 5, 6.

20. Idowu, *African Traditional Religion*, 135.

21. Robin Horton, "A Definition of Religion, and its Uses," *The Journal of the Royal Anthropological Institute of Great Britain and Ireland* 90 no. 2 (Jul.–Dec. 1960), 211.

22. Horton, "A Definition," 212.

23. Robin Horton "Judeo-Christian Spectacles: Boon or Bane to the Study of African Religions?" in *Patterns of Thought in Africa and the West: Essays on Magic, Religion, and Science* (Cambridge: Cambridge Univ. Press, 1993), 177–78.

24. Horton, "Judeo-Christian Spectacles," 176.

25. Sjoerd Hofstra, "Ancestral Spirits of the Mendi," *Internationale Archiv für Ethnologie* Band 39, Heft 1–4 (Leiden, 1940), 184–85.

26. Horton, "A Definition," 222.

27. Ibid., 211.

28. Michael Jackson, *Allegories of the Wilderness: Ethics and Ambiguity in Kuranko Narratives* (Bloomington: Indiana Univ. Press, 1982), 16.

29. Ibid., 15.

30. Ibid.

31. Ibid., 16–17.

32. Ibid., 17.

33. W.T. Harris and Harry Sawyerr, *The Springs of Mende Belief and Conduct* (Freetown: Sierra Leone Univ. Press, 1968), hereafter SMBC.

34. Sawyerr tabulates exactly which passages he added, and my subsequent references to this book will attribute passage references to Sawyerr or to Harris accordingly.

35. See "Foreword," to Harry Sawyerr, *The Practice of Presence: Shorter Writings of Harry Sawyerr*, edited by John Parratt (Grand Rapids, Mich.: Eerdmans, 1994), viii–xvi.

36. See Sawyerr's discussion of Sundkler in *Practice*, 100–107; the other major source is Kenneth Little, *The Mende of Sierra Leone: A West African People in Transition* (London: Routledge, 1951).

37. Pronounced *ŋgewɔ*.

38. Kenneth Little, "The Mende in Sierra Leone," in *African Worlds*, edited by Daryll Forde, 111–137 (London: Oxford Univ. Press, 1954), 119.

39. SMBC, 11.

40. SMBC, 8–9.

41. SMBC, 6–7. Pronounced *leve*.

42. SMBC, 10, 12.

43. SMBC, 8–9.

44. SMBC, 6, 61, 132.

45. SMBC, 11.

46. SMBC, 3, 10, 12, 61.

47. SMBC, 12–13, 17.

48. Harry Sawyerr, *God Ancestor or Creator? Aspects of Traditional Belief in Ghana, Nigeria, and Sierra Leone* (Harlow: Longmans, 1970), 81.

49. Sawyerr, *God*, 68ff.

50. SMBC, 3.

51. Pronounced *ŋga-fa*, Sawyerr, *God*, 82.

52. Pronounced *kpila-gbualɛi*.

53. SMBC, 31.

54. SMBC, 32.

55. Sawyerr, *God,* 84.

56. Pronounced *tewenjamεi.*

57. Hofstra, "Ancestral Spirits," 186.

58. Little, "The Mende in Sierra Leone," 115.

59. Pronounced *ŋgombi-mε-hun,* SMBC, 88–89.

60. SMBC, 188–89.

61. SMBC, 32, 89.

62. Hofstra, "Ancestral Spirits," 186.

63. Howard Mueller, "Oral Data on the Development of the United Brethren in Sierra Leone, Gathered 1971–72," 405 (hereafter MOD).

64. MOD, 405.

65. MOD, 406.

66. MOD, 349.

67. MOD, 350.

68. MOD, 433.

69. MOD, 400.

70. Little, "The Mende in Sierra Leone," 115.

71. Little, "The Mende in Sierra Leone," 115; Hofstra, "Ancestral," 188.

72. SMBC 14; Hofstra "Ancestral Spirits," 192; Little, *The Mende of Sierra Leone,* 219; Little, "The Mende in Sierra Leone," 116.

73. MOD, 402.

74. Hofstra, "Ancestral Spirits," 192; Sawyerr, *Practice,* 44–45; Little, "The Mende in Sierra Leone," 119.

75. Pronounced *kεkεni.*

76. Sawyerr, *Practice,* 44–45.

77. SMBC, 18–19.

78. SMBC, 20–22.

79. Pronounced *kεkεni.*

80. Sawyerr, *Practice,* 45.

81. SMBC, 26.

82. W.T. Harris, "The Idea of God among the Mende," in *African Ideas of God,* edited by Edwin Smith (London: Edinburgh House Press, 1950), 282.

83. SMBC, 29; Sawyerr, *Practice* 45.

84. See Sawyerr, *God: Ancestor or Creator?,* esp. "Conclusion," 95–105.

85. Sawyerr, *God,* 6.

86. Jackson, *Allegories,* 16–17.

87. SMBC, 103.

88. SMBC, 109.

89. Pronounced *simɔŋgama,* SMBC, 104, 106.

90. SMBC, 94–95, 105.

91. SMBC, 99.

92. SMBC, 112.

93. SMBC, 113.

94. Pronounced *kpεbgeli,* SMBC, 113.

95. SMBC, 114.

96. SMBC, 114.

97. SMBC, 115.

98. See MOD, 368, interview with Saboleh.

99. Pronounced *humɔi,* SMBC, 96.

100. SMBC, 112–13.

101. SMBC, 114.

102. SMBC, 108–109.

103. SMBC, 115.

104. Isaac Ndanema, "The Rationale of Mende 'Swears,'" *The Sierra Leone Bulletin of Religion* 6 (December 1964), 21.

105. See M.C. Jedrej, "Medicine, Fetish, and Secret Society in a West African Culture," *Africa* 46 no. 3 (1976), 249.

106. Ndanema, "Rationale," 24.

107. SMBC, 67; see also Ndanema, "Rationale."

108. Sawyerr, *Practice*, 73–84.

109. Ndanema, "Rationale," 23.

110. SMBC, 64.

111. SMBC, 110.

112. Pronounced *mɛɛ-nde*, SMBC, 96–98.

113. M.C. Jedrej, "Medicine, Fetish, and Secret Society in a West African Culture," *Africa* 46 no. 3 (1976), 248.

114. Little, "The Mende in Sierra Leone," 127; see also Little, *The Mende of Sierra Leone*, 227–28.

115. Beryl Bellman, *The Language of Secrecy: Symbols and Metaphors in Poro Ritual* (New Brunswick, N.J.: Rutgers Univ. Press, 1984), 10.

116. Beryl Bellman, *Village of Curers and Assassins: On the Production of Fala Kpelle Cosmological Categories* (The Hague: Mouton, 1975), 113.

117. Ibid., 121–22.

118. Ibid., 122.

119. Ibid.

120. Ibid., 122–23.

121. Ibid.

122. Keith Thomas, *Religion and the Decline of Magic* (New York: Scribner, 1971), 27.

123. Ibid., 26.

124. Ibid., 29.

125. Ibid.

126. Ibid., 30.

127. Ibid., 41.

128. Ibid., 44.

129. Ibid., 79.

130. Ibid., 89.

131. Ibid., 110.

132. Harry Sawyerr, *Creative Evangelism* (London, Lutterworth, 1968), 117.

133. Max Weber, in *The Protestant Ethic and the Spirit of Capitalism*, trans. Talcott Parsons (New York: Scribners, 1958), emphasizes that the popular perception and reaction to Calvin's doctrines was not really consistent with those doctrines themselves: For Calvin, God has eternally foreordained which souls shall be saved and which shall be damned, and there is no way for human beings, using any human capacity, be it rational or emotional, or even be it a matter of our human moral conscience, to determine who is saved and who is damned, and why some should be saved and others damned. Salvation is not earned through good works, and has nothing to do with our human feelings or intentions (110). But, as Weber points out, "quite naturally this attitude was impossible for his followers...and, above all, for the broad mass of ordinary men. For them the certitudo salutis in the sense of the recognizability of the state of grace necessarily became of abso-

lutely dominant importance" (110). "Thus, however useless good works might be as a means of attaining salvation...they are indispensable as signs of election" (115). In practice, Calvinists came to view the fact of their own incessant hard work according to a rationally planned system, directed to the end of the most profitable material gain, as the best sign of their membership in the group of God's elect (see 162). The attitude that hard, systematic work aiming at ever increasing material profit was a sign of God's grace spread beyond Calvinism to many other protestant movements (Chap 4, passim). It is very likely that the subtle distinction between "sign of" and "cause of" was, in practice, for the most part, readily overlooked. And while the emphasis was laid upon hard, systematic, work itself as a sign of grace, it is also very likely that in the popular imagination the worldly success resulting from hard work should be viewed as a reward bestowed by God right along with that of eternal salvation. That virtuous hard work might indeed go unrewarded in this life is perfectly consistent with Calvin's own theology of the human incomprehensibility of God's ways—and the inconsistency of this obvious fact with the popularized version of Calvinism must have been often simply overlooked.

134. Adeleye Ijagbemi, "Rothoron (the Northeast) in Temne Tradition and Culture: An Essay in Ethnic History," *Journal of the Historical Society of Sierra Leone* 2 no. 1 (1978), 7.

135. A.K. Turay, "Temne Supernatural Terminology," *The Sierra Leone Bulletin of Religion* 9 no. 2 (1967), 50–51; see also C.F. Schlenker, *A Collection of Temne Traditions, Fables, and Proverbs* (London: Church Missionary Society, 1861, rpt. Nendeln/Liechtenstein: Kraus, 1970), ix.

136. Frederick Lamp, *Temne Rounds: The Arts as Spatial and Temporal Indicators in a West African Society* (Diss. Yale Univ. 1982), 39.

137. Turay, "Temne," 52. Pronounced *kərfi*. Also spelled *krifi*.

138. James Littlejohn, "Temne Space," *Anthropological Quarterly* 36 no. 1 (1963), 2–3. Pronounced *rokərfi, rosɔki*.

139. Also spelled *ro-shiron.*

140. Lamp, *Temne Rounds*, 36.

141. Turay, "Temne," 52–53; see Schlenker, *A Collection*, xi.

142. Lamp, *Temne Rounds*, 45.

143. David E. Skinner, *Islam in Sierra Leone During the Nineteenth Century* (Diss. Univ. of California, Berkeley, 1971), 206.

144. Turay, "Temne," 52.

145. Turay, "Temne," 54; the words *melakas* and *Sethani* are also of Arabic origin, see Skinner, *Islam*, 206.

146. Schlenker, *A Collection,* 12–15.

147. Ibid., 14–19.

148. Ibid., 25–33.

149. Lamp, *Temne Rounds*, 48.

150. Pronoucned *rothorɔŋ.*

151. Littlejohn, "Temne Space," 9.

152. Ibid., 10.

153. Ijagbemi, "Rothoron," 2–3.

154. Pronounced *nɔru, rokərfi, rosɔki, roserɔŋ.*

155. Littlejohn, "Temne Space," 2.

156. Rosalind Shaw, "Splitting Truths from Darkness: Epistemological Aspects of Temne Divination," in *African Divination Systems: Ways of Knowing,* edited by Philip M. Peek, 137–52 (Bloomington: Indiana Univ. Press, 1991), 143.

157. Littlejohn, "Temne Space," 13.

158. Ibid., 13–14.

159. Pronounced *kaŋtha.*

160. Ibid., 6–8.

161. See, for example, Edmund Husserl, The *Crisis of European Sciences and Transcendental Phenomenology*, trans. David Carr (Evanston, Il.: Northwestern Univ. Press), sec. 9.

162. Louis B. Schlesinger, "Physiognomic Perception: Empirical and Theoretical Perspectives," *Genetic Psychology Monographs* 101 (1980), 79.

163. Heinz Werner, *Comparative Psychology of Mental Development* (New York: International Universities Press, 1973), 72.

164. Ibid., 71.

165. See for example, Rudolf Arnheim, "The Gestalt Theory of Expression," *Psychological Review* 56.3 (May 1949): 156–71.

166. Littlejohn, "Temne Space," 14.

167. Ibid., 13.

168. Lamp, *Temne Rounds*, 102–103.

169. Ibid., 104–106.

170. Pronounced *aŋ-bempa, aŋ-waŋka, aŋ-seŋa.*

171. Ibid., 118.

172. Ibid., 112–113.

173. Ibid., 122.

174. Ibid., 123.

175. Ibid., 127.

176. Ibid., 131.

177. Ibid., 132.

178. Ibid., 105.

179. Ibid., 106.

180. Ibid. And it seems likely that the action of the religious specialist would involve the invocation of spirits.

181. Ibid., 107.

182. Lamp does not discuss in any detail the notion of *ma-sem* (*ma-səm*), which appears to be the Temne equivalent of the Mende notion of *hale*. He translates *ma-sem* as "sacred," and equates *ma-sem* with "the realm of *ro-soki*" (Ibid., 183).

183. Pronounced *aŋsɔki.*

184. Shaw, "Splitting," 143.

185. Ibid., 143.

186. Ibid., 145.

187. Ibid., 147.

188. Ibid., 148.

189. Bellman, *Language*, 16–17; Kenneth Little, "The Political Function of the Poro," in *Africa and Change,* edited by Colin M. Turnbull (New York: Knopf, 1973), 257.

190. Frederick Lamp, "Frogs Into Princes: The Temne Rabai Initiation," *African Arts* 11 no. 2 (1978): 38–49.

191. Frederick Lamp, "Cosmos, Cosmetics, and the Spirit of Bondo," *African Arts* 18 no. 3 (1985), 28 (but Ahmadu refers to the Kono society as Bundu, "Rites and Wrongs," 288). Lamp shows shows that the spelling "Bondo" reflects more accurately than "Bundu" the actual pronunciation of the word not only in Temne, but also in the Mende, Limba, Bullom, and Gola languages; see *Temne Rounds: The Arts as Spatial and Temporal Indicators in a West African Society* (Ph.D. Dissertation, Yale Univ. 1982), 281.

192. Pronounced *polɛi hale*, Jedrej, "Medicine," 248.

193. Little, *The Mende of Sierra Leone*, 226, 246.

194. Emile Durkheim, *The Elementary Forms of Religious Life*, trans. Karen E. Fields (New York: Simon & Schuster, 1998), 229.

195. Ibid., 216–225.

196. Ibid., 217–218.

197. Ibid., 217–218, 220.

198. Ibid., 222, 223.

199. Ibid., 226–27.

200. Camara Laye, *The Dark Child [L'Enfant noir]*, trans. James Kirkup and Ernest Jones (New York: Farrar, 1954), 112, 113, 111–135. Note that "Camara" is the author's family name.

201. Camara, *The Dark Child*, 114.

202. Camara, *The Dark Child*, 113.

203. Bellman, *Language*, 80.

204. Little, *The Mende of Sierra Leone*, 119.

205. Little, "Political Function," 264.

206. Lamp, "Frogs Into Princes," 38.

207. Little, *The Mende of Sierra Leone*, 119.

208. Bellman, *Language*, 80.

209. Bellman, *Language*, 81; Little, *The Mende of Sierra Leone*, 120.

210. Lamp "Frogs Into Princes," 42.

211. Little, *The Mende of Sierra Leone*, 120–21.

212. Bellman, *Language*, 96.

213. Little, *The Mende of Sierra Leone*, 121.

214. Lamp, "Frogs Into Princes," 42.

215. Little, *The Mende of Sierra Leone*, 123; A problem in Little's account is that he also reports that non-members may not see the Poro spirit—but Little's description of this celebration does not seem to involve the Poro spirit being hidden from anyone. Perhaps a lesser spirit of the society was responsible for entering the village—see Little, "Political Function," 276.

216. Pronounced *mabɔlɛ*.

217. Little, *The Mende of Sierra Leone*, 124.

218. Ibid.

219. Lamp, "Frogs into Princes," 44.

220. Ibid., 46.

221. Ibid., 47.

222. Warren D'Azevedo, "Gola Poro and Sande: Primal Tasks in Social Custodianship," *Ethnologische Zeitschrift Zürich* 1 (1980), 14.

223. Carol MacCormack, "Sande: The Public Face of a Secret Society," in *The New Religions of Africa*, edited by Bennetta Jules-Rosette, 27–37 (Norwood, N.J.: Ablex, 1979), 28, 29.

224. Ibid., 36.

225. Ibid., 33.

226. Little, *The Mende of Sierra Leone*, 129.

227. Frederick Lamp, *Temne Rounds: The Arts as Spatial and Temporal Indicators in a West African Society* (Ph.D. Dissertation, Yale Univ. 1982), 142–61. "Some writers have maintained that [the lobes] signify sexual organs, either male or female. This seems to represent, however, the phantasy of European observers rather than indigenous perception" (158). "It is said by some informants that the neck rings of the mask suggest the

ripples of water radiating about a-Nɔwo [the Bondo spirit] as she is drawn from the stream" (151). "Many informants agreed that the zoological form [of the chrysalis] was identified with the mask but they could not tell whether the mask was named for the chrysalis or vice versa" (145).

228. MacCormack, "Sande," 29.

229. Ibid., 34.

230. Ruth B. Phillips, *Representing Woman: Sande Masquerades of the Mende of Sierra Leone* (Los Angeles: UCLA Fowler Museum of Cultural History, 1995), 81.

231. Ibid.

232. Lamp, "Cosmos," 28.

233. Sylvia Ardyn Boone, *Radiance From the Waters: Ideals of Feminine Beauty in Mende Art* (New Haven: Yale Univ. Press, 1986), xx, quoted in Phillips, *Representing Woman*, 30.

234. Ibid.

235. Phillips, *Representing Woman*, 30.

236. Ibid., 102, 105.

237. I explore this idea in more detail in "Perceptions, Propositions, and Ideals: The Problem of Truth in the Novel," *Studies in the Humanities* 13.2 (1986): 93–102, and "Religious Experience and Literary Form: The Interrelation of Perception, Commitment, and Interpretation," *Religion and Literature* 21.3 (Autumn 1989): 61–83.

238. Lamp, *Temne Rounds*, 154. "If the rings represent water, they represent, again, the serpent as well" (151).

239. Ibid., 161.

240. Ibid., 153.

241. Bellman, *Language*, 83.

242. Ibid., 143.

243. Joseph Campbell, *The Hero with a Thousand Faces* (New York: Meridian, 1956), 11.

244. Phillips, *Radiance*, 81–84.

245. Lamp, "Cosmos," 28.

246. Pronounced *Nɔwo.*

247. Pronounced *Na-soko.*

248. Ibid., 33.

249. Ibid., 30.

250. Ibid., 34.

251. Fuambai Ahmadu, "Rites and Wrongs: An Insider/Outsider Reflects on Power and Excision," in *Female "Circumcision" in Africa: Culture, Controversy, and Change,* edited by Bettina Shell-Duncan, 283–312 (Boulder, Colorado: Renner, 2000), 301.

252. Ibid., 300.

253. Lamp, *Temne Rounds*, 292.

254. Jackson, 15.

255. Ibid., 17.

CHAPTER FIVE

The Interaction of Cultures:
Society and Religion

Mende and Temne Sociopolitical Systems
and the Poro Society: The Household,
Gender Roles, and Division of Labor

Among the Mende, the basic unit of economic organization is and was the household, or *mawe*.[1] The *mawe* includes a family over three generations, but might also, at least before 1927, include slaves and may still include clients. The elder grandfather who is the primary holder of the land of the *mawe* (known as the *mawee-mo*[2]) has the responsibility to allocate the land to members of the *mawe*, in consultation with his brothers. He may also allocate land to strangers for a season—at the end of the season, it reverts to him.[3] Ownership of land is thus not a simple relation of one individual to one spatial expanse. The *mawee-mo* or head of the household "owns" the land, but a three-generation group has rights to it. He owns the land *as* the head of that group and must manage it *for* the group. Land has never been a commodity which he or anyone can sell. The *mawee-mo* also has responsibilities to the group at the next higher level of social organization, *kuwui*, which Little defines the as "local group of kinsmen" who must be involved in decisions such as "major allocation of land."[4]

In the nineteenth century as well as today, the economy of Sierra Leone has been a predominantly agricultural one whose basis is the cultivation primarily of a staple crop (rice) primarily for subsistence, with a system of land tenure based on traditional rights to land ascribed to families and households in which land is not a commodity. Farming is accomplished by manual labor largely without the assistance of wheeled vehicles or plows and animals domesticated for pulling them. Anthony G. Hopkins demonstrates that the lack of plows and wheeled vehicles was determined not by cultural backwardness but by the exigencies of the natural environment, and that traditional methods of agriculture in West Africa are well adapted to its natural conditions.[5] If capitalism is defined as the pursuit of the accumulation of wealth through the maximization of profit as a result of investment in trade or manufacture, the precolonial, and indeed the present day, economy of Sierra Leone, as well as of much of Africa, is clearly pre-capitalist.[6]

The social inequalities among the Mende appear to have existed primarily within the household. (The exception would be slave villages.) The *mawee-mo* has the most privileged position, younger male family members and their wives have lower status, and clients and slaves the lowest position. Studies of late twentieth-century Mende village agriculture, along with what data is available on gendered division of labor in precolonial Africa, challenge the notion that there was and is an unambiguous division of labor between genders in Africa, with certain definite tasks carrying prestige assigned to men, and certain other definite tasks regarded as menial and contemptible exclusively assigned to women and (in an earlier era) slaves.[7] Koopman cites a study done in 1928 of "the sexual division of labor in 140 African societies described in anthropological studies and travelers' reports form the pre-colonial and colonial periods."[8] This study identified three categories of labor division with corresponding percentages: 1) men clear, women plant and harvest—40%; 2) "men do most of field work"—15%; 3) "mixed sex farming systems"—45%.[9] The pattern of cultivation in which these tasks have their place is the predominant one in West Africa. Each year a new area of cultivated land is cleared from the bush, and last year's land is allowed to return to bush. Clearing involves tasks ranging from the felling of trees to burning. The Government anthropologist Northcote Thomas reported in 1916 that among the Temne, thirty men and boys would spend two days clearing land for a large rice farm, then five or six days burning. A group of thirty men and thirty women cooperate to hoe, otherwise prepare the ground, and plant—a task which takes one or two days.[10]

Melissa Leach studied the agricultural practices of the Mende in Madena and Malema chiefdoms during 1987-91, with special attention to gender roles. She reports that before 1960, there was already a gendered division of labor in which, while males and their work had relatively greater power and prestige, there was also cooperation and complementarity. This cooperation was evident even between the *mawee-mo* and his senior wife: "While the *mawee-mo* took responsibility for decisions such as farm-site location and size, a male head's senior wife (*nyaha-wa*) shared (and occasionally took over) decisions about *mawee* labor and product use."[11] The division of labor among the members of a *mawe* and a *kuwui* was determined not only by gender, but also by age and kinship status: "High-status men participated in the socially significant male tasks involved with bush clearance but would then turn to hunting and local political activity, leaving subsequent 'men's work,' such as fencing the farm-site against cane rats, to young men, strangers, and clients. These 'junior' men worked with women to plant and harvest the rice."[12] At least in the era before the outlawing of slavery in 1927 slaves may well have joined the young men, women, and strangers.

Kinship and age, along with gender and condition of servitude, are also very significant determinants of status, and 'slavery' involved many degrees and types of dependence and subservience, which often persisted even after the legal abolition of slavery. In the contemporary Mende communities that Leach studied, bush clearing is an exclusively male activity, and the processing and cooking of rice an exclusively female one. However, for other tasks, such as planting, bird-scaring, harvesting and to some extent even weeding, there is a great deal of flexibility as far as gender participation is concerned.[13] Leach notes that "Mende emphasize that these gender-divided roles are complementary and interdependent."[14] Women do not share equally in the proceeds from cash crop production. Even though both men and women work to produce cocoa, coffee, and plantation palm-oil, "women have received disproportionately few of the benefits" from the sale of those cash crops, while for rice and wild-palm oil production, "husbands and wives who work together both receive rewards for their labor."[15] The reason that income is not distributed equally between husband and wife is not simply that men have more power, but also because, "as in most parts of West Africa, there is no notion of a pooled conjugal budget. Mende husbands and wives have always maintained separate income streams and expenditures, whether in cash or kind."[16] Yet financial decisions and arrangements are not simply carried out independently by husband and wife: "Amidst these ideals and ambiguities, conjugal financial arrangements are very varied and subject to a great deal of more or less explicit bargaining."[17]

One aspect of African culture that colonial officials and missionaries often criticized was indeed its pattern of gender relations—specifically polygamy, patriarchy, and an alleged exploitation of women. Mignerey at one point asserts that women do all the work, while men laze around the village all day. A consideration of the available evidence strongly suggests that the perception of the exploitation of women in Africa shared by many colonial officials and missionaries was exaggerated. Women are clearly in a subordinate position, but within that overall subordination, in many ways their role in the economy is in a collaborative and complementary relationship with men, and not necessarily a subservient one. Also, women at the household level are in a position to share decision making power and to negotiate.

Mende Local Political Organization: Kuwuisia, Towns, Villages, Chiefs, and Poro

A Mende town does not simply consist of a certain number of *maweisia*. The *maweisia* are grouped into a number of *kuwuisia*.[18] The members of each *kuwui* generally have multiple kinds of family connections, although neither the *mawe* nor the *kuwui* is simply limited to relatives of any particular kind. Little translates *kuwui* as 'compound,' but 'neighborhood' might also be appropriate. Of course the *kuwui* as neighborhood is not merely a spatial classification—it also essentially involves family relations and traditions among families. Also, with each town are associated a number of villages which are connected to the town by pathways. And each village is associated with a particular *kuwui*. Villages are founded in the area surrounding the town by *kuwuisia* for a variety of reasons, and a village need not be spatially close to its *kuwui*. The members of a village also belong to the founding *kuwui* but the village members are socially subordinate to the town members. Authority in the *kuwui* centers on what Little calls its 'nuclear descent group.' That group consists of those closest to the patrilineal descent line of those who are considered to have founded the *kuwui*. The leader of the *kuwui* is the *kuloko*. The *kuloko* is generally the oldest male member of the *kuwui* in the nuclear descent group, but it is perfectly possible for someone outside of that inner circle to lead, and also for a woman to lead.[19]

Little claims that the position of chief was strictly hereditary and that leadership was drawn from the descent line of those who were considered to have founded the chiefdom.[20] However, Abraham decisively refutes Little on this point. The view that there were ruling houses gradually came to be propagated by the colonial government as if it were the Mende tradition, simply in order to provide that government with a simple system for appointing chiefs. (By the time Little was working, this invented tradition was taken for granted.) Abraham shows that early in the colonial period, even many colonial officials clearly recognized that the system was very flexible.[21] Abraham concludes that, in the nineteenth century,

> the political system was fluid to allow anyone the channel to achieve it [the position of chief] by merit through the manifestation of the greatest skill in leadership. Where there appears to be hereditary succession, it was more a coincidence than a consciously accepted principle in Mende law of succession, because the late chief's son must have had better opportunities to train in leadership."[22]

Even Little acknowledges that on the level of the *kuwui*, leadership was not always determined simply by family position, so it appears possible that he may be exaggerating the role of the 'nuclear descent group' there as well.

Little includes among the duties of the precolonial chief those of military leader; of judge; of provider of help to strangers and the needy; and of cooperation with the chief's council, the chiefdom council, and the Poro society. The chief had the right to exact labor on his rice farms and for his compound, to collect a sort of tax of rice and palm oil, and to collect fines and fees as a judge.[23] As in many African societies, the chief's power was limited by a number of checks and balances. Before taking any major step, the chief was traditionally required to consult both with the chief's council, which consisted of "the Speaker, the sub-chiefs, and a number of the big men of the chiefdom," and, where it existed, a larger body known as the chiefdom council, which also included "the headmen of larger towns and villages, and representatives of the principal *kuwuisia*."[24] But the role of the Poro society was even more important, and its tradition reaches back at least 400 years.[25]

The Poro was the organization including all adult male members of the community. Initiation into the Poro was in fact what defined one's status as an adult and a full member of the community. Poro traditions and the Poro itself have a religious basis, indeed, one later writer considers that the Poro is very like what outsiders would call a church. The Poro itself has an inner hierarchy, and an extremely important fact for understanding Mende political organization is that the Poro hierarchy does not simply reproduce the political hierarchy otherwise, and that the chief is not the head of the Poro. In the Mende tradition, there is a clear separation between sacred and secular—the chiefship does not carry with it the mystical power or religious role that chiefship does among, for example the Temne, or that "divine kingship" did for example, in the kingdom of Benin. The chief cannot ascend to power, and once in power, cannot take any major action, without the consent and involvement of the Poro society. According to Little: "The upshot of all this is that no person can hope to occupy any position of authority in the chiefdom without being a Poro member and receiving Poro support. It is probable, in the old days, that each fresh successor to the chiefly office needed Poro approval, and the contemporary situation is much the same."[26] However, Little also points out that the majority of the Poro members remained at the most junior grade of its hierarchy, had no voice in any Poro decisions, and were absolutely obligated to carry out the commands of the Poro elders.[27] Regarding both the connection and distinction between the sacred and the secular, "the [Poro] society signalizes the respect due to secular authority by parading at the funeral or coronation of a chief its principal and most sacred spirit, the *Gbeni*, which ordinarily 'comes out' in public only on the most important type of occasion."[28] In Little's view, "the best way of summing up the situation" is that "political power was normally balanced between the Poro and the chieftainship."[29]

Temne Political Organization: Divine Chiefship and Religious Associations

The powers of Temne chiefs, and the limitations placed upon those powers, were quite similar to those of Mende chiefs. According to Wylie, the chiefs had the power to make war, to collect tribute, to demand labor, and to be the final judge of civil and criminal cases.[30] Also, as for the Mende, the chiefs' power was limited by that of other officials and of the associations including the Poro society, or, in many areas of Temne country, the Ramene, or Ragbenle societies. The Ragbenle society is the tradition most widely practiced among the Temne.

The Temne system of local government differed from that of the Mende in two ways. Traditionally, the chief is believed to be invested with *mesem* or mystical power, so that with him is associated some of the sacred power which is concentrated solely in the Poro society among the Mende. The second difference relates to the influence of Islam, which became most prominent in the northern areas of Temne country.[31] One of the aspects of this influence is the adoption of a slightly different approach to the appointment of sub-chiefs. The traditional Mende term for chief is *Obai*, and for sub-chief is *Kapr*. One aspect of the influence of Islam was the replacement of the term *Obai* by the term *Alkali or Alikali*, and the term *Kapr* by the terms *Almami* or *Alimami* and *Santigi*. This change in terminology was accompanied by a revision of appointment procedures and powers as well.[32] The traditional system was in place for most of the nineteenth century, Islamic influence only making itself felt toward the end of that century.[33]

In the traditional, pre-colonial and pre-Islamic system, the procedures for the selection, and the selection itself, of a new chief, are the responsibility of the Ragbenle, Poro, or Ramene, which in this context I will call *religious associations*. In a meeting of the religious association and in accordance with its laws, "all the chiefdom elders, that is, representatives of the various clans, gather together to elect a successor from among the recognized royal families in the chiefdom."[34] The head is severed from the departed chief's body, and that body is buried with the head of the previous chief, which has been carefully preserved in a special box. The preserved head of the chief is considered to bring beneficent influence.[35] The sacred status of the chief is expressed partly through the religious interpretation placed upon his death. It is announced to the people not that the chief has died but that he is ill and that he has traveled to *ro-toron* or the East, often named as "Futa" or "Futa Jallon," the kingdom that lies to the Northeast, in order to be cured. The switching of heads also serves to express the idea that the new chief is the same person as the old. As Ijagbemi points out, "it is this very chief that is supposed to have returned from Futa, fully cured, when new installation ceremonies are being performed and ready to be reinstated in his chiefdom."[36] For the Temne, *ro-toron*, the Northeast, is "the source of all good things—the sun rises in the east; the moon appears in the east; all the major rivers through the Temne country flow roughly south-westwards, toward the sea." Both ancestors and chiefs come from there, and the ancestors still are there.[37] Ijagbemi points out that these legends may rest on historical memories of invasions and impositions of power from the east.[38] But clearly the notion of "*ro-toron*" as the source of all good things is a mythical idealization. It is an expression or a symbol of the experience of the ideal.

Once the new chief is chosen, he nominates his *Kapr*. The *Kapr* title is a lifetime appointment—so the new chief must inherit the *Kapr* already in office in addition to appointing new ones.[39] The new chief with his *Kapr* are then placed in *an-kantha*—seclusion or confinement—which could last from three months to a year or more.[40] This period of *an-kantha* corresponds to the journey of the chief and the several *Kapr* to *ro-toron* or Futa. During this time they are initiated into the religious association. Initiation involves teaching the new chief "the names of the heads of the various families and the boundaries of the chiefdom, the late chief's enemies and problems, the installation ritual, his special dances, his rights and obligations as chief," etc.[41] As a result of this period of seclusion, the chief acquires mystical power or *mesem*. This mystical power manifests itself through a whole host of ritual obligations and prohibitions, both regarding the behavior of others and of the chief himself. The members charged with this initiation into, for example, the *Ragbenle* society include spirit members known as *Maneke*, and three male and four female officials who are in charge of the society. Though the chief and *Kapr* are initiated into the society, "they take little part in society activities."[42]

So it is evident that even though the Temne chief has the mystical aura the Mende chief lacks, his power is by no means absolute. His legitimacy as chief derives from the power of the religious association to confer his *mesem* and he is in fact selected through the workings of that association. In addition, in the nineteenth century the *Kapr* "were empowered to kill their chief if he fell ill, and a wicked man was dispatched after the slightest decline in health or well being."[43] Not only the *Kapr*, but also the Ragbenle or Poro societies had the power to assassinate the chief, or kill him with magical means.[44] The religious association could instigate unified group action against a chief, for example by using swearing medicines or "refusing to aid [the chief] in ritual matters." Appeals could be made to subchiefs or religious association officials, and appeals could be made to another chief.[45]

The Islamic influence especially in northern Temne country somewhat strengthened the power of the chiefs. The *almami*, unlike the *Kapr*, could be directly appointed at any time by the chief without the period of *an-kantha*.

> The real changes which occurred in the northern chiefdoms (and much later in the south and east) were not changes in mere titles, but in the power relations between the chief and his various subchiefs. In areas such as Port Loko...a chief could rule more arbitrarily...Patterns of authority based on material rewards and clientship would be a natural consequence of growing commerce. But in the non-Muslim areas, where Poro or Ragbenle held sway, and where a shari'a regulated trade had not intruded, authority was still derived from a traditional base. In Marampa, Masimera, and Yoni the changes resulting from the adoption of new titles were less significant than in Port Loko, where society practices had lapsed under Muslim influence.[46]

The traditional political organization of both the Mende and the Temne thus consisted of an interlocking network of groups and powers within which the considerable powers of the chiefs were nevertheless limited by the power of various groups and by other kinds of power. The authority of the religious associations, which represented the authority of the ancestors, of spirits, and of God, was the source that granted chiefs the authority they had and that also demanded their continued allegiance. This authority was believed to express itself in the ability to inflict disease and misfortune upon those who reject it. Those same religious associations were also organizations of people that did include all male adult members of the community (apparently even slaves[47]). But as Little points out "the great majority of initiates did not advance beyond the most junior grade."[48] Those at the top of the hierarchy were responsible for discussing issues affecting the community and deciding upon action to be taken. The Poro elite does not seem to necessarily be a group identical to the chief's advisers. Finally, the subchiefs and officials with whom the chief worked were not always entirely beholden to him, and represented a power bloc whose cooperation he needed to maintain.

This context makes it abundantly clear just how disastrous the British colonial system would prove to be for Sierra Leone. For under the colonial system, the chiefs were essentially selected by the government. It is true that to some extent traditional systems of selection were allowed to continue, but the selection was always subject to the veto of the colonial government, and the government's understanding of the workings of traditional government was often defective to say the least. Once selected, the chiefs were in the employ of the colonial government, and could be deposed by that government at will. At the same time, the colonial government completely ignored the role of subordinate officials and of the religious associations as checks on the chiefs' powers.[49] In doing so, the colonial government radically disempowered those groups, and severed the network of interconnections of power that was the very life of the traditional system. The chiefs were essentially no longer accountable to their own people. Having eviscerated the indigenous democratic traditions, the colonial government attempted to take over the impossible task of simultaneously guaranteeing the power of the chief and protecting the interests of the people. The main effect of the new system was to open the doors wide to chiefly corruption.[50]

Long Term Political and Economic Effects of the Imposition of Colonial Rule (1898–1961)

The main effects of the imposition of colonial rule over the Protectorate did not include modernization in any recognizable sense of the term, nor did they include the development of capitalism as Marxists would have predicted, nor did they involve the creation of a national order where before there had only been tribal or regional chaos, as was the putative intention of the colonialists. Rather, the mode of production remained distinctly pre-modern and pre-capitalist, traditional political arrangements were corrupted rather than developed, and the pre-colonial states that had been emerging were systematically undermined and dismantled. British colonization did introduce wage-labor, a transportation system, trade by sea with industrialized countries, and a state. But only a small minority of those in the Protectorate directly participated in such "modern" activities. In many ways, the effect of these changes upon society as a whole was quite superficial, and in many ways, the effect, though powerful, was simply disruptive.

Abraham attacks Kilson for claiming that the establishment of the colonial state was both an agent and a form of "modernization." Abraham argues that the notion of "modernization" as Kilson employs it, is vague, confused, and misleading.[51] Kilson does define what he means by modernization: "the particular features of colonial political change that render it 'modern' in the context of indigenous African societies are (1) the process of rationalization and (2) the increase in access to political authority and power on the part of the average person."[52] But Kilson provides no evidence either that politics or the economy became either more "rationalized" or more democratic than it had been prior to colonization. The evidence he does provide tends in fact to suggest the opposite. He indicates for example that one aspect of social change was the new opportunity for education available to a few. "Education necessarily contributed to a rise of a new system of social stratification."[53] He also says that

> there is a tendency for some facets of a social or cultural system to change in a modern direction while other facets remain intact or simply lag. Values (and attitudes toward traditional rulers fall within the realm of values) would appear to be one fact of culture least likely to change rapidly or in the first instance, as compared to such things as the mode of economy, dress, food, and the like.[54]

He notes that "chiefs' involvement in cash crop production and marketing created a competitive relationship between chiefs and the peasantry that had no precedent in tradition." But then he says that "the relationship was essentially modern or Western in nature."[55] But why specifically would one want to call the relationship modern or Western? The specific situation was that the chiefs became clients of a colonial government which at the same time completely failed to acknowledge, thereby short-circuiting, the traditional checks that indigenous communities exercised over the power of their chiefs. The chiefs were then in a position to more freely exploit traditional prerogatives such as labor tribute and the obligations of household dependents in order to personally profit from cash crop production. Chiefs also took advantage of their position as tax collectors for the colonial government to enrich themselves through tax extortion. The fact that this situation did arise as a result of contact with the West does not in itself mean that society was thereby becoming more like the West. Society was simply becoming less democratic, less autonomous, and more exploitative. As Abraham puts it, "that 'fundamental political innovations occur in response to' the imposition of colonial rule is admissible enough, but that this was synonymous with modernization is hardly acceptable except in a very negative sense."[56]

Abraham points out that before 1914 the colonial government frequently deposed chiefs and that these depositions were initiated by the government itself rather than as a result of complaints by the people.[57] But after 1914, the colonial government realized that these frequent depositions were undermining the authority of the chiefs, thereby undermining its own policy of ruling through the chiefs. From 1916, the colonial government pursued a policy of strengthening the position of the chiefs, while at the same time reserving the right to depose them unilaterally. "From 1916 to 1942 there were in all less than ten depositions."[58] Abraham summarizes the situation like this:

> The powers of the chiefs had been drastically reduced, and the greatest restraint in the exercise of their authority stemmed from the ultimate sanction of the colonial state which could depose them. All the same, the rather paradoxical situation arose that while a chief's powers were but a shadow of the pre-colonial ones, the chief who enjoyed the confidence of the administration, and therefore the security of his tenure in office, could oppress his people without the traditional sanctions operating. The function of control was taken over by the colonial state and while it sought to preserve the chiefs, it found itself at the same time safeguarding the rights of the subjects who could no longer operate the traditional sanctions against the chiefs.[59]

But the colonial government did nevertheless to some extent take seriously its avowed responsibility to look after the interests of the people over against those of the chiefs. The ten cases of deposition from 1916–1942 were all government actions taken in response to complaints about oppression made by the people of the chiefdoms affected.[60] At the same time the stories of these depositions clearly show chiefs using their new positions to enrich themselves at the expense of their subjects, especially through excessive taxation, fines, and labor levies. The magnitude the problem had assumed by the 1950s suggests that the extent of exploitation went far beyond the cases of the ten chiefs who were in fact deposed. And it is likely that the low number of depositions reflects the government's hesitation to act forcefully given its concern about undermining the authority of the chiefs.

Wylie reaches the same conclusions for the case of the Temne that Abraham reaches for the case of the Mende. Even before 1898, "as the British increasingly made clients of certain chiefs, they not only undermined the chiefs' ancient powers but, paradoxically, removed them from the controls which had always kept them in check."[61] After 1898, "It was immediately apparent that in this area the paramount chief was rendered largely independent of his traditional sources of revenue, indeed often to the extent that he could ignore the advice of the traditional councilors and use his new-found wealth to enhance his position at their expense."[62] "For the most part, if Dorjahn is correct, this new-found power was largely based on wealth gained through 'extortion and corruption,' which was more easily carried on and extended because of the loss of the subchiefs' prestige and of their powers in checking an *obai*'s actions."[63] Dorjahn describes the case of a chief in Kolifa in the early 1940s who had increased labor levies to such an extent that the people of his chiefdom were unable to attend to their own farms. The people attempted to persuade him to change his ways through the action of the *Ragbenle* and Poro societies, but the chief remained unmoved. When the people repeatedly appealed to the colonial government to have the chief removed, the government supported the chief.[64] This case is especially interesting because it shows explicitly how the colonial situation ruined the traditional workings of democracy. It also suggests that the associations such as the Poro and the *Ragbenle* could operate to promote not only the interests of an oligarchic elite, but also the interests of the community at large.

Eliphas G. Mukonoweshuro shows that the economic changes brought by colonization in Sierra Leone resulted from the application of political power through conquest and colonial administration, constituting a counterexample to the Marxist conception of political power as fundamentally an expression of economic forces. In the case of Sierra Leone,

> the idea that trade induces capitalist accumulation which in turn leads to innovation and transformation of the pre-capitalist to the capitalist mode of production and social formation is a particularly misleading proposition when analyzing social and economic change during the colonial and post-colonial periods.[65]

The accumulation of capital by chiefs resulted from the position they were granted by the colonial administration. That position involved in some respects an enhancement of their traditional powers, in other respects a limitation of their traditional powers, and also an elimination of traditional checks on their political power. Even so, the chiefs did not develop large scale plantations, "land was not turned into a commercial commodity," and the traditional land tenure system remained in place. The colonial government also turned down proposals from foreign capital for investment in plantations.[66] The chiefs took advantage of the colonial situation to exploit the traditional system more lucratively than before, rather than to develop a new system, or through investment to pursue innovation in methods of agricultural production. The system of production itself remained and remains pre-capitalist.[67]

The establishment of Paramount Chiefdoms fomented increasing political fragmentation rather than integration. The initial institution of the Paramount Chiefdoms entailed the breakup of states, and political fragmentation was continually exacerbated as those chiefdoms multiplied over time. "The ordinance defined a Paramount Chief as 'a chief who is not subordinate in his ordinary jurisdiction to any other chief,'"[68] so that there was to be no unit of indigenous political authority higher than the Paramount Chiefdom. There were nine states in 1880, but 27 Paramount Chiefdoms in 1899, 82 by 1912, and 115 in 1924.[69] "Thus" Abraham observes, " a clearly discernible picture emerges of a systematic policy of 'divide and rule.'"[70] The colonial government did not at all acknowledge the existence of the precolonial states, and actively stymied the development of any African political organization at a level higher than the Chiefdoms the government itself had established.

Kilson identifies one aspect of "modernization" as "the increase in access to political authority and power on the part of the average person." Yet the British government of Sierra Leone was completely autocratic from the start, and remained so until the very last minute. No changes that could be interpreted as giving any kind of real power at all to Africans were instituted until 1958, just shortly before independence. Constitutional changes in 1924 and 1947 increased African participation, but only in bodies that were purely consultative. Legally, the Governor, representing the Crown, retained absolute power, any action by anybody being subject to his veto. (W.S. Marcus Jones, in *Legal Development and Constitutional Change in Sierra Leone*, provides a complete accounting of the evidence for the persistently autocratic nature of the British colonial constitutional system in Sierra Leone.) British authority was unambiguously established over the original Colony in 1791.[71] From that time, the Governor, who had absolute authority, worked with what was called the Advisory Council. The constitution of 1863 instituted a Legislative Council and an Executive Council in their place.[72] The Executive Council consisted entirely of British Officials (Governor, Chief Justice, Colonial Secretary, Queen's Advocate, Officer Commanding the Troops). The Legislative Council consisted of the members of the Executive Council plus, in practice, usually two nominated members who were not officials, one African and one European. This arrangement ceded no power to Africans. The Governor's power was not limited even by the judiciary. The British turned a deaf ear to Krio demands for representation and self-government.[73]

The declaration and establishment of the Protectorate, by proclamation in 1895 and by detailed ordinance in 1896, did not alter this system of councils. The proclamation "empowered the legislature of the colony to legislate for the Protectorate in the same way as it did for the colony,"[74] and this was reaffirmed in 1913, when the Colony Legislative Council was officially granted "full authority to legislate on behalf of the Crown, for the Protectorate."[75] The Protectorate was divided into five districts (Karene, Ronietta, Bandajuma, Panguma, and Koinadugu), each headed by a District Commissioner.[76] The ordinance established three types of courts in each District: the Court of the District Commissioner, the Court of the District Commissioner and Chiefs, and the Court of Native Chiefs. The first two courts had jurisdiction over most criminal matters and all matters involving non-natives. The Court of Native Chiefs was "a sort of residuary one" dealing with "disputes arising exclusively between natives."[77] While the Paramount Chiefs were appointed by the Governor, and could be deposed by him at any time, the idea behind the system was that the British would rule through the Paramount Chiefs. However, since the system of justice had been taken largely out of the chiefs' hands, the action of "ruling" seems to have become tantamount to no more than "collecting taxes." To legitimate its rule, the British Government depended upon the chiefs, who were in fact the most prestigious and economically powerful members of their communities. The Government became therefore quite reluctant to depose chiefs, and eager to buy their favor. The fact that the chiefs had the support of the Government over against their own people meant the increasing impotence of traditional checks on the chiefs' power, as through the Poro Society. This situation opened the doors to chiefly corruption.

The 1924 Constitution still restricted membership in the Executive Council to Government Officials, and expanded the membership of the Legislative Council without adding to its powers. The Legislative Council could pass laws, but the Governor had veto power with no recourse by the Council. The Legislative Council now included, in addition to eleven official members: five Africans from the Colony, two appointed by the Governor and three elected; three Paramount Chiefs from the Protectorate, appointed by the Governor; and two Europeans appointed by the Governor.[78] While these changes had the appearance of slight liberalization, the policy of the Government was in fact becoming more repressive. In response to the challenge posed by the first stirrings of nationalism by The West African Youth League and its leader Isaac Wallace-Johnson, the Government instituted in 1939 a series of measures inimical to human rights including: The Sedition Ordinance; The Incitement to Disaffection Ordinance; The Aliens Expulsion Ordinance; The Undesirable Publications Ordinance; The Undesirable British Subjects Control Ordinance; The Production of Telegrams Ordinance; and the Trade Union Ordinance. The fact that nowhere were the crucial terms "sedition" and "undesirable" defined makes the authoritarian force of these ordinances unmistakable. In effect, those acts or words were seditious which the government judged to be seditious, and those persons were undesirable whom the government judged to be undesirable.[79] The trial, itself of questionable legality, and imprisonment of Wallace-Johnson put an end to the West African Youth League as a major force in Sierra-Leonean politics.

In 1943, the Governor appointed two Africans to the Executive Council: a lawyer, J. Fowell Boston, and Paramount Chief A. G. Caulker, who had been a member of the legislative council (and whom Mignerey had known in Rotifunk). According to Jones, Caulker "had not shown himself to be a nationalist. Nor had he contributed much, if anything at all, to the debates of the Legislative Council. He was more or less, like all other chiefs, a silent member of the legislature."[80] The Protectorate Assembly and the District Councils were established under the Legislative Council in 1945. Unlike the Council the resolutions of the Protectorate Assembly "did not have the force or effect of law."[81] The Protectorate As-

sembly consisted of 10 official representatives, 6 appointed unofficial representatives of which 4 were to be Africans, and finally 26 additional representatives,
two elected by, and from, each of the 13 Protectorate District Councils. Each
District Council consisted of two representatives of each chiefdom in that district, one being the chief, the other one, as things turned out, chosen by the
chief.[82] All of this more or less made a mockery of the pretense that these
changes represented progress toward democracy, since the Protectorate Assembly was little more than a meeting of chiefs, all of whom served, of course, only
at the pleasure of the Government.

Changes to the Legislative Council were not enacted until 1951. Under a
new constitution, there were seven instead of eleven Official members (including the Governor, Chief Commissioner, etc.), and the list of unofficial members
was much expanded, including seven elected from the Colony and fourteen
elected from the Protectorate. Genuine elections did take place in the Colony.
But in the Protectorate, the District Councils were to select Legislative Council
representatives. The Executive Council was to have four Official and six Unofficial members. The Governor appointed Africans to fill all the Unofficial
seats.[83] Yet even at this late date, as the Attorney General could accurately state,
"the governor of this colony is both in form and fact the Executive....The governor may....constitutionally reject the advice of the Executive Council. This is
provided for in the [1951] constitution."[84]

From the 1920s until independence, once the Government had disposed of
the West African Youth League, the political struggles within Sierra Leone involved three groups: the urban Krio elite of the Colony, the Paramount Chiefs,
and the growing educated elite of the Protectorate. These groups competed to
influence the British government as it putatively worked to make its merely consultative bodies more representative while carefully preserving their merely consultative character. The colonial state and the business interests that developed
along with it were the forces behind the emergence of the new elites. Western
education provided mostly by missions but to an extent also by Government
prepared individuals for entry into the elites that emerged as a result of colonization. The creation of the Protectorate opened the doors to this new middle and
upper class to those of its residents who could obtain a Western education. The
types of work which brought this new middle or upper class status included
Law, Medicine, Business, Teaching, Government service, and the Church. Employment often involved working for Western entities—whether for the Government, missions, or business concerns. Kilson notes that "of the sixty companies registered in Sierra Leone during the period 1937–56, only about a quarter
were exclusively African owned."[85]

The proportion of people belonging to these elites was quite small. Kilson
estimated in 1960 that "hardly 2 percent of Sierra Leone's population can be
included in the new-elite category."[86] Adding lower paid teachers and junior
civil servants to the category of middle and upper income "elites," Kilson estimated in 1960 that only about 14,000 individuals earned incomes that would
place them in that category. In 1960 the population of the Protectorate was about
2,150,000, and of the Colony, about 100,000. If one estimates family size at 5,

the total size of the combined middle and upper class would be only 3% of the population. Of course, the obligations of extended family directly affect the relationships between the elites and the rest of society. More prosperous individuals incur the unavoidable obligation to assist their poorer relatives,[87] a practice which, by the way, inhibits capital accumulation.

The new elite only became politically active after World War Two, and its aim was to challenge the monopoly of the chiefs on the government's various consultative bodies. As early as 1929, members of the emerging new elite along with some educated Paramount Chiefs had formed the Protectorate Educational Progressive Union (PEPU). Its early members included Dr. Milton Margai (1894–1964), Chief Julius Gulama (1893–1951), and Chief A.G. Caulker. Margai and Gulama were both graduates of Albert Academy. Margai had attended the UBC primary school at Bonthe, and Margai the school at Rotifunk. The purpose of PEPU "was to provide scholarships for Protectorate boys,"[88] and its successor organization, The Sierra Leone Organization Society (SOS), founded in 1946, also had an "ostensibly educational" purpose. But, as Cartwright points out, "its leaders tended to view education as a process of developing popular political awareness of what they regarded as an unsatisfactory constitutional position.[89] Its founders included Dr. John Karefa-Smart (1915–2010), Doyle Sumner (1907–1999), Siaka Stevens (1905–88), and Frank Anthony, as well as Chief Gulama, all graduates of Albert Academy.[90] In response to the new opportunities offered by the 1951 constitution, the PEPU and SOS merged to form the Sierra Leone Peoples Party.[91] A third party, Laminah Sankoh's People's Party, also took part in the merger. Sankoh, also an Albert Academy graduate, had founded the People's Party in 1948 as a minority Krio party making common cause with the Protectorate. (The National Council was the dominant Krio party.)[92] Gulama, as the leader of the Protectorate Chiefs, and Margai, as the leader of the new elite, worked closely together to unify these two groups under the SLPP.

Milton Margai was the single most influential and respected leader of the period, finally serving as the first prime minister of independent Sierra Leone. He received a medical degree in 1927, the first person from the Protectorate to do so, and served as a medical officer for 22 years, working in almost every Protectorate district. In 1946, he and Gulama initiated the chiefs' conferences that led to the formation of the Protectorate Assembly and District Councils. He endeavored successfully to promote public health by working with the local Sande society chapters in several districts to spread modern medical practice relating to midwifery. Abraham sums up Margai's character and his political contribution succinctly:

> Uninterested in material values, he had very little property and cared little for accumulating personal wealth. Despite occasional shake-ups in the political system, Sierra Leone maintained a strong stability during Sir Milton's leadership. When he died on April 28, 1964, that stability was threatened, and the days of his rule are remembered with nostalgia as an epoch of social well-being.[93]

These parties engaged in their first real campaign in the 1951 election. The National Council and the SLPP competed in a genuine election in the Colony for seven seats on the Legislative Council. The National Council won five and the SLPP, one. The constitution did not provide for genuine elections in the Protectorate, since the 12 Legislative Council members were voted on by the members of the District Councils only. Eight chiefs, not SLPP candidates, were elected, along with SLPP members Milton Margai, his brother Albert, and Siaka Stevens. The real bone of contention became the six seats on the Executive Council that were to be allocated to Africans. To make this determination, the Governor met with the new Legislative Council informally. He chose to mimic the tradition that the majority party should form a government—in this case, should be allocated positions on the Executive Council. But most of the chiefs did not have a party affiliation. As Jones describes the episode,

> the governor asked, it is submitted illegally, all those who supported the SLPP to stand on one side and those supporting the National Council to stand on the other side. All the chiefs who had not been elected on the basis of the SLPP support, then joined the SLPP. The governor then concluded that the SLPP had a majority and proceeded to appoint members of the Executive from among them.[94]

In 1953, the Governor "grouped the various government departments into five divisions" and appointed the African members of the Executive council as the "ministers" of those divisions.[95] But Jones makes it clear that even at this point, when Sierra Leone was supposedly being prepared for independence, the African leaders were granted little, if any, real power. The authoritarian bureaucratic structure of the colonial government remained firmly in place, despite the trappings of elections and ministerial appointments. The Governor

> in essence …was still the only policy maker. He controlled finance, the judiciary, the civil service, defense, and foreign affairs. The ministers were obliged to act in accordance with the advice tendered them by their secretaries. The heads of the major government departments were still expatriate officials, and they not only determined what government policy was, but were also dedicated and determined to see it scrupulously carried out.[96]

There was to be no real semblance of democracy until very shortly before independence. Constitutional changes in 1957 provided for the first direct franchise in the Protectorate, which was exercised in the elections of 1958.[97] Not until March 1960 was any substantial power granted to the African cabinet. Milton Margai became head of a "United Front" which represented Sierra Leone in negotiations for independence. Margai gained the cooperation of all political groups, including the Peoples' National Party (later All Peoples Congress or APC) which, under the leadership of Albert Margai and Siaka Stevens, had split away from the SLPP in 1958.[98] The Sierra Leone Independence Bill was passed by the British House of Commons in March, 1961, after only two hours of debate.[99]

As one considers the historical evidence gathered by Jones, Kilson, and Cartwright, together with the Cox report, regarding the elaborate and confusing structural changes instituted over time by the Colonial Government, the conclusion becomes unavoidable that, especially in the case of the Protectorate, the changes in reality moved neither in the direction of making institutions more representative, nor of granting more real power to Africans. In the Protectorate, until the election of 1951, the only Africans the British officially even consulted were chiefs. The chiefs were appointed by the British, and the chiefs themselves had no real power over Government policy. After 1951, the "cabinet" appointed by the governor included members of the Protectorate elite, but still had no real power.

The chiefs, however, did have a great deal of power over their own people. And it appears that power only became more and more oppressive as time went on. As has been pointed out, indirect rule rendered impotent traditional checks on chiefly power through colonial support of chiefs and the exclusion from official power of the Poro society. The institution of Native Administrations in 1937 shows clearly how the colonial government, enamored of the pretense of democratic development, in fact only strengthened chiefly autocracy. Tribal Authorities were supposed, by statute, to be representative bodies, including not only chiefs but a headman or representative for every 20 taxpayers.[100] After the riots of 1956, the Cox commission made an extraordinarily thorough and careful survey of the conditions in the country that led up to the unrest. The commission summed up the actual functioning of the Native Administration (Tribal Authorities) succinctly: "It has become accepted during the years that the powers vested in Tribal Authorities as bodies have been exercised by the Paramount Chief (sometimes acting with the approval of sycophantic caucus)."[101]

> The legislative power of issuing formal orders and making formal bye-laws is hardly used. There is much less resort to the judicial machinery in the shape of Native Courts than there should be. Local affairs have been in fact governed by arbitrary and summary executive action, and as there is no adequate executive in the shape of staff, all action has been taken by individual members of the authority—chiefs....There has been much evidence that no one will raise a voice against the Paramount Chief at the few formal meetings of the Tribal Authority....There has been much evidence that the Chief would not always take, or even listen to, the advice of elders....The Authorities hardly exist effectively even as deliberative bodies.[102]

In other words, local government was effectively no more than chiefly autocracy.

Also, it appears the chiefs had in practice been able to reclaim much of the judicial authority which the Government had co-opted through the original Protectorate Ordinance. Since Native Administrations had responsibility for law enforcement, and were also in effect mere puppets of the chiefs, the chiefs were in fact in a very good position to arbitrarily impose fines and punishments in disregard for the three tiered system of courts established by the Colonial Government, at the top of which was the District Commissioner's court.

> Chiefs do not always see that culprits are brought to court and it seems to be recognized that the smaller cases are decided by the Chief on what he considers to be his own authority and in his own premises. Nor is it only Paramount Chiefs who enjoy the exercise of power; Section Chiefs are not backward in this respect and even headmen indulge [in] it....With regard to irregularities within the Native Courts we find them to be frequent and widespread. There is evidence which

we believe that cases tried in open 'barri' are not always recorded and fines are not always credited to the Chiefdom Treasury, or only partly credited.[103]

And as time went on and the pretense of democratization became the order of the day, the power and influence of the District Commissioners became more and more attenuated. As Cox put it,

In their execrated and partly disabled state, District Commissioners have been too few and of necessity their contacts have been mostly with District Councils and Tribal Authorities which themselves have not been in close contact with the people. Small wonder then that illegalities are introduced to the people by the assertion that the Government has ordered the step or that unpopular moves are at the wish of the Government. Small wonder to that, for the same reason, complaint to the government's agent is regarded as futile.[104]

The Cox Commission concluded that the impetus for the riots came from the nearly universal perception that the Chiefs were extremely corrupt and oppressive both in their dispensing of justice and in their collection of taxes and fees. The Commission also came to the conclusion that these popular perceptions were quite accurate, and marshaled a great deal of evidence to that effect. Chiefs had the responsibility for tax collection. Until 1937, Paramount Chiefs derived their income from: land farmed for them; tribute; a five percent rebate on tax collections; and finally "various collections...when necessity arose."[105] With the establishment of Native Administrations and Chiefdom Treasuries, a new tax, the Chiefdom tax, was instituted. The purpose of this tax, to be paid into the Chiefdom treasury, was to, among other things, provide salaries to Chiefs in lieu of their earlier forms of income, which became mostly illegal.[106] The original house tax was retained at 5 shillings and the chiefdom tax was set originally at 4 shillings However, the Native Administrations—in practice, the chiefs themselves—were responsible for setting the rate. The total tax remained at 9 shillings until 1950, when it rose to between 10 shillings and 13 shillings, 6 pence. When the dual tax was replaced by a single Local Tax in 1954, the rate skyrocketed "to between 20s. and 30s. and in one chiefdom to 40s."[107] Cox estimates that 25 shillings would equal a laborer's earnings for about one week, but acknowledges that such payment would be much more problematic for subsistence farmers who were much less involved in the cash economy.[108] Cox acknowledges that the discontent over taxation was not merely due to the rate or even the increase in the rate. The real outrage came from the belief that much of the proceeds were going merely to enrich the chiefs; little if any was going to better the community; and due to corruption, a much higher level than the one legally authorized was being collected. The Commission found convincing evidence that all three claims were justified.

In the case of corruption in tax collection, the commission concluded that

no chiefdom is free from the taint of unlawful levies of tribute although it is often difficult to distinguish these levies from unauthorized fines, from payments in lieu of forced labor, from illegal additions to the Local Tax, or from customary "hand shakes." Witnesses have affirmed that whatever may be the lawful Local Tax the amount actually taken from the people is twice the tax. We doubt the arithmetical accuracy of these statements but it is not an unlikely approximation.[109]

Tax assessors—with the chiefs to back them up—required a lavish reception wherever they went, often collecting so much food that the excess had to be taken away or even sent back to the chief.[110] Practices such as assessing vacant plots of land, the deceased, and underage individuals not subject to tax, were common. Additional money was often extorted, for example, to remove a deceased person from the list.[111]

And what did the Native Administrations contribute to people's lives? Kilson shows, for example, that between 1937 and 1949, "the administrative expenditure head (the main subheads of which were personal emoluments of Paramount Chiefs, Section Chiefs, Headmen, Court Presidents, and Court Members) invariably claimed about 50 percent or more."[112] And it should be remembered that these figures are, of course, based on official revenue—the probably equally large illegal revenue undoubtedly going directly to the same administrators. And in return, the activities of these administrators were apparently limited to those of dispensing—often arbitrary—justice, and...collecting taxes. As Cox puts it:

> The government of a chiefdom at present is so attenuated in its duties that its misfeasance in respect of those few that remain becomes exaggerated. We shall describe the "maintenance" of law and order by Tribal Authorities as having proved very defective but the task is not one to evoke enthusiasm even when it is properly performed. In the past two years the only other single duty performed by Tribal Authorities on any appreciable scale has been the highly unpopular one of tax collection.[113]

The fundamental parameters of the colonial situation were that chiefs were a respected elite, and the colonizer required their cooperation in order to prevent rebellion. Such was the level of tradition-bound respect that it took years of ever more flagrant abuse for the Temne to rebel against their chiefs, and even then they maintained respect for the office while attacking its holders.[114] Government required a means to keep the chiefs on its side—and that means was taxation. So the role of the chiefs became largely to collect taxes. By doing so they could legally and illegally enrich themselves. However, the expenditure of Native Administrations on public services was more than nil, and grew steadily between 1937 and 1949. In 1937, administrative expenses were about 70% of revenue, and public services were less than 1%. By 1949, administrative expenses had fallen to about 57% of total expenditures, and public services were somewhere between about 20% and 46% of revenue (depending on how one classifies "misc." and "extraordinary expenses"[115]).

Cox provides a succinct account of why the riots finally broke out. The commission, he says, discovered

> a degree of demoralization among the people in their customary institutions and in their approach to their statutory duties which they have been entrusted, which has shocked us. Dishonesty has become accepted as a normal ingredient of life to such an extent that no one has been concerned to fight it or even complain about it. The ordinary peasant or fisherman seems originally to have accepted a degree of corruption which was tolerable; at a later stage he has been cowed into accepting it; finally he rebelled.[116]

The unrest began on November 17, 1955, with a protest to the District Commissioner against the actions of a chief in Rofenka in Maforki Chiefdom. Cox records the testimony of Peter Kamara, who came to be regarded as a leader by the protesters. His story sums up the whole experience of corruption that the Commission found to be generally prevalent:

> The Paramount Chief asked the whole Chiefdom to help him in building a house and he told the District Commissioner that the people agreed...and that 5s. was to be added to the £1 12s. 6d. to build the house....When I heard this I gathered my own men and said: "What are we going to do? Should we subscribe...money...to meet the Chief? We shall have to ask pardon as the tax is too much—we cannot earn it."...the Chief has a brother, Foday Samu...who went to the Chief and said that Peter Kamara is not going to pay and that he will kill anyone who goes on assessment. Then the Chief sent for me...and said he wanted to see me; he sent one of his Messengers....the Messenger met me ill...and I said I was ill....Then his own brother came and said that the Chief had sent his Messenger...and he had come to take me. I said "I won't go as I am suffering from headache" and...I asked if I were summoned to Court and the answer was "no." They called the rest of the Messengers and I went to my own room and got my machet and said "...today our lives are going to be at an end." I went out and said "If you touch me I will show you I am a man." He called the rest of the Messengers....in the evening the townspeople came and I informed them of the incident. Next day...the Messengers came again but they did not meet me...they brought my brother to the Chief and when they returned they said that if I refused to go I should be beaten...and the Chief...would come kill me if I didn't pay...I said I was going to see the D.C....and ask him...when I found the D.C. out...I told the Clerk that the Chief had sent twelve men to beat me and I had done nothing wrong to the Chief...I said if you don't send an escort through the town there will be a fight.[117]

Later, the District Commissioner proposed to the Chief that he withdraw the 5 shilling assessment. Such was the arrogance of the Chief that he would agree only "if the people agreed that traditional labor to the house would include sawing boards, breaking stone, and carrying sand." The District Commissioner refused to accept the chief's proposal. On November 21st he met a crowd of 3000 at Port Loko. Peter Kamara and others had been addressing the crowd. The D.C. is reported to have said to them "it is your own brothers who are taxing you, not the Government" although he later denied that.[118] On November 25 a further public meeting was held at Port Loko, this time with a crowd of 8,000. Peter Kamara, the District Commissioner, and others addressed the crowd, which dispersed peacefully. Cox points out that Peter Kamara was "not a leader of unlawful assemblies," that "he never advocated violence," and that there was "no damage to property in Maforki Chiefdom."[119]

But the sequel was to be quite violent and destructive. The riots took place mostly in the Temne area of Sierra Leone in December of 1955 and January of 1956, affecting five of the twelve districts in the country.[120] While rioting was confined to these areas, the Commission assigned blame to factors generally prevalent throughout the country. Cox places the number of rioters in the tens of thousands.[121] During the riots, police killed twenty two people and wounded seventeen.[122] The rioters focused their activity on the destruction of houses of members of the Native Administration. Cox estimates the damage to property at about three quarters of a million pounds sterling.[123]

Near the beginning of the report, Cox noted that "the extent of the malpractices to which the rioters took exception was not apparently appreciated prior to our inquiry"[124]—and appreciated neither by the government, nor the country's African leadership. However, both groups substantially rejected the report itself, despite the scrupulous care with which it had been prepared and the wealth of detailed evidence it marshaled. The government chose instead to blame the "unsettlement following upon the war, the decline of moral standards in general, the undermining of respect for law and order following on widespread discoveries of diamonds."[125] The government asserted an explanation for disobedience to the chiefs, but simply did not address the question of whether the chiefs' behavior itself was at all objectionable.[126] However, the government did take some very limited action: "it prohibited a large number of types of fees and licenses, forbade any forced labor, and promised to institute inquiries into the conduct of chiefs, sub-chiefs, and headmen whose conduct might have contributed to the uprisings."[127] Eleven individuals were investigated, of whom nine were relieved of office. But within four years, five of the eleven were reinstated.[128]

The country's African leadership was as unwilling as the British government to accept the Cox commission's criticisms. In the Legislative Council debates arising from the riots and the Cox report, "almost all SLPP members who spoke claimed that the chiefs were being made scapegoats."[129] Some council members claimed that British officials, and others that opposition parties, "were responsible for fostering the trouble." One founder of the SLPP privately told Cartwright that "British officials had fomented the riots as revenge against the chiefs for the latter's role in starting the SLPP."[130] Milton Margai was evidently the only member of the Legislative Council who showed, in this debate, any appreciation of the problem of chiefly oppression. He puts his criticism of the chiefs in extremely diplomatic terms:

> I have often spoken in this House that if we have to move toward progress we must move hand in hand with our chiefs, and I feel a little bit hurt when some of them get up and say they have a doubt in their minds. I think they are doubting the one who is their greatest friend. I do not ask that they should go on pressing their subjects but that they should continue ruling their people....My conscience would not allow me to uphold a chief who goes on oppressing his people. But a chief who has not done any wrong, I am always there to uphold him.[131]

Likewise, in a debate over the Cox report's recommendations, Margai attempts to support those recommendations, but in a very ambiguous way, clearly calculated to bring the least possible offense to the chiefs:

> The impression has been given that the chiefs have been very much dissatisfied, or have been made scapegoats. We have to understand that if we are running the country as a Government there are certain recommendations which would be doing more harm to the country by not implementing them and that is one....if we have a Commission which comes all out and says that an inquiry should be held

in a certain number of chiefdoms, we shall be doing more harm to ourselves as a country and to even chiefs, if we say no.[132]

I have attempted to trace aspects of the social and political history of Sierra Leone until the time of independence in order to convey a sense of how the situation of colonial rule Mignerey was involved in played out over the course of some years. Independence was a turning point at which in a sense a new story begins. There is no doubt that the British colonial assault on African society played a large role in Sierra Leone's future troubles. But I cannot here endeavor to present in detail the story of the country's post-colonial decline. Suffice it to say that the decline began with the death of Milton Margai and the accession to power of his brother Albert in 1964, and continued unabated throughout the rule of Siaka Stevens from 1967 to 1985. Stevens, a graduate, like Milton Margai, of the Albert Academy, is today almost universally vilified as the single man most responsible for the situation that led to the virtual collapse of Sierra Leone in the 1990s. A rebel war, waged by Foday Sankoh and his "Revolutionary United Front" at the behest of Charles Taylor of Liberia, devastated the country from 1991–2002. The RUF consisted largely of abducted children and deserters from the army of Sierra Leone. Indeed, segments of the Sierra Leone army were probably cooperating with the RUF. The RUF literally had no aim but to plunder and terrorize the country.[133] Many, many towns and villages were attacked and destroyed, including Rotifunk. Freetown was invaded, sacked, and terrorized twice by the RUF.

Earl Conteh-Morgan sums up the situation in Sierra Leone at the end of the twentieth century. Even before the war, the situation was grim: "A 1988 World Bank assessment placed life expectancy in Sierra Leone at 42 years, with close to 200 children out of 1,000 dying before age one, and close to 50 out of every 1,000 dying between the ages of one and four."[134] The effects of the war are evident in the massive human displacement it caused:

> By May 1993, the number of displaced Sierra Leoneans was estimated at over one million. By March 1996, the civil strife, attributed mostly to the atrocities committed by the RUF, had displaced nearly forty seven percent of the country's pre-war population of 4.47 million persons, according the United Nations.[135]

Conteh-Morgan sums up his assessment of the reasons for this situation as follows:

> In the late 1990s Sierra Leone is in a deplorable state, gripped by abject poverty and a virtual breakdown of law and order in a substantial portion of the country. The contributory factors have no doubt been the unrestrained accumulation of riches by politicians and powerful businessmen through illicit means, the deterioration of the formal economy because of the parallel informal economy, the enormous debt burden due to government overexpenditure, the virtual collapse of many state institutions.[136]

And yet, national elections were successfully held not only with the coming of peace in 2002, but already in the middle of the war in 1996. I will never forget sitting in the dining room in the Paramount hotel in Freetown on March 17, 1996, as the presidential runoff election results were announced on the radio at precisely 9:00 PM. I was talking to the waiters whom I had gotten to know when suddenly we heard through the open veranda the enormous shout of the combined voices of thousands and thousands of Freetown residents. Alhaji Ahmad Teejan Kaaba had been victorious over John Karefa-Smart. (Karefa-Smart had been active in Sierra Leone politics his whole life, and happened to be the son of the Rev. John-Karefa Smart with whom Mignerey had worked at Rotifunk.) But I sensed, as we went outside to see the people streaming into the streets, that the celebration was not so much for the winner, as for the fact that the military leaders of the country had this time kept their promise, and allowed the election to come off as planned.

The African Encounter with Missionary Christianity

The United Brethren missionary venture in Sierra Leone is a case study in the confrontation and interaction of Western and African cultures, each of which had and has its own notions of God and morality, its own sets of rituals, and its own ways of defining and valuing social groups. According to a common stereotype, Western missionaries, with the power of the colonial state behind them, single-handedly compelled Africans to submit to an alien religion and culture. This stereotype is an injustice both to the missionaries and to Africans.

The missionaries in Sierra Leone did depend upon the protection of the colonial state, and they often did support its measures (such as the hut tax in the late 1890s), but there is very little evidence that anyone was ever forced to convert to Christianity. In fact, the missionaries had to have the permission of local chiefs in order even to establish their compounds on village land. At worst, chiefs at times conscripted children to attend mission schools, but this was not a common practice. A form of indirect pressure probably did motivate many conversions to Christianity: in the colonial state, advancement in the new system required a Western education, Western education was available primarily through missions, and religious instruction was an essential part of the curriculum of mission education. But the missions did not simply teach Christianity: rather, religious instruction and proselytization was thoroughly integrated into a standard educational curriculum. Many graduates of mission schools (especially secondary schools) became teachers in the mission school system, and this itself was an avenue of advancement in the new colonial system.

The common stereotype that has Western missionaries simply imposing Christianity upon Africans also fails to take into account the role of African agency in the spread of Christianity. Indeed, it is probably a fair generalization that Africans had the primary role, and Western missionaries a secondary one. The evidence certainly bears this out in the case of the United Brethren in Sierra Leone. Howard Mueller's unpublished dissertation "The Formation of a Mission Church in an African Culture: The United Brethren in Sierra Leone" is a careful study of the interaction of United Brethren missionaries and African Christians from 1855–1946. Mueller's conclusions are based on extensive interviews, conducted in 1971 and 1972, with 52 African informants, the majority of whom "were pastors and lay people in the former United Brethren Church."[137] (The transcript of these interviews runs to 450 single-spaced pages.) Most had attended United Brethren schools, many at the secondary as well as primary level; and the interviewees included many teachers as well as pastors (in fact, most pastors had started out as teachers.) The pastors Mueller interviewed included many of the most prominent United Brethren pastors in the country, the acknowledged leaders of their denomination. And often these were the pastors who had the most to say to him about African culture, conversion strategies, and mission politics. Mueller's dissertation, and the extensive interviews upon which it is based, provide a clear picture of the role the mission workers played in the spread of Christianity in Sierra Leone, as well as how Christianity became adapted to African culture. My interpretation of this situation is based upon my own analysis of the interview transcripts, as well as upon Mueller's conclusions.

The station at Rotifunk in 1922 provides a good example of how proselytization was organized. Only four missionaries were located at the station: Mignerey, his wife, the nurse Nora Vesper, who ran the dispensary, assisted by Maud Hoyle. The work of the mission was largely carried out by Africans, including the African pastor (John Karefa-Smart) and four African teachers. Karefa-Smart headed the church, Nurse Vesper the dispensary, and Ross Lohr was head teacher. 113 boys and 31 girls attended the school at Rotifunk. The Rotifunk church had 98 "communicant" members and 148 "seeker" members. In Sierra Leone as a whole, there were 21 United Brethren missionaries in 1922, and the church employed 18 African pastors and 72 African teachers. There were 1531 "communicant" and 950 "seeker" members of the church. The work of proselytization was by no means confined to missionaries and pastors. Teachers had definite responsibilities in that area as well, both as an essential aspect of their teaching duties, and in the activity of "itineration" in the wider community. Indeed, the brunt of the responsibility for proselytization was borne by the teachers. All teachers were required to itinerate, and were required to prepare for the missionaries a weekly report of their itineration activities. This requirement sometimes lead to falsification of reports. Students at United Brethren secondary schools were also required to itinerate.

Mueller's interviews make it clear that the African pastors and teachers were able to communicate the meaning of Christian ideas and ritual practices in ways that were completely inaccessible to the missionaries themselves. This communication took place in terms of analogies to traditional African religious ideas and ritual practices. Mueller's informants also make it clear that most African converts continued to hold to many traditional African religious beliefs and ritual practices. As a matter of fact, most of the pastors and teachers themselves continued to hold to at least some of those traditional beliefs and practices.

The missionaries were probably not aware of the full extent to which African tradition persisted within the Christian community. The missionaries did directly attack polygamy—and their attack had little support among African Christians. But on the other hand, the missionaries were perfectly willing to accept some of the African traditions of which they were aware. When Mignerey writes that "it is practically impossible to pass judgment upon the Porro," he is not a lone voice of tolerance, but in fact reflects the consensus of United Brethren missionaries.

Of the 14 African informants who speak of the issue, only two say that the missionaries openly opposed the Poro. Eleven say that the missionaries never spoke against Poro, and two say that the missionaries opposed it privately but not publicly. From the informants' comments it is also evident that most African teachers and even pastors were in fact active members of the Poro society.

Only two of Mueller's African informants expressed a fairly thorough rejection of African tradition—to the point of openly preaching against, or example, ancestor worship, the use of traditional "medicine," and traditional beliefs about dreams. These two individuals both worked under the very conservative missionary Charles Leader. Both were pastors and teachers. One (J. S. Kamanda), as opposed to tradition as he was, had nevertheless joined Poro as a youth. The other (Peter P. Pieh) was willing to oppose traditional customs in his personal life even when his opposition provoked family resentment over matters that many other Christians might not even have made an issue of. Pieh's rejection of traditional custom even down to minor details, in the case of the birth of his first child for example, appears to be very much the exception:

> When I got my first child, Matthew Pieh, in 1934, in Tungei, where native customs prevailed very much. When the mother brought him down from Tungei they dressed him in many many robes. I took off them all and tied them into bundles and sent them back to the mother-in-law. I said that as long as you have given me your daughter and we have gotten an issue [child] now it is ours. All this you have done for her you did not know. But I will know how to take care of my own child. So they didn't like it. They wrote me a letter, a stinker. They said that I have taken myself to be a white man.[138]

Pieh's willingness to provoke conflict was unusual even among those who opposed much of African tradition. Seven informants (including two pastors) more or less took the position that it is necessary for them as Christians in African society to tolerate and even sometimes participate in traditional practices that they privately do not accept. But this group also accepts much more of traditional African belief than Pieh and Kamanda did. Their expressed attitude toward the presence of ancestors and the efficacy of "medicine" is in some cases clearly positive, and in other cases ambiguous. The attitude of Rev. T. S. Bangura[139] is typical of those who appreciate the importance of harmony despite their private disagreement:

> Becoming Christians we do not cut off all of our cultural heritage. This is true in what you have just mentioned—keeping in contact with the dead. Here our Christians go to the graves on a New Year's Sunday. They put flowers. They sit by the grave and talk to their parents and intimate friends on the other side. They feel that there is this contact. In the case of a husband the wife will say: "Your children are growing. I am doing my best to take care of them, but your spirit must continue with us encouraging them so that they do what is right." ....And since I became a Christian I go to my folks and they make sacrifice. I will sit with them. And they will pray on this bread and then divide it.....And this makes them feel Christianity does not really make you sever from your people, but brings you together.

When Mueller then asked Bangura whether he participated in the family sacrifice in order to "maintain relationships with the living" or also "because you feel you are communicating with those who have died," Bangura replied:

> No. I don't feel this any more. But I do not want to hurt their feelings. When I am with them I have to participate so that they feel that I am alright with them. But I myself do not feel that this has any particular spiritual value or communication with the dead.[140]

Bangura feels not only that the preservation of family harmony is more important than speaking out against erroneous beliefs, but also that not making an issue of such errors is *more* in accordance with Christianity, which stands for "bringing people together."

A third group of 8–10 informants, including five pastors, expresses a much higher level of acceptance of traditional African beliefs and practices, including beliefs about communication with ancestors and the pouring of libations, beliefs about dreams, and beliefs about the efficacy of "medicine," curses, swearing, and witchcraft. For example Rev. David Shodeke frankly describes the extent of the persistence of traditional beliefs about ancestors:

> If you take ancestor worship out of Africa you take out the heart. We have not come to the place where we can honestly say that we are not all involved in one way or the other in the worship of ancestors. Whether it be pastor or bishop. Unlike the West, we strongly believe and have practiced ancestor worship over the centuries. If you come to a cemetery on New Year's Day or on Easter Monday you will find literally hundreds of people. And to a degree we pastors believe in that.[141]

Rev. M.E.S. Gbundema[142] describes many traditional beliefs, and contrasts them with what he as a Christian is supposed to believe. But he points out that many Africans continue to hold traditional beliefs, and he does not make any point of excluding himself from those many Africans. For example, when Mueller, seeking a clarification, asks "So it is the ancestors and not God who punishes?" Gbundema replies:

> Yes, but now that some of us are Christians we have de-tribalized ourselves. At times we don't want to expose the truth to you people. Never mind, we believe the ancestors punish us. Even if we are B.A., B.D., Ph.D., we still believe the ancestors punish us.[143]

Gbundema also speaks very positively of the tradition of the "big cook"—the kind of feast held several times a year in honor of the ancestors during which a portion is always reserved for them:

> All Christians as far as I know do "cooking." But because of our position we conceal it; we say that we are just remembering our parents, that it is just memorial. But there is always some chop reserved! Even though we know the dead is finished we do not eat it. Habits are hard to break.....When we are in front of the missionaries or Europeans, we try to feel that we are like them. It is not proper; we have our own culture, despite our Western cultural status. But one thing I believe is to express my mind.

Gbundema tells Mueller that he does a "big cook" *as a minister* "on festive days, like Christmas, New Year, Easter, and Whit Sunday."[144] Gbundema does not seem to think that the persistence of African religious traditions among Christians is at all a bad thing. He is in fact somewhat annoyed by the need to put up a false front to the missionaries. And while he holds to these traditional African beliefs about the afterlife, he also expresses a very orthodox view of the last judgment:

> We believe that the judgment will be one great and grand day wherein the sheep will be divided from the goats. All of us will meet somewhere....And then God will make a statement....Then we shall know each other better when the scales have fallen from our eyes.[145]

Gbundema also maintains traditional African beliefs about dreams: "What I dream will come to pass....There are many many instances."[146] And apparently as a minister, his role at times becomes very like that of a traditional diviner—church members bring him their dreams, which he is quite willing to interpret for them.[147] He also has traditional beliefs about magic:

> Our people are very clever. They can bewitch you. You can say that you don't believe it, but something will happen to you. Here in Africa ministers will say this and that. But they will know the fact. It is there. We are trying to bring it into disrepute because we don't believe in it now. But we were born in it. But we grew out of it. Since we have accepted Christianity we don't believe in it. But that doesn't mean that it is not operating.[148]

Gbundema's statements do seem somehow contradictory. But the contradictions he expresses are precisely the contradictions of the cultural situation he is living out. Christianity did not come close to destroying the cultural world in which magic and the presence of the ancestors is simply assumed.

Seven of the ministers and teachers that Mueller interviewed discussed conversion strategies at some length. In response to Mueller's questions about how they would explain Christianity to members of a seekers class and/or to people who were illiterate, five of the seven clearly espoused the philosophy that it is necessary to "begin with the known" in order to "move to the unknown." That is, they either explicitly believed, or apparently assumed, that it is necessary to begin with analogies drawn from African culture in order to lead "seekers" to understand and accept various Christian rituals and beliefs. From their discussion of the use of these analogies, one has the impression that they regard these analogies as *valid*; that there is a meaning or idea that links together the "pagan" with the Christian practice. But two ministers, in somewhat briefer comments, seem to place more emphasis on the importance of impressing upon the "seekers" the *difference* between the "pagan" and Christian rituals and beliefs, and seem less convinced of the usefulness of the analogies themselves. These two may seem to represent a more anti-traditional viewpoint, but even the very anti-traditional J.S. Kamanda, who served happily under Leader, in practice made active use of such analogies.

The discovery of analogies and shared meanings represented an effective means, almost completely inaccessible to the missionaries themselves, of introducing a new religious system. All five informants emphasize the analogy between Christian baptism and traditional washing. Three mention specifically the similarity between baptism as initiation into the society of Christians and the traditional ritual washing that climaxes initiation into the Poro and Bondo societies. Four mention specifically the analogy between Christian baptism as the washing away of sins and the traditional ritual washing that follows upon confession of incest (evidently *simongama*) prohibitions. Other connections the informants make include that between Christ as a mediator and ancestors as mediators; and between the notion of the death of Christ as a sacrifice and traditional African sacrifice.

Rev. David Shodeke's comments provide a particularly clear and thorough illustration of the perspective these African Christians had toward linking Christianity and traditional African culture. This is what he has to say about the connection between Christian baptism and African initiation rituals (and his account of those rituals agrees with Harris and Sawyerr's):

> The idea of baptism to the Sierra Leonean is not new. I say this with a certain amount of authority because I know. You will find out that in every bit of our societies from the time a child is born to the time a man is buried there are certain traditional rites where washing comes in.... The last traditional rite of the Bundu society, on the day these girls are brought to town, as early as five o'clock in the morning the entire group is taken to some brook or some river (Kesay brook in Freetown is a usual place) and this ceremonial washing takes place. If you lived in the country you would notice that the very last day of the Poro and Wundu societies are always held by a stream or river.... So there is this idea of immersion which is traditional with us. We built from that. We said baptism is more meaningful and more powerful. And instead of being washed in a society and coming back into life as it were, you must get this washing which is symbolized in our act of baptism. And from there you go to teach them that this is of the spirit. I have always used the dove descending at the baptism of Christ. You don't want to be too abstract; give the story of that day when John the Baptist in the river Jordan baptized Christ and something like an actual dove actually came down. And the voice, "This is my beloved son." You try to play up all of these things because you want the entire thing to have some meaning. You say that you have been washed from your sins. This is why we like immersion. It is more meaningful because it is nearer to the native traditions.[149]

Even the more anti-traditional J.S. Kamanda seems perfectly comfortable with using links and analogies with African tradition in order to explain ideas and rituals in Christianity. The explanation to "seekers" that he mentions relates baptism to ritual washing for incest (evidently *simongama*):

> I will tell you that first of all in baptism we use water. Water is a symbol of washing the outside, to clean the outside. But when we use it in a spiritual sense the inside is also washed. That is the way we tell people when they are being baptized. In fact here in Africa that kind of ceremony is also used sometimes.... Here in Africa one way to observe the custom of washing is when somebody commits what they call incestery (sic). When the ceremony is performed, washing comes in. After you confess that particular sin they wash you so that you are free from

it. I do use this when I teach people to be baptized. Water can help them to wash away their sins.[150]

Shodeke connects the idea of Christ as a mediator between humanity and God with the traditional idea of ancestors as mediators:

The man in the bush there is not without knowledge of God; he has an idea of some supernatural being. And if you talk to any native man in this country you will find him thinking very much about somebody bigger than himself....All the rites of our societies must invoke the spirit. Because we believe traditionally that there must be some relationship between us, this middle person, and God. When the African offers his sacrifice... We believe that our departed relatives must act as an intermediary because they are now in the spirit world with God. They don't believe that they themselves in this mortal flesh can go straight. We as Christians believe that there is an intercessor, and intermediary, in Jesus Christ. It may not cut as deep as that. But most of these rites are based on these intermediaries. And most of these rites are sacrifices. When you are born there is a ceremony recommending this new-born baby to God through our intercessors, who are the spirits of our departed ones. The Christian comes with a better concept. We say that we have a good man who can be intermediary. Our Lord Jesus Christ fits very beautifully into that pattern. And I have used the illustration many times.[151]

As he indicates, both in Christianity and in traditional African religion, the idea of a mediator or intercessor is connected with the idea of sacrifice: in Christianity, Christ's death is often seen as a sacrifice that in some way restores a relationship between humans and God, and in traditional African religion, food is offered to the ancestors in order to get their attention or to keep the relationship alive between the ancestors and the living.

When Mueller asked "As you have just said, most people in Sierra Leone believe that their ancestors are mediators between them the living and God. From their standpoint, what is the necessity for a mediator called Jesus Christ?" Shodeke replied that "we presented Christ as a very superior mediator. Now these people who left us knew nothing better than ourselves. And we cannot see how by suffering death you become that superior in your knowledge. But here [in Christ] we have somebody. And I have used it many times in my sermons. Jesus Christ is the only person who died and came back."[152] And, as Shodeke points out, the idea of the efficacy of a blood sacrifice is a belief deeply rooted in African tradition:

The idea of sacrifice, especially blood, is nothing foreign. We do it. My people do it. If a man is going on a journey a chicken is sacrificed to the gods believing that the blood spilt to the ground will protect him as long as he travels on earth. Christ, the biggest of sacrifices, the passover, has been offered for us. And there the story of the first passover comes in vividly. That they did offer some sacrifice and the blood of some animal was put on the door posts and when the angel came he passed over. Our people believe that when the sacrifice is offered something takes place.[153]

There is some disagreement among Mueller's informants about how important it is for Christians to abandon traditional African beliefs and practices— only two seem at all zealous to eliminate tradition, the rest retain tradition to varying degrees, and do not believe in provoking conflict by endeavoring to eliminate traditions they do not personally accept. When it comes to proselytization, what is remarkable is the general absence of any attempt by the African Christians interviewed to demonize African tradition. Even when some informants report on their attempts to stop traditional practices, their attitude seems to be not that the tradition is demonic, but simply that it has now been superseded—and evidence for this attitude lies in their willingness to use analogies from tradition in order to explain Christianity. The attitude of all of the informants is that Christianity is like a seed that has fallen on soil in Africa on which it may well take root. The Christian message has not fallen in some kind of desert; it is not trying to make its way in an utterly alien or diabolical environment. So many of the basic ideas of Christianity are already there in a kind of preliminary form: the idea of a creator God in the myths about Ngewo and Kuru; the idea of forgiveness and cleansing from sin in rituals for the lifting of curses and purification from *simongama*; the idea of joining a society ordained by God in the Poro and Sande/Bondo initiation process; the idea of an intermediary between God and humans in beliefs about the ancestors; the idea of sacrifice as a way of renewing a relationship with an intermediary; the idea of sacrifice as an action that genuinely affects the relationship between humans and ancestors and God. In introducing Christianity to others, these African Christians did not believe they were introducing something absolutely unprecedented. Rather, they believed that Christianity took what was already there and raised it to a higher level.

How widespread in Sierra Leone were and are the attitudes of the African United Brethren pastors towards the relationship of traditional African religion and Christianity? That Mueller's interviews include a significant proportion of United Brethren African pastors, and include many of the most prominent among them, is in itself strong evidence for the typicality of their beliefs. Their approach also turns out to be congruent with that advocated by a number of other Sierra Leonean theological writers and/or prominent church leaders, both within and outside of the United Brethren Church, including a United Methodist Mende theologian (Emanuel Munda Wilson), the relatively conservative Anglican Bishop Samuel Ajayi Crowther (1807–91), the relatively liberal Congregationalist minister Orishatukeh Faduma (1857–1946), and the relatively conservative Anglican theologian Harry Sawyerr (1909–87).

Emanuel Munda Wilson is a Mende United Methodist minister who was a teacher and Evangelical United Brethren pastor at Moyamba in the 1960s, studied, taught, and/or served congregations at various schools and churches in Sierra Leone, England, Canada, the United States, and Nigeria, and eventually went on to complete the Doctor of Missiology degree at Fuller Theological Seminary in 1982. He attended the EUB school in Moyamba and graduated from Albert Academy. He was chaplain of Albert Academy from 1975–76. His dissertation *Toward a Mende Christian Theology* concludes with a recommendation that reflects a way of thinking very similar to that of the teachers and ministers Mueller interviewed. Wilson points out that the growth of Christianity among the Mende has been very slow. He also believes that Christianity has not struck very deep roots among the Mende. He suggests that the reason for these failings is that "the missionaries and their trained church leaders consider Mende traditional institutions 'pagan,' forms unworthy of Christian use."[154] And the primary cultural institution of the Mende is the Poro and Sande. Wilson points out that the Poro and Sande in fact perform many of the social and also religious functions that a church does. The reason that Christianity has not struck deeper roots, Wilson suggests, is that the Mende, including the Christian Mende, already have a church—the Poro and Sande. The Christian Church has at worst opposed, and at best been uninvolved with, Poro and Sande. Wilson proposes that the church instead take on the admittedly difficult and delicate project of *Christianizing* Poro and Sande. Wilson sees an analogy between the Jewish heritage of belief among the earliest Christians and traditional Mende belief, i.e. between Poro/Sande and the synagogue. And it is because of these real analogies that it is possible for Poro/Sande to be Christianized just as the synagogue was Christianized:

> The attributes of Yahweh are similar to those of Ngewou. The role of Yahweh as the power capable of sustaining his people, the Jews, is similar to that of Ngewou, in relation to the Mende, although in the case of Ngewou he has made His power (*Kpaya*) and *Hale* (Medicine) available for this purpose. The concept of "baptism" or "initiation" as the symbol or form that means a transition from a state of "not-belonging" to a state of "belonging", and a belief system and peoplehood, exists in Poro/Sande. The laws of Poro/Sande are said to have been brought down (*Njini*) by *Leve* (God). These Laws which bind the covenant relationships between God and His people, and between individuals and the group are similar to Biblical laws and therefore, usable as a Christian's starting place.[155]

Wilson holds that while "it is false to try to equate Mende Ngewo with the Biblical notion of *Yahweh*," it is nevertheless "equally unsatisfactory to hold that the Jewish concept of Yahweh is utterly different from the Mende concept of Ngewo."[156] *Hale* is not utterly different from the power of Yahweh (and, he implies, their experience of *hale* indeed has made them "ready" to receive the Holy Spirit[157]). Initiation is not utterly different from baptism. The laws and covenants of Poro/Sande are not utterly different from the laws and covenants of Yahweh. Ngewo as creator is not utterly different from Yahweh as creator. And these analogies are due to the fact that God is already communicating with humans through these Mende beliefs and practices. Wilson quite explicitly states that he is "suggesting that God does communicate his meaning through Mende sociocultural institutions just as he did and continues to do through Jewish cultural institutions. These cultural institutions are not static, they are dynamic. They are changing. This is a good reason why God chose to communicate through cultural forms, for he can transform them gradually, even without the people knowing." "The Biblical message to the Mende is that God who left them and took residence in the sky has now returned to them. He is with them, in God-in-Jesus-Christ present in the Holy Spirit."[158] The Mende sense of the presence of ancestor-spirits is a valid analogy for the presence of Jesus Christ, and evidently prepares Mende people for that presence. But the presence of Christ itself radically *transforms* the sense of the presence of an ancestor spirit:

The Mende [Christians] believe that an ancestor spirit (if we can refer to the res-urrected Christ as such) is not limited by space and time, since He is a transcen-dent Being. Thus, Jesus Christ is not limited. He can, after His resurrection, be with the Mende in the twentieth century.....Secondly, by sending His disciples to all the nations (*ta ethne*), Jesus Christ has made all the nations his extended fam-ily for whom He accomplished salvation....We can say, therefore, that the Mende are the descendants of Jesus Christ, who is working to save them.[159]

Wilson's views show the influence both of the Nigerian Methodist theolo-gian and churchman E. Bolaji Idowu (1913–93), and Harry Sawyerr. Idowu's work is similar to Sawyerr's in that both have extensively researched traditional African beliefs (in Idowu's case, Yoruba beliefs), with the aim of understanding their relationship to Christianity and of promoting the indigenization of Chris-tianity in Africa. Both have a great deal of respect for traditional beliefs, and hold it imperative that those who would evangelize in Africa take those beliefs into account. However, their theological understandings of the relationship of those beliefs to Christianity differ significantly. Idowu unambiguously takes the position that God—the God that Christians worship—had in fact begun to reveal himself, for example to the Yoruba, long before the arrival of Christianity. Yo-ruba religion, especially with its emphasis on the supreme creator god Olodu-mare, represents a genuine, though imperfect, revelation of God:

The big question to which neither the European educators nor Christian Nigerians have yet given any consideration is that of where, ethnically, Nigerians come in this one world which belongs to God and which He so loved that He sent His only begotten Son to redeem; whether in the past pre-Christian history of Nigeri-ans, God has ever in any way revealed Himself to them and they have appre-hended His revelation in however imperfect a way; whether what happens in the coming of Christianity and as a result of evangelism is that Nigerians have been introduced to a *completely* new God Who is absolutely unrelated to their past his-tory. This is a fundamental question and there will no doubt be various brilliant and theoretical answers to it. On the basis of the Bible taken as a whole, however, there can only be one answer. There is only one God, the Creator of heaven and earth and all that is in them; the God who has never left himself without witness in any nation, age, or generation; Whose creative purpose has ever been at work in this world; Who by one stupendous act of climactic self-revelation in Christ Jesus came to redeem a fallen world.[160]

Wilson evidently shares Idowu's view on this point: "God does communicate his meaning through Mende socio-cultural institutions just as he did and contin-ues to do through Jewish cultural institutions."[161] But Sawyerr sees this issue somewhat differently. While Sawyerr's approach could not be further from one that would disdain or demonize traditional Mende beliefs, he is nevertheless uncomfortable with the notion that, for example, the Mende creation myths con-stitute a divine revelation even of an imperfect sort. Sawyerr is critical, for ex-ample, of Bengt Sundkler's view that African myths "constitute an 'original revelation,' which is re-enacted in annually recurrent festivals, in a rhythm which forms the cosmic framework of space and time."[162] "Granted," Sawyerr retorts, "that the African myths relate to the Beginning of Things and therefore provide material for what he has called 'an original revelation,' has he

[Sundkler] not fore-shortened the total *raison d'etre* of the Old Testament?...No doubt Africans who read the biblical accounts will readily silhouette them against their own indigenous stories. But will they necessarily pass on to the Hebrew concept of history?"[163] Sawyerr acknowledges that the Biblical creation stories may call to mind for Africans their traditional stories. But for Sawyerr, this association is not enough to justify the assertion that the traditional African stories also constitute revelation in any sense. And Sawyerr is struck much more by the differences between African and biblical creation stories than by their similarities. Idowu is deeply impressed by the many witnesses to divine revelation in the vast variety of the world's cultures. But Sawyerr is not, apparently because it is his view that only that which saves us can qualify as revelation—and only Christian revelation can save us. Sawyerr's goal is not to show how God has never been without a witness, but rather—as he states at the very end of his work *Creative Evangelism*—to show that "if we are patient enough to distill from the corpus of African traditional beliefs and practices such factors as are consonant with Christianity, we shall ultimately redeem them unto the obedience of Christ."[164] Evidently, in Sawyerr's view, human religion, rather than constituting an "original revelation," is merely capable, in some cases, of being redeemed by Christianity, through its consonance with Christian faith. And interestingly, for Sawyerr, not the Mende creation myth, but rather the traditional emphasis upon family and community, represents the aspect of traditional Mende belief most consonant with Christianity:

> All of us Africans feel that our deceased parents and other ancestors are close to us. In the present context, therefore, Christian doctrinal teaching should be directed towards, first, presenting the Church as a corporate body with a unique solidarity transcending by far anything akin to it in pagan African society; and, second, discovering a means of preserving the tribe, solidarity of living and dead, as Africans understand that relationship, but in a new idiom, that of the community of the Church. In any case, ancestors are thought of in relation to their tribes or clans or families. They could, therefore, be readily embraced within the framework of the universal Church and be included within the communion of saints.[165]

Along the same lines, Sawyerr believes that most appropriate image for Christ that may be derived from African tradition is not that of Christ as "chief," but rather as "elder brother."[166] Sawyerr also finds in the community bond created through Poro and Sande initiation rituals a tradition particularly consonant with Christianity:

> The initiates have been born again together and for ever they remain united in one body, i.e. concorporate. The concorporateness is indeed a key element in the puberty initiation ceremonies, and as we have noted, it is essentially based on a blood-covenant relation. Its religious significance is an aspect of the initiation ceremonies which the anthropologists do not seem to have grasped.[167]

Sawyerr unites the themes of the elder brother, the concorporate community, and ancestor worship, in a rather startling formulation:

> If we, as Christians, have been adopted in to Sonship by God, then we have a stronger case than the pagan African for believing that God our Father is indeed our Ancestor.... In the language of Christian theology the Church is the mother of all Christians, but the Church owes its origin to Jesus Christ, whose Body it is. Therefore membership of the family of the Church brings us into a foetal bond based on Jesus Christ.[168]

Sawyerr, in his unmistakable emphasis on the doctrine of atonement as the center of Christian belief, and his apparent insistence that only Christianity can bring salvation, clearly represents the orientation I have labeled as "conservative." But it should also be noted that he explicitly rejects fundamentalism. He presents three reasons for rejecting it: 1) "[Fundamentalism] accepts the story of the Creation in the first three chapters of Genesis as literally true and ignores the discoveries of geologists and astronomers." 2) "Some fundamentalists tend to lay emphasis on 'a comfortable certitude of heavenly bliss hereafter,' whilst they offer little or no guidance on the meaning in this life, here and now, of the Gospel Sayings of Jesus." 3) "Extreme fundamentalism is anti-Church."[169] In addition, while he does hold that salvation can come only through Christianity, he is unwilling to exclude the possibility of conversion beyond this life. He points out that this issue is particularly poignant for African Christians because of the closeness they feel to their ancestors nearly all of whom, of course, died as non-Christians.[170]

Sawyerr looks for inspiration to the most influential West African churchman of the nineteenth century, Samuel Ajayi Crowther. Crowther was born a Yoruba in what is now Nigeria. He was abducted into slavery at age 13, liberated by the British navy, and released in Freetown, becoming in effect a first generation Krio. Crowther was one of the very first students to enroll in and graduate from Fourah Bay College. Upon graduation he became a schoolmaster and evangelist, was eventually sent to England to study and was then ordained an Anglican priest. He became very prominent in the Anglican church, establishing a mission at Abeokuta in his Yoruba homeland, and was finally ordained the bishop of "the countries of Western Africa beyond the limits of the Queen's dominions."[171] Crowther's orientation was of course clearly "conservative." He preached that "Christianity has come into the world to abolish and supersede all false religions, to direct mankind toward the only way of obtaining peace and reconciliation with their offended God."[172] But Crowther was nevertheless a pioneer in the "indigenization" of Christianity in Africa: of the idea that African Christianity should be recognizably African rather than a mere copy of European models; that evangelization should take place on the basis of understanding for African traditions rather than wholesale demonization; and that the African church should develop African leadership. For example, he advocated, like Wilson, not the destruction, but the reformation of institutions like Poro: "Their native mutual-aid clubs should not be despised, but where there is any connection with superstitions, they should be corrected and improved after a Christian model."[173] He did not believe that women in polygamous marriages should be denied baptism—because, he believed, their social system had forced them into polygamy. Also, he did not believe that slave owners should be denied baptism either—because there is no prohibition of slavery in the Bible, and because he saw that African slavery was very different from slavery in America.[174] He believed that African traditional religious language and ritual can be adopted and employed by Christianity: "Their religious terms and ceremonies should be carefully noticed: a wrong use made of such terms does not depreciate their real value, but renders them more valuable when we adopt them in expressing Scriptural terms in their right senses and places, though they may have been misapplied."[175] Crowther in fact made a careful study of the traditional beliefs especially of the Yoruba.[176] His attitude toward conversion is summed up in a speech he made to a conference of all the CMS clergy in Nigeria: "With the heathen population we have mostly and chiefly to do. Them you must not censure as ignorant, stupid, and foolish idolaters; your dealing with them must be that of sympathy and love, as you would deal with the blind who errs out of the way."[177] And Crowther was also unwilling to categorically assert that the ancestors who had died as non-Christians were therefore condemned: "With all submission, I will remark that it is not the will of God to reveal unto us what shall become of such persons."[178]

There are two other religious figures of the late nineteenth and early twentieth century closely associated with Sierra Leone with whom Sawyerr clearly does not identify as he does with Crowther: E.W. Blyden (1832–1912) and Orishatukeh Faduma (1857–1946). Both were outspoken and widely known proponents of liberalism in Christian theology. Faduma, originally a Yoruba, was taken captive and enslaved together with his parents, and the intact family was, when liberated by the British navy, sent at first to British Guyana. Faduma's family had converted to Christianity shortly before his birth, and he was christened William J. Davis. They did not remain in British Guyana long, but soon emigrated to Freetown. There Faduma attended Wesleyan Boys High School from 1876 and boarded with J.C. May, who had founded that school in 1874. May was closely associated with Blyden, and was a strong proponent of his ideas about African self-consciousness and self-development. Blyden resided in Freetown from 1871–74, in Liberia from 1874–85, and again in Freetown from 1885–88, and helped May to found *The Sierra Leone Weekly News* in 1884. Blyden was already acquiring an international reputation as spokesman for Africans by 1871, and his rejection of the ideology of racial inferiority combined with his affirmation of African culture found support among Freetown's Krios, who were chafing under the increasingly racist policies of the British colonial government.[179] Blyden's short lived periodical *The Negro,* founded with May's assistance, provided a forum for this viewpoint, and later *The Sierra Leone Weekly News* "became a major conduit of Blyden's ideas and writings to the West African community"[180]

Through May, Faduma came into contact with, and was deeply influenced by, Blyden's ideas.[181] Faduma went on to college in England in 1882, and returned to Freetown upon graduation in 1885, to teach at Wesleyan Boys High School. In 1887 he officially changed his name from William J. Davis to Orishatukeh Faduma—a move meant to affirm his African heritage, which provoked both criticism and support in Freetown.[182] From 1891–1913 he resided in the

United States, graduating from Yale Divinity school and then working as a minister and educator. From 1916–23 he was an educator in Freetown, and from 1924–46, an educator in North Carolina and Virginia. He delivered the graduation address at Albert Academy in 1916.[183] The United Brethren *Sierra Leone Outlook* printed his address in full.

During his years in Freetown, Faduma was a prominent figure, frequently contributing to *The Sierra Leone Weekly News*. His contributions to that periodical culminated in a long series published in 1923 titled "The Faith That Is in Me." These articles clearly set forth Faduma's liberal theological outlook. That his forthright statement of that outlook also prompted controversy on the pages of the same periodical clearly indicates that both liberal and conservative religious viewpoints had support and were taken seriously in Freetown at that time. Also, his "ecumenism allowed him to be welcomed and at home in most of Sierra Leone's churches."[184] An "appraisement of Professor Faduma," summing up his reputation, appeared in *The Sierra Leone Weekly News* in 1923: "That he is appreciated by members of his race in both continents cannot be denied....In both continents he has inspired Negro boys and girls to noble action." The article goes on to call for a published compilation of his writings.[185] In his book-length study of Faduma, Moses Moore calls attention to the fact that, in the United States, Faduma belonged to a "small though significant minority" of African-American "clerical activists" who "selectively and critically appropriated the tenets of theological liberalism."[186] The kind of diversity of theological outlook which existed at the time in The United Brethren Church and American Protestantism as a whole evidently belonged to the milieu of African and African-American Protestantism as well.

Faduma summed up his support for theological liberalism in an article in the *African Methodist Episcopal Church Review* of 1890:

> The substance of Christ's teaching is "Love to God and man"; "On these two commandments hang all the law and the prophets." If the Fatherhood of God and the brotherhood of man are not practically demonstrated in our every-day life, in our social, political, and religious environments, our religion is a farce, our metaphysical speculations on the attributes of the Deity a nonsense, and ourselves a huge deception of the name Christian.[187]

His liberal understanding of the nature of Christ as revelation of God is evident in the installment of "The Faith That Is in Me" devoted to that topic. While unambiguously affirming the divinity of Christ, he places little emphasis on the atonement, stressing instead the status of Jesus as "the only sinless man held up for imitation and true copy."[188]

He clearly adopts Blyden's central teaching about the relationship between Christ and the racial or ethnic identity of his followers—in order to truly follow Christ, each people must find its own way, and not artificially adopt the forms that have originated with other peoples:

> It is unchristian and unscientific to present Christ to the Negro under an European or a Hebrew coloring, as it leaves the wrong impression in the mind and finally in the action that *the religion of Christ* is not what the Bible says it is, but it is, on

the contrary, *the white man's religion*....No second-hand inspiration, no second-hand metamorphosis of our inner life, can bring the change that Christ desires.[189]

Faduma also affirms the progressive nature of revelation:

> The fatherhood of God and the brotherhood of man, in spite of political hate and ecclesiastical pride, are being better though slowly understood, because her conceptions of God are being elevated, and the teachings of His Word are being better grasped. What men a few centuries back thought and believed to be the infallible teachings of the Word of God with respect to the rights of humanity, are by reason of a clearer revelation, being discovered to be erroneous.[190]

And then Faduma bases his understanding of the relationship of Christianity to other religions on just that notion of the progressive historical development of religious consciousness. "The idea of God, the religious sense, the moral sentiment are innate in man. They are not fictions of the mind, but grow with man's growth, and assume various forms according to his culture and development."[191] Faduma's evaluation of traditional African religion in this context is not unlike that of the liberal United Brethren J. S. Mills—those religions represent a relatively undeveloped stage of religious consciousness, within which yet lie the germs of future progress. (But Faduma includes no suggestion that traditional African religion is somehow degraded, as Mills does.) In positive terms, Faduma goes further, but not much further, than Mills in acknowledging a theistic element in traditional African religion, somewhat presaging Idowu's notion of 'diffuse monotheism':

> The Oludumare, Orisha, or Ifa of the Yorubas, and the Unkulunkulu of the Zulus are not mere names or phantoms, they are gross representations of a blurred conception of a real God....If you deny reality as underlying the conception of God in these ethnic religions, you are forced to deny the same in all religions, and in doing so you deprive them all of God.[192]

Ideas about God and about gods throughout the world's cultures are evidence of reflection on the question of the origins of things, and all of these ideas have their origin in God himself: "There is reality underlying all beliefs in a deity. Jupiter or Zeus is more than the sky, it represents a power behind the sky. Neptunus or Poseidon is more than a personification of water, it represents the power which imparts physical life."[193] The revealed God of Christianity is the culmination both of humankind's struggle to understand God and of God's progressive self-revelation: "The Christian idea takes up all that is best in the ethnic and the revealed religions of the world. It is the progressive development of the ideas of God in all ages, and the latest and fullest revelation of God to man through Christ. It is essentially the religion of love."[194]

In this section I have attempted to trace the interaction of missionaries and Africans in terms of religious experience. The attitudes of missionaries toward traditional African culture varied. All, of course, assumed that Christian faith was superior to African traditional religion. Most understood that Africans were already religious, and not all missionaries were completely opposed to every aspect of traditional African culture and belief. African Christians of course agreed that Christian faith was superior to traditional religious life. And they obviously understood their own cultures in a way impossible for missionaries. What is remarkable is that the African Christians involved in conversion efforts—specifically the ministers and teachers Mueller interviewed—for the most part did not demonize traditional African culture as some missionaries did. They regarded African religious traditions as providing the seeds for Christian understanding, and regularly used analogies from those traditions to introduce key Christian ideas. Also, to varying degrees, they retained traditional African beliefs and maintained traditional practices.

I have also attempted to set these interviews in the wider context of Christian theology in West Africa. I show that different West African thinkers espoused versions both of the liberal and the conservative theological traditions. But here again, neither liberals nor conservatives demonized African tradition. The most that can be said is that they interpreted its positive value in different ways. The conservative Anglican Sawyerr, in the tradition of Crowther, is willing to understand African tradition on its own terms, and he believes it is possible to find within African tradition elements which can be taken up and redeemed for Christian purposes. Wilson (whose affiliation is EUB-UMC) has a position close to Sawyerr's. The liberal Congregationalist Orishatukeh Faduma, unlike Sawyerr, does see an original revelation of God in traditional African religion. However, he does not value that revelation as highly as E. Bolaji Idowu does.

It is evident that the attitudes and beliefs of the leading United Brethren pastors in Sierra Leone that Mueller interviewed are congruent with the reflections of twentieth century West African theologians. This lends even further support to the assertion that those attitudes were widespread and typical of pastors in West Africa.

The Legacy of Missions and Colonial Rule

The mission established by the United Brethren Church experienced steady growth throughout its career in the twentieth century. The mission consisted of three institutions: churches, schools, and medical facilities. The scope of each grew steadily from the beginning of the century through the 1960s. This mission continued in existence through two church mergers in the United States: the 1946 merger of the United Brethren Church with the Evangelical Church to form the Evangelical United Brethren, and of the latter in 1968 with the Methodist Church to form the United Methodist Church. Representative figures for communicant church membership in Sierra Leone during the twentieth century through the second merger are (as reported by Mueller from the *Sierra Leone Outlook*):

Year	UB Communicant Membership
1901	327
1922	1525
1930	2364
1940	3077
1946	4735

1967	18,677

School enrollment as reported in the *Outlook* grew as follows:

Year	UB School Enrollment
1921	1459
1935	8495
1956	7846
1964	19,236
1967	28,630

In 1923 the mission maintained a dispensary at Rotifunk and at Jaiama, and a third was added at Taiama in 1926. By 1947, the dispensary at Rotifunk had become a hospital. The mission kept records on the numbers of treatments provided, which had increased steadily since 1926:

Year	Rotifunk Treatments
1926	16,933
1935	46,982
1942	103,421
1947	114,379

During 1947, more than half of the treatments were provided at Rotifunk.

The above growth should be considered in the context of the larger picture. Estimates of Christian and Muslim adherents vary widely.[195] The figures cited in *The World Christian Encyclopedia* are probably the most accurate, and show steady growth in numbers of Christian adherents through the course of the twentieth century, but much more dramatic growth in numbers of Muslim adherents.[196] In the case of Sierra Leone, Blyden's prediction about the relative success of Muslim and of Christian missionaries proved quite accurate. The *Encyclopedia*'s figures are as follows:

Year	Muslims	Christians	"Ethnoreligionists"
1900	10%	4.6%	85.4%
1970	38.1%	8.2%	53.7%
2000	45.9%	11.5%	40.4%

The missionaries, of course, dreamed of much more than just establishing a school system. Their aspiration was to spread Christian belief and to radically transform societies. They assumed, in fact, that Christianity and social transformation would naturally go hand in hand. The activity of colonization would lead "primitive" societies to join in the march of progress which was in fact bringing ever greater material benefits to increasingly large numbers of people in the industrializing societies of Europe and the United States. This picture was not merely cynical propaganda obfuscating the reality of self-interest and exploitation. The idealistic practitioners of colonization, including missionaries and many colonial officials, sincerely believed in what they were doing. By the close of the twentieth century, Africa as a whole remained by far the poorest continent in the world. According to its United Nations Human Development Index ranking, Sierra Leone itself was the single poorest country in the world by the year 2000.[197] Were all the missionaries' efforts in vain?

The enduring legacy of British colonial power is highly problematic. How can one then today evaluate the contribution of missions in the context of colonialism? The establishment of the conditions for the emergence of a new Krio society in Freetown must be seen as a thoroughly positive contribution. But the democratic tradition of British political culture which educated Sierra Leoneans did imbibe was nevertheless contradicted by the authoritarian nature of British rule. The institution of the army, another legacy of colonial authoritarianism, has had a post-colonial career that is, of course, checkered, to put it mildly. The effect of missions was disruptive and destructive to the extent that they cooperated with and depended upon the political and military intrusion of British colonial power. But the missions also made a contribution that was both creative and enduring in two areas: religion and education.

The efforts of European and United States missionaries in the nineteenth and twentieth centuries were indispensable to the emergence of Christianity as a major religion in sub-Saharan Africa. The value one assigns to this contribution of course depends upon how one evaluates Christianity itself. The evidence from Sierra Leone at least demonstrates (as I have shown in Chapter Four) that the emergence of Christianity did not by any means imply the extirpation of traditional African culture or religion. It also shows that Africans were at least as indispensable to the spread of Christianity as missionaries were.

The missions were also essential in the establishment of Western educational systems in Africa. Their contribution to this endeavor far overshadows the role of colonial governments. The importance of missions in this regard, including the United Brethren mission, is especially clear in the case of Sierra Leone. Doyle Sumner's study of education in Sierra Leone provides a wealth of statistics demonstrating the relative roles of missions and government in the field of education. The primary school that the Government had maintained in Freetown from the founding of the Colony closed in 1889.[198] In the succeeding years until independence, the only government schools to open were: a primary school at Bo in 1906, with a secondary department added in 1937,[199] and a new Model School in Freetown in 1916, at first primary, with a secondary department added in 1923 which was transferred to the new Prince of Wales school in 1925.[200] Also, in 1910 the government expanded its system of grants to non-government schools to include the Protectorate as well as the Colony.[201] The grants increased year by year, and were contingent upon an annual inspection, but at least during the 1920s never came to cover more than a small portion of school budgets. Government activity was merely a supplement to the very extensive educational work carried out by missions. By 1910 there was a total of 71 schools in the Protectorate—of which 70 were mission schools—with a total enrollment of

2,229.[202] In 1918 the two largest proprietors of Government-inspected schools in the Protectorate were the (British) Church Missionary Society and the United Brethren Church. The complete list of church organizations with schools in the Protectorate is as follows:[203]

Church Organization	Protectorate Schools in 1918
(British) Church Missionary Society	16
United Brethren Church	15
(British) Wesleyan Methodist Society	7
Roman Catholic	5
United Methodist Free Churches	5
African Methodist Episcopal	3
American Wesleyan Mission	2
Society for the Propagation of the Gospel	1

Between 1924 and 1929, the number of government assisted mission primary schools in the Protectorate grew from 57 to 76, enrollment from 3,003 to 4,811, and attendance from 2,208 to 3,471.[204] The total enrollment in all Colony and Protectorate Primary schools had reached 16,686 by 1930, including 11 government schools, 128 government-aided schools, and 64 unaided schools.[205] Statistics on school enrollment of children ages 5–16 from 1937 give a clear picture of the eventual impact of Western education upon Sierra Leone by region. Note that the United Brethren had concentrated their efforts in the Southern Province:

Region	% of Children in School in 1937
Colony including Freetown	57.4%
Southern Province	4.75%
Northern Province	.097%

In 1937, Freetown and the Colony had 86 schools, the Southern Province, 143, and the Northern Province, 26. With 11,197 enrolled in Freetown and the Colony, and 9,828 in the Protectorate, the overall percentage of children enrolled in 1937 came to 6%.[206] The United Brethren were responsible for a substantial proportion of this development: total United Brethren school attendance had grown steadily from 1900 to 1933.[207]

Year	UB School Enrollment
1900	460
1922	925
1923	928
1924	863
1933	2,437

Without the contributions and efforts of the missions, the development of education in Sierra Leone would have been truly negligible. The missions pioneered and built a system which educated an elite—but to this day Western education has never reached more than a small percentage of the population.

The primary social impact of the United Brethren missions was to contribute to the formation of a Western-educated elite. Graduates of United Brethren schools played a disproportionate role in the political developments accompanying the end of formal colonization. The United Brethren definitely played a role in the transmission of Western ideals of democracy and human rights contradicted by the reality of colonial authoritarianism. This contradiction came to light especially clearly within the mission, as the African pastors struggled for a real voice in their own church. And the United Brethren obviously had an important role to play in the establishment of Christianity as a self-sustaining institution in Sierra Leone, even though Christians form a distinct minority of the population.

But it does not appear that the United Brethren mission, and for that matter, Christian missions in general, were a really major agent of social change, for good or for ill, in the history of Sierra Leone. The one exception would be of course, the impact of Christianity on the Krio. The missionaries' hopes for social change—whether in terms of economic development, the overcoming of poverty, or the end of polygamy—were never fulfilled. The British system of "indirect rule," and not missionary activity, was the major disruptive force in colonization. From the available evidence relating to United Brethren missions, it does not appear that their effect was particularly disruptive. There was little conflict between the Poro society and the church. Indeed, most pastors were active members of Poro. African Christians, including African pastors, tended for the most part to avoid conflict with non-Christians. African pastors even maintained traditional African beliefs to varying degrees. Missionaries were often tolerant of this. They were often oblivious as well. Moreover, African Christians tended to put up a front for the missionaries, hiding certain traditional beliefs and practices they continued to maintain.

I think it can be argued that the most destructive *religious* effect upon African traditional religion and society was exercised not by missions but by the colonial government. If the core of traditional African religions is loyalty and trust in one's immediate human community, then a system which marginalizes an institution like the Poro society, by that very fact, attacks religious faith which is in this case the very substance of social cohesion. Indirect rule marginalized the Poro society by freeing chiefs from the check on their power that Poro traditionally maintained. The chiefs were the only effective connection between the people and the colonial government, but the effect of the colonial system was for the most part to simply make the chiefs more independent of the people over whom they ruled. The Cox Commission investigation into the causes of the riots in the 1950s clearly showed the extent to which chiefly corruption had grown by that point. Their report eloquently sums up the degree of distrust in the chiefs which had emerged as a result of that corruption. They discovered a degree of demoralization among the people in their customary institutions and in their approach to their statutory duties which they have been entrusted, which has shocked us. Dishonesty has become accepted as a normal ingredient of life to such an extent that no one has been concerned to fight it or even complain about it. The ordinary peasant or fisherman seems originally to have accepted a degree of corruption which was tolerable; at a later stage he has been cowed into accepting it; finally he rebelled.[208]

The Cox commission itself was oblivious to the meaning of the Poro society, but the work of Abraham and Wylie clearly demonstrates that the colonial government's effective dismissal of the Poro society in favor of the chiefs was the single aspect of colonial rule most destructive of the traditional social order. For now African leaders had lost legitimacy, and the people had little recourse against oppression.

The Struggle for an Autonomous African Church (1920–1973)

The mission organizations explicitly acknowledged from the beginning that their purpose was to establish Christian churches which would eventually stand on their own.[209] By the 1940s the United Brethren Church in Sierra Leone had developed a core of educated African pastoral leadership who were gradually wresting some authority from the missionaries. But independence for the church lagged far behind political independence for the nation. Even in 1968, at the time of the merger, the church in Sierra Leone still did not have a status in church governance equal to that of United Methodist churches in the United States. Autonomy was not to come until 1973.

The organization of the United Brethren church, school, and medical institutions was from the beginning very much top-down, with American missionaries and their Mission Board at the top. Only very slowly were any of the African participants in these institutions to gain any measure of power or influence. Howard Mueller devotes a chapter of his dissertation to a careful study of the "struggle for authority" between missionaries and African pastors, as it played out between 1920 and 1946. He demonstrates that the initiative for greater African authority came from the Africans themselves, and to a lesser extent, eventually, from the Mission Board in the U.S. The missionaries in Sierra Leone were mostly very resistant to ceding any power to Africans. Though a minority of missionaries were in favor of the idea of greater African authority, they themselves were not responsible for any of the initiatives for change.

The mission board in the U.S. was responsible for all six of the overseas United Brethren missions. According to Mueller, it was responsible for "appointing missionaries and selecting one of them as superintendent" and "it determined the amount of money each field received."[210] It was not in complete control of every aspect of each mission, but rather "formulated general mission policy...and then left the implementation of it to the missionaries in each field."[211] The missionaries in the field had "ability to control the decision making process, including the assignment of all Africans and the allocation of funds."[212] As a formal decision-making body, the missionaries met annually as the Mission Council.[213] The Mission Council worked with the Conference, whose membership included the African pastors. In the 1920s the Conference usually approved "without any opposition" the recommendations of the Mission Council, "but in the 1930s pastors began to challenge certain policies."[214] The missionaries were divided on the question of granting authority to Africans.

Annual Conference 1909

Front row: Zella King, J.R. King, T.B. Williams, C.A.E. Campbell; The standing figure behind them may be A.T. Sumner; the female missionary in the second row is probably Miss Eaton; the man with the mustache just behind her is J. F. Musselman; the African with a mustache behind Musselman is T.F. Hallowell. A.T. Sumner was assistant principal at Albert Academy before he became pastor at Bonthe, where he served at least until 1943. T.B. Williams served as a United Brethren pastor at Sembehun, Pendembu, Taiama and then at Rotifunk until his retirement in 1952. T.F. Hallowell served as a pastor at Ronietta, Yonibana, Rokon, and at Rotifunk until 1935 when he became an Emeritus pastor, not retiring completely until the 1950s; C.A.E. Campbell served as a pastor at Shenge until 1920, and thereafter no longer appears in the stationing committee reports.

Musselman and H. H. Thomas were in favor of granting some authority to Africans, but Schutz and Leader were opposed.[215] John Karefa-Smart (a Temne with whom Mignerey worked at Rotifunk, and whose son, of the same name, became prominent in Sierra Leone politics), S. B. Caulker (probably a Sherbro), S. M. Renner and J. K. Ferguson (both Krios) emerged in the early 1930s as leaders among the pastors. Musselman, who was superintendent from 1922 to 1947, supported and worked closely with these four.[216] Both the missionaries and the pastors were voting members of the conference, but as time went on the proportion of pastors increased. As Mueller puts it, "by 1932 there were twenty-three missionaries and twenty-two pastors, but thereafter the number of pastors remained stable or increased while the number of missionaries declined."[217] Though this gave the pastors the ability to begin to challenge the missionaries, they availed themselves of this opportunity only gradually.

One reason that the pastors were hesitant to challenge the missionaries was that the missionaries controlled pastoral appointments, and could and did retaliate against pastors who challenged their authority. On the basis of his extensive interviews, Mueller concludes that:

> Pastors who dared to suggest that Africans were capable of assuming positions held by missionaries were frequently the target for vindictive action aimed at intimidating them from further challenges. Many pastors, particularly the Creoles who were more aggressive on this issue, were appointed to less desirable stations as punishment for questioning the missionary's assumption of superiority. E.K. Ferguson remarked that missionaries attempted to make any pastor who opposed them 'unhappy in the work.' He continued, 'You were bound to agree with all they said and did. Woe to you if you did not!'[218]

S.M. Renner describes the attitudes of missionaries toward pastors, including their prejudice against Krio pastors like himself. Given this prejudice, it is remarkable that 18 out of the 41 individuals who entered the conference as pastors between 1912 and 1946 were Krios, especially since the vast majority of United Brethren adherents were not Krios. Among the reasons for this was the fact that Krios had a much longer tradition of Western and Christian education, and of aspiration to and participation in Christian ministry.[219] So the missionaries' need for educated pastors lead them to accept Krios despite their discomfort. And Musselman actively supported and promoted them. As Renner puts it:

> The tension between missionaries and Musselman came about because the average missionary in those days did not have much of a liking for Creoles. Because the average white man cannot stand being argued and being told what to be by the African. He resents it. The Creoles did not swallow all that the missionaries said. They questioned them and argued them. So that brought some tension. In the Provinces the boys were more obedient to them. But the Creoles having dealt with the white man more than the people up-country did not hit very much with them. I know certain missionaries always looked upon us as heading for hell. We just said what we felt.[220]

Renner also describes a specific incident in which he experienced retaliation for his outspokenness, retaliation Musselman was not able to prevent:

> I have a lot of gratefulness for what missionaries have done and sometimes I hesitate to criticize them. But it is true [that retaliation could occur]. In my own case I knew the *Discipline* then. I should say, more than the presiding elders of

the Conference. They didn't think studying the *Discipline* to run an African conference was necessary. They just ran the conference as they felt. But [J. K.] Ferguson and I studied the *Discipline* of the church and now and then we called them
to order and quoted the *Discipline* and said they were wrong. Maybe that is one
of the reasons I was removed from this church. I was enjoying the pastorate here
very much. I didn't like to go up-country, but I fell out with the missionary at
conference and he said, "Well, you know in Freetown Renner gets good support
as the missionaries pay good support, but we will send him to Moyamba and let
him go on full support without any grant in aid from the mission. We will give
him both sides of the barrel."[221]

E.K. Ferguson names only three missionaries who were "progressive enough
to face facts without prejudice": Musselman, Hursh, and H.H. Thomas. Renner
felt that H.H.Thomas was the only one who could be called progressive.[222]

Renner challenged the missionaries from the beginning of his career. He was
aware that the missionaries were not following the established rules of their denomination, and he used this fact as a basis for his challenges. The missionaries
evidently tacitly believed that African Christians and their church organizations
were simply not to be respected as the equals of American Christians and their
church organizations. In particular, the African pastors became aware of a specific provision added to the *Discipline* in 1925 which the missionaries chose to
completely ignore. This provision allowed for the creation of an "Administrative
Committee" composed of both missionaries and pastors whose main responsibility would be "to interpret the needs of the field to the Board and to administer
the funds contributed by the Board."[223] Such a committee would for the first
time grant some real power to the African pastors, even though the majority of
the committee was to be elected by the missionaries until such time as half of
the churches became self supporting.[224] Most significantly, the African pastors
would "elect their own representatives in contrast to the earlier procedure whereby the mission superintendent appointed the African members of the Business
Committee."[225] The pastors finally decided to act at the conference of 1930. As
Renner recalls the scene:

> We said in Conference: "You have got to run this Conference according to the
> *Discipline* of the Church. All that you have done this morning is not in accor-
> dance with the *Discipline* of the Church. And we are insisting that it be done [ac-
> cording to the *Discipline*]." It took the missionaries by storm that we dared to say
> that. But we had the *Discipline*. But strange to say, he did not have a *Discipline*.
> He [Charles Leader] was running the Conference his own way; the *Discipline*
> was at the Mission House. So he got the *Discipline* and said we were right. And
> so that day the Conference was organized according to the *Discipline*. Instead of
> his Business Committee, a Council of Administration was elected. And we ran
> according to how it is run in the United States. Dr. Leader was a good mission-
> ary; he worked very hard to develop the church here. But you had to do things
> according to the way he wanted it.[226]

But even though the pastors now had real voting power, the rules for the
committee still guaranteed the missionaries a majority. If the pastors were to
control their own church they would have "either to gain an equal vote in the
powerful administrative committee or eliminate it altogether."[227] In 1942, they

chose to attempt the latter. The Conference, in which the pastors had the majority, voted to ask the Mission Board in the U.S. to amend the Discipline to "replace the Administrative Committee with the Council of District Superintendents," [228] placing the functions of that committee in the hands of the African pastors. But the superintendent, Musselman, chose to misinterpret the resolution as simply intending the Council of District Superintendents to serve as the African members of the Administrative Committee.[229] Writing to the secretary of the Mission Board, Musselman said: "Do not take the matter too seriously that the men brought forward relative to the Administrative Committee and its membership." The Mission Board accepted Musselman's recommendation to them that no changes be made.[230] But two years later, in 1945, Renner visited the U.S. and met with the Mission Board:

> When he inquired about the fate of the pastors' resolution he was told that the Board's failure to present it to the General Conference had been an 'oversight.'....In December 1945 the secretary of the Board wrote to the mission superintendent, stating that he had reviewed the proposed budget for 1946 and noted that more than half the total budget came from sources in West Africa. "Therefore,' he concluded, 'I shall recommend to the Executive Committee at its meeting in January that the number of members on the administrative committee be increased to ten, half of whom shall be elected by the mission and half by the conference.'[231]

For the first time, the African pastors had gained an equal voice in running their church.

The mission teachers made up a much larger share of the African workers in the church. Their number grew from 68 in 1920 to 200 in 1946. Mueller points out that their duties went far beyond education:

> In 1946 there were sixty-two local churches (stations) and forty-two of them were under the supervision of teachers, who were called agents. The agent's duties included not only teaching in the day school but performing all ministerial functions except administering the sacraments, officiating at weddings, and receiving communicant members into the church.[232]

Their position in the mission hierarchy was even lower than that of the pastors. But unlike the pastors, they never gained any real voice in mission affairs. As Mueller summarizes the situation, "generally speaking, neither missionaries nor pastors solicited teachers' advice about mission policy and there was no provision in the conference structure for them to be more than observers of a system that regulated all aspects of their work."[233] The creation of the Administrative Committee in 1930 inspired the teachers to agitate for a greater voice. A petition for "greater lay representation in a mission conference" was thwarted.[234] In 1938 the teachers became "advisory members" of the West African Conference. They were allowed to speak at the Conference, but not to vote.[235] But soon after that, as Mueller reports, the "government established a pay scale for all teachers and ordered that mission teachers be paid according to the new schedule." This meant that the teachers were paid more than the pastors, who were in authority over them. "In response, the pastors became more protective of their dominance in the institutional church and defeated every effort by the teachers to gain additional participation in the conference authority structure."[236]

In 1950 the General Conference of the Evangelical United Brethren changed the status of their church in Sierra Leone. The new Sierra Leone Conference was now no longer a "missionary conference" but a conference on a par with those in the United States, which would have representation in what was now the Evangelical United Brethren General Conference. (The United Brethren had merged with the Evangelical Church to form the EUB in 1946.) Missionaries would now be members of their home conferences in the U.S., and advisory members of the Sierra Leone conference.[237] The 1951 Conference of the church in Sierra Leone was the first to introduce these changes. Carl D. Heinmiller, Executive Secretary of the Department of World Missions, traveled to Sierra Leone to participate in the conference. Samuel Ziegler, associate general secretary of the Department of World Missions, had written in 1946 in the denomination's journal that "it has been the policy of the board to build up a strong indigenous church and to turn over responsibility for leadership as rapidly as possible."[238] In this spirit, Heinmiller proposed some changes in the governance of the Sierra Leone conference. Walter Schutz had been General Superintendent of the mission in Sierra Leone since 1947. Mueller questioned Renner about the changes occurring at this time, referring to the direction the American mission board was taking:

> Mueller: "It seems to me that Dr. Ziegler was pressing for more African leadership. Were Africa pastors aware of this and what was their feeling about it?"
> Renner: "A few of us knew about it. About two or three of us knew about it. From the questions that the Board secretaries asked in the Conference we could sense that there was a desire by the home board that there be more African responsibility." [239]
> "For example Heinmiller suggested a joint council and he wanted an African majority. Before he knew it Dr. Schutz had appointed a joint council. He appointed the men that he thought would serve on the council. But Heinmiller did not accept that. He said it should be done by election. And that brought about a serious argument between Schutz and Heinmiller. And right there in the Mission Office Schutz resigned."[240]

Schutz was upset enough by this turn of events not only to resign as superintendent, but to leave the mission field altogether. His aversion to the idea of greater African authority must have been strong indeed for him to so suddenly abandon the field he had served since 1923. The editor of the *Sierra Leone Outlook*, Solomon Caulker, in the usual editorial statement about the conference, summed up the contributions of Schutz and Heinmiller in a way that shows how much the African pastors welcomed the new joint council arrangement, and that contains strong hints of their impatience with Schutz's paternalism:

> A good deal of credit for these achievements of the 1951 Annual Conference must go to Dr. W. Schutz, our Mission Executive Secretary, who presided over the sessions of the Conference. The many years of faithful service Dr. W. Schutz has devoted to our country has developed in him a sympathetic understanding of our problems and failings and a deep appreciation of our efforts to rise up to the Christian challenge. His fatherly accessibility and enthusiastic desire and willing-

ness to help and counsel will secure his position as our constant contemporary through the years, in the task of spiritual reconstruction of this our land.

Then to Dr. Carl D. Heinmiller, the Executive Secretary of the Department of World Missions, of our denomination, must also go the credit for the victories of the 1951 Annual Conference. Actually, it is very easy for official delegations to come here, and, at the time of their return, leave us with more problems and misunderstandings than when they first arrived. But of Dr. Heinmiller it can be said that throughout his stay with us, he remained objective without being impersonal; positive without being dictatorial; interested without being partisan and sentimental; fraternal without being patronizing. He spoke to us not as to children; but as to a Conference which has come of age.[241]

And some of the tension which Schutz must have felt comes across in his conference sermon: "Our Conference Theme is 'Taking Stock of Our Stewardship.' This immediately suggests looking at ourselves and our work and evaluating it for what it really is. This is a particularly appropriate thing to do at this Conference as we are now stepping from the old order into the new in this very Annual Session." "Now we stand at the threshold of full Annual Conference standing for our work. What an opportunity! What a responsibility? *Are we able?*"[242] In this sermon, Schutz bears down hard on the theme of the lack of ability of men to move forward without God—and the way he insistently drives this theme home strongly suggests the subtext of the inability of Africans to move forward without missionaries. Some of his anxiety and pique may be reflected in his remark that "we make our biggest mistake when we take over from another man and we have in mind belittling his work or determining to uproot what has been done."

Upon Schutz's resignation, and according to the new plan for conference organization, the conference was divided into two districts, each with its own superintendent. The superintendents would henceforth be African. Renner was elected to the Freetown district, and Benjamin Carew was elected to the Bo district. They served in this capacity until 1968.[243] Renner served as the first African chair of the Annual Conference in 1952. In 1961 the Joint Council proposed a five year plan to complete the transition to African control. This included reducing the role of the Joint Council itself to that of a committee whose responsibility would be limited to assigning posts to missionaries.[244] An editorial in the *Sierra Leone Outlook* in 1960 suggests that these changes still encountered resistance among missionaries:

> The Joint Council of the EUB Conference and Missions of Sierra Leone was in its semi-annual session at the Bible-Training Institute, Bo, February 6th and 8th, respectively.
>
> The basic purpose of the Council should be kept in mind: its membership is composed of Missionary and Conference personnel; it was initiated to assist both the Missionaries and their African comrades to grow up.
>
> Some of the missionaries need to grow up from feelings of paternalism—that is, the desire to continue with their converts as a father would with his infant child. On the other hand, native Sierra Leoneans need to grow up too from the flaws of secured feelings of forever gathering the 'manna' of charity from Amer-

ica. It means for the people of this land to begin to assume the measured self-help, self-direction that are usually part of the word, 'responsibility.'

Let us first refresh our minds concerning current definitions of terms. 'Conference' is used to represent all the parts of the EUB Church over which native Sierra Leoneans have been granted responsibility, which includes the running of our Churches, our schools, medical work, church extension or the opening up of new areas and fields of activity, etc. The word 'mission' now stands for its true meaning more than before. It means one sent out to help spread the knowledge of God's salvation through Christ. The word 'help' is important in this idea. It does not mean to do all for a people, but help them do what they are able to do for themselves.[245]

While African control grew steadily through the 1950s and 1960s, the Sierra Leone Conference had not gained "autonomous" status. Official autonomy only came in 1973, after the Evangelical United Brethren Church had united (in 1968) with the Methodist Church to form the United Methodist Church. Shortly after church union, in 1969, the Sierra Leone conference returned to a single superintendent system. There was a somewhat heated contest for the new position, among Renner, Carew, and J. K. Ferguson. Renner withdrew his name from contention, and Carew was elected over Ferguson. The 1969 conference in which this election took place was presided over, as all conferences had been, by an American Bishop, in this case, J. Gordon Howard.[246] With official autonomy in 1973, the Sierra Leone Conference no longer had an American Bishop, but an African one. Benjamin Carew was the first Bishop of the newly autonomous church.

The exact term for the church's new status was "Affiliated Autonomous Church." The 1976 *Discipline* defines this status as that of "a self-governing church in whose establishment The United Methodist Church or one of its constituent members has assisted." The *Discipline* also stipulates that "relations between the United Methodist Church and an affiliated church shall be such as may be mutually agreed upon by the two churches." Ministers in one church will be recognized as ministers in the other, and the affiliated church will send two delegates to the General Conference of the UMC, but those delegates will not have the right to vote.[247]

However, as the move toward autonomy had gained speed in the 1960s, there were signs of some misgivings on the African side. Greater independence evidently also involved reduced financial support from the United States. Two editorials in the *Sierra Leone Outlook* in 1963 deal with "the new financial policy of the church": "The cold facts and figures sum up in this: that gradually, all operating costs and expenses which come in the annual budget under the heading, General Administration, or up-keep of the Conference, must be raised locally."[248] This policy was evidently of some concern, and the editorial writers urged *Sierra Leone Outlook* readers to face the situation squarely and take on greater responsibility for their own church. One editorial reassures the reader that "the policy does not imply any cut of aids on capital requests from the E.U.B. Department of World Missions in America."[249] At the beginning of 1971, the *Outlook* included an article entitled "Autonomy: Two Views."[250] The "pro" view was basically that of the American Robert Martin of the Committee on

Structure of United Methodism Overseas (COSMOS), who spoke at the Annual Conference. The "con" view, that of most of the pastors, was one that had serious reservations about autonomy. At issue was the amount of aid that could be expected from America. Conference participants repeatedly asked Martin whether autonomy would mean less aid. Most of the pastors did in fact fear that this would be the result. Martin repeatedly tried to assure them that aid and autonomy were unrelated. He came away sounding rather exasperated: "'I don't understand why it is so hard to convince them that autonomy is a good thing,' Mr. Martin said later. 'The American Church has been running the show out here for 115 years, and if Sierra Leoneans are not ready to take over, when will they ever be?'" What made Martin's situation awkward was that the American church had in fact recently cut back on aid. "He said that Americans are giving less because of their own problems at home, and therefore the budget for Sierra Leone had to be cut." On the "con" side the *Outlook* provides the response: "Much of the fear centered on autonomy comes not from disbelief in the good faith of the Board of Missions on this particular issue, but from caution that has been learned through the years from other incidents where Sierra Leoneans feel they have been deceived or told only half truths." The "con" side quotes several pastors including one who

> expressed a feeling that much of the caution Sierra Leoneans feel in dealing with the Board of Missions comes from the fact that so much important information seems to come to Conference leaders second hand through missionaries. He seemed to feel that the Board sometimes tells Sierra Leoneans only what it thinks they should know and tells the whole story to the missionaries.

The United Methodist Church of Sierra Leone remained autonomous for twelve years. In 1981 it chose to reunite with the United Methodist Church, becoming now part of a new West Africa Central Conference of Methodist churches in Sierra Leone and Liberia, and retaining its Bishop, Rev. T.S. Bangura. Carew, now retired as Bishop, was not in favor of this change. He expressed his opposition in words which cannot but sound somewhat poignant, given the course of events that was to ensue in the history of Sierra Leone over the next twenty years:

> Is there any good reason to sacrifice autonomy at this point? We have, in all areas of church life, made considerable progress since autonomy. Autonomy has helped us tremendously because we have got relationships that we did not have before. We have cordial partnerships in mission with the Swedish, German, and Canadian churches. All these show God is with us. Why should we retract when our flowers are blooming and everything going fine?[251]

Notes

1. Pronounced *mawɛ* or *mawɛɛ*.
2. Pronounced *mawɛɛ-mɔ*.

3. Kenneth Little, *The Mende of Sierra Leone: A West African People in Transition* (London: Routledge, 1951), 88, 89.

4. Ibid., 101.

5. Anthony. G. Hopkins, *An Economic History of West Africa* (New York: Columbia University Press, 1973), 32-37.

6.. See, e.g., Eliphas G. Mukonoweshuro, *Colonialism, Class Formation, and Underdevelopment in Sierra Leone* (New York: University Press of America, 1993), 84. The debate between the economic historian Anthony Hopkins and the anthropologist Paul Bohannan does much to illuminate the exact sense in which West African economy is pre-capitalist. Hopkins disputes Bohannan's claim that African societies are ones that: 1) may or may not have traditional market places; and 2) in which market principles operate not at all or only peripherally. Bohannan contrasts these kinds of societies with properly capitalist societies, "societies which are dominated by the market principle and the price mechanism." Bohannan defines the market principle as "the determination of prices by the forces of supply and demand regardless of the site of transactions." (Paul Bohannan and George Dalton, "Introduction," in *Markets in Africa* [Evanston, Il.: Northwestern Univ. Press, 1962], 1-3). Hopkins refers to evidence (which he does not explicitly cite) that Bohannan underestimated the significance of the law of supply and demand in his analysis of traditional African economic structures. On the basis of the evidence that Bohannan has underestimated the relative significance of market principles, Hopkins jumps to the conclusion that "it has been shown...that sociological explanations relating to family structure, social mobility, the status-hierarchy and supposedly anti-capitalist values are unacceptable" (Hopkins, *An Economic History*, 76). Hopkins has shown no such thing. He has only pointed to evidence that market principles might be more important than Bohannan has considered. In then considering Bohannan's claim that African economies are multi-centric—i.e. are economies in which not only market principles, but also religious and community values have an economic impact—Hopkins points out that capitalist economies are also multi-centric in this sense. So apparently Hopkins concedes that non-economic factors including religious and moral beliefs can have an economic impact. So apparently sociological explanations relating to values are acceptable after all. There remains the task, on Hopkins' own assumptions (assumptions toward which he adopts contradictory attitudes) of considering the relative importance of economic and non-economic factors. Hopkins fails to pursue this task. Also, a capitalist system is not simply a system in which the law of supply and demand operates. It is one dominated by the pursuit of profit without limit through investment. There is clear evidence that traditional African cultures—such as that of the Mende of Sierra Leone—are anti-capitalist in the sense that their value systems disapprove of the individual pursuit of wealth in isolation from the family and community to which one belongs. Long distance trade and capital accumulation on that basis definitely existed in pre-colonial west Africa but this simply indicates that economic diversity was indeed present. Hopkins himself shows that while long distance trade was significant for centuries, there were very definite limits on its expansion, and that the precolonial African economy was hardly dominated by this form of economic activity.

7. Catharine Coquery-Vidrovitch, in her study *African Women: A Modern History*, trans. Beth Gillian Raps (Boulder, Col.: Westview, 1997), asserts that, during the nineteenth century "a slave man was an individual made to do a job that a woman ordinarily would do. There is no clearer way to describe the condition of women, slave or free, at the dawn of colonization" (26). (In later chapters she claims that the situation has done anything but improve since that time.) If Coquery-Vidrovitch is asserting that there was an unambiguous division of labor between genders in Africa, with certain definite tasks

carrying prestige assigned to men, and certain other definite tasks regarded as menial and contemptible exclusively assigned to women and (in an earlier era) slaves, her generalization is probably incorrect. (She offers, by the way, almost no evidence, and certainly no review of research, to substantiate her claim.)

8. Jeanne Koopman, "Women in the Rural Economy: Past, Present, and Future," in *African Women South of the Sahara,* edited by Margaret Jean Hay and Sharon Stichter (London: Longman, 1984), 5, in reference to Hermann Baumann, "The Division of Work According to Sex in African Hoe Culture," *Africa* 1 no. 3 (July 1928): 289-319.

9. Koopman says that Baumann's 1928 article "gives a good indication of the relative importance of women's, men's, and mixed sex farming systems." But while pointing out that Baumann's data indicate that women's (men clear, women do the rest) represents 40%, men's represents 15%, and mixed represents 45%, Koopman also says that "women usually carried out all the major farming tasks...with little or no male help" (4), which contradicts Baumann. Koopman does not evaluate the conflicts in the evidence she presents about precolonial gendered division of labor. Koopman's claim that "women usually carried out all the major farming tasks...with little or no male help" (4) is in reference to Ester Boserup, *Woman's Role in Economic Development* (New York: St. Martin's, 1970). Boserup also refers to Baumann's study, concluding from it that "female farming was far more widespread than systems of male farming and it also seems to have been more widespread than systems of predominantly female farming with some help from the males in cultivation" (17). Boserup has evidently misread Baumann. Baumann's three categories are "I. Men and women work together at the actual hoe culture; II. Men undertake hoe culture nearly or entirely alone; III. Women alone do field work (except clearing)." Baumann presents a comprehensive review of research on 201 ethnic groups. He lists 107 (51%) in category I (Men and women); 22 (11%) in category II (Men alone); and 72 (36%) in category III (Women alone)—so it is unclear how Koopman calculated her somewhat different percentages. Boserup equates Baumann's category I, stated by Baumann as, "Women and men work together at the actual hoe culture," with her statement in somewhat different terms: "systems of predominantly female farming with some help from the males in cultivation." Baumann's account of the data in his table does not justify the conclusion Boserup appears to draw about the relative share of labor within the "mixed" category. In addition, Boserup refers to a map of Africa showing the regional distribution of three categories. This map appears on page 303 of Baumann's article, and on Baumann's published version of that map, one category is: "Man only prepares ground, women do all the other work." The other two are in effect subcategories of : "Man takes part in actual hoe culture (prepares ground, hoes, sows, weeks, harvests alone or with women)." This category includes a lighter and a thicker shading, with the explanation that "the thicker shading indicates that man takes most part." In Boserup's reproduction of this map on page 18 of her book, the category for the area of lighter shading becomes: "Men take part in cultivation, but women do most of it."

10. Northcote Thomas, *Anthropological Report on Sierra Leone* (London: Harrison, 1916. Rpt. Westport, Conn.: Negro Universities Press, 1970), 172-73.

11. Melissa Leach, *Rainforest Relations: Gendered Resource Use Among the Mende of Gola, Sierra* Leone (Washington D.C.: Smithsonian Institution Press, 1994), 82; Leach here refers to K.H. Crosby, "Polygamy in Mende Country," *Africa* 10 no. 3 (1937): 249-64.

12. Leach, *Rainforest Relations,* 83-84.

13. Ibid., 77.

14. Ibid., 79.

15. Ibid., 120.

16. Ibid., 189-90.

17. Ibid., 191.

18. *mawesia* is plural of *mawe; kuwuisia*, plural of *kuwui.*

19. Little, *The Mende of Sierra Leone,* 101-108.

20. Ibid., 176, 179, 181.

21. Arthur Abraham, *Mende Government and Politics Under Colonial Rule* (Freetown: Sierra Leone Univ. Press, 1978), 274-75.

22. Abraham, *Mende Government,* 240.

23. Little, *The Mende of Sierra Leone,* 182-83.

24. Ibid., 183.

25. Little, "Political Function," 258.

26. Little, *The Mende of Sierra Leone,* 185.

27. Little, "Political Function" 268.

28. Little, *The Mende of Sierra Leone,* 184.

29. Little, "Political Function," 285.

30. Kenneth Wylie, *The Political Kingdoms of the Temne* (New York: Africana, 1977), 33.

31. David E. Skinner, in *Islam in Sierra Leone During the Nineteenth Century* (Diss. Univ of California, Berkeley, 1971) estimates that Muslims formed 16% of the population of Sierra Leone by 1931. By that year, "the figures indicate that the Mandingo, Susu, Fula, Koranko, and Temne were the most Islamicized ethnic groups" (190).

32. Wylie, *Political Kingdoms,* 34-35, 40-41.

33. Ibid., 45.

34. Adeleye Ijagbemi, "Rothoron (the Northeast) in Temne Tradition and Culture: An Essay in Ethnic History," *Journal of the Historical Society of Sierra Leone* 2 no. 1 (1978), 2-3; see also Vernon R. Dorjahn, "The Changing Political System of the Temne," in *Social Change: The Colonial Situation,* edited by Immanuel Wallerstein, 171–209 (New York: Wiley, 1966).

35. Dohrjahn, "Changing," 180.

36. Ijagbemi, "Rothoron," 2.

37. Ijagbemi, "Rothoron," 1; see also James Littlejohn, "Temne Space," *Anthropological Quarterly* 36 no. 1 (1963), 9.

38. Ijagbemi, "Rothoron," 2-3.

39. Wylie, *Political Kingdoms,* 35.

40. Ijagbemi, "Rothoron," 2-3.

41. Vernon Dorjahn, "Organization and Function of the Ragbenle Society of the Temne," *Africa* 29 (1959), 165.

42. Dorjahn, "Organization," 161.

43. Dorjahn, "Changing System," 175.

44. Ibid., 198.

45. Dorjahn "Changing System," 197-98, and "Organization and Function," 167.

46. Wylie, *Political Kingdoms,* 49.

47. See John J. Grace, *Domestic Slavery in West Africa, with Particular Reference to the Sierra Leone Protectorate, 1896–1927* (New York: Barnes and Noble, 1975), 9: "In Sierra Leone the Poro of the Mende admitted slaves to the lowest grade of membership only and tried to keep them in their lowly place."

48. Little, "Political Function," 268.

49. See Little, "Political Function," 260.

50. See Wylie, Political *Kingdoms,* 182, 202, 204; Abraham, *Mende Government,* chap. 5, esp. 289-90.

51. Abraham, *Mende Government,* 233.

52. Martin Kilson, *Political Change in a West African State: A Study of the Moderni-zation Process in Sierra Leone* (New York: Athenaeum, 1969), 8.

53. Ibid., 39.

54. Ibid., 62.

55. Ibid., 63.

56. Abraham, *Mende Government,* 235.

57. Ibid., 280.

58. Ibid., 290.

59. Ibid., 289-90.

60. Ibid., 290.

61. Wylie, *Political Kingdoms,* 182.

62. Ibid., 202.

63. Ibid., 204.

64. Dorjahn, "Changing System," 198-200.

65. Mukonoweshuro, *Colonialism,* 84.

66. Ibid., 73.

67. See Mukonoweshuro, esp. 55-81.

68. Abraham, *Mende Government,* 178.

69. Ibid., 175.

70. Ibid., 176.

71. W. S. Marcus Jones, *Legal Development and Constitutional Change in Sierra Leone* (Ifracombe, Devon: Stockwell, 1981), 39.

72. Ibid., 108-09.

73. Ibid., 108-112.

74. Ibid., 122.

75. Ibid., 130.

76. Ibid., 122.

77. Ibid., 123.

78. Jones, *Legal Development,* 137; Kilson, *Political Change,* 124-25.

79. Jones, *Legal Development,* 149-158.

80. Ibid., 167-68.

81. Ibid., 174.

82. John R. Cartwright, *Politics in Sierra Leone 1947-1967* (Toronto: Univ. of To-ronto Press, 1970), 38-39.

83. Jones, *Legal Development,* 180-183.

84. Quoted in Jones, *Legal Development,* 187.

85. Kilson, *Political Change,* 84.

86. Ibid., 87.

87. Kilson, *Political Change,* 88.

88. Cartwright, *Politics,* 38.

89. Ibid., 38.

90. Carwright, *Politics,* 38; Cyril P. Foray, *Historical Dictionary of Sierra Leone* (Metuchen, N.J.: Scarecrow Press, 1977); C. Magbaily Fyle, *Historical Dictionary of Sierra Leone,* New Edition (Lanham, Md.: Scarecrow Press, 2006); L. H. Ofosu-Appiah, *The Encyclopaedia Africana Dictionary of African biography* (New York: Reference Publications, 1977); Kilson, *Political Change,* 229.

91. Cartwright, *Politics,* 54; Fyle, *Historical Dictionary,* 123.

92. Cartwright, *Politics,* 56; Fyle, *Historical Dictionary,* 170; Kilson, *Political Change,* 228.

93. Arthur Abraham, "Margai, M.A.S," in *The Encyclopaedia Africana Dictionary of African Biography,* edited by L. H. Ofosu-Appiah, 111-12 (New York: Reference Publications, 1977), 112.

94. Jones, *Legal Development,* 184.

95. Jones, *Legal Development,* 187; see also Kilson, *Political Change,* 172-73.

96. Jones, *Legal Development,* 187.

97. Ibid., 190-91.

98. Jones, *Legal Development,* 192; Arthur Abraham and C. Magbaily Fyle, "Sierra Leone: An Historical Introduction," in *The Encyclopaedia Africana Dictionary of African Biography,* edited by L. H. Ofosu-Appiah, 17-34 (New York: Reference Publications, 1977), 32.

99. Ibid., 195.

100. Herbert Cox, A.T.A. Beckley, and A.J. Loveridge, *Sierra Leone Report of Commission of Inquiry into Disturbances in the Provinces, November 1955 to March 1956* (London: The Crown Agents for Overseas Governments and Administrations on behalf of the Government of Sierra Leone, 1956), 170.

101. Ibid., 171.

102. Ibid., 172.

103. Ibid., 187-188.

104. Ibid., 221.

105. Ibid., 98.

106. Ibid., 99-100.

107. Ibid., 126.

108. Ibid., 131.

109. Ibid., 155.

110. Ibid., 122.

111. Ibid., 111-12; 123.

112. Kilson, *Political Change,* 29.

113. Cox, *Sierra Leone Report,* 174-75.

114. Ibid., 150.

115. Kilson, *Political Change,* chart on page 30.

116. Cox, *Sierra Leone Report,* 9.

117. Ibid., 20.

118. Ibid., 21.

119. Ibid., 25.

120. Ibid., 80.

121. Ibid., 9-10, 15.

122. Ibid., 85.

123. Ibid., 14, 13.

124. Ibid., 15.

125. Quoted in Cartwright, *Politics,* 82.

126. Cartwright, *Politics,* 83.

127. Ibid.

128. Ibid.

129. Ibid.

130. Ibid., 84.

131. quoted in Cartwright, *Politics,* 84.

132. quoted in Cartwright, *Politics,* 85.

133. Arthur Abraham, in "Dancing with the Chameleon: Sierra Leone and the Elusive Quest for Peace," in *Journal of Contemporary African Studies* 19 no. 2 (2001): 205-228,

provides an exhaustive account of the causes and nature of the war. Abraham lays a good deal of the blame on Stevens, who "weakened the democratic structure of the state, limiting and eventually dominating the autonomy of civil society. State intervention in elections, both local and national, *removed* competitiveness and accountability, successfully eliminating opposition parties from functioning and reducing parliament to a rubber stamp" (206).

134. Earl Conteh-Morgan, *Sierra Leone at the End of the Twentieth Century* (New York: Peter Lang, 1999), 116-117.

135. Ibid., 129.

136. Ibid., 117.

137. Howard Ernest Mueller, *Formation of a Mission Church in an African Culture: The United Brethren in Sierra Leone* (Ph.D. Dissertation in Religion, Northwestern University, 1973), 7.

138. Howard Ernest Mueller, "Oral Data on the Development of the United Brethren in Sierra Leone, Gathered 1971-72," 354 (hereafter MOD).

139. Bangura attended primary school at Rotifunk, graduated from the Albert Academy in 1944, was ordained in 1951 and began his work as a UB pastor at Moyamba. From 1979-92, he served as Bishop of the Sierra Leone Conference.

140. MOD, 75.

141. MOD, 180.

142. Gbundema was born in 1910, graduated from Albert Academy in 1939, and began working as a pastor, initially at Bo, about 1951.

143. MOD, 294.

144. MOD, 236.

145. MOD, 297.

146. MOD, 234.

147. MOD, 235.

148. MOD, 245.

149. MOD, 173.

150. MOD, 199-200.

151. MOD, 108.

152. MOD, 397-98.

153. MOD, 174.

154. Emanuel Munda Wilson, *Toward a Mende Christian Theology* (Fuller Theological Seminary Dissertation, 1982), 222.

155. Ibid., 253.

156. Ibid., 162.

157. Ibid., 195.

158. Ibid., 224, 213.

159. Ibid., 179.

160. E. Bolaji Idowu, *Towards an Indigenous Church* (London: Oxford Univ. Press, 1965), 24-25.

161. Wilson, *Toward a Mende*, 224.

162. Bengt Sundkler, *The Christian Ministry in Africa* (London: Charles Burchall, 1962), 100, quoted in Sawyerr, *Practice*, 100.

163. Sawyerr, "The Basis of a Theology for Africa," in *The Practice of Presence: Shorter Writings of Harry Sawyerr*, edited by John Parratt (Grand Rapids, Mich.: Eerdmans, 1994), 102.

164. Sawyerr, *Creative Evangelism* (London, Lutterworth, 1968), 158.

165. Ibid., 94.

166. Ibid., 72-73.

167. Ibid., 89.

168. Ibid., 102, 105.

169. Ibid., 69-70.

170. Ibid., 94-95.

171. Andrew F. Walls, "Samuel Ajayi Crowther (1807-1891)," in *The Cross Cultural Process in Christian History: Studies in the Transmission and Appropriation of Faith*, 155-64 (Maryknoll, N.Y.: Orbis, 2002).

172. Sawyerr, *Practice,* 125.

173. Quoted in *Practice*, 126; and in P.R. McKenzie, *Inter-religious Encounters in West Africa: Samuel Ajayi Crowther's Attitude Toward Traditional Religion and Islam* (Leicester, England: Blackfriars, 1976), 56.

174. McKenzie, *Inter-religious Encounters*, 37.

175. Quoted in Sawyerr, *Practice,* 126.

176. See McKenzie, *Inter-religious Encounters*, e.g. Appendix A, 98-101.

177. McKenzie, *Inter-religious Encounters,* 49.

178. Quoted in Sawyerr, *Practice,* 130.

179. Moses N. Moore, *Orishatukeh Faduma: Liberal Theology and Evangelical Pan-Africanism 1857-1946* (Lanham, Md.: The American Theological Library Association, 1996), 32. See also Edith Holden, *Blyden of Liberia: An Account of the Life and Labors of Edward Wilmot Blyden L.L.D. as Recorded in Letters and in Print* (New York: Vantage, 1966).

180. Moore, *Orishatukeh Faduma*, 34.

181. Ibid., 35.

182. Ibid., 41.

183. Ibid., 159; see Orishatukeh Faduma, "The Man of Dreams," *Sierra Leone Outlook* 7 (April 1916): 3-8.

184. Moore, *Orishatukeh Faduma*, 199.

185. Quoted in Moore, *Orishatukeh Faduma*, 200-201.

186. Moore, *Orishatukeh Faduma,* 67.

187. Orishatukeh Faduma, "Thoughts for the Times, or The New Theology," *A.M.E. Church Review* 7 (Oct. 1890), 143, quoted in Moore, *Orishatukeh Faduma*, 80.

188. Orishatukeh Faduma, "The Faith that is in Me, III," *The Sierra Leone Weekly News* (July 14, 1923).

189. Faduma, "Thoughts," 142-43.

190. Ibid., 140.

191. Orishatukeh Faduma, "Materials for the Study of World Religions," *A.M.E. Church Review* 12 (April 1896), 471.

192. Ibid., 470.

193. Quoted in Moore, *Orishatukeh Faduma*, 86.

194. Quoted in Moore, *Orishatukeh Faduma,* 87.

195. In 1962, one estimate places Christians at 3.6 percent of the population. The Krios are the only group whose majority (62%) was Christian (Gilbert W. Olson, *Church Growth in Sierra Leone* [Grand Rapids, Mich.: Eerdmans, 1969], 72). The Adherents.com website, which collects figures from a wide variety of sources, for the end of the twentieth century, includes estimates of the proportion of Christians in Sierra Leone ranging from ten to twenty five percent, and estimates for Muslims ranging from thirty to sixty percent. http://www.adherents.com/adhloc/Wh_296.html#682. December 7, 2009.

196. David B. Barrett, George T. Kurian, and Todd M. Johnson, eds., *World Christian Encyclopedia: A Comparative Survey of Churches and Religions in the Modern*

World, Second Edition (Oxford: Oxford Univ. Press, 2001), vol.1, pp. 658-660. The Encyclopedia is a product of the compilation of much of the data from annual census conducted by "most of the Christian world's denomination and agencies"—data collected by as many as 10 million church workers. Becky Hsu, Amy Reynolds, Conrad Hackett, and James Gibbon tested "the reliability of the WCD [World Christian Database—online succesor of the World Christian Encyclopaedia] by comparing its religious composition estimates to four other data sources (World Values Survey, Pew Global Assessment Project, CIA World Factbook, and the U.S. Department of State)," and found that "estimates are highly correlated" (679). They also find a "tendency" for Christian estimates to be "slightly higher in the WCD"—but nevertheless "the percentage Christian estimates are closely related among the data sets" (684). "Estimating the Religious Composition of All Nations: An Empirical Assessment of the World Christian Database" in *Journal for the Scientific Study of Religion* 47, no. 4 (December 2008).

197. United Nations Development Program, *Human Development Report 2000* (New York: Oxford Univ. Press, 2000), 160.

198. Doyle Sumner, *Education in Sierra Leone* (Freetown: The Government of Sierra Leone, 1963), 131.

199. Richard Corby, "Bo School and its Graduates in Sierra Leone," *Canadian Journal of African Studies* 15 no. 2 (1981), 330; Sumner, *Education*, 140.

200. Sumner, *Education*, 181-82.

201. Ibid., 158.

202. Ibid., 157.

203. Ibid., 158-59.

204. Ibid., 185.

205. Ibid., 259.

206. Ibid., 228.

207. Glen Rosselot, *The Origin, Growth, and Development of the United Brethren in Christ Mission Schools in Sierra Leone, West Africa* (M.A. Thesis in Education, University of Chicago, 1936), table 1 on pages 117-18.

208. Cox, *Sierra Leone Report*, 9.

209. See Mueller, *Formation*, 137.

210. Ibid., 138.

211. Ibid.

212. Ibid., 139.

213. Ibid.

214. Ibid.

215. Ibid.

216. Ibid., 140.

217. Ibid., 139-140.

218. Ibid., 109-110.

219. Ibid., 116-117.

220. MOD, 65.

221. MOD, 64.

222. MOD, 52, 424.

223. Mueller, *Formation*, 143.

224. Ibid.

225. Ibid., 144.

226. MOD, 147.

227. Mueller, *Formation*, 151.

228. Ibid., 152.

229. Ibid.

230. Ibid.

231. Ibid., 153.

232. Ibid., 141.

233. Ibid., 142.

234. Ibid., 149-50.

235. Ibid., 151.

236. Ibid.

237. J. Steven O'Malley, *"On the Journey Home": The History of Mission of the Evangelical United Brethren Church, 1946-1968* (New York: General Board of Global Ministries, United Methodist Church, 2003), 68-69.

238. Quoted in O'Malley, *On the Journey Home,* 11.

239. MOD, 66.

240. MOD, 423.

241. "From the Editorial Desk: Annual Conference—1951," *Sierra Leone Outlook,* Jan.-Feb., 1951, 3.

242. Dr. W. Schutz, "Conference Sermon: Untapped Strength," *Sierra Leone Outlook,* Jan.-Feb., 1951, 6.

243. "Editorial: The Current Leadership of the United Methodist Conference in Sierra Leone," *Sierra Leone Outlook,* Jan.-Mar., 1969, pp. 2-3.

244. O'Malley, *On the Journey Home,* 76.

245. "Missionaries and Africans Must Grow Up," *Sierra Leone Outlook,* Feb., 1960, 2-3.

246. "Editorial: The Current Leadership of the United Methodist Conference in Sierra Leone," *Sierra Leone Outlook,* Jan.-Mar., 1969, pp. 2-3.

247. United Methodist Church (U.S.), Board of Discipleship, *The Book of Discipline of the United Methodist Church, 1976* (Nashville: United Methodist Publishing House, 1976), 253-54.

248. "Editorial: What the Financial Policy Means," *Sierra Leone Outlook* 54 no. 6, June 1963, 3; and "Editorial: The New Financial Policy of the EUB church," *Sierra Leone Outlook* 54 no. 16, April 1963, 2-3.

249. "Editorial: Financial Policy with Christian Fortitude" *Sierra Leone Outlook* 54 no. 18, July-Aug. 1963.

250. "Autonomy: Two Views." *Sierra Leone Outlook,* 1971, no. 1, pp. 2-3.

251. Quoted in Robert J. Harman, *From Missions to Mission: The History of Mission of the United Methodist Church, 1968-2000* (New York: General Board of Global Ministries, The United Methodist Church, 2005), 146.

EPILOGUE

Lloyd Mignerey 1896 – 1988

When I met Lloyd Mignerey's daughter Elinor in 1995, she told me that she thought the reason that he was continually transferred among a series of out of the way churches for years after he returned from Sierra Leone in 1924 was that his views were unpopular and the church wanted to minimize his influence. I also asked her if his views of Africa changed as he got older. The painful disappointment of "the closing of the mission door" may be measured by the fact that there were two subjects, she told me, her father never spoke of: World War One, and Africa.

However, Lloyd remained an active and fairly well-known minister in his denomination. His activity included a great deal of what he once called "printed-page preaching," that eventually associated him with the denomination's magazine, *The Religious Telescope*. The editorship of the *Telescope* had been in the hands of Joseph M. Phillippi through the 1920s. During that time, overtly fundamentalist voices were given a great deal of play. But even at the height of the fundamentalist controversy, the *Telescope* still included a variety of voices calling for moderation. When Phillippi died in 1926, the editorship passed into the hands of William E. Snyder, and the publication took a decidedly more liberal tone. From 1933–35 Mignerey wrote a weekly column on "Youth and the Church" which was presented as a regular religious study guide. In 1930 he had also founded a South East Ohio conference publication, which he edited until 1935. As a minister, in 1929 he managed to get into at least one extended epistolary altercation with a traveling fundamentalist preacher, and he earned the enmity of the KKK in Lancaster, which was trying to get him removed in 1926.

It is worth recalling that number four and five on his 1935 list of "challenges to my faith" are:

4. Corruption among the Ministry—(cf. Apathy of, to Moral Questions)
5. Treachery Among the Laity of the Church

Perhaps in reaction to precisely these frustrations, he became a chaplain in the Air Force in 1942. In 1946, he was awarded an honorary Doctor of Divinity degree by Otterbein College. In the Air Force, he was stationed at various bases in the U.S., and eventually in Tokyo, visiting units all over East Asia and the Pacific. When stationed in Duluth, Minnesota he broadcast, between 1951 and 1953 at least 96 episodes of a religious radio program titled "Your Skypilot" on the station EWBC. He retired in 1953—at about age 59. He served a church for two more years, and retired from active ministry in 1962. He continued editorial work for the American Issue Publishing Company (a temperance organization) until 1964. His wife Ruth died in 1968.

Mignerey was seventy two in 1968. During the 1960s, he must have heartily welcomed the vigorous advance of the Civil Rights Movement. He had been waiting for a very long time for something like this to happen. On his own, he had long before done the spiritual work of recognizing and grappling with the racism in himself and in his society, a task that the vast majority of his contemporaries had pursued very sluggishly if at all, and were now finding themselves pressured to catch up on. The occasion of the assassination of Martin Luther King prompted him to write a radio script entitled "The Gospels and the Latest News." Since the extant copy is marked "Reader C," it seems likely that the script must have been performed in some venue or other.

The script has three sections, and under each section, New Testament quotations alternate with news items and commentary on contemporary society and religion. The news topics include the Vietnam war, the Civil Rights Movement, and King's assassination. The first section is titled: "Is the Church Relevant or Irrelevant?":

READER A - News note, continued: "Because the underground church is not encumbered with buildings and budgets it can enlist in unpopular causes and take radical stands on such issues as peace and racial injustice…This is much closer to the spirit of Christ…than is the 'establishment church' which is essentially committed to the status quo."

The third section is titled "Peace or War":

ANNOUNCER - "…And, behold, one of those who were with Jesus stretched out his hand and drew his sword, and struck the slave of the high priest, and cut off his ear. Then Jesus said to him, 'Put your sword back into its place; for all who take the sword will perish by the sword.'" (Mt. 26:52)
READER C - Now hear this! Saigon. They killed two of us, but we killed 99 of them.
READER B - "You have heard it said, 'You shall love your neighbor and hate your enemy.' But I say to you, 'Love your enemies, and pray for those who per-

secute you, so that you may be sons of your father who is in heaven.'" (Mt. 5:43-45a)
READER C - Now hear this! Since January 1961 they have killed 21,000 of us, but we have killed an estimated several hundred *thousand* of them.

The second section is titled "Brotherhood or Bigotry?" In this section he has Jesus retell the story of the good Samaritan in contemporary terms: "A certain man from an exclusive, white residential suburb of Chicago" drove to Birmingham, but he was attacked and beaten on the way. The first passerby was "a parish priest from Dayton," who chooses not to get involved. "I think I had best stick to my pulpit and keep preaching the old-time gospel. That's always safe and sound, and anyway, it's what they want." The second passerby was "a high church executive," who had left "his plush office suite in the Ecclesiastical Ivory Tower building in Cincinnati" to drive to Birmingham. "What a mess! I would like to help the poor Whoever-he-is, but I simply haven't time. Our executive board will meet in half an hour. We *must* get the ecclesiastical union machinery going without delay." The third passerby was "a small-store merchant from a ghetto in Nashville—a Negro" who dressed the man's wounds from the first aid kit in his car and took him to a motel, "where he himself looked after him throughout the night" and promised to pay for his room.

Mignerey's script may well have been inspired by Martin Luther King's sermon on the good Samaritan, titled "On Being a Good Neighbor," which appears in the 1963 volume *Strength to Love*. King reminds us that the Samaritan was "a half-breed from a people with whom the Jews had no dealings."[1] King's implicit analogy between Blacks and Samaritans is unmistakable, and in the sermon King makes vivid the parable's relevance to the struggle for racial justice. The lesson King draws from the parable is that the Samaritan showed altruism—an altruism that is "universal," and "dangerous," and "excessive." The motive for altruism's willingness to risk danger and unwillingness to limit its responsibility is precisely its universality. "The good Samaritan will always remind us to remove the cataracts of provincialism from our spiritual eyes and see men as men.... The good neighbor looks beyond the external accidents and discerns those inner qualities that make all men human, and therefore, brothers."[2]

Martin Luther King in fact belongs to exactly the same theological tradition of Protestant liberalism as Mignerey. In the essay that concludes *Strength to Love*, King makes it clear that he rejected fundamentalism very early, never to return. He at first embraced liberalism, and his acceptance later became somewhat qualified. His final position was that of a liberalism modified, but not rejected, as a result of contact with neo-orthodoxy. The crucial point for him was that "if liberalism was too optimistic about human nature, neo-orthodoxy was too pessimistic." He even criticizes neo-orthodoxy for veering toward fundamentalism: "In its revolt against the overemphasis on the power of reason in liberalism, neo-orthodoxy fell into a mood of antirationalism and semi-fundamentalism, stressing a narrow, uncritical biblicism."[3]

That King embraced Gandhi's philosophy of non-violent resistance is of course very well known. Less well known is that King's first hero was the same as Mignerey's: Robert Rauschenbusch. King says that *Christianity and the So-cial Crisis* "left an indelible imprint on my thinking":

> Rauschenbusch gave to American Protestantism a sense of social responsibility that it should never lose. The gospel at its best deals with the whole man, not only with his soul but also his body, not only his spiritual well being but also his material well being. A religion that professes a concern for the souls of men and is not equally concerned about the slums that damn them, the economic conditions that strangle them, and the social conditions that cripple them, is a spiritually moribund religion.[4]

And what places King and Mignerey and Rauschenbusch ahead not only of their own time but also ours, is their unflinching challenge to capitalism. As King puts it in his sermon "What Should a Christian Think of Communism?"

> In all fairness, we must admit that capitalism has often left a gulf between superfluous wealth and abject poverty, has created conditions permitting necessities to be taken from the many to give luxuries to the few, and has encouraged small-hearted men to become cold and conscienceless so that, like Dives before Lazarus, they are unmoved by suffering, poverty stricken humanity.... God intends that all his children shall have the basic necessities for meaningful, healthful life. Surely it is unchristian and unethical for some to wallow on the soft beds of luxury, while others sink in the quicksands of poverty.

> The profit motive, when it is the sole basis of an economic system, encourages a cut-throat competition and selfish ambition that inspires men to be more concerned about making a living than making a life.... Capitalism may lead to a practical materialism that is as pernicious as the theoretical materialism taught by Communism.[5]

Non-violent resistance—whether it confronts racial or economic injustice, requires courage:

> The ultimate measure of a man is not where he stands in moments of comfort or convenience, but where he stands at times of challenge and controversy. The true neighbor will risk his position, his prestige, even his life for the welfare of others. In dangerous valleys and hazardous pathways, he will lift some bruised and beaten brother to a higher and more noble life.[6]

Notes

1. Martin Luther King, *Strength to Love* (Philadelphia, Fortress Press, 1981), 27.
2. Ibid., 29.
3. Ibid., 148.
4. Ibid., 150.
5. Ibid., 102.
6. Ibid., 31.

BIBLIOGRAPHY

UBC Church Publications Consulted

Sierra Leone Outlook
Religious Telescope

Archival Material

J.R. King Collection, Otterbein University Archives, Westerville, Ohio
Lloyd Mignerey Collection, Otterbein: Diaries, Correspondence, Autobiographical outlines, Miscellaneous papers, Photographs
Charles Snavely file, Otterbein archives
Mignerey Collection, Center for EUB Heritage, United Theological Seminary, Dayton, Ohio: Diaries, Correspondence
Ziegler Collection, Center for EUB Heritage

Abbreviations

SMBC: Harris, *The Springs of Mende Belief and Conduct*
MOD: Mueller, "Oral Data"
HSL: Fyfe, *A History of Sierra Leone*
SHSL: Fyfe, *A Short History of Sierra Leone*
OFME: Mills, *Our Foreign Missionary Enterprise*

Abraham, Arthur. "Dancing with the Chameleon: Sierra Leone and the Elusive Quest for Peace." *Journal of Contemporary African Studies* 19 no. 2 (2001): 205–228.

_____. *An Introduction to the Pre-colonial History of the Mende of Sierra Leone*. Lewiston, N.Y.: Mellen, 2003.

_____. "Margai, M.A.S." In *The Encyclopaedia Africana Dictionary of African Biography, vol. 2, Sierra Leone-Zaire,* edited by L. H. Ofosu-Appiah, 111–12. Algonac, Mi.: Reference Publications, 1979.

_____. *Mende Government and Politics Under Colonial Rule*. Freetown: Sierra Leone Univ. Press, 1978.

_____. "Pattern of Warfare and Settlement Among the Mende in the Second Half of the Nineteenth Century." *Africa* 2 (1975): 120–40.

_____, and C. Magbaily Fyle. "Sierra Leone: An Historical Introduction." In *The Encyclopaedia Africana Dictionary of African biography, vol. 2, Sierra Leone-Zaire,* edited by L. H. Ofosu-Appiah, 17–34. Algonac, Mi.: Reference Publications, 1979.

Ahmadu, Fuambai. "Rites and Wrongs: An Insider/Outsider Reflects on Power and Excision." In *Female "Circumcision" in Africa: Culture, Controversy, and Change,* edited by Bettina Shell-Duncan, 283–312. Boulder, Colorado: Renner, 2000.

Alldridge, T. J. *The Sherbro and its Hinterland.* London: Macmillan, 1901.

Anderson, Benjamin. *Narrative of a Journey to Musadu, the Capital of the Western Mandingoes.* New York: n.p., 1870.

Arnheim, Rudolf. "The Gestalt Theory of Expression." *Psychological Review* 56 no. 3 (May 1949): 156–71.

Baker, Earl D. *The Development of Secondary Schools in Sierra Leone.* Ph.D. Thesis, University of Michigan, 1963.

Banks, Louis Albert. *The Lincoln Legion: The Story of its Founder and Fore-runners.* New York: Mershon, 1903.

Barrett, David B., George T. Kurian, and Todd M. Johnson. *World Christian Encyclopedia: A Comparative Survey of Churches and Religions in the Modern World.* Second Edition. Oxford: Oxford Univ. Press, 2001.

Baumann, Hermann. "The Division of Work According to Sex in African Hoe Culture." *Africa* 1 no. 3 (July 1928): 289–319.

Behney, J. Bruce, and Paul H. Eller. *The History of the Evangelical United Brethren Church.* Nashville: Abingdon, 1979.

Bellman, Beryl. *The Language of Secrecy: Symbols and Metaphors in Poro Ritual.* New Brunswick, N.J.: Rutgers Univ. Press, 1984.

_____. *Village of Curers and Assassins: On the Production of Fala Kpelle Cosmological Categories.* The Hague: Mouton, 1975.

Bemesderfer, James O. *Pietism and its Influence upon the Evangelical United Brethren Church.* Annville, Pa.: Bemesderfer, 1966.

Blyden, Edward Wilmot. *African Life and Customs.* Chesapeake, N.Y.: ECA Associates, rpt. 1990.

_____. *Black Spokesman: Selected Published Writings of Edward Wilmot Blyden.* Edited by Hollis R. Lynch. London: Cass, 1971.

_____. *Christianity, Islam, and the Negro Race.* Baltimore, Maryland: Black Classic Press, 1994.

_____. *The Three Needs of Liberia.* London: Phillips, 1908.

Boahen, Adu. *Topics in West African History.* Essex: Longman, 1986.

Bohannan, Paul, and George Dalton. "Introduction." In *Markets in Africa.* Evanston, Il., Northwestern Univ. Press, 1962.

Boone, Sylvia Ardyn. *Radiance From the Waters: Ideals of Feminine Beauty in Mende Art.* New Haven: Yale Univ. Press, 1986.

Boserup, Ester. *Women's Role in Economic Development.* New York: St. Martin's, 1970.

Camara, Laye. *The Dark Child.* Trans. James Kirkup and Ernest Jones. New York: Farrar, 1954.

Campbell, Joseph. *The Hero with a Thousand Faces.* New York: Meridian, 1956.

Cartwright, John R. *Politics in Sierra Leone 1947–1967.* Toronto: Univ. of Toronto Press, 1970.

Caulker-Burnett, Imodale. *The Caulkers of Sierra Leone: The Story of a Ruling Family and Their Times.* Xlibris, 2010.

Cauthen, Kenneth. *The Impact of American Religious Liberalism.* Washington, D.C.: University Press of America, 1983.

Conteh-Morgan, Earl. *Sierra Leone at the End of the Twentieth Century.* New York: Peter Lang, 1999.

Coquery-Vidrovitch, Catharine. *African Women: A Modern History.* Trans. Beth Gillian Raps. Boulder, Colorado: Westview, 1997.

Corby, Richard. "Bo School and its Graduates in Sierra Leone." *Canadian Journal of African Studies* 15 no. 2 (1981): 323–33.

Cox, Herbert., A.T.A. Beckley, and A.J. Loveridge. *Sierra Leone Report of Commission of Inquiry into Disturbances in the Provinces, November 1955 to March 1956.* London: The Crown Agents for Overseas Governments and Administrations on behalf of the Government of Sierra Leone, 1956.

Cronon, E. David. *Black Moses: the Story of Marcus Garvey and the Universal Negro Improvement Association.* Madison, Wis.: Univ. of Wisconsin Press, 1969.

Crosby, K.H. "Polygamy in Mende Country." *Africa* 10 no. 3 (1937): 249–64.

Crowder, Michael. *West Africa Under Colonial Rule.* London: Hutchinson, 1968.

D'Azevedo, Warren. "Gola Poro and Sande: Primal Tasks in Social Custodianship." *Ethnologische Zeitschrift Zürich* 1 (1980): 13–23.

"Dedication of Martyr's Memorial Church Rotifunk, West Africa." *Women's Evangel* 23, Nov. 1904, 164.

Denzer, LaRay, and Michael Crowder. "Bai Bureh and the Hut Tax War of 1898." In *Protest and Power in Black Africa,* edited by Robert I. Rotberg and Ali A. Mazrui,169–212. New York: Oxford Univ. Press, 1970.

Domingo, George Maxmillan. "The Caulker Manuscript." Pt. 2. *Sierra Leone Studies* (old series) 6 (1922): 1–30.

Dorjahn, Vernon R. "The Changing Political System of the Temne." In *Social Change: The Colonial Situation,* edited by Immanuel Wallerstein, 171–209. New York: Wiley, 1966.

_____. "Organization and Function of the Ragbenle Society of the Temne." *Africa* 29 (1959): 156–70.

Dorn, Jacob H. *Washington Gladden: Prophet of the Social Gospel.* Columbus: Ohio State Univ. Press, 1967.

Drury, A. W. *Outlines of Doctrinal Theology.* Dayton, Oh.: Otterbein Press, 1914.

Durkheim, Emile. *The Elementary Forms of Religious Life.* Trans. Karen E. Fields. New York: Simon & Schuster, 1998.

Ely, Richard T. "Christianity as a Social Force," [United Brethren] *Quarterly Review* 5 (Jan. 1894): 66–73.

_____. *Socialism: An Examination of Its Nature, Its Strength And Its Weakness, With Suggestions For Social Reform.* New York: Crowell, 1894.

Faduma, Orishatukeh. "The Faith That Is in Me, III." *The Sierra Leone Weekly News,* July 14, 1923.

_____. "The Man of Dreams." *Sierra Leone Outlook* 7 (April 1916): 3–8.

_____. "Materials for the Study of World Religions." *A.M.E. Church Review* 12 (April 1896): 461–73.

_____. "Thoughts for the Times, or The New Theology." *A.M.E. Church Review* 7 (Oct. 1890): 121–26.

Fisher, George Park. *Grounds of Theistic and Christian Belief.* New York: Scribner, 1883.

_____. *Grounds of Theistic and Christian Belief.* New York: Scribner, 1909.

Flickinger, D.K. *Ethiopia: Or Twenty Six Years of Missionary Life in Western Africa.* Dayton, Ohio: United Brethren Publishing House, 1882.

_____. *Off Hand Sketches of Men and Things in Western Africa.* Dayton, Ohio: United Brethren Printing Establishment, 1857.

_____. *Our Missionary Work from 1853 to 1889.* Dayton, Ohio : United Brethren Publishing House, 1889.

Flickinger, D.K., and William McKee. *History of the Origin, Development, and Condition of Missions Among the Sherbro and Mendi Tribes.* Dayton, Ohio: United Brethren Publishing House, 1885.

Foray, Cyril P. *Historical Dictionary of Sierra Leone.* Metuchen, N.J.: Scarecrow Press, 1977.

Forman, Charles W. "A History of Foreign Mission Theory in America." In *American Missions in Bicentennial Perspective,* edited by R. Pierce Beaver. South Pasedena, California: William Carey Library, 1977.

Funk, William R. *Life of Bishop J.S. Mills, D.D.* Dayton, Ohio: Otterbein Press, 1913.

Fyfe, Christopher. *A History of Sierra Leone.* Oxford: Oxford Univ. Press, 1962. [HSL]

_____. *A Short History of Sierra Leone.* London: Longmans, 1962. [SHSL]

Fyle, C. Magbaily. *Historical Dictionary of Sierra Leone.* New Edition. Lanham, Md.: Scarecrow Press, 2006.

Fyle, Clifford, and Eldred D. Jones. *A Krio-English Dictionary.* Suffolk: Oxford Univ. Press, 1980.

Garvey, Marcus. *Philosophy and Opinions of Marcus Garvey.* Ed. Amy Jacques-Garvey. New York: Atheneum, 1992.

Gennep, Arnold van. *Rites of Passage.* Trans. Monika B. Vizedom and Gabrielle L. Caffee. Chicago: Univ. of Chicago Press, 1960.

Gosset, Thomas F. *Race: The History of an Idea in America.* New York: Oxford Univ. Press, 1997.

Grace, John J. *Domestic Slavery in West Africa, with Particular Reference to the Sierra Leone Protectorate, 1896–1927.* New York: Barnes and Noble, 1975.

_____. "Slavery and Emancipation among the Mende in Sierra Leone." In *Slavery in Africa,* edited by Suzanne Meiers and Igor Kopytoff, 415–31. Madison: Univ. of Wisconsin Press, 1977.

Groenendyke, Ellen. "Three Early African Experiences." *The Evangel* 40 nos. 7–8 (July–August, 1921), 201–203.

Harman, Robert J. *From Missions to Mission: The History of Mission of the United Methodist Church, 1968–2000.* New York: General Board of Global Ministries, The United Methodist Church, 2005.

Harnack Adolf. *What is Christianity?* Trans. Thomas Bailey Saunders. New York: Putnams, 1901.

Harris, William Thomas. "The Idea of God among the Mende." In *African Ideas of God,* edited by Edwin Smith. London: Edinburgh House Press, 1950.

_____, and Harry Sawyerr. *The Springs of Mende Belief and Conduct.* Freetown: Sierra Leone Univ. Press, 1968. [SMBC]

Hart, James G. *The Person and the Common Life.* Dordrecht: Kluwer, 1992.

Henry, Michel. *Phénoménologie matérielle.* Paris: Presses Universitaires de France, 1990; *Material Phenomenology.* Translated by Scott Davidson. New York: Fordham Univ. Press, 2008.

Hesiod. *Theogony.* Trans. Norman O. Brown. New York: Liberal Arts Press: 1953.

Hofstra, Sjoerd. "The Ancestral Spirits of the Mendi." *Internationale Archiv für Ethnologie* Band 39, Heft 1–4. Leiden, 1940. 177–96.

Hogg, W. Richie. "The Role of American Protestantism in World Mission." In *American Missions in Bicentennial Perspective,* edited by R. Pierce Beaver, 366–402. South Pasadena, California: William Carey Library, 1977.

Holden, Edith. *Blyden of Liberia: An Account of the Life and Labors of Edward Wilmot Blyden L.L.D. as Recorded in Letters and in Print.* New York: Vantage, 1966.

Hopkins, A.G. *An Economic History of West Africa.* New York: Columbia University Press, 1973.

Horton, Robin. "A Definition of Religion, and its Uses." *The Journal of the Royal Anthropological Institute of Great Britain and Ireland* 90 no. 2 (Jul.–Dec. 1960): 201–226.

_____. "Judeo-Christian Spectacles: Boon or Bane to the Study of African Religions?" In *Patterns of Thought in Africa and the West: Essays on Magic, Religion, and Science.* Cambridge: Cambridge Univ. Press, 1993.

Hough, Samuel S. *Our Church Abroad.* Dayton: United Brethren Publishing House, 1918.

Howard, Allen M. "Production, Exchange, and Society in Northern Coastal Sierra Leone." In *Essays on the Economic Anthropology of Sierra Leone,* edited by Vernon R. Dorjahn and Barry L. Isaac, 45–61. Philadelphia: Institute for Liberian Studies, 1979.

Hsu, Becky, Amy Reynolds, Conrad Hackett, and James Gibbon. "Estimating the Religious Composition of All Nations: An Empirical Assessment of the World Christian Database." *Journal for the Scientific Study of Religion* 47, no. 4 (December 2008): 678–693.

Husserl, Edmund. *The Crisis of the European Sciences and Transcendental Phenomenololgy.* Trans. David Carr. Evanston, Il.: Northwestern Univ. Press, 1972.

Hutchinson, William R. *Errand to the World: American Protestant Thought and Foreign Missions.* Chicago: University of Chicago Press, 1987.

_____. "A Moral Equivalent for Imperialism." In *Missionary Ideologies in the Imperialist Era, 1880–1920: Papers from the Durham Consultation, 1981,* edited by Torben Christensen and William R. Hutchinson, 167–77. Århus, Denmark: Aros, 1983.

Idowu, E. Bolaji. *African Traditional Religion: A Definition.* Maryknoll, New York: Orbis, 1975.

_____. *Olodumare: God in Yoruba Belief.* New York: Wazobia, 1994 (Rpt. Of 1962 ed.).

_____. *Towards an Indigenous Church.* London: Oxford Univ. Press, 1965.

Ijagbemi, Adeleye. "The Freetown Colony and the Development of Legitimate Commerce in the Adjoining Territories." *Journal of the Historical Society of Nigeria* 5 no. 2 (1970): 243–56.

_____. *A History of the Temne in the Nineteenth Century.* Diss. Univ. of Edinburgh, 1968.

_____. "Rothoron (the Northeast) in Temne Tradition and Culture: An Essay in Ethnic History." *Journal of the Historical Society of Sierra Leone* 2 no. 1 (1978): 1–15.

Jackson, Michael. *Allegories of the Wilderness: Ethics and Ambiguity in Kuranko Narratives.* Bloomington: Indiana Univ. Press, 1982.

James William. *The Varieties of Religious Experience.* New York: New American Library, 1958.

Jedrej, M.C. "Medicine, Fetish, and Secret Society in a West African Culture." *Africa* 46 no. 3 (1976): 247–57.

_____. "Structural Aspects of a West African Secret Society." *Journal of Anthropological Research* 32 no. 2 (1976): 234–45.

Jones, W. S. Marcus. *Legal Development and Constitutional Change in Sierra Leone.* Ifracombe, Devon: Stockwell, 1981.

Kilson, Martin. *Political Change in a West African State: A Study of the Modernization Process in Sierra Leone.* New York: Athenaeum, 1969.

King, J.R. "The Death of Chief Caulker." *Women's Evangel* 22 no. 11, Nov. 1903, 169.

King, Martin Luther. *Strength to Love.* Philadelphia: Fortress Press, 1981.

King, Zella. "Martyr's Memorial Church." *Women's Evangel* 23 no. 12, Dec., 1904, 179–80.

Koopman, Jeanne. "Women in the Rural Economy: Past, Present, and Future." In *African Women South of the Sahara,* edited by Margaret Jean Hay and Sharon Stichter. London: Longman, 1984.

Kopytoff, Igor and Suzanne Meiers. "African 'Slavery' as an Institution of Marginality." In *Slavery in Africa,* edited by Suzanne Meiers and Igor Kopytoff, 3–84. Madison: Univ. of Wisconsin Press, 1977.

Lamp, Frederick J. "Cosmos, Cosmetics, and the Spirit of Bondo." *African Arts* 18 no. 3 (1985): 28–43.

_____. "Frogs Into Princes: The Temne Rabai Initiation." *African Arts* 11 no. 2 (1978): 38–49.

_____. *Temne Rounds: The Arts as Spatial and Temporal Indicators in a West African Society.* Diss. Yale Univ. 1982.

Lavelle, Louis. *De l'âme humaine.* Paris: Aubier, 1951.

_____. *Psychologie et Spiritualité.* Paris: Albin Michel, 1967.

Leach, Melissa. *Rainforest Relations: Gendered Resource Use Among the Mende of Gola, Sierra Leone.* Washington D.C.: Smithsonian Institution Press, 1994.

Levy-Bruhl, Lucien. *The Notebooks on Primitive Mentality.* Trans. Peter Rivière. Oxford, UK : Basil, 1978.

Lewis, C.S. *The Discarded Image: An Introduction to Medieval and Renaissance Literature.* Cambridge, England: Cambridge Univ. Press, 1964.

Lisk, L.O.G. *The History of the Albert Academy and its Contribution to the Development of Sierra Leone.* Diploma in Education Thesis, Fourah Bay College, 1965. At Fourah Bay College Library, Freetown, Sierra Leone.

Little, Kenneth. "The Mende in Sierra Leone." In *African Worlds,* edited by Daryll Forde, 111–137. London: Oxford Univ. Press, 1954.

_____. *The Mende of Sierra Leone: A West African People in Transition.* London: Routledge, 1967.

_____. "The Political Function of the Poro." In *Africa and Change,* edited by Colin M. Turnbull, 257–288. New York: Knopf, 1973.

Littlejohn, James. "Temne Space." *Anthropological Quarterly* 36 no. 1 (1963): 1–17.

MacCormack, Carol. "Sande: The Public Face of a Secret Society." In *The New Religions of Africa,* edited by Bennetta Jules-Rosette, 27–37. Norwood, N.J.: Ablex, 1979.

Marsden, George M. *Fundamentalism and American Culture: The Shaping of Twentieth Century Evangelicalism, 1870–1925.* New York: Oxford Univ. Press, 1980.

_____. *The Soul Of The American University: From Protestant Establishment To Established Nonbelief.* New York: Oxford Univ. Press, 1994.

Mbiti, John *Concepts of God in Africa.* New York: Praeger, 1970.

_____. *African Religions and Philosophy.* New York: Praeger, 1969.

McKee, William. *History of the Sherbro Mission, West Africa, Under the Direction of the Missionary Society of the United Brethren in Christ.* Dayton, Ohio: United Brethren Publishing House, 1874.

McKenzie, P.R. *Inter-religious Encounters in West Africa: Samuel Ajayi Crowther's Attitude Toward Traditional Religion and Islam.* Leicester, England: Blackfriars, 1976.

Mignerey, Lloyd. *Crumbs* [Otterbein, xeroxed bound selections]; *Crumbs* [post Otterbein]; *African Notes*; *Progress*; Otterbein University Archives.

_____. Diaries and Letters in Otterbein University Archives, Westerville, Ohio, and The Center for Evangelical United Brethren Heritage, United Theological Seminary, Dayton, Ohio.

_____. "Friendship with Other Races." *Religious Telescope* (July 22, 1933): 22.

_____. "Some First Impressions." *Sierra Leone Outlook* (March 1922): 5–7.

Mills, Job Smith. "The Essence of Christianity." [United Brethren] *Quarterly Review* 6 (Jan. 1895): 33–47.

_____. *A Manual of Family Worship With an Essay on the Christian Family.* Dayton, Oh.: United Brethren Publishing House, 1900.

_____. *Mission work in Sierra Leone, West Africa.* Dayton, Oh.: United Brethren Publishing House, 1898.

_____, W. R. Funk, and S. S. Hough. *Our Foreign Missionary Enterprise.* Dayton, Oh.: United Brethren Publishing House, 1908. [OFME]

Moore, Moses N. *Orishatukeh Faduma: Liberal Theology and Evangelical Pan-Africanism 1857–1946.* Lanham, Md.: The American Theological Library Association, 1996.

Mott, John R. *The Decisive Hour of Christian Missions.* New York: Student Volunteer Movement for Foreign Missions, 1910.

_____. *The Evangelization of the World in this Generation.* New York: Student Volunteer Movement, 1905.

_____. *The Present World Situation: With Special Reference to the Demands Made upon the Christian Church in Relation to Non-Christian Lands.* New York: Student Volunteer Movement, 1915.

Mueller, Howard Ernest. *Formation of a Mission Church in an African Culture: The United Brethren in Sierra Leone.* Diss. Northwestern University, 1973.

_____. "Oral Data on the Development of the United Brethren in Sierra Leone, Gathered 1971–72." [MOD]

Mukonoweshuro, Eliphas G. *Colonialism, Class Formation, and Underdevelopment in Sierra Leone.* New York: Univ. Press of America, 1993.

Nassau, Robert. *Fetichism* [sic] *in West Africa: Forty Years' Observation of Native Customs and Superstitions.* New York: Young Peoples' Missionary Movement, 1904.

Naumann, William Henry. *Theology and German-American Evangelicalism: The Role of Theology in the Church of the United Brethren in Christ and the Evangelical Association.* Diss. Yale Univ., 1966.

Ndanema, Isaac. "The Rationale of Mende 'Swears.'" *The Sierra Leone Bulletin of Religion* 6 (December 1964): 21–24.

Niebuhr, H. Richard. *Christ and Culture.* New York: Harper, 1951.

_____. *Radical Monotheism and Western Culture,* New York: Harper, 1970.

Niebuhr, Reinhold. *The Nature and Destiny of Man.* Vol. 1. New York: Scribner's, 1964.

Nott, Josiah Clark, and George R. Gliddon. *Types of Mankind.* Philadelphia: Lippincott, 1854.

Okonkwo, R.L. "The Garvey Movement in British West Africa." *The Journal of African History* 21, issue 1 (1980): 105–17.

Olson, Gilbert W. *Church Growth in Sierra Leone.* Grand Rapids, Mich.: Eerdmans, 1969.

O'Malley, J. Steven. *"On the Journey Home": The History of Mission of the Evangelical United Brethren Church, 1946–1968.* New York: General Board of Global Ministries, United Methodist Church, 2003.

_____. "The Role of African Americans in the Millenial Vision of the United Brethren in Christ: The Case of Joseph and Mary Gomer." *The A.M.E. Church Review* 119, no. 389 (Jan.–Mar. 2003): 56–65.

Pfleiderer, Otto. "The Essence of Christianity." *The New World: A Quarterly Review of Religion, Ethics, and Theology* 1 no. 3 (Sept. 1892): 401–430.

Phillips, Clifton J. "Changing Attitudes in the Student Volunteer Movement of Great Britain and North America, 1886–1928." In *Missionary Ideologies in the Imperialist Era, 1880–1920,* edited by Torben Christensen and Willliam R. Hutchinson, 131–45. Århus, Denmark: Aros, 1983.

Phillips, Ruth B. *Representing Woman: Sande Masquerades of the Mende of Sierra Leone.* Los Angeles: UCLA Fowler Museum of Cultural History, 1995.

Polanyi, Michael. *Personal Knowledge.* New York: Harper, 1964.

Rauschenbusch, Walter. *The Social Principles of Jesus.* New York: National Board of the Young Women's Christian Associations, 1916. New York: Association Press, 1916.

Reeck, Darrell. *Deep Mende: Religious Interaction in a Changing African Rural Society.* Leiden: Brill, 1976.

_____. "Oral Data Regarding the History of the Process of Modernization and Related Mission Influences in Sierra Leone (1968–69)."

_____. *A Socio-Historical Analysis of Modernization and Related Mission Influences in Two Chiefdoms in West Africa, 1895–1940.* Diss. Boston Univ., 1970.

Ritschl, Albrecht. *Instruction in the Christian Religion.* Translated by Alice Mead Swing. In *The Theology of Albrecht Ritschl,* edited and introduced by Albert Temple Swing. New York: Longmans, 1901.

Rosselot, Glen. *The Origin, Growth, and Development of the United Brethren in Christ Mission Schools in Sierra Leone, West Africa.* M.A. Thesis in Education, Univ. of Chicago, 1936.

Rupp, George. *Culture-Protestantism: German Liberal Theology at the Turn of the Twentieth Century.* Missoula, Montana: Scholar's Press, 1977.

Sanders, Thomas Jefferson. *The Philosophy of the Christian Religion: A Thesis.* (Ph.D. Thesis, Univ. of Wooster). Dayton, Ohio: United Brethren Publishing House, 1890.

Sanneh, Lamin. *West African Christianity*. Maryknoll, N.Y.: Orbis Books, 1983.

Sawyerr, Harry. *Creative Evangelism*. London, Lutterworth, 1968.

_____. *God Ancestor or Creator? Aspects of Traditional Belief in Ghana, Nigeria, and Sierra Leone*. Harlow: Longmans, 1970.

_____. *The Practice of Presence: Shorter Writings of Harry Sawyerr*, edited by John Parratt. Grand Rapids, Mich.: Eerdmans, 1994.

Schleiermacher, Friedrich. *The Christian Faith*. Trans. H. R. Macintosh and J.S. Stewart. Edinburgh: Clark, 1989.

Schlenker, C.F. *A Collection of Temne Traditions, Fables, and Proverbs*. London: Church Missionary Society, 1861. Rpt. Nendeln/Liechtenstein: Kraus, 1970.

Schlesinger, Louis B. "Physiognomic Perception: Empirical and Theoretical Perspectives." *Genetic Psychology Monographs* 101 (1980): 71–97.

Shaw, Rosalind. "Splitting Truths from Darkness: Epistemological Aspects of Temne Divination." In *African Divination Systems: Ways of Knowing*, edited by Philip M. Peek, 137–52. Bloomington, Ind.: Indiana Univ. Press, 1991.

Skinner, David E. *Islam in Sierra Leone During the Nineteenth Century*. Diss. Univ. of California, Berkeley, 1971.

Smith, Jeremy H. "Husserl, Derrida, Hegel, and the Notion of Time." *International Philosophical Quarterly* 36. no. 3 (Sept. 1996): 287–302.

_____. "Michel Henry's Phenomenology of Aesthetic Experience and Husserlian Intentionality." *International Journal of Philosophical Studies* 14.2 (April 2005): 191–219.

_____. "Perceptions, Propositions, and Ideals: The Problem of Truth in the Novel." *Studies in the Humanities* 13.2 (1986): 93–102.

_____. "Religious Experience and Literary Form: The Interrelation of Perception, Commitment, and Interpretation." *Religion and Literature* 21.3 (Autumn 1989): 61–83.

Snavely, Charles. *A History of the City Government of Cleveland Ohio*. Ph.D. Thesis, Johns Hopkins Univ., 1902.

Spargo, John. *Socialism: A Summary and Interpretation of Socialist Principles*. New York: MacMillan, 1912.

Speer, Robert E. *Christianity and the Nations*. New York: Laymen's Missionary Movement, 1910.

Stevens, Siaka. *What Life has Taught Me*. Abbottsbrook, Eng.: Kensal Press, 1984.

Sumner, Doyle. *Education in Sierra Leone*. Freetown: The Government of Sierra Leone, 1963.

Sundkler, Bengt. *The Christian Ministry in Africa*. London: Charles Burchall, 1962.

Szasz, Ferenc Morton. *The Divided Mind of Protestant America: 1880–1930*. University, Alabama.: Univ. of Alabama Press, 1982.

Thomas, Keith. *Religion and the Decline of Magic*. New York: Scribner, 1971.

Thomas, Northcote. *Anthropological Report on Sierra Leone*. London: Harrison, 1916. Rpt. Westport, Connecticut: Negro Universities Press, 1970.

Timberlake, James H. *Prohibition and the Progressive Movement: 1900–1920.* Cambridge, Mass.: Harvard Univ. Press, 1963.

Turay, A.K. "Temne Supernatural Terminology." *The Sierra Leone Bulletin of Religion* 9 no. 2 (1967): 50–55.

Ukpabi, S.C. "British Colonial Wars in West Africa: Image and Reality." *Civilizations* 20 no. 3 (1970): 379–404.

_____. "Recruiting for the British Colonial Forces in West Africa in the Nineteenth Century." *Odu* 10 (July 1974): 79–97.

United Methodist Church (U.S.), Board of Discipleship. *The Book of Discipline of the United Methodist Church, 1976.* Nashville: United Methodist Publishing House, 1976.

United Nations Development Program. *Human Development Report 2000.* New York: Oxford Univ. Press, 2000.

Walls, Andrew F. "Samuel Ajayi Crowther (1807–1891)." In *The Cross Cultural Process in Christian History: Studies in the Transmission and Appropriation of Faith,* 155–64. Maryknoll, N.Y.: Orbis, 2002.

Weaver, Jonathon. *Christian Theology: A Concise and Practical View of the Cardinal Doctrines and Institutions of Christianity.* Dayton, Oh.: United Brethren Publishing House, 1900.

Weber, Max. *The Protestant Ethic and the Spirit of Capitalism.* Trans. Talcott Parsons. New York: Scribners, 1958.

Werner, Heinz. *Comparative Psychology of Mental Development.* New York: International Universities Press, 1973.

Wilson, Emanuel Munda. *Toward a Mende Christian Theology.* Diss. Fuller Theological Seminary, 1982.

Wylie, Kenneth. *The Political Kingdoms of the Temne.* New York: Africana, 1977.

Wyse, Akintola. *The Krio of Sierra Leone: An Interpretive History.* London: Hurst, 1987.

Ziegler, Samuel R. *History of the United Brethren Board of Missions.* Ms. at Center for EUB Heritage, United Theological Seminary, Dayton, Ohio.

General Index

CPSIA information can be obtained
at www.ICGtesting.com
Printed in the USA
LVHW031327240121
677344LV00002B/222

9 781609 470166